T0185026

Lecture Notes in Computer Science   11673

Founding Editors

Gerhard Goos
Karlsruhe Institute of Technology, Karlsruhe, Germany
Juris Hartmanis
Cornell University, Ithaca, NY, USA

Editorial Board Members

Elisa Bertino
Purdue University, West Lafayette, IN, USA
Wen Gao
Peking University, Beijing, China
Bernhard Steffen
TU Dortmund University, Dortmund, Germany
Gerhard Woeginger
RWTH Aachen, Aachen, Germany
Moti Yung
Columbia University, New York, NY, USA

More information about this series at http://www.springer.com/series/7409

Irfan Awan · Muhammad Younas ·
Perin Ünal · Markus Aleksy (Eds.)

Mobile Web and Intelligent Information Systems

16th International Conference, MobiWIS 2019
Istanbul, Turkey, August 26–28, 2019
Proceedings

 Springer

Editors
Irfan Awan
University of Bradford
Bradford, UK

Muhammad Younas
Oxford Brookes University
Oxford, UK

Perin Ünal
Teknopark Ankara
Ankara, Turkey

Markus Aleksy
ABB AG Forschungszentrum
Ladenburg, Germany

ISSN 0302-9743   ISSN 1611-3349   (electronic)
Lecture Notes in Computer Science
ISBN 978-3-030-27191-6   ISBN 978-3-030-27192-3   (eBook)
https://doi.org/10.1007/978-3-030-27192-3

LNCS Sublibrary: SL3 – Information Systems and Applications, incl. Internet/Web, and HCI

© Springer Nature Switzerland AG 2019
This work is subject to copyright. All rights are reserved by the Publisher, whether the whole or part of the material is concerned, specifically the rights of translation, reprinting, reuse of illustrations, recitation, broadcasting, reproduction on microfilms or in any other physical way, and transmission or information storage and retrieval, electronic adaptation, computer software, or by similar or dissimilar methodology now known or hereafter developed.
The use of general descriptive names, registered names, trademarks, service marks, etc. in this publication does not imply, even in the absence of a specific statement, that such names are exempt from the relevant protective laws and regulations and therefore free for general use.
The publisher, the authors and the editors are safe to assume that the advice and information in this book are believed to be true and accurate at the date of publication. Neither the publisher nor the authors or the editors give a warranty, expressed or implied, with respect to the material contained herein or for any errors or omissions that may have been made. The publisher remains neutral with regard to jurisdictional claims in published maps and institutional affiliations.

This Springer imprint is published by the registered company Springer Nature Switzerland AG
The registered company address is: Gewerbestrasse 11, 6330 Cham, Switzerland

Preface

Welcome to the proceedings of the 16th International Conference on Mobile Web and Intelligent Information Systems (MobiWis 2019), which was held in Istanbul, Turkey, during August 26–28, 2019. Istanbul is one of the major cities in Turkey and is unique as it is located both in Asia and Europe. It is one of the economic centers and metropolitan cities of Turkey. Istanbul has a rich cultural heritage and its historic peninsula is among the UNESCO World Heritage sites.

The Program Committee put together an interesting technical program, which includes papers that cover timely topics in the area of mobile Web and intelligent information systems. The area of mobile Web has gained significant attention from users, researchers, developers, and technology providers. This is evidenced through the enormous use of mobile devices such as smart phones, tablets, and wearable devices. People across the world are using mobile devices not only for conventional phone calls and messaging but for complex Web-based applications such as processing business transactions, sharing and manipulating critical data and documents. The number of people accessing the Internet/Web from mobile devices has surpassed conventional computers.

The research and development community therefore faces enormous challenges as they attempt to gain insights from highly complex mobile Web infrastructure and to design effective solutions that can benefit users as well as technology providers. The MobiWis conference therefore aims to advance research on and practical applications of mobile Web, intelligent information systems, and related mobile technologies. It includes interesting and timely areas such as mobile Web systems, recommender systems, security and authentication, context-awareness, mobile Web and advanced applications, cloud and IoT, mobility management, mobile and wireless networks, and mobile Web practice and experience.

This year MobiWis attracted a good number of submissions from different countries across the world. A total of 74 papers were submitted to the conference. All submitted papers were reviewed by multiple members of the Program Committee. Based on the reviews, 26 papers were accepted for the conference, that is, an acceptance rate of 35%. The accepted papers covered a range of topics related to the theme of the conference. These include: mobile Web and apps, wireless sensor networks, security and privacy, Web services, cloud services, Web applications, and various mobile Web technologies. Also included were papers on practical applications of technologies in areas of virtual reality, social media, agriculture, and textile industries.

Many people contributed their time and effort in the organization of the conference and in making this conference a successful event. We thank all the Program Committee members who provided timely, constructive, and balanced feedback to the authors. We are grateful to the authors for their contributions to the conference.

We thank Prof. Tor-Morten Grønli (Workshop Coordinator), Dr. Aneta Poniszewska-Maranda (Publicity Chair), Prof. George Ghina (Journals Special Issues

Chair), and Dr. Muhammad Younas (Publication Chair) for their help and support. We would like to thank the local organizing chairs, Dr. Tacha Serif and Dr. Sezer Gören Uğurdağ.

We sincerely thank the keynote speakers, Prof. Pierangela Samarati (Università degli Studi di Milano, Italy), Mr. Gökhan Büyükdığan (Arçelik A.S., Turkey), and Dr. Soumya Kanti Datta (EURECOM, France), for delivering interesting talks.

Our sincere thanks also go to the Springer LNCS team for their valuable support in the production of the conference proceedings.

August 2019   Irfan Awan
                                                                                            Perin Ünal
                                                                                         Markus Aleksy
                                                                                   Mohammed Ghazal

Organization

MobiWis 2019 Organizing Committee

General Co-chairs

Markus Aleksy   ABB, Germany
Perin Ünal   Teknopar, Turkey

Program Co-chairs

Irfan Awan   University of Bradford, UK
Mohammed Ghazal   Abu Dhabi University, UAE

Local Organizing Co-chairs

Sezer Gören Uğurdağ   Yeditepe University, Turkey
Tacha Serif   Yeditepe University, Turkey

Publication Chair

Muhammad Younas   Oxford Brookes University, UK

Journal Special Issue Coordinator

George Ghina   Brunel University London, UK

Workshop Coordinator

Tor-Morten Grønli   Kristiania University College, Norway

Publicity Chair

Aneta Poniszewska-Maranda   Lodz University of Technology, Poland

Program Committee

Abdel Lisser   University Paris Sud, France
Agnis Stibe   ESLSCA Business School Paris, France
Andrea Omicini   University of Bologna, Italy
Aneta Poniszewska-Maranda   Lodz University of Technology, Poland
Carlos Calafate   Technical University of Valencia, Spain

Chi (Harold) Liu	Beijing Institute of Technology, China
Christophe Feltus	Luxembourg Institute of Science and Technology, Luxembourg
Dan Johansson	Umea University, Sweden
DO van Thuan	Linus AS, Norway
Fatma Abdennadher	National School of Engineering of Sfax, Tunisia
Florence Sedes	Paul Sabatier University, France
Hiroaki Kikuchi	Meiji University, Japan
Ivan Demydov	Lviv Polytechnic National University, Ukraine
Jorge Sa Silva	University of Coimbra, Portugal
Jozef Juhar	Technical University of Košice, Slovakia
Jung-Chun Liu	TungHai University, Japan
Katty Rohoden	Jaramillo Universidad Técnica Particular de Loja, Ecuador
Lianghuai Yang	Zhejiang University of Technology, China
Lidia Ogiela	Pedagogical University of Cracow, Poland
Lulwah AlSuwaidan	King Saud University, Saudi Arabia
Marek R. Ogiela	AGH University of Science and Technology, Poland
Masahiro Sasabe	Nara Institute of Science and Technology, Japan
Michal Gregus	Comenius University in Bratislava, Slovakia
Mikko Rissanen	Improventions, Malaysia
Muslim Elkotob	MB TDF Group, Germany
Nor Shahniza Kamal Bashah	Universiti Teknologi MARA, Malaysia
Norazlina Khamis	Universiti Malaysia Sabah, Malaysia
Novia Admodisastro	Universiti Putra Malaysia, Malaysia
Ondrej Krejcar	University of Hradec Kralove, Czech Republic
Pablo Adasme	University of Santiago de Chile, Chile
Paolo Nesi	University of Florence, Italy
Perin Unal	METU, Turkey
Philippe Roose	IUT de Bayonne, France
Pınar KIRCI	Istanbul University, Turkey
Riccardo Martoglia	University of Modena and Reggio Emilia, Italy
Sajad Khorsandroo	The University of Texas at San Antonio, USA
Sergio Ilarri	University of Zaragoza, Spain
Shinsaku Kiyomoto	KDDI R & D Laboratories Inc., Japan
Stephan Böhm	Rheinmain University, Germany
Thanh Van Do	Telenor, Norway

Contents

Mobile Apps and Services

Web and Mobile Applications

Mobile Web and Practical Applications

Mobile Apps and Services

A Variable Neighborhood Search Algorithm for Massive MIMO Resource Allocation

Pablo Adasme[1](✉) and Abdel Lisser[2]

[1] Universidad de Santiago de Chile,
Avenida Ecuador 3519, Estación Central, Santiago, Chile
pablo.adasme@usach.cl
[2] Laboratoire de Recherche en Informatique, Université de Paris-Sud,
Bât. 650, 91405 Orsay Cedex, France
abdel.lisser@lri.fr

Abstract. In this paper, we consider the problem of maximizing capacity for a Massive Multiple Input Multiple Output (MIMO) system subject to power and antenna assignment constraints. Massive MIMO technology has gained increased attention by the research community within last decade as it has become a strong candidate for 5G wireless communications. Some advantages of this new technology include better performance in terms of data rate and link reliability, transmitting in higher frequency bands which improves coverage, strong signal indoors, and the possibility of more resistant systems to intentional jamming attacks, to name a few. The optimization problem is formulated as a mixed integer nonlinear programming problem for which exact methods cannot be applied efficiently. Consequently, we propose a variable neighborhood search (VNS for short) meta-heuristic algorithm which allows to obtain significantly better solutions compared to a state of the art algorithm. Although, at a higher computational cost for most tested instances.

Keywords: Mixed integer nonlinear programming ·
Resource allocation of Massive MIMO systems · Greedy algorithm ·
Variable neighborhood search meta-heuristic

1 Introduction

Multiple Input Multiple Output (MIMO) technology basically consists of a wireless communication method that allows to transmit and receive more than one signal simultaneously over the same radio channel. For this purpose, MIMO uses several antennas at the transmitter and receiver sides. As reported in the literature, MIMO technology has proved to be highly efficient in order to increase significantly data rate throughput in wireless communications compared to a single input single output system which uses only one antenna at both, the transmitter and receiver sides. As a consequence, better quality of service can

© Springer Nature Switzerland AG 2019
I. Awan et al. (Eds.): MobiWIS 2019, LNCS 11673, pp. 3–15, 2019.
https://doi.org/10.1007/978-3-030-27192-3_1

be achieved. The IEEE 802.11n Wireless Standard is an example of this technology. Massive MIMO appears as an extension of MIMO where a significantly large number of antennas is utilized. Commonly, traditional MIMO networks use two or four antennas at most. Whilst Massive MIMO reaches up to tens or even hundreds of antennas. For instance, Huawei and Facebook have shown that a Massive MIMO system can operate with up to 126 antennas correctly [7]. It has also been shown that the more antennas the transmitter and receiver is working with, the more signal paths, link reliability, coverage and security aspects can be achieved compared to traditional MIMO systems making Massive MIMO a perfect candidate for 5G wireless communications. Thus, it is widely expected that this improved technology will play a key role as an extra complement of 5G technology in order to handle the huge increase in data usage which is estimated by Cisco to reach up to 5.5 billion mobile users around the globe by 2020. It is also estimated that each user will consume approximately 20 GB of data per month without including Internet of Things (IoT) future networks which will certainly increase these demands.

Some few relevant works related with resource allocation of Massive MIMO networks can be described as follows. In [8], the authors investigate energy efficient power allocation for downlink Massive MIMO systems. They propose a constrained nonconvex optimization problem in order to maximize the capacity of the network. By the use of fractional programming techniques and computing a lower bound for each user data rate, the nonconvex problem is transformed into a tractable convex one. Finally, they propose an iterative algorithm to obtain the optimal power allocation. Similarly, the authors in [3] propose an energy efficient resource allocation method for a Massive MIMO system under the assumption of imperfect channel state information at the base station (BS). In this case, the authors formulate a mathematical programming model to maximize capacity while considering Beam Forming (BF) design, antenna selection, power allocation and time division protocol. In order to find the optimal power and time allocation, a solution approach based on nonlinear fractional programming is also proposed. Finally, they present extensive simulation studies to demonstrate the effectiveness of their solution method.

In particular, in this paper we consider the same antenna selection problem studied in [1] where the objective is to maximize the sum of broadcasting data rates achieved by mobile users in one cell served by a Massive MIMO transmitter. This assignment problem is relatively new in the literature and has gained increased attention due to the many favorable properties of Massive MIMO technology. The authors propose a greedy approach that efficiently solves the formulated problem while obtaining benefits from both the spatial selectivity and multiuser diversity offered by antenna selection and user scheduling, respectively. Finally, they conduct performance evaluation showing that their proposed algorithm is able to achieve near optimal performance at low computational cost. Although, only small instances of the problem with up to 30 antennas are solved. In this paper, we consider the case when all users are served simultaneously by the BS while using a significantly large number of transmitting antennas.

The arising combinatorial optimization problem is NP-hard and formulated as a mixed integer nonlinear programming problem for which exact methods cannot be applied efficiently. Consequently, we propose a variable neighborhood search (VNS for short) meta-heuristic algorithm which allows to obtain significantly better solutions compared to the greedy approach proposed in [1], although at a higher computational cost for most tested instances.

As far as we know, this is the first time a VNS algorithm is proposed for the resource allocation problem of a Massive MIMO system. Variable neighborhood search is a meta-heuristic that is mainly based on the idea of neighborhood change during the ascent toward local optima while simultaneously escaping from local valleys. We choose VNS due to its simplicity, low memory requirements and proven efficiency when solving hard combinatorial optimization problems [5,6].

The paper is organized as follows. In Sect. 2, we present a brief system description of a Massive MIMO system and the mathematical formulation for the resource allocation problem. Then, in Sect. 3, we present our VNS algorithm and describe the greedy approach reported in the literature which is used as a reference for comparison. Subsequently, in Sect. 4 we conduct preliminary numerical results in order to compare the performances obtained with both algorithms. Finally, in Sect. 5 we give the main conclusions of the paper and provide some insights for future research.

2 System Description and Mathematical Formulation of the Problem

In this section, first we give a brief system description of a Massive MIMO system and then, we present the mathematical programming model for the resource allocation problem we are dealing with.

2.1 System Description

We consider a single cell area composed of a BS and mobile users. The BS is equipped with a set of antennas $\mathcal{N} = \{1, \ldots, N\}$ whilst each user uses only one antenna to receive data from the BS using Massive MIMO technology. The optimization problem at hand consists of assigning a predefined number of antennas, say m out of N to a set of $\mathcal{K}$ users in such a way that the total capacity of the network is maximized subject to a power constraint on the BS. Notice that the combinatorial nature of the problem arises from the fact that we intend to find an optimal subset of antennas $\mathcal{A}$ from $\mathcal{N}$ that maximizes the capacity of the network. Let K be the cardinality of $\mathcal{K}$, there are $\sum_{m=K}^{N} \binom{N}{m}$ possible subsets of antennas. In general, it is required that the number of antennas be greater than or equal to the number of users, i.e., $N \geq K$ [1]. Although, for practical systems setting $m = K$ antennas would suffice in order to reduce hardware costs at the transmitter while satisfying distortion limits at the receivers [4]. Obviously, the combinatorial nature of the problem leads to a challenging optimization problem. In Fig. 1, we show a Massive MIMO cell network where the BS has N antennas and each user is equipped with one antenna. In order to select m out of N available antennas, the BS module requires the input channel matrix $\mathbf{H} = (\mathbf{H}_{nk})$, $n \in \mathcal{N}$, $k \in \mathcal{K}$ where each entry is a complex number representing a channel value which is assumed to behave as a quasi static independent and identically distributed Rayleigh fading channel.

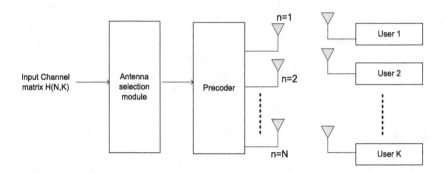

Fig. 1. Massive MIMO system.

We denote by $\mathbf{h}_k$ the kth column of matrix $\mathbf{H}$. Consequently, $\mathbf{h}_k^H$ denotes the Hermitian transpose of $\mathbf{h}_k$ in Eq. (1) whereas s_k represents the data symbol sent to user $k \in \mathcal{K}$. Similarly, the complex vector $\mathbf{w}_k$, for each $k \in \mathcal{K}$, denotes the kth column of the pseudo inverse channel matrix formed by the set of users in $\mathcal{K}$ while using selected antennas in $\mathcal{A} \subseteq \mathcal{N}$. Finally, $\eta_k \sim \mathcal{CN}(0,1)$, for each k, represents a noise term which behaves according to an independent complex Gaussian distribution with zero mean and unit variance. When a particular subset of antennas $\mathcal{A}$ is selected, each user signal is passed through a linear precoding scheme called Zero Forcing Beam Forming (ZFBF). Thus, the complete transmitted signal is a summation of the products formed by the desired signal and the associated precoding vector. Formally, the signal received by user k can be written as

$$r_k = \mathbf{h}_k^H \mathbf{w}_k s_k + \sum_{\substack{k \in \mathcal{K} \\ i \neq k}} \mathbf{h}_k^H \mathbf{w}_i s_i + \eta_k \qquad (1)$$

where the first and second terms on the right hand side correspond to the signal received by user k and the interference caused by remaining users, respectively. Since ZFBF is used and assuming that channel state information is perfectly known at the transmitter, then the second term equals zero and can be removed from (1).

2.2   Mathematical Formulation

A mathematical formulation which allows to maximize the whole capacity for the Massive MIMO system previously described can be written as follows

$$\max_{\{p,\mathcal{A},\mathcal{K}\}} \sum_{k\in\mathcal{K}} \log_2\left(1 + p_k|\mathbf{h}_k^H\mathbf{w}_k|^2\right) \tag{2}$$

$$\text{s.t.} \sum_{j\in\mathcal{A}}\sum_{k\in\mathcal{K}} p_k \leq P \tag{3}$$

$$K \leq |\mathcal{A}| \leq m \tag{4}$$

$$p \in [0,\infty)^K \tag{5}$$

where the complex vectors $\mathbf{h}_k$ and $\mathbf{w}_k$, $k \in \mathcal{K}$ in the objective function (2) only retain the entries related with selected antennas in $\mathcal{A}$. Constraint (3) is a power constraint imposed on the BS and ensures that the total power consumed by the BS cannot exceed P. Constraint (4) indicates that the number of selected antennas in $\mathcal{A}$ must be greater than or equal to the number of users which is handled by the means of parameter m. As mentioned before and w.l.o.g. setting $m = K$ is a correct choice for practical Massive MIMO systems [4]. Consequently, hereafter we solve the optimization problem (2)–(5) using $m = K$. Finally, constraints (5) are domain constraints for the power decision variables $p_k, \forall k$.

Notice that the maximum capacity in the objective function (2) will be achieved when constraint (3) is active, i.e., when the maximum available power P is used for transmission. Thus, for a particular subset of antennas $\mathcal{A}$, the Lagrangian function of the above mathematical model can be written as

$$L(p_k,\lambda) = \sum_{k\in\mathcal{K}} \log_2\left(1 + p_k|\mathbf{h}_k^H\mathbf{w}_k|^2\right) + \lambda\left(P - \sum_{j\in\mathcal{A}}\sum_{k\in\mathcal{K}} p_k\right) \tag{6}$$

where λ is a nonnegative Lagrangian multiplier. Now, it is easy to show by establishing the Karush-Kuhn-Tucker conditions [2], that the partial derivatives $\frac{\partial(L)}{\partial(p_k)}$ for each $k \in \mathcal{K}$ allow one to compute the optimal power for each user by using the following equation

$$p_k = \left(\mu - \frac{1}{|\mathbf{h}_k^H\mathbf{w}_k|^2}\right)^+ \tag{7}$$

where $(x)^+ = \max(0,x)$ and $\mu = \frac{1}{\lambda}$ represents a water filling level which must satisfy

$$\sum_{j\in\mathcal{A}}\sum_{k\in\mathcal{K}}\left(\mu - \frac{1}{|\mathbf{h}_k^H\mathbf{w}_k|^2}\right)^+ = P \tag{8}$$

In particular, $(x)^+$ ensures that the power constraints (5) are satisfied. Next, we present two algorithms that allow to obtain feasible solutions for the resource allocation problem (2)–(5).

3   Algorithms

In this section, first we present and explain the greedy algorithm proposed in [1] and subsequently, we present and describe our VNS algorithm.

3.1   Greedy Algorithm

The pseudo code of the greedy approach proposed in [1] is depicted in Algorithm 3.1. As it can be observed, it requires the input channel matrix $\mathbf{H}$ and it outputs a selected subset of antennas $\mathcal{A}^*$. The algorithm is simple and works as follows. In Step 1, variable t is set to $t = 1$ while set $\mathcal{A}$ is initialized to $\mathcal{A} = \mathcal{N}$. Then, in Step 2, a while loop iterates in order to reduce the size of the current set $\mathcal{A}$. Notice that the underlying idea of Algorithm 3.1 is to successively remove at each iteration the worst antenna, i.e., the one that may cause the worst performance degradation. The algorithm iterates until the number of removed antennas equals $N - K$. Notice that in [1], Algorithm 3.1 is used simultaneously for antenna selection and user scheduling. In this paper, we restrict our attention only to the case where antenna selection is performed while providing connectivity to all users simultaneously.

Algorithm 3.1. Algorithm proposed in [1]

Data: Input channel matrix $\mathbf{H}$ and total number of antennas and users.
Result: Selected set of antennas $\mathcal{A}^*$.
Step 1;
Set $t \leftarrow 1$;
$\mathcal{A} = \{1, \ldots, N\}$;
Step 2;
while $(t \leq N - K)$ **do**
  $\quad maxRate \leftarrow 0$;
  $\quad$ **foreach** $j \in \mathcal{A}$ **do**
    $\quad\quad R_m \leftarrow R_{sum}(\mathcal{A} \setminus \{j\})$;
    $\quad\quad$ **if** $R_m > maxRate$ **then**
      $\quad\quad\quad maxRate \leftarrow R_m$;
      $\quad\quad\quad j_{bad} \leftarrow j$;
  $\quad \mathcal{A} \leftarrow \mathcal{A} \setminus \{j_{bad}\}$;
  $\quad t \leftarrow t + 1$;
$\mathcal{A}^* \leftarrow \mathcal{A}$;
Return $\mathcal{A}^*$;

3.2   Variable Neighborhood Search Algorithm

In order to propose a VNS algorithm for the Massive MIMO system previously described, first we define the neighborhood structure $N_h = \{1, \ldots, h_{max}\}$ which

---

Algorithm 3.2. Proposed VNS algorithm

Data: Input channel matrix $\mathbf{H}$ and total number of antennas and users.

Result: Selected set of antennas $\mathcal{A}^*$.

Step 1: Randomly generate an initial set of antennas $\mathcal{A}$. Denote by $\mathcal{A}_c$ the complement set of $\mathcal{A}$, i.e., the set of inactive antennas. Using $\mathcal{A}$, compute each user power value using formulas (7) and (8). Let $f(\mathcal{A})$ be the objective function value obtained with $\mathcal{A}$.;

$BestObj \leftarrow f(\mathcal{A})$;

$\mathcal{A}^* \leftarrow \mathcal{A}, \mathcal{A}_c^* \leftarrow \mathcal{A}_c$;

Set $h \leftarrow 1, Cont \leftarrow 0$;

Step 2;

while $h \leq h_{max}$ do

    for $i = 1$ *to* h do

            Randomly swap an element of $\mathcal{A}$ with an element of $\mathcal{A}_c$;

    Set $i \leftarrow 1, j \leftarrow 1, sw \leftarrow 0$;

    while $i \leq K$ do

        while $j \leq N - K$ do

            $B \leftarrow \mathcal{A}, B_c \leftarrow \mathcal{A}_c$;

            $aux \leftarrow B(i)$;

            $B(i) \leftarrow B_c(j)$;

            $B_c(j) \leftarrow aux$;

            if $f(B) > BestObj$ then

                $BestObj \leftarrow f(B)$;

                $i \leftarrow 1, j \leftarrow 0$;

                $sw \leftarrow 1, \mathcal{A} \leftarrow B, \mathcal{A}_c \leftarrow B_c$;

            $j \leftarrow j + 1$;

        $i \leftarrow i + 1$;

    if $sw = 1$ then

        $\mathcal{A}^* \leftarrow \mathcal{A}, \mathcal{A}_c^* \leftarrow \mathcal{A}_c, h = 1, Cont \leftarrow 0$;

    else

        $\mathcal{A} \leftarrow \mathcal{A}^*, \mathcal{A}_c \leftarrow \mathcal{A}_c^*, Cont \leftarrow Cont + 1$;

        if $Cont > \beta$ then

            $h = h + 1, Cont \leftarrow 0$;

Return $\mathcal{A}^*$;

---

consists of performing h random swap moves between the sets of active and inactive antennas. Notice that the size of the neighborhood structure N_h allows one to ensure diversification of the search space. In order to ensure intensification, we propose a deterministic local search procedure which consists of performing swap moves between all pairs of active and inactive antennas while keeping the best current solution found. In case a better solution is obtained, the local search phase is re-initialized with the hope of finding better solutions. On the opposite, if no better solution is obtained, the local search phase stops and returns to the diversification step using the neighborhood structure N_h.

The detailed pseudo-code of our VNS procedure is depicted in Algorithm 3.2. In Step 1, we generate an initial feasible solution by choosing randomly K antennas which are saved in $\mathcal{A}$. Next, we compute the objective function value according to $\mathcal{A}$ and save this value as best found so far. Subsequently, in Step 2, we start an iterative process which is performed while $h \leq h_{max}$ where h refers to the size of the neighborhood structure N_h and h_{max} represents the maximum value for which the neighborhood structure N_h will proceed. Inside the while loop, we randomly modify the best current solution found so far by swapping h elements between subsets $\mathcal{A}$ and its complement $\mathcal{A}_c$. Subsequently, we perform the local search procedure and update the best solution found when required. If so, we reset $h = 1$, otherwise we increment $h = h + 1$ in order to continue with a larger neighborhood structure favouring diversification. Finally, notice that we only increment h when β trials have been accomplished. Otherwise, we keep the size of the neighborhood structure. As such, parameter β acts as a persistent parameter used to control the number of times we randomly affect the best current solution found in order to obtain improved solutions.

4   Preliminary Numerical Results

In this section, we perform preliminary numerical results in order to compare the proposed VNS algorithm with the greedy approach proposed in the literature. We generate instances using different number of antennas and users with parameter values ranging from $N = 50$ to $N = 500$ and $K = 15$ to $K = 100$, respectively. Each complex value in the input matrix $\mathbf{H} = (\mathbf{H}_{n,k})$, $k \in \mathcal{K}$, $n \in \mathcal{N}$, is generated randomly according to an independent and identically distributed Rayleigh fading channel. In our simulations, the maximum power values used in constraint (3) go from $P = 50$ to $P = 500$ dBm. The parameter values of h_{max} and β are arbitrarily set to $h_{max} = 10$ and $\beta = 50$ in Algorithm 3.2. We implement a Matlab program in order to test Algorithms 3.1 and 3.2. The numerical experiments have been carried out on an Intel(R) 64 bits core(TM) with 3.40 Ghz and 8 gigabytes of RAM.

Notice that larger power values can be straightforwardly used in constraint (3) for a particular solution obtained with any algorithm. Consequently, in Table 1, we report numerical results for Algorithms 3.1 and 3.2 using only a maximum power value of $P = 50$ dBm. The legend of Table 1 is as follows. In columns 1–3, we present the instance number and the dimensions of each instance. Next, in columns 4–5, we present the solution obtained with Algorithm 3.1 and CPU time in seconds it requires to obtain that solution. Subsequently, in columns 6–8, we report the initial and best solutions obtained with VNS, and the CPU time in seconds it requires to obtain the best solution. Finally in column 9, we report gaps that we compute by $\left[\dfrac{\text{VNS}_{Best} - \text{Greedy Alg.}}{\text{VNS}_{Best}} * 100 \right]$.

Table 1. Numerical results for Algorithms 3.1 and 3.2 using 50 dBm.

#	K	N	Greedy Alg.	CPU(s)	VNS_{Ini}	VNS_{Best}	CPU(s)	Gap (%)
Small-medium size instances								
1	15	100	70.71	1.54	12.72	174.81	15.96	59.55
2	15	110	138.71	1.98	12.99	198.72	15.10	30.20
3	15	120	128.94	2.35	5.52	177.39	9.28	27.32
4	15	130	41.49	2.73	11.14	178.62	13.76	76.77
5	15	140	116.31	3.39	6.79	201.24	7.97	42.20
6	15	150	118.63	4.03	24.21	241.05	9.59	50.78
7	30	100	201.11	3.14	12.51	328.82	26.15	38.84
8	30	110	193.97	3.85	4.10	348.72	3.36	44.38
9	30	120	263.55	4.53	18.64	327.78	5.29	19.60
10	30	130	322.14	5.80	8.11	423.66	29.52	23.96
11	30	140	227.78	6.85	12.85	277.74	4.20	17.99
12	30	150	151.57	8.30	8.04	376.97	44.04	59.79
Large size instances								
13	80	100	397.92	4.01	28.77	433.69	34.97	8.25
14	80	110	764.50	6.52	46.61	823.50	81.02	7.16
15	80	120	531.12	9.28	13.88	609.81	98.43	12.90
16	80	130	382.42	12.63	3.51	675.10	102.33	43.35
17	80	140	509.62	16.30	61.55	622.47	48.10	18.13
18	80	150	514.91	21.99	46.62	818.19	62.83	37.07
19	50	100	518.25	5.02	33.96	701.25	19.33	26.10
20	50	150	341.14	14.20	12.08	477.17	101.49	28.51
21	50	200	351.83	31.10	5.95	449.17	39.81	21.67
22	50	250	522.14	49.53	3.64	592.57	50.34	11.89
23	50	300	397.35	83.88	5.41	551.78	73.24	27.99
24	50	400	385.31	160.55	8.99	534.06	85.89	27.85
25	50	500	491.37	276.92	3.40	581.66	269.77	15.52
26	100	150	439.75	22.47	2.88	747.75	523.23	41.19
27	100	200	689.74	61.07	7.09	1229.18	258.86	43.89
28	100	250	759.80	115.22	9.42	1052.02	56.14	27.78
29	100	300	800.34	206.82	1.21	874.86	368.34	8.52
30	100	400	910.23	415.62	24.39	1187.26	355.52	23.33
31	100	500	911.68	790.10	2.05	953.97	353.78	4.43

In Table 1, two sets of instances are tested. The first one includes the small and medium size instances #1–12 whilst the second one contains the larger ones (i.e., instances #13–31). From Table 1, we observe that VNS allows to obtain better solutions for all the instances of the first set with gap values going from 19.6% to 76.7%. These are high gaps and clearly demonstrate the effectiveness of our proposed VNS algorithm compared to Algorithm 3.1. In general, we see that the initial solutions obtained with VNS are very poor compared to their best counterparts.

Regarding CPU times, we observe that VNS requires larger CPU times than Algorithm 3.1 for most of the instances. Similarly, we observe that the gap values for the second set of instances go from 4.43% to 43.89%. Again, this fact evidences that VNS significantly outperforms the greedy approach. Although, in this case there are some few instances for which the greedy approach obtains tighter solutions compared to VNS. This is the case for the instances #13–#14, #29 and #31 with gap values lower than 10%. Finally, we observe that the CPU times required by VNS are larger than those required by the greedy approach. Although, there are some few instances for which the CPU times obtained with VNS are lower. This is the case for the instances #23–#25, #28 and #30–#31. In Fig. 2, we plot capacity values for two instances with dimensions of $K = \{30, 80\}$ users and $N = 150$ antennas. By doing so, we intend to give some insight regarding the capacity improvements that can be achieved when the maximum available power P in constraint (3) is incremented. Consequently,

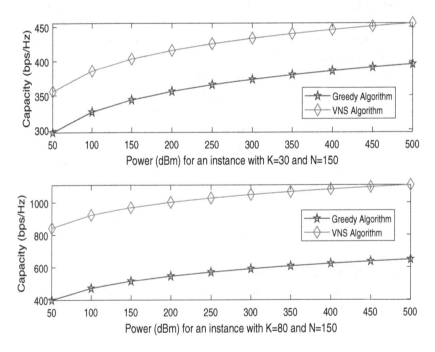

Fig. 2. Capacity improvements achieved by Algorithms 3.1 and 3.2 while incrementing power.

Table 2. Numerical results for Algorithms 3.1 and 3.2 using $P = 50\,\text{dBm}$ and equal power values for each user.

#	K	N	Greedy Alg.	CPU(s)	VNS_{Ini}	VNS_{Best}	CPU(s)	Gap (%)
Small-medium size instances								
1	15	100	75.94	1.85	2.17	197.89	21.63	61.63
2	15	110	30.44	1.97	11.21	215.54	7.16	85.88
3	15	120	65.96	2.48	10.01	244.68	27.70	73.04
4	15	130	55.64	2.86	3.78	198.51	11.66	71.97
5	15	140	93.47	3.44	4.89	194.93	3.47	52.05
6	15	150	122.07	3.83	19.74	223.19	60.10	45.31
7	30	100	202.67	3.11	3.12	381.79	26.09	46.91
8	30	110	155.85	3.90	2.49	384.69	47.16	59.49
9	30	120	206.28	4.76	9.89	326.51	27.31	36.82
10	30	130	153.95	5.77	5.21	352.58	31.32	56.34
11	30	140	282.61	6.84	1.32	461.17	75.71	38.72
12	30	150	266.83	7.98	9.14	375.69	130.58	28.98
Large size instances								
13	80	100	574.30	4.17	3.13	924.49	157.05	37.88
14	80	110	647.89	6.53	1.10	823.91	199.15	21.36
15	80	120	692.71	9.34	1.58	892.84	249.35	22.42
16	80	130	722.78	12.68	0.85	744.70	238.52	2.94
17	80	140	803.49	16.41	8.77	867.73	71.23	7.40
18	80	150	799.56	21.31	0.49	1049.43	588.04	23.81
19	50	100	537.96	4.73	5.76	599.06	149.75	10.20
20	50	150	369.93	14.50	1.07	433.94	52.60	14.75
21	50	200	267.33	29.26	1.93	534.20	11.22	49.96
22	50	250	395.61	51.43	1.82	597.96	290.30	33.84
23	50	300	402.63	81.24	1.42	463.24	86.85	13.08
24	50	400	258.39	166.25	1.25	359.34	2.98	28.09
25	50	500	415.08	284.43	4.16	717.92	64.13	42.18
26	100	150	633.78	22.72	1.04	726.45	193.70	12.76
27	100	200	774.67	59.73	0.80	841.97	295.52	7.99
28	100	250	802.92	112.90	1.04	869.61	341.88	7.67
29	100	300	817.48	191.18	2.16	844.78	1314.42	3.23
30	100	400	721.21	409.75	0.68	799.90	419.86	9.84
31	100	500	964.26	724.04	1.17	1335.76	1589.59	27.81

the capacity values in Fig. 2 are obtained while increasing P and using the same set of antennas found by each algorithm when a power value of 50 dBm is used.

From Fig. 2, as one would expect, first we observe that the capacity values increase according to a logarithmic scale. Next, we see that the whole capacity of the system increases in about 100 and 300 bps/Hz when the maximum power P goes from 50 to 500 dBm for $K = 30$ and $K = 80$ users, respectively. These values show that the capacity of the system is increased in approximately 4 bps/Hz for each extra user in the system. Finally, we confirm that VNS algorithm significantly improves the solutions obtained with the greedy approach and hence the capacity values for the Massive MIMO system. Ultimately, in Table 2 we present numerical results for the Algorithms 3.1 and 3.2 for $P = 50$ dBm while using equal power values for each user in constraint (3). Notice that this constraint allows one to assign power to each user following any assignment criteria. In particular, using equal power values guarantees that each user has a positive signal to noise ratio which might not always be the case when Eqs. (7) and (8) are used.

The legend in Table 2 is exactly the same as in Table 1. From Table 2, we mainly confirm the observations drawn from Table 1. In this case, the gap values, in which VNS outperforms the greedy approach, go from 28.98% to 85.88% for the small and medium size instances. Whilst for the larger ones, these values go from 2.94% to 49.96%. Similarly, we observe that the initial solutions obtained with VNS are poor compared to their best counterparts, and in particular these objective function values are worse for the large instances. Regarding CPU times, in general we observe higher values for VNS as well.

5 Conclusions

In this paper, we consider the problem of maximizing the whole capacity of a Massive MIMO system subject to power and antenna assignment constraints. Massive MIMO technology has emerged as an extended version of traditional MIMO systems. Due to its many favorable properties, it has become a strong candidate for 5G wireless communications and has gained increased attention by the research community within last decade. Improvements that can be achieved with this new technology are better performance in terms of data rate and link reliability, transmitting in higher frequency bands, strong signal indoors, and resistant systems to interference and intentional jamming attacks. The optimization problem considered is formulated as a mixed integer nonlinear programming problem for which exact methods cannot be applied efficiently. In order to overcome this difficulty, we propose a variable neighborhood search meta-heuristic algorithm which allows to obtain significantly better solutions compared to a state of the art greedy algorithm. Although, at a higher computational cost for most tested instances.

As future research, we plan to propose new mathematical models in order to deal with this important resource allocation problem. New formulations should include other criteria in the objective function such as fairness, utility functions and quality of service constraints while taking into account the uncertainty of wireless channels. Finally, new algorithmic approaches should be developed while avoiding the computational effort required to compute pseudo inverse matrices within each iteration. This would allow solving larger size instances of the problem.

Acknowledgments. The first author acknowledges the financial support of Fondecyt Project 11180107.

References

1. Benmimoune, M., Driouch, E., Ajib, W., Massicotte, D.: Joint transmit antenna selection and user scheduling for massive MIMO systems. In: IEEE Wireless Communications and Networking Conference (WCNC), pp. 381–386 (2015)
2. Boyd, S., Vandenberghe, L.: Convex Optimization. Cambridge University Press, Cambridge (2004)
3. Chang, Z., Wang, Z., Guo, X., Han, Z., Ristaniemi, T.: Energy-efficient resource allocation for wireless powered massive MIMO system with imperfect CSI. IEEE Trans. Green Commun. Netw. **1**(2), 121–130 (2017)
4. Fischer, T., Hegde, G., Matter, F., Pesavento, M., Pfetsch, M. E., Tillmann, A. M.: Joint Antenna Selection and Phase-Only Beamforming using Mixed-Integer Nonlinear Programming (2018). https://arxiv.org/abs/1802.07990v1
5. Hansen, P., Mladenovic, N.: Variable neighborhood search: principles andapplications. Eur. J. Oper. Res. **130**(3), 449–467 (2001)
6. Mladenovic, N., Brimberg, J., Hansen, P., Moreno Pérez, J.A.: The p-median problem: a survey of metaheuristic approaches. Eur. J. Oper. Res. **179**(3), 927–939 (2007)
7. Mundy, J., Thomas, K.: https://5g.co.uk/guides/what-is-massive-mimo-technology/. Accessed 21 Mar 2019
8. Zhang, J., Jiang, Y., Li, P., Zheng, F., You, X.: Energy efficient power allocation in massive MIMO systems based on standard interference function. In: IEEE 83rd IEEE Vehicular Technology Conference (VTC Spring), pp. 1–6 (2016)

A Play-Based Interactive Learning Approach for Fostering Counting and Numbers Learning Skills for Early Childhood Education Using QR Codes Mobile Technologies

Yaser Mowafi[✉], Ismail Abumuhfouz, and Jenni Redifer

Western Kentucky University, Bowling Green, KY 42101, USA
{Yaser.mowafi,ismail.abumuhfouz,Jenni.redifer}@wku.edu

Abstract. Preschool education is vital to children's social, physical, intellectual, cognitive, and motor skills. In this paper, we propose an interactive learning approach that allows preschool children to learn while they play based on a pedagogical concept for basic skills related to numbers and counting. To assess our proposed learning approach for basic skills related to the number core, we have developed a Quick Response (QR) code mobile application using the Android SDK that allows for children to navigate and count a set of QR tagged learning objects using a 1-to-1 counting correspondence and the cardinal counting principles. We evaluate the application with preschool children ages 3–5. Evaluation results indicate the viability of an interactive and entertaining learning experience that allows children to learn while they play. The results show that such a learning environment can have an influence on preschool children's perception and learning related to numbers and counting.

Keywords: Mobile application · Human computer interaction · Interactive learning · Early childhood education · QR codes technologies · Numbers and counting

1 Introduction

Preschool education refers to the formal teaching of young children before the standard age of schooling by people outside the family and typically in settings outside the home. These early learning experiences help children's intellectual, social, and emotional development which lays the foundation for later school success [1]. Studies have shown that high quality or high rated preschools can have a long term effect in improving the educational outcomes of children [2], and play has been shown to be a contributor to healthy social, emotional and cognitive growth [3].

The rise of the presence of mobile devices has paved the way for pervasive learning content associated with personalized learning contexts, content quality, richness of interaction, and adaptability for potential learners [4–6]. With mobile devices becoming more prevalent in the hands of young learners, enhancing the impact of mobile technology learning tools with relevant learning content requires integrating the learning environment with real-time interaction and stimulating materials [7, 8]. A considerable

© Springer Nature Switzerland AG 2019
I. Awan et al. (Eds.): MobiWIS 2019, LNCS 11673, pp. 16–26, 2019.
https://doi.org/10.1007/978-3-030-27192-3_2

body of literature demonstrate the positive impact of mobile technology on learning and suggests greater potential in facilitating access to information and increasing engagement to learning in classrooms [7–10]. For example, [11–13] find that mobile technology can positively improve motivation and engagement of young primary school learners. Equally, research studies on the use of mobile technology tools with young children (age 3–5) also highlight the importance of designing and developing learning applications that can motivate children's engagement and learning for such applications to be educationally valuable [14–17].

Continual advances in mobile technologies have allowed for enriching users interaction with their surroundings by linking users with their real-world content. One such development is Quick Response (QR) code technologies of two-dimensional barcodes that allow easy access to information through mobile devices [18]. This technology encourages learning by appealing to what [19] call the trilogy of mobile learning—time independence, location independence, and meaningful content, all of which are afforded by QR codes. Other review studies point to the potential of integrating QR codes for encouraging learners to become more accountable for their own learning by quickly and easily engaging with the learning content in which the gap between the classroom and the real world becomes "closer" [20, 21]. At younger ages, children can achieve significant learning gains related to learning outcomes through a variety of formats ranging from multiple interaction and with real-world learning content [22]. Similarly, [23, 24] discern that QR code mobile technology usage has increased the level of self-driven autonomous learning and engagement of children, along with their interest to accomplish the learning tasks.

In this paper, we propose an interactive learning approach that aims to augment the number and counting learning skills of preschool children. The proposed learning approach in this study aims to develop and evaluate a fun educational environment for preschool children to learn while they move and play based on a pedagogical concept for basic skills related to the numbers and counting. The approach also seeks to further preschool children's engagement with the learning content by stimulating children's autonomous learning and engagement with their educational environment.

2 Study Approach

According to Piaget's classic theory of cognitive development, the mental tools available for information processing increase with age [25]. This implies that learning based on personal experiences and interaction with their surroundings may allow children to master basic concepts in one domain before they can learn more advanced concepts in the same domain [26]. Early stages pedagogical environment emphasizes the following inextricable aspects: learning is fun; choices are important; the learning environment is linked to interests and everyday life's experiences; and learning avoids pressure and stress when based on play, exploration and discovery [27]. As interaction is important in both inquiry-based methods and social construction of meaning [26], our approach offers a range of possibilities that are complemented by allowing children's interaction with their environment along with their educators and peers. We base our approach on the learning paths of numbers, relations, and operations presented in work on mathematical learning in early childhood education [1].

The proposed approach of the present study focuses on fostering preschool children's learning of the number core and the cardinal counting principles[1]. The learning process builds on children's exploration of their surroundings by allowing them to use their environment to observe and probe a set of learning objects. Our approach attempts to prompt children to identify and count objects, and to provide instant feedback on the counted number of real world objects. Instead of counting objects displayed on a tablet screen, as is the case in many existing numeral learning applications, children can use the application to search for, identify, and count the objects of their interest. This format promote and stimulate children's interest in learning by inviting them to move around and search for learning objects in their surrounding environment. Equally, our proposed approach is not meant to substitute preschool classroom teachers' role in helping children explore their learning environment, resolve any possible conflicts between children, or prevent frustration with their learning environment.

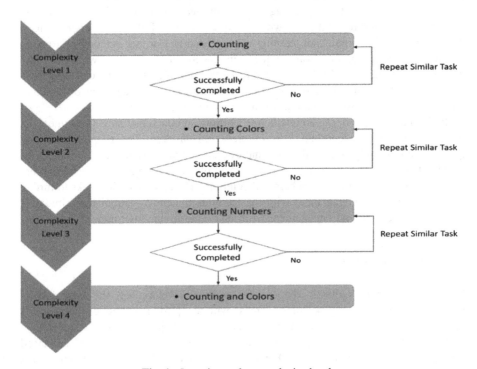

Fig. 1. Learning tasks complexity levels

---

[1] The number core concerns the list of counting numbers 1, 2, 3, 4, 5, … and is used in describing how many things are in collections. Cardinal counting refers to knowing the total number of items in the set.

The learning approach proposed in this study allows children to perform four different levels of progressive complexity for learning the number core and cardinal counting (Fig. 1). The interactive learning setting models levels of complexity and is meant to encourage and motivate participants' learning, as well as stimulate their learning process. Each level of complexity setting adjusts to adapt with the learner's progress, and remains unchanged until successfully completed by the learner prior to proceeding to the next level. Successful completion is defined in assessing numeracy skills of achieving a minimum 80% accuracy score in accordance with the Kindergarten Math Proficiency Rubric's learning indicators [28]. The levels of complexity analyzed in this study are as follows:

- Counting: the first level focuses on the learner's counting skills to identify and count a set number of five objects regardless of the color of these objects.
- Counting Colors: the second level focuses on the learner's counting skills and identification of five objects of a specific color.
- Counting Numbers: the third level focuses on the learner's counting cardinality skills to identify a defined number between one and five of a specific color.
- Counting and Colors: the fourth level focuses on the learner's counting and cardinality skills to identify and count two different colors between one and five objects of two specific colors.

As interactive learning is important in both inquiry-based methods and social construction of meaning, we thus propose the following hypothesis:

The complexity levels of the interactive learning tasks will have an impact on children's perception and performance on counting and number learning skills.

3 Methodology

The goal of this study is to explore a fun, educational, interactive learning approach that can allow preschool children to learn while they play based on a pedagogical concept for basic skills related to the numbers and counting. The study mainly focuses on early childhood learning of the number core that includes the number word list from one to five, 1-to-1 counting correspondence, and the cardinal counting principles. The study is designed to empirically assess the viability of different levels of progressive complexity for learning the number core and cardinal counting with the use of QR code mobile technologies interaction.

3.1 Apparatus

To evaluate the influence of our proposed interactive learning approach for children's basic skills related to the number core and to test our study hypothesis, we have developed a mobile application running on seven-inch Samsung Tablet Android OS devices equipped with QR code readers. This app works in conjunction with QR code tags attached to colored learning objects. The architecture of the application (Fig. 2) is comprised of the user control interface that provides the required interface to the QR code tag reader and audio speaker. The QR code tag database stores information about the QR tags as well as data on the users' counting progress. When the user brings the handheld device in close proximity of the QR code tag, the handheld device produces display feedback and an audio-based information relevant to the learning object and task. The user assessment management is set to track each child's learning progress and adjust the complexity of the learning level according to their individual progress.

Fig. 2. Application architecture.

3.2   Participants

The target learners of the study are preschool children whose ages are between three and five years. Children at this age are typically able to identify colors, shapes, letters and numbers, are in the process of developing numeracy and literacy skills, and have started to show interest in counting [26]. Twenty children between the ages of three and five years were selected from a preschool (11 boys, 9 girls). Basic demographic characteristics of the participants are summarized in Table 1. Most of the children in the sample were familiar with mobile devices and tablets. However, no prior experience with handheld mobile devices or tablets was required.

Table 1. Participants demographic summary.

N	Age (years)	Gender	N	Age (years)	F-value test statistic	p-value
20	Average: 4.35 Std. Dev.: 0.56	Girl	9	Average: 4.33 Std. Dev.: 0.5	0.06[§]	0.81
		Boy	11	Average: 4.36 Std. Dev.: 0.63		

[§]An ANOVA test was employed between gender groups.

3.3   Procedure

The classroom-learning environment in our study included learning objects (i.e., colored rubber puzzle mats) labeled with QR tags. Each object has a unique QR code tag that stores information about that object color (Fig. 3). The interactive learning approach allows participants to perform their learning activities, which entails navigating and exploring certain learning objects and colors. Participants performed their learning tasks on the Samsung Tablet handheld devices. All learning sessions took place in the classroom and were administered by classroom teachers who were informed in advance about the goals and objectives of the study. The classroom teachers explained the learning activity and instructions to the participants. Participants were assigned a unique login identification number associated with their logged learning tasks in order to track their learning progress and performance.

Fig. 3. Classroom learning environment setup. (Color figure online)

The learning tasks required participants to identify and count a specific number (ranging from one to five) of colored rubber mats by tagging with their tablet devices the specific color specified in that task. When the participants approach the learning object of their interest and bring their handheld devices close to the object which they can view through the tablet's screen, the QR tag reader displays the information associated with that task's counting progress on the tablet. Depending on whether the identification of the selected learning object was correct or not, the application will provide the participant with the counting progress that appears on the tablet device along with verbal feedback of the counting progress and further guidance towards fulfilling that task ("Try again"). The process is repeated for each task until it has been successfully completed with a minimum of 80% accuracy in identifying and counting the specified object(s) over the last three trials for each task, as demonstrated in Fig. 4.

The learning activities evaluated in the study consist of four different levels of complexity:

- Task one (counting) requires the participant to identify and count five objects of any of three colors (red, blue, and green) from a set of five colors (red, blue, green, yellow, and pink). The current task will continue until the learner successfully identifies the set number of objects of the specified colors for this task.
- Task two (counting colors) requires the participant to identify and count five objects of a specific color at a time (five reds, or five blues, or five greens). Similar to the earlier task, the current task will continue until the learner successfully identifies the set number of objects of each of the three specified colors.
- Task three (counting numbers) requires the participant to identify and count a specific number of objects (between one and five) of a specific color (e.g. three reds, or four blues, or two greens). Similar to the earlier task, the current task will continue until the learner successfully identifies the set number of objects of each of the specified colors.
- Task four (colors and counting) requires the participant to identify and count two different colors and a specific number of objects (between one and five) of each color for a total of five across two colors (e.g. three reds and two blues, or two greens and three blues). Similar to the earlier task, the current task will continue until the child identifies the set number of objects of each of the two specified colors.

Fig. 4. Demonstration of learning task process. (Color figure online)

3.4   Recorded Measures

Two objective performance and comprehension measures were used to measure learning: time and accuracy score (see Table 2). Subjective post-task assessment was not used, because children between 3 and 5 years often lack the metacognitive skills necessary to reflect on their experiences, and few guidelines for this type of measurement exist [29]. Children in this age group may not clearly express their experience and satisfaction levels and/or may try to impress the adults by showing what they can do without any help [30].

Table 2. Objective performance and comprehension measures gathered in the study.

Measure	Description
Completion time	Duration of the time from when the participant starts identifying and counting the specific objects set for each task until successfully[*] completing the task
Accuracy score	The number of correct counting of the specific number of objects and color of the total counting trials during each task

[*]Achieving a minimum of 80% accuracy score in identifying and counting the specified object(s) over the last three trials for each task.

4   Results and Analysis

We evaluated both the participants' performance and comprehension of the learning tasks during the study (see Table 3). The means and standard deviations for completion time and score are provided in Table 4. A one-way analysis of variance (ANOVA) was used to compare the average completion time and average accuracy score among the four learning tasks. The data met the assumptions required for using ANOVA. There were significant differences among the four learning tasks categories ($p < 0.01$), supporting the study hypothesis of the impact of the complexity levels of the interactive tasks on the participants' perception and performance of learning counting and numbers.

Table 3. Means and std. dev. with ANOVA results among the learning tasks measures.

Task measure	Mean	Standard dev.	F-value test statistic	p-value
Completion time (minutes)			24.48	<0.0001[*]
Counting	1.31	0.51		
Counting colors	1.16	0.39		
Counting numbers	0.37	0.17		
Colors and numbers	1.02	0.41		
Accuracy score			7.9	0.0001[*]
Counting	0.84	0.13		
Counting colors	0.87	0.09		
Counting numbers	0.96	0.08		
Colors and counting	0.77	0.23		

[*]Statistically significant ($P \leq 0.01$) with differences between groups.

An additional analysis was performed to assess the participants' perception and retention of the processed learning tasks, namely (counting and counting numbers) and (counting colors and colors and counting). The results of the paired t-tests used to compare participants' performance on the counting vs. counting numbers tasks and counting colors vs. colors and counting tasks are presented in Tables 4 and 5 respectively.

Table 4. Means difference between counting and counting numbers tasks measures.

Task Measure	Mean	_Paired t_-value Test Statistic	_p_-value
Completion time (minutes)		9.46	<0.0001*
Counting	1.31		
Counting numbers	0.37		
Accuracy score		−3.46	0.0014*
Counting	0.84		
Counting numbers	0.96		

*Statistically significant ($p \leq 0.01$) with differences between groups.

Table 5. Means difference between counting colors and colors and counting tasks measures.

Task Measure	Mean	_Paired t_-value test statistic	_p_-value
Completion time (minutes)		1.31	0.21
Counting colors	1.16		
Colors and counting	1.02		
Accuracy score		2.55	0.02
Counting colors	0.87		
Colors and counting	0.77		

*Statistically significant ($p \leq 0.01$) with differences between groups.

These results indicate significant difference in participants' completion time and scores between counting and counting numbers learning tasks ($p < 0.01$), as shown in Table 4. A considerably significant difference was found in the accuracy score between counting colors and colors and counting ($p = 0.02$). The results might indicate the impact of the various complexity levels of autonomous learning tasks on the participants' perception and performance of counting and numbers learning skills. However, no significant difference was found in the completion time between counting colors and colors and counting ($p = 0.21$), as shown in Table 5.

5   Conclusion

In this paper, we propose an interactive learning approach for early childhood learning of numbers and counting founded on related didactical and pedagogical concepts. The proposed method uses handheld devices equipped with QR code mobile technology.

The approach aims at improving children's ability to play, and fostering their understanding of their surroundings. In addition, the approach allows children to learn how to count objects using a 1-to-1 counting correspondence and the cardinal counting principles. We evaluate the application on preschool kindergarten children between three and five years old. Evaluation results indicate the viability of the application in fostering children's engagement in a fun and entertaining learning environment.

The results of this study are able to further the state of knowledge in understanding the influence of interactive learning using handheld mobile devices on children's learning ability and behavior related to numbers and counting. The study provides guidelines to be proposed for creating a fun, educational, interactive environment for preschool and kindergarten children, based on a pedagogical concept for learning basic skills related to the numbers and counting. For future work, there remain several areas of inquiry to further illuminate the impact of the interactive learning approach proposed in the study related to early childhood learning of numbers and counting. For example, additional studies would be necessary to determine how valid such results could be compared with traditional learning methods to count objects using a 1-to-1 counting correspondence and the cardinal counting principles.

References

1. Committee on Early Childhood Mathematics, N.R.C., Mathematics Learning in Early Childhood: Paths Toward Excellence and Equity. The National Academies Press (2009)
2. Shaefer, S., Cohen, J.: Making Investments in Young Children: What the Research on Early Careand Education Tells Us, N.A.O.C. Advocates, Editor, Washington, DC (2000)
3. Wenner, M.: The Serious Need for Play. Scientific American (2009)
4. Drigas, A., Kokkalia, G., Lytras, M.D.: Mobile and multimedia learning in preschool education. J. Mob. Multimed **11**(1–2), 119–133 (2015)
5. Gabrielle, A.C.-H., Gary, F., Xingyu, P.: Tablet-based math assessment: what can we learn from math apps? J. Educ. Technol. Soc. **18**(2), 3–20 (2015)
6. Seifert, T.: Pedagogical applications of smartphone integration in teaching: lecturers, pre-service teachers and pupils' perspectives. IJMB **7**(2), 1–16 (2015)
7. Zomer, N.R., Kay, R.H.: Technology use in early childhood education: a review of literature. J. Educ. Inform. **1**, 1–25 (2016)
8. Herodotou, C.: Young children and tablets: a systematic review of effects on learning and development. J. Comput. Assist. Learn. **34**(1), 1–9 (2018)
9. Domingo, M.G., Garganté, A.B.: Exploring the use of educational technology in primary education: teachers' perception of mobile technology learning impacts and applications' use in the classroom. Comput. Hum. Behav. **56**, 21–28 (2016)
10. Devers, C., Panke, S.: Learning with mobile devices: an overview, in e-learn: world conference on e-learning in corporate, government, healthcare, and higher education 2017. In: Dron, J., Mishra, S. (eds.) Association for the Advancement of Computing in Education (AACE), Vancouver, British Columbia, Canada, pp. 1709–1717 (2017)
11. Gerger, K.: 1:1 Tablet Technology Implementation in the Manhattan Beach Unified School District: A Case Study. California State University, Long Beach (2014)
12. Jagušt, T., et al.: Gamified digital math lessons for lower primary school students. In: 6th IIAI International Congress on Advanced Applied Informatics (IIAI-AAI). IEEE (2017)

13. Jagušt, T., Botički, I., So, H.-J.: Examining competitive, collaborative and adaptive gamification in young learners' math learning. Comput. Educ. **125**, 444–457 (2018)
14. Aronin, S., Floyd, K.K.: Using an iPad in inclusive preschool classrooms to introduce STEM concepts. Teach. Except. Child. **45**(4), 34–39 (2013)
15. Flewitt, R., Messer, D., Kucirkova, N.: New directions for early literacy in a digital age: the iPad. J. Early Child. Lit. **15**, 289–310 (2014)
16. Lee, L.: Digital media and young children's learning: a case study of using iPads in American preschools. IJIET **5**(12), 947 (2015)
17. McManis, L.D., Gunnewig, S.B.: Finding the education in educational technology with early learners. Technol. Young Child **67**, 14–24 (2012)
18. Ashford, R.: QR codes and academic libraries: reaching mobile users. Coll. Res. Libr. News **71**(10), 5 (2010)
19. Law, C., So, S.: QR codes in education. J. Educ. Technol. Dev. Exch. **3**(1), 85–100 (2010)
20. Thorne, T.: Augmenting classroom practices with QR codes. TESOL J. **7**(3), 746–754 (2016)
21. Kossey, J., Berger, A., Brown, V.: Connecting to educational resources online with QR codes. FDLA J. **2**(1), 1 (2015)
22. Furió, D., et al.: Mobile learning vs. traditional classroom lessons: a comparative study. J. Comput. Assist. Learn. **31**(3), 189–201 (2015)
23. Looi, C.-K., et al.: Bridging formal and informal learning with the use of mobile technology. In: Chai, C.S., Lim, C.P., Tan, C.M. (eds.) Future Learning in Primary Schools, pp. 79–96. Springer, Singapore (2016). https://doi.org/10.1007/978-981-287-579-2_6
24. Boticki, I., et al.: Usage of a mobile social learning platform with virtual badges in a primary school. Comput. Educ. **86**, 120–136 (2015)
25. Piaget, J.: Piaget's theory. In: Mussen, P. (ed.) Handbook of Child Psychology, 4th edn., vol. 1. Wiley, New York (1983)
26. Ormrod, J.E.: Human Learning, 5th edn. Pearson Education, London (2009)
27. Lee, J.S.: Preschool teachers' shared beliefs about appropriate pedagogy for 4-years-olds. Early Child. Educ. J. **33**(6), 433–441 (2006)
28. Kindergarten Math Proficiency Rubrics (2014). www.tomah.k12.wi.us/ReadResourcePubl icForm.aspx?resourceid=131
29. McKnight, L., Cassidy, B.: Children's interaction with mobile touch-screen devices: experiences and guidelines for design. Int. J. Mob. Hum. Comput. Interact. (IJMHCI) **2**(2), 18 (2010)
30. Hanna, L., Risden, K., Alexander, K.: Guidelines for usability testing with children. Interactions **4**(5), 9–14 (1997)

Detecting Defected Crops: Precision Agriculture Using Haar Classifiers and UAV

Mehmet Doğan Altınbaş$^{(\boxtimes)}$ and Tacha Serif$^{(\boxtimes)}$

Yeditepe University, Atasehir, 34755 Istanbul, Turkey
{daltinbas,tserif}@cse.yeditepe.edu.tr

Abstract. According to recent studies, the world's population has doubled since 1960. Furthermore, some projections indicate that the world's population could reach more than ten billion in the next half of this century. As the world is getting increasingly crowded, the ever-growing need for resources is rising. It appears that depletion of natural resources will be three times more than current rates by the mid-century. People would not only consume more resources but also will need more agricultural produce for their everyday life. Hence, in order to meet the ever-increasing demand for farming products, yield should be maximized using top-end technologies. Precision agriculture is the application of technologies and methods to obtain data driven crop management of the farmland. In the middle of the 1980s, precision farming techniques initially were used for soil analysis using sensors and evolved to advanced applications that makes use of satellites, handheld devices and aerial vehicles. Drones commonly referred as unmanned aerial vehicles (UAVs) and have been extensively adopted in precision farming. Consequently, in the last two decades, 80 to 90% of the precision farming operations employed UAVs. Accordingly, this paper proposes a prototype UAV based solution, which can be used to hover over tomato fields, collect visual data and process them to establish meaningful information that can used by the farmers to maximize their crop. Furthermore, the findings of the proposed system showed that this was viable solution and identified the defected tomatoes with the success rate of 90%.

Keywords: Haar classifiers · Image processing · Machine learning · Mobile application

1 Introduction

According to the latest studies, the world population could reach 9.6 billion by 2050 [1]. Because of the aforementioned projection, it is clear that the increase in the demand for overall agricultural products is imminent.

Agricultural production is one of the main human activities for survival, and people currently use 50% of the habitable terrains for farming [2]. Using advanced technologies in farming could improve the well-being of the farming land; reduce the need for pesticides and increase the productivity. Precision agriculture aims to increase productivity and sustainability by reorganizing, managing and analyzing the crop production lifecycle. By doing so, the farmers and landowners can keep track of their crops daily bases, considering their production target.

© Springer Nature Switzerland AG 2019
I. Awan et al. (Eds.): MobiWIS 2019, LNCS 11673, pp. 27–40, 2019.
https://doi.org/10.1007/978-3-030-27192-3_3

As part of this paper, a system that would observe the agricultural terrain and detect defected tomatoes is developed and described. The proposed system uses a smartphone-controlled drone to gather information from the terrain and analyzes its visual findings using Haar. Accordingly, this paper is structured as follows; Sect. 2 starts with a brief introduction to agriculture and elaborates on its practices. Section 3 details the image processing techniques and methodologies, and Sect. 4 describes the requirements and system design. Section 5 depicts the prototype implementation, and Sect. 6 analyzes and highlights the outcomes of the test results and evaluations. Finally, Sect. 7 summarizes the findings, and discusses future development areas.

2 Background

Farming processes has changed dramatically in the last couple of decades and evolved immensely from what it was a century ago. As the population grows and the numbers of middle classes increase, the need for optimized yield production rises exponentially.

Agriculture or farming is about cultivating animals, plants and raising crops for sustaining human life. According to archeological studies, all people were hunter-gatherer until about 10.000 years ago [3]. After people have learned how to preserve meat cool, cook with fire and taming wild animals, they have achieved inhabiting for longer periods in the same geographical areas. As a result, they started using the soil and producing agricultural goods. As an example, Chinese farmers were one of the first farmers who have cultivated wild rice for their survival [4].

In the 1800s, the invention of internal combustion engines has accelerated development of farming tools. People have started using tractors for labor-intensive tasks, such as plowing, tilling and planting fields. Using engines and machinery at the beginning of the 19th century was also the beginning of a new era in agriculture. From that milestone and onwards, farming improved greatly by the help of soil enrichment, chemical aids such as pesticides and mechanical tools and irrigation pipe networks [5].

In the early 1990s, information and communication technologies once again changed the farming rules and the processes surrounding it by the realization of precision agriculture [6]. According to new technology-aided concept, the land should be in constant observation, starting from soil preparation, to harvesting. Following this trend, Wang et al. [7] have implemented a system, which used low-altitude remote sensing (LARS) to observe the capacity field and analyzed the crop yield information using an UAV. Similarly, Ivushkin et al. [8] determined soil salinity by the help of an UAV sensors. In this study, the authors used three different sensors, which were attached to the UAV, such as thermal camera, hyperspectral camera and Light Detection and Ranging (LiDAR) scanner. These sensors were utilized to detect water and salt stress in quinoa plants. Their findings concluded that the hyperspectral Reflectance Index (PRI) performed with the best results.

From different perspective, Senthilnath et al. [9] aimed to detect tomatoes using spectral-spatial methods from RGB (red, green and blue) photos that were taken by an UAV. Spectral clustering was performed using algorithms such as; K-means, expectation maximizations (EM) and self-organizing maps (SOM). The images were shot from different heights using an UAV and the impact of the height differences on the performance of the overall system was observed. As a result, their findings showed that the EM outperformed the other two classification algorithms that were used. Similarly, Kerkech, Hafiane and Canals [10] designed a system that evaluated the diseases in the vineyard fields using deep learning methods. In this study too, the RGB images were taken by an UAV. Moreover, Rieka et al. [11] developed a high-precision positioning system that determines the position of a micro-sized UAV. To do that a Real Time Kinematic (RTK) positioning system was integrated into the UAV. As a consequence, position error of micro-sized UAV is calculated around 90 cm.

3 Methodology

This section discusses the tools, methodologies and algorithms that are needed to implement a UAV based data collection and defected produce identification system.

3.1 Algorithms

This study aims to identify and distinguish fresh, healthy tomatoes from the defected ones. Therefore, a list of possible useful algorithms is examined and considered for this purpose. Accordingly, the following section details the image processing and machine learning algorithms that should be taken into consideration in order to achieve the task.

Image Processing Algorithms. Digital image processing algorithms deliver extensive solutions such as; distortion/noise removal, color enhancement and compression [12]. For instance, image smoothing is a base method that is mainly applied to reduce noise and resolution of an image. The linear filtering is a process that linear combination of the values of the pixels in the input pixel's neighborhood is used to calculate the value of an output pixel. As depicted by the Eq. 1, $g(i,j)$ refers output pixel value whereas $f(i+k,j+l)$ denotes input pixel values also $h(k,l)$ represent kernel which is less than filter's coefficient.

$$g(i,j) = \sum_{k,l} f(i+k,j+l)h(k,l) \qquad (1)$$

On the other hand, every image has a dimension value, which can be visualized by rows and columns. Each row and column pairs represent a pixel, and each pixel has a RGB value that indicates its color. By determining value of color, the image pixels can be changed as desired. For example, consider an image that contains multiple colors such as blue, red and green (Fig. 1a). This image can be transformed to an image that only contains red pixels (Fig. 1b). To achieve this, the image is sliced into a grid using columns and rows and after that every row-column pair is analyzed in terms of its color content. Using this approach, RGB colors of each pixel can be determined. Consequently, each pixel that contains a color different than red is altered into a white color.

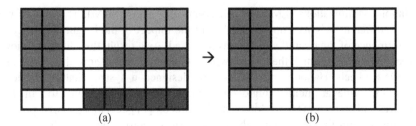

Fig. 1. Accessing Image's pixels and changing some of them (Color figure online)

Threshold binary is another practical technique which is commonly used. The basic idea is to check whether the source pixel is above the threshold value or not. If the source pixel is above the threshold value, the pixel will be set to the maximum value which is also specified as a parameter of the threshold algorithm. If not, the source pixel is set to 0. The following equation (Eq. 2) indicates how threshold binary works (Fig. 2).

$$dst(x,y) = f(x) = \begin{cases} maxVal, & if\ src(x,y) > thresh \\ 0, & otherwise \end{cases} \tag{2}$$

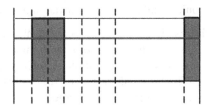

Fig. 2. Threshold binary

Machine Learning Algorithms. Machine learning is a field of computer science and an application of artificial intelligence that gives learning ability to computers by extracting information from raw data. Machine learning algorithms are the group of algorithms that enables software applications to become more accurate in forecasting results without being programmed individually.

Machine learning algorithms can be categorized into two groups – supervised and unsupervised. Supervised learning is the process of algorithm learning from the dataset. The target is to obtain specific relationships or patterns in the input data that allows generating correct output data. In unsupervised learning, data is qualified generally by assigning its features [13]. For example, tens of thousands of banana image samples are included in the database. Each banana has several features like color, surface strength and offset from other bananas are estimated.

Haar-based classifier, which is a machine learning object detection algorithm that is used in unsupervised learning tasks, is a highly successful method that is used for detecting a specific object in images. Haar classifier uses Haar-features that are achieved by detecting edges and lines [14]. The following figure shows the aspects of the features (Fig. 3).

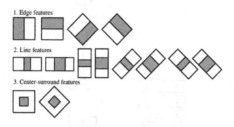

Fig. 3. Haar-like feature

3.2 Essential Tools

One of the core software elements that makes image processing algorithms more accessible is the Open Source Computer Vision Library (OpenCV), which is an open source computer vision and machine learning library that can be integrated to both desktop and mobile development platforms. This library has more than 2000 algorithms that can be used for detecting and recognizing faces, tracking objects, extracting 3D models and so on. The other core component that need to be utilized is the Xcode integrated development environment. Xcode is a OSX software that enable programmers design, preview and create applications for both OSX and iOS systems. The development platform also allows developers to integrate third-party libraries, such as OpenCV, and software development kits for additional functionality.

On the other hand, there will be need for three different types of hardware to realize this prototype. These are: (a) high-end computers that can be used in the development of the mobile application and its integration with the computer vision libraries. (b) A drone with a high-resolution video camera and; (c) a mobile phone that will be used in operating the drone and analyzing the collected photographic data.

4 Analysis and Design

As mentioned in the previous section, the proposed precision agriculture solution is composed of a smartphone, storage area (database) and multi-rotor drone. For prototyping purposes, the proposed solution will be using the internal storage area of the smartphone to implement a local database and store its data and user's commonly used preferences (Fig. 4).

According to this architecture, the system is designed for the maximum ease of use, where a smartphone controls the drone. Also, system operates a database in smartphone that keeps user credentials. The main functionality of the system is divided as functional and non-functional requirements. Accordingly, functional requirements point out that what system does, whereas, non-functional requirements specifies how system accomplishes features that it proposes.

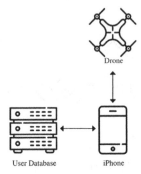

Fig. 4. System architecture

As it is shown below (Table 1), there are several qualified functional needs in the system. In order to determine tomatoes, the drone camera should capture one or multiple tomatoes on in the farming area. Additionally, the pictures taken by drone should be transferred to the smartphone. At this point, the application running on the smartphone should evaluate the image to check whether there are any tomatoes in the collected data. If the findings are positive, it should check for defected products. Furthermore, the application should be able to store credentials and preferences for every user.

Table 1. Functional and non-functional requirements of the system

Functional requirements	Non-functional requirements
Drone should capture images that includes one or more tomatoes on land	Smartphone must have iPhone Operating System (iOS). Also, iOS version should be 9.0 or later
Detecting ratio of defected tomatoes on land The drone should be controlled with the smartphone	The drone should provide an SDK to communicate with the smartphone over the Wi-Fi
Taking multiple pictures at a time. Transferring taken pictures from the drone to the smartphone	Quality of image should be at least 10 megapixels to recognize colors and get precise results
Saving and monitoring data for every user	iOS core libraries should be implemented to save user credentials

On the other hand, the system also needs to satisfy some non-functional requirements. First of all, the drone should have mobile SDK libraries that enables easy access to the drone's features through the smartphone. Using the drone's SDK, it would be possible to access drone's camera, control drone and transfer image files to/from the drone to the smartphone. Furthermore, the drone's camera quality should be set to minimum of 10 megapixels, so that using these high resolution images most accurate results can be obtained. Lastly, drone's SDK requires iOS 9.0 or later due to operating system compatibility requirements.

5   Implementation

At the very beginning, before any processing can be undertaken, the OpenCV Haar classifier needs to be trained. For this purpose, a group of positive images, photographs that contain tomatoes, and negative images, photographs do not contain tomatoes, are collected (Fig. 5). The positive images that contain tomatoes are either taken by a camera or extracted from open access Internet databases. Also for variety purposes, the positive images are photographs that do have different hue, contrast and background. Similarly, to the positive images, the negative images that do not contain any tomatoes are obtained from the Internet.

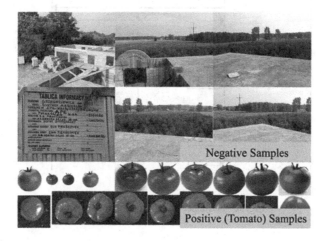

Fig. 5. Haar classifier samples

As a rule of thumb, while determining the size of the training data with the positive and negative images, three factors are taken into consideration. These factors are: the size, the quality of the images in hand, and the capacity of the underlying computing platform – such as random access memory (RAM) and the central processing unit (CPU). Using trial and error approach, it has been identified that the system produces the best predictions when trained with 5000 negative and 1100 positive samples. To reduce the CPU load and processing time, all images are converted to black and white during training phase. The training is conducted with the following steps:

- The path to each negative sample is stored in a text file.
- The path to each positive sample is stored in a text file; with additional information such as the dimension of the image, number of tomatoes in the image and dimension of the tomatoes.

- A vector map file (*.vec) is created using the 1100 positive.
- The vector map file, which is created in the previous step, is trained with negative samples and an XML file is generated. This process can take up to couple of hours depending to the hardware used.

After the training process, the classifier data is generated and stored in an XML file. This file is then transferred to the smartphone to be used by the implemented mobile application during tomato detection phase.

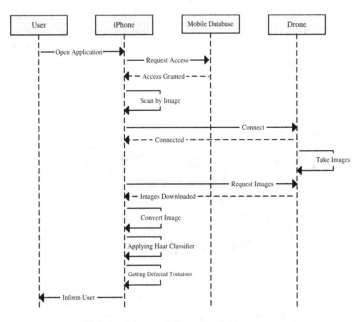

Fig. 6. Sequence diagram of the system

As depicted in the sequence diagram (Fig. 6), the system should start once the application is launched on the smartphone and the user is required to log on to the system. Hence at this stage, the user either types his/her credentials and logs in or registers. After the user is authorized and s/he has selected image scanning, the connection between phone and drone is established through Wi-Fi. Following this step, the on-screen control is enabled (Fig. 8b) and user can lift off the drone. After takeoff, the user can propel the drone to the target area using the same mobile app's on-screen control panel. As soon as the drone is landed, all the images shot during the flight are transferred to the smartphone via Wi-Fi. At this stage, user packs an image from the recently taken picture collection for identification. The selected image is converted to Mat object to apply the Haar classifier algorithm.

After Haar classifier is run on the image, it results with possible areas with target objects – in this case tomatoes. A series of algorithms are performed on the previous identified target areas to eliminate any false positives. For example, median blur is used to reduce noise in the image. Furthermore, target areas are examined by based on their pixels to ensure the number of tomatoes. As a result of these steps, target areas are treated as new images and added to an array. By accessing pixels of these images, dark areas, which are defect candidates, are identified. Also, are implemented to get rid of shadow removal algorithm is applied to reduce false positives. As a result of these processes, the user is informed with the final outcome.

In the development of the mobile application, the assets, OpenCV libraries, and also generated classifier files are added to the project environment. After that, the user authentication system is implemented to register users in the application. In other words, users must be authenticated with their username/password credentials. To achieve this, the login and sign up screen (Fig. 7) is created.

After the user registration and login modules are implemented, the main menu is created where the user will be able to choose with the base functions (Fig. 8a). As it can be seen in the figure, there are three buttons on the screen. An exit button is implemented to sign out from the application, whereas, the statistic button shows statistics about the pictures taken during the current session. These statistics also entail the number of tomatoes identified and its timestamp. The "Scan by Image" button starts the connection with the drone and brings piloting screen to the view. Piloting screen has some GUI elements that enable interaction with drone (Fig. 8b). The right-hand side buttons control yaw rotation, which rotates the drone around the vertical axis. On the other hand, the left-hand side buttons are responsible for roll rotation, which rotates the drone around the front-to-back axis.

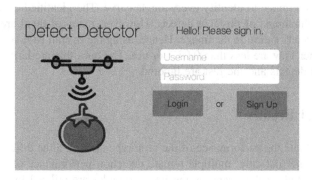

Fig. 7. Login and sign up view

After the mobile application is featured by drone controlling, images which contain tomatoes are taken by the drone. Then, the Haar classifier is executed that detects tomatoes in the image. As a result of this, every possible area that is tomato-like is called a region of interest (ROI) as referenced from in the OpenCV documentation [15]. These areas are considered to be parts of the image that need further detailed processing.

All ROIs are added to an image list to apply following algorithms for further investigation. Initially, an algorithm is used to reduce the number of the ROIs from the list if it is covered entirely by another ROI. To do that, coordinates and dimensions of ROIs are compared, and overlapped areas are eliminated. Additionally, ROIs are handled with their pixel values, so that if a region consists more than 40% of red pixels is classified as a tomato. The red color RGB range are defined as constant. Hence, any remaining ROIs in the list are accepted as tomatoes.

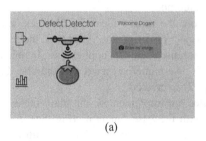
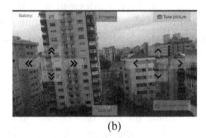

(a)   (b)

Fig. 8. User menu and drone view

So far, the system should have accomplished distinguishing any existing tomatoes in the images. Since the final objective is to identify any defected tomatoes within the images, as the next step the application needs to process and pinpoint tomatoes with defects. The defects are considered to be black dots on a tomato. Thus, an algorithm works to distinguish dark colors on any given image that contains at least one tomato. By checking each pixel in the given ROI, all dark pixels are set to remain the same but the rest are converted to white color. Following this, the contouring algorithm is performed on the image to identify every single curve. The identified curves could be translated into hundreds of possible defects. However, many of them are small pixel groups due to deterioration in the image. Hence, using the overall ROI size, defects are checked whether they are less than 0.03% or not. The ones that are larger than 0.03% are counted as defects and the rest are ignored.

6   Tests and Results

In order to evaluate the performance of the prototype system, three different test cases are created. In the first case, multiple tomato detection performance of the prototype system is evaluated. In this scenario, ten image samples are utilized for evaluation of ten tests results. The drone takes off and hovers off the given area to take pictures on the land and captures images that consist of two or more tomatoes from different angles and positions. After the images are collected, they are analyzed with the classifier and additional algorithms as described in the implementation section, to determine the number of tomatoes. The error rate is calculated as shown in the formula (Eq. *3*):

$$Error\ rate(\%) = 100 - \left(\left(\sum_n \frac{x_n/y_n}{n} \right) x\ 100 \right) \tag{3}$$

In error rate calculation, n represents the number of test environments, whereas x_n depicts the number of defected tomatoes, and y_n stands for the number of real tomatoes for n^{th} environment.

Accordingly, using the formula above (Eq. 3), the error rate is calculated as 11.6%. The graphical representation of the results is provided in Fig. 9. The arrangement of tomatoes, the intensity of the sun and the height of drone above ground level may cause aforementioned error in the findings.

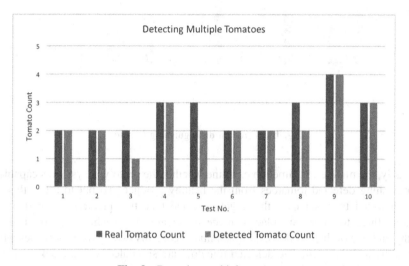

Fig. 9. Detecting multiple tomatoes

The aim of the second test is to evaluate the object identification performance of the proposed system. Hence, in this scenario two similar shaped objects are positioned in the target area. These objects – tomato and oranges – are selected since they are similar in size and shape. To test this, the drone is lifted off the air and taken five different images. The pictures that are taken by the drone is transferred to the smartphone and each image is processed with the classifier to detect ROIs. The identified ROIs could be very small area or can be overlapping by another ROI. In that case, an algorithm is used to neglect those ROIs. After algorithms have applied to the image, the remaining ROIs are accepted as tomatoes.

As can be seen in Fig. 10, as part of this test, if an orange is assumed to be a tomato, then we can consider this as algorithm's failure. On the other hand, if the number of tomatoes are identified correctly, algorithm is assumed to be successful. Accordingly, after the previous described test, the overall error rate of the algorithm is calculated to be 20%.

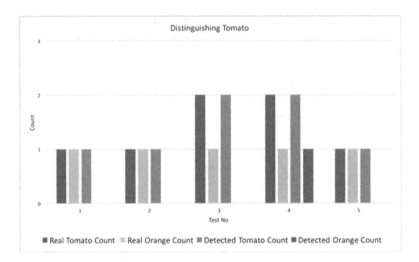

Fig. 10. Error on distinguishing tomato

Lastly, the final test is aimed to examine whether the prototype system is capable of distinguishing defected tomatoes from the healthy produce. To put to a test this, the drone is asked to hover over the target area and take five pictures. As part of this scenario, three tomatoes are placed in the target area from which two of them are healthy and one of them is defected. Each image contains two kinds of tomatoes which are healthy and defected. The defected tomatoes are simulated with a black sticker on them (see Fig. 11).

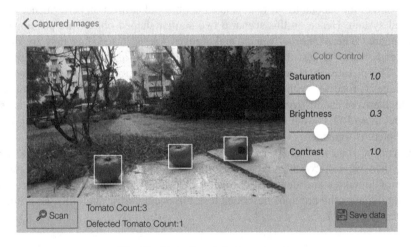

Fig. 11. Detecting defects on tomato

The error rate is calculated based on whether the algorithm can detect defected tomatoes or not. If the real number of defected tomato count is equal to detected defected tomato count, it is accepted as a successful test. Considering that, the overall error rate is calculated being as 20%. In this test, possible defected tomatoes are pointed by analyzing black-dotted in tomatoes. However, training an additional model could be more accurate than using dark color schemes to obtain defected tomatoes in images. This model could be generated by following the same steps that were used to train model for finding regular tomatoes (Fig. 12).

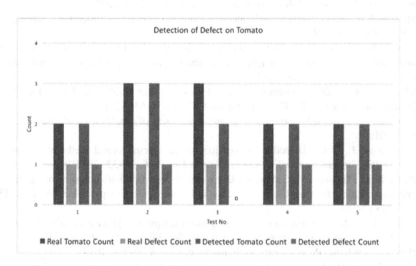

Fig. 12. Error on detecting defects on tomato

7   Conclusion

This paper proposed, developed and tested a prototype smartphone-controlled drone system that detects defected tomatoes on a farming field. The main idea behind this was to pinpoint any issues with the crop in real-time and enable farmers to keep track of their produce on a daily basis. This solution would also enable farmers to determine defected crops before go rotten and identify the reasons and find solutions to the problem.

According to the findings, the Haar classifier can be a viable solution in detecting agricultural objects, if it is prepared with well-selected samples. Also, Haar classifier and additional image processing algorithms could give accurate results in such scenarios. Moreover, our findings show that, access the pixel of images and contouring algorithms enhance the resulting product and increase the success rate of the proposed system.

As a future work, based on the experience gained throughout the tests and evaluations, it would be possible to get more accurate results by using a more precise color scale. Furthermore, by improving the algorithms used in the tomato identification phase, researches would be able to identify overlapping tomatoes in the images.

References

1. Alexandratos, N., Bruinsma, J.: World agriculture towards 2030/2050: the 2012 revision. FAO: ESA Working paper No. 12-03 (2012)
2. Roser, M., Ritchie, H.: Yields and land use in agriculture. Our World in Data (2018). https://ourworldindata.org/yields-and-land-use-in-agriculture#breakdown-of-global-land-area-today. Accessed 01 Apr 2019
3. Smith, V.L.: Hunting and Gathering Economies: The World of Economics, pp. 330–338. Palgrave Macmillan, London (1991)
4. Pringle, H.: The Slow Birth of Agriculture. Science **282**, 1446 (1998)
5. Matson, P.A., et al.: Agricultural intensification and ecosystem properties. Science **277** (5325), 504–509 (1997)
6. Tran, D.V., Nguyen, N.V.: The concept and implementation of precision farming and rice integrated crop management systems for sustainable production in the twenty-first century. Int. Rice Comm. Newsl. **55**, 91–113 (2006)
7. Wang, X., et al.: Development of visualization system for agricultural UAV crop growth information collection. IFAC-PapersOnLine **51**(17), 631–636 (2018)
8. Ivushkin, K., et al.: UAV based soil salinity assessment of cropland. Geoderma **338**, 502–512 (2019)
9. Senthilnath, J., et al.: Detection of tomatoes using spectral-spatial methods in remotely sensed RGB images captured by UAV. Biosyst. Eng. **146**, 16–32 (2016)
10. Kerkech, M., Hafiane, A., Canals, R.: Deep leaning approach with colorimetric spaces and vegetation indices for vine diseases detection in UAV images. Comput. Electron. Agric. **155**, 237–243 (2018)
11. Rieke, M., et al.: High-precision positioning and real-time data processing of UAV systems. Int. Arch. Photogramm. Remote Sens. Spat. Inf. Sci. **38**(1/C22), 119–124 (2011)
12. Berkner: Academic Press Library in Signal Processing **4**, 79–94 (2014)
13. Zhao, Z., Liu, H.: Spectral feature selection for supervised and unsupervised learning. In: Proceedings of the 24th International Conference on Machine Learning, pp. 1151–1157. ACM (2007)
14. Lienhart, R., Maydt, J.: An extended set of haar-like features for rapid object detection. In: Proceedings of the International Conference on Image Processing, vol. 1, p. I. IEEE, Rochester (2002)
15. Deepthi, R.S., Sankaraiah, S.: Implementation of mobile platform using Qt and OpenCV for image processing applications. In: IEEE Conference on Open Systems, pp 284–289. IEEE, Langkawi (2011)

An Efficient Tool for Learning Bengali Sign Language for Vocally Impaired People

Muhammad Nazrul Islam(✉), A. M. Shahed Hasan, Tasmiah Tamzid Anannya, Tani Hossain, Marium Binte Ibrahim Ema, and Shoab Ur Rashid

Department of Computer Science and Engineering,
Military Institute of Science and Technology, Mirpur Cantonment,
Dhaka 1216, Bangladesh
nazrulturku@gmail.com, amsh.himu@gmail.com

Abstract. The sign language is the only mean of communication for the vocally impaired people throughout the world. This is possible for a vocally impaired person who has undergone special training. In Bangladesh, learning sign language is a hard job because not enough institutes are available for teaching sign language, and not enough supporting materials or tools are available online. In this paper, an efficient learning tool was developed for vocally impaired people of Bangladesh to learn Bengali alphabet without any assistance or supervision of another person. The system consists of a computer software and a special sensor-fitted glove. The software shows various letters with associated signs to the user. The user can imitate the sign using the glove, while the system can detect the bending of the fingers and tilt of the hand and check whether the sign is correct or not. A between-subject experiment with 18 vocally impaired people were conducted to assess the performance and user experience of the proposed learning tool. The study results showed that the tool is effective for the vocally impaired people to learn Bengali alphabet comparing to the traditional learning approach. The results also showed the developed system is efficient, useful and acceptable to users.

Keywords: Sign language · Flex sensor · Arduino · Learning tool · Vocally impaired people

1 Introduction

Speech impairment is a disability where a person is unable to speak. At present, roughly 466 million people in the world are vocally and hearing impaired, among them around 34 million are children [1]. Spoken language is the principal mode of communication among humans. Being unable to speak, vocally impaired people are deprived of this mean of communication which affect them immensely.

© Springer Nature Switzerland AG 2019
I. Awan et al. (Eds.): MobiWIS 2019, LNCS 11673, pp. 41–53, 2019.
https://doi.org/10.1007/978-3-030-27192-3_4

Without an effective mean of communication, it is quite impossible to survive properly in society, which in turn leads to the evolution of sign language.

The sign language is a mode of communication using hand gestures and various signs. Although vocally impaired people all around the world use sign language for communication, sign language is not universal. Just like spoken language, different countries have different sign languages with different alphabets, words and grammar. For example, sign language used in USA (American Sign Language) and in France (French Sign Language) are not the same [3,5]. Bengali spoken language has 50 letters in its alphabet, including 11 vowels and 39 consonants. Moreover, it has its own set of words and grammar just like any other language. The sign language used in Bangladesh is called Bengali Sign Language (BdSL).

Learning sign language is similar to learning a spoken language. One has to learn the alphabet, the words and the grammar in order to communicate using sign language. But depending on the country or region, learning a particular sign language can be very difficult. Learning American Sign Language is fairly easy as there are numerous sources available offline and online. StartASL is a platform which provides offline and online courses, mobile app and various other multimedia contents to teach American Sign Language [4]. Memrise is another platform that teaches many spoken languages. It also has courses for various sign languages including American Sign Language, French Sign Language etc. [2]. Bengali sign language is comparatively new. As a result, not many sources are available offline or online which help in learning Bengali sign language. Similarly, there are almost no institutes or multimedia contents available for Bengali sign language and people with knowledge of BdSL are also very rare. Thus a person with speech impairment doesn't have an efficient and convenient way of learning sign language. Moreover, most cases in Bangladesh, disabilities such as vocal impairment is neglected and necessities like sign language are seen as luxury instead. With all these hindrances, learning sign language in Bangladesh is really difficult.

Therefore, the objective of this research is to develop a cost-effective and efficient learning tool for vocally impaired people to learn Bengali sign language alphabet. The proposed learning tool will encompass a wearable glove and an application.

The remaining section of this paper is organized as follows. The existing works focusing on learning and evaluation system for vocally impaired people are presented in Sect. 2. Both the hardware and software implementation with highlighting the key features are discussed in Sect. 3. The Sect. 4 presents the empirical evaluation study with data collection procedure, analysis and findings. Discussion, future work plan and concluding remarks are presented in Sect. 5.

2   Related Works

This section briefly presents the existing works on sign language. Some papers focus on the conversion of speech into signs for speech impaired people. For example, in [17], a Spanish speech to sign language conversion system was developed using a speech converter and a 3D avatar animation module. The system was used to translate sentences spoken by an official into Spanish sign language for speech impaired people at the time of assisting people applying for or renewing their ID cards. The best configuration of the system showed 31.6% sign error rate. A similar kind of system was developed in [15] to provide bus related information in Spanish sign language for vocally impaired people with less than 10% sign error rate. In another work [9], a system was developed for speech to sign transformation using machine translation and 3D avatar modelling to help vocally impaired people to understand multimedia contents by including sign language video tracks into them. The delay of translation was the key limitation of this system.

3D poses and shapes can be estimated using silhouette images [18]. Using this method and Beam search, a system was implemented for tracking sign language [16]. Based on these two systems, a conversion system to convert American Sign Language to text was developed using two hidden Markov models, one with a camera on the desk that observes the user's unadorned hand and another with a camera mounted in a cap worn by the user. The first system has achieved 92% accuracy where the second one has achieved 98% accuracy, but they have used only 40-word lexicon [19]. An almost same work has been done for Taiwanese Sign Language [14]. In several other researches, image processing has been used for sign language recognition [7]. However, the problem with image processing is that hand tracking gets affected easily by complex background and some other conditions which ruins the accuracy. Thus, in 2013, a group of Chinese authors have developed a sign language recognition system using Kinect sensor [8] which was a line motion sensing device. Kinect tracks the body and hand movements and thus recognizing sign languages becomes easier. The problem is that the kinect is expensive. In another work [10], a sign to speech converter system was developed using flex sensors that can recognize signs by analyzing the bending of hands. This flex sensor based system was cost-friendly and much effective.

A Bengali Sign Language (BdSL) identifier system was built using Fingertip finder algorithm [12]. The average accuracy of this system was 88.6% which was much promising than the existing systems at that time [12]. Again, in [11], image processing was used to identify BdSL. In this system, hand gesture was identified using HOG (Histogram of Oriented Gradients) and the output text was also converted to sound using a TTS (Text-to-Sign) converter. Similarly, in [6], a Bengali sign language recognition system was proposed that uses image processing. The model was built in such a way that it could recognize every skin type. The authors used their own data set of both male and female hands. In another work [13], a similar approach was proposed using Neural Network Ensemble (NNE) technique. The NNE makes the training time faster.

In sum, some of the works converted speech to sign language, various others converted sign language to spoken language. Again, a very limited number of works related to Bengali sign language have been carried out in Bangladesh, while most of them are for detecting the sign language, not for teaching.

Although a lot of works have been done in the area of communication using various technologies, but as of now, there is no system that works as a learning kit for Bengali sign language. Therefore, this research does not concentrate on building a communication device rather focuses on building a learning tool which can be used by speech impaired people to learn Bengali sign language alphabets. The tool proposed in this work tries to use the existing technology in a new manner to help vocally impaired people learn the sign language easily and efficiently.

3   Development of the System

A learning tool was developed for vocally impaired people that comprises both the hardware and software parts. The hardware part was implemented using five flex sensors, a gyro sensor (accelerometer), Bluetooth module and micro-controller (Arduino Uno). A wearable glove was used to fit the sensors. The five flex sensors were placed on the five fingers of the wearable glove. The accelerometer/gyro sensor was placed on the back of the glove. Each of these components was connected to the micro-controller, which takes the data from the sensors and transmits them to the computer using the Bluetooth module. Figure 1 showed how the hardware system (wearable glove) looks like. The estimated cost of developing the hardware part reaches only 50 US dollars.

The software part (desktop application) was built to interact with the sensors through micro-controller to match the signs and give the user a user interface. The application was implemented on java platform and Derby database was used to store the test results. Figure 2 shows an example screenshot of the application. The application acts as mediator for the end users to learn the alphabet and to test the learning performance.

Figure 3 shows how a user can learn the letters. In this case, a page with all the letters of Bengali alphabet appears when learn button is clicked. From there, when one letter is being chosen,the corresponding sign of that letter appears. The user can see the sign and try to imitate the sign wearing the glove. When the "Match" button is pressed, the imitated sign is checked. If the sign is correct, the application's UI shows the "Matched" message, otherwise it shows the "Not Matched" message. The user can go back to the page showing all the letters and learn a different letter.

To ensure that the user is learning all the signs correctly, a test feature is implemented in the system, where the user can try to match the signs without seeing the pictures of the signs. Figure 4 shows how a learner can test the learning performance. The test feature has three levels: easy level, medium level, and hard level. In the easy level of testing, all letters are shown just like the learn page and the user can select any of them. But unlike the learn page, no picture of the sign is shown. Instead, the user needs to match the sign on his/her own. There is no scoring here, nor any limit on the number of trials. In the medium level, a scoring system is applied. The letters appear randomly one by one. If the user succeeds in matching the letter, the score is increased by one, otherwise, the

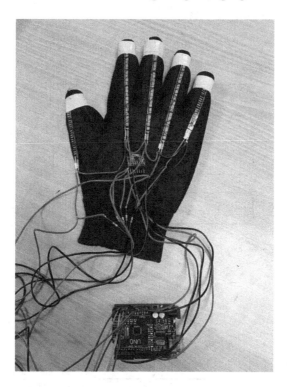

Fig. 1. The wearable glove of the learning tool

Fig. 2. Matching page of learning tool application

score stays the same. The user can stop at any time, at which point, the total number of trials and associated successes are shown to the user. These values are stored in the database along with the name of the user so that his/her highest score can be shown later. The hard level is similar to the medium one. The only difference is that the user cannot make more than 3 mistakes in one go. In one

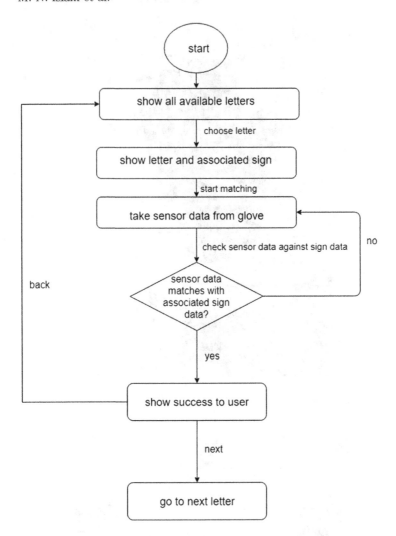

Fig. 3. Workflow of learning Bengali Alphabet

test, when the user fails to match more than 3 signs, that particular test session is over. The score is calculated and stored in the database.

The key features of the proposed system include the following:

1. The user-interface is simple and user-friendly: Designing intuitive and interactive user interfaces are crucial to develop any usable application [20,21]. Thus, the user interfaces of the proposed system are designed as simple, user-friendly and instinctive so that anyone can easily use the software without any effort.
2. All the signs of the Bengali alphabet are provided: Bengali alphabet has total 50 letters including 11 vowels and 39 consonants. These letters have 38

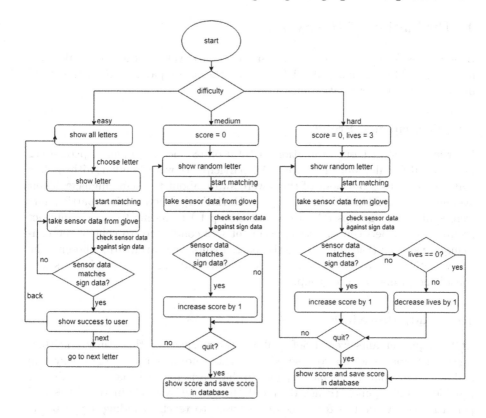

Fig. 4. Workflow of testing the learning performance

corresponding signs due to some similar sounding letters having similar signs. All the signs of the letters are available in the proposed system. The user can access any letter and see the corresponding sign.

3. The signs are detected using the wearable glove: In sign language, each sign is done by a unique positioning and movement of the hand, or individual fingers. The system includes a special sensor-fitted glove which can detect the movement and positioning of the fingers and the hand. Thus, the system can detect the signs done by the person wearing the glove.

4. The detected signs can be evaluated using wearable glove: The proposed system can check the signs performed by the user (wearing the glove) against the actual sign and can tell the user whether he/she has successfully imitated the sign or not.

5. The learners can test themselves: To ensure that the user is learning the signs properly, user can take tests where he/she can try to match the signs without the help of the pictures of the signs. Several tests are available, some with scoring systems to show the user learning progress.

6. A user can check his/her learning progress time to time: The progress report of each learner are stored in the database so that he/she can see their progress.

4   Evaluation of the System

A between-subject experiment was carried out to evaluate the proposed learning system. This section will briefly discuss the participants' profile, the study procedure and the evaluation outcomes.

4.1   Participants' Profile

In order to conduct our evaluation, a total of 18 vocally impaired people (12 male and 6 female) were recruited. All participants were familiar with mobile and computer uses but none of them were aware about the sign language. Their average age was 23 ± 2.65 (mean $\pm$ Std. Deviation). The recruited participants were split in two groups (Group A and Group B) including 9 participants per group. Since a between-subject experiment was conducted, to control the confounded variable (learning effect) the participants were arbitrarily chosen. The age variation in two groups was not significant and balancing gender was also considered in making the group.

4.2   Study Procedure

At first, participants were briefed about the purpose of this study and their roles. Participants were also ensured that, this study is for assessing the system and not for evaluating the participants so that participants behave normally and provide honest opinion (if asked) about the overall system functionalities and performance. A total of 8 letters were chosen to teach including 4 Shorborno (vowels in Bengali) and 4 Banjonbonno (consonants in Bengali) (see Fig. 5). Group A was assigned the manual approach and Group B used the learning tool to learn the letters and testing their learning performances. In manual approach, two authors of this article performed the role of instructor and taught sign language to the participants of Group A and evaluated their learning performance by interviewing. Participants were taught the letters for 20 min following the traditional approach, where instructors taught/showed the signs using their hands and fingers. To examine them, instructors showed the letters in a paper and participants were asked to imitate the sign to express that letter. Data of accurately imitating sign was collected for each participant for further analysis. In case of using the learning tool, two other authors of this article performed as moderators who provided a short (2–3 min) training on the learning tool to the participants of Group B. The participants of Group B were also allowed to use the learning tool for 20 min to learn the letters. After that, each participant gave a (easy level) test using the learning tool; and the frequency of the sign matched for each participant was recorded. Moderators were present to assist them for whole session for each participant. Finally, participants of Group B were asked to complete a set of questionnaires. The questionnaires include 5 topics: (a) satisfaction level, (b) ease of use, (c) easy to learn, (d) recommend to others, and (e) willingness to use the system in future. These questions were closed questions and asked to rate in a scale of 1 (strongly disagree) to 5 (strongly agree). Apart from these, Group B participants were asked an open question to share their experiences about the expected benefits and the possible ways of improvement.

Shoroborno

অ, আ, এ, ও

Banjonborno

ক, ঝ, প, ব

Fig. 5. Selected Bengali letters for evaluation

4.3 Data Collection and Analysis

The summary data related to the number of letters matched accurately for both cases (with and without the learning tool) is presented in Table 1. The results showed that the participants who used the learning tool performed well in learning the sign language for Bengali letters. The participants who used the learning tool could imitate the signs properly because when the bending of the finger properly matched then the software UI showed that the alphabet is matched. Again, the learning tool was user-friendly and easy to learn for them. The results also showed that, the performance of learning the Banjonborno was comparatively higher than the Shorborno in both cases (see the Fig. 6).

Table 1. Result of learning accuracy

	Number of letters matched accurately (learning accuracy)	
	Manual approach	Learning tool
Mean	5.78	7.22
Std. deviation	1.30	0.67
Percentage	72.22%	90.28%

The user experience of the proposed learning tool is depicted in Table 2. The result showed that the average score to each UX measure was comparatively higher. All participants found the system easy to learn and use; though the 'easy to use' received a little marginal score (3.4 ± 0.68) comparing to the 'easy to learn' (4.2 ± 0.26). It may be due to the fact that the participants used such kind of tool for the first time. They were willing to use the system in future (4.2 ± 0.81) and interested to recommend the system to others (3.6 ± 0.71). The overall satisfaction score was more than 4 which represents a good level of satisfaction.

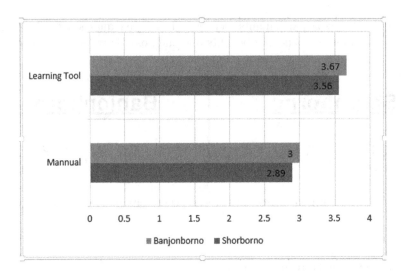

Fig. 6. Learning accuracy of Shorborno and Bangonborno

Table 2. Scores of different statements related to user experience

Ser	Questions related to	Score ($M \pm SD$)
a	Satisfaction level	4.1 ± 0.54
b	Ease of use	3.4 ± 0.68
c	Easy to learn	4.2 ± 0.26
d	Recommend to others	4.3 ± 0.71
e	Future use	4.3 ± 0.67

From the open-ended questions, the study found that all agreed to say that the tool will introduce an effective and motivated means to learn the Bengali sign language for the vocally impaired people. They also highlight the following benefits:

1. The application is user-friendly.
2. The learning and testing features of the system and the user interface makes the learning process fun.
3. No extra effort is required to search the offline and online learning resources.
4. The hassle of enrolling any course becomes redundant.
5. One can learn to operate the tool easily and also can learn sign language without any help.

In a nutshell, the outcome of the evaluation study showed that the system is effective, efficient, useful as well as satisfactory to end users. However, participants also opined that the learning tool can be improved by including some features. For example, making the tool wireless and portable. Some of them also mentioned that an android version of the application would also be useful for them. A few other participants stated that reducing the time of matching the signs can also be an improvement.

5   Discussion and Conclusion

In this research, a learning tool that includes an application and a wearable glove was developed for vocally impaired people of Bangladesh to learn the Bengali alphabet and evaluate their learning performance in three levels: novice, medium, and expert. The study also found that the proposed tool was effective to learn the Bengali alphabet comparing to the traditional approach. The participants found the tool enjoyable and easy to learn. Participants were highly interested to use the system in future and the overall satisfaction was also prominently high.

In Bangladesh, vocally impaired people are greatly ignorant about sign language. The required resources like institutions, NGOs, teachers, online materials, etc. to learn sign language are rare and costly. The proposed learning tool is affordable. Moreover, with this tool, a child can learn sign language without any skilled guide or supervision. Furthermore, a very little attention has been paid to develop ICT means for teaching the vocally impaired people and thus this tool also would be a great initiative to motivate them to adopt ICTs and overcome the challenges of digital divide.

The developed tool can eradicate the problem of learning sign language in Bangladesh. At present, there are no online sources for learning Bengali Sign Language. Enrolling in an institute which teaches sign language may be impossible because there are so few. Even after that, there are flaws in the teaching process because one teacher has to deal with a lot of students. As a result, all the students cannot absorb the knowledge completely, also the teacher cannot pay the same amount of attention to all the students. In contrast, the developed tool is used personally, so all the signs can be learned and tested very thoroughly and efficiently. Moreover, a student can revisit the letters at any time. The learning tool is a complete guide in the sign language learning process. Not to mention, the tool is removing all the other difficulties involved in the process such as, searching for signs of Bengali alphabet, the hassle of personally attending classes of an institute, substantial amount of cost etc. Therefore, the learning tool will hopefully make a positive impact in learning the sign language.

However, the proposed tool has a few limitations also. At present, the proposed tool can help only for alphabet, the tool does not teach signs of words. The tool was built with a certain sized wearable glove which may not be suitable for everyone. A limited number of participants (only 9 out of total 18) were recruited to use and test the proposed tool. Another limitation was that only 8 letters were taught and examined during the evaluation study. Apart from these, only a desktop application was developed, while mobile application would be another useful option. In future, the functionality of the proposed tool can be extended by incorporating signs of words and sentences. Though there are huge numbers of words in any language, at the beginning, basic words will be added for day-to-day communication. Gradually, more and more words can be added.

Future research may be conducted focusing to designing the wearable glove to make it customizable so that people of different hand sizes can use the tool comfortably. In addition to the desktop application, developing a mobile application and exploring its learning performance and user experience would be another open issue for future research. Thus the system would be more materialistic to open a new horizon in the process of learning sign language in Bangladesh.

References

1. Deafness and hearing loss. World Health Organisation. https://www.who.int/news-room/fact-sheets/detail/deafness-and-hearing-loss. Accessed 29 May 2019
2. Naruvir. Memrise - Sign Languages (n.d.). https://www.memrise.com/courses/english/sign-languages/. Accessed 6 Apr 2019
3. American Sign Language—NIDCD, 7 June 2010. https://www.nidcd.nih.gov/health/clearinghouse. Accessed 6 Apr 2019
4. Learn American Sign Language. StartASL.com (n.d.). https://www.startasl.com/. Accessed 6 Apr 2019
5. French Sign Language, 24 February 2019. https://en.wikipedia.org/wiki/French_Sign_Language. Accessed 6 Apr 2019
6. Arko, F., Tabassum, N., Trisha, T., Ahmed, F.: Bangla sign language interpretation using image processing. Ph.D. dissertation. BRAC University (2017)
7. Bauer, B., Karl-Friedrich, K.: Towards an automatic sign language recognition system using subunits. In: Wachsmuth, I., Sowa, T. (eds.) GW 2001. LNCS (LNAI), vol. 2298, pp. 64–75. Springer, Heidelberg (2002). https://doi.org/10.1007/3-540-47873-6_7
8. Chai, X., et al.: Sign language recognition and translation with kinect. In: IEEE Conference on AFGR (2013)
9. Araujo, T., et al.: An approach to generate and embed sign language video tracks into multimedia contents. Inf. Sci. 281(2014), 762–780 (2014)
10. Gunasekaran, K., An, R.: Sign language to speech translation system using PIC microcontroller (2013)
11. Hasan, M., Sajib, T., Dey, M.: A machine learning based approach for the detection and recognition of Bangla sign language. In: 2016 International Conference on Medical Engineering, Health Informatics and Technology (MediTec), pp. 1–5. IEEE (2016)
12. Jarman, A., Arshad, S., Alam, N., Islam, M.: An automated bengali sign language recognition system based on fingertip finder algorithm. Int. J. Electron. Inform. 4, 1–10 (2015)
13. Karmokar, B., Alam, K., Siddiquee, M.: Bangladeshi sign language recognition employing neural network ensemble. Int. J. Comput. Appl. 58, 16 (2012)
14. Liang, R., Ouhyoung, M.: A real-time continuous gesture recognition system for sign language. In: Proceedings of the Third IEEE International Conference on Automatic Face and Gesture Recognition, pp. 558–567. IEEE (1998)
15. López-Ludeña, V., González-Morcillo, C., López, J., Barra-Chicote, R., Córdoba, R., San-Segundo, R.: Translating bus information into sign language for deaf people. Eng. Appl. Artif. Intell. 32(2014), 258–269 (2014)
16. Shimada, Y., Shirai, Y.: 3-D Hand Pose Estimation from Image Sequence Using Probability-Based Search and Matching. https://ci.nii.ac.jp/naid/110003227566. Accessed 6 Apr 2019

17. San-Segundo, R., et al.: Speech to sign language translation system for Spanish. Speech Commun. **50**(11–12), 1009–1020 (2008)
18. Shirai, Y.: Estimation of 3-D pose and shape from a monocular image sequence and real-time human tracking. In: Proceedings of the International Conference on Recent Advances in 3-D Digital Imaging and Modeling, pp. 130–139. IEEE (1997)
19. Starner, T., Weaver, J., Pentland, A.: Real-time American sign language recognition using desk and wearable computer based video. IEEE Trans. Pattern Anal. Mach. Intell. **20**(12), 1371–1375 (1998)
20. Islam, M.N., Bouwman, H.: Towards user-intuitive web interface sign design and evaluation: a semiotic framework. Int. J. Hum.-Comput. Stud. **86**(2016), 121–137 (2016)
21. Islam, M.N.: Semiotics perception towards designing users' intuitive web user interface: a study on interface signs. In: Rahman, H., Mesquita, A., Ramos, I., Pernici, B. (eds.) MCIS 2012. LNBIP, vol. 129, pp. 139–155. Springer, Heidelberg (2012). https://doi.org/10.1007/978-3-642-33244-9_10

Web and Mobile Applications

Monitoring Driver Behaviour
with BackPocketDriver

Ian Warren[1]([⊠])(iD), Andrew Meads[1](iD), Chong Wang[1], and Robyn Whittaker[2](iD)

[1] Department of Computer Science, University of Auckland, Auckland, New Zealand
{i.warren,a.meads,c.wang}@auckland.ac.nz
[2] National Institute for Health Innovation, University of Auckland,
Auckland, New Zealand
r.whittaker@auckland.ac.nz

Abstract. Road safety is an international public health issue with youth drivers being grossly overrepresented in road crash fatalities and injuries. Our work centres on the use of smartphone technology to deliver an intervention that aims to improve driving behaviour. In this paper we describe the technical design of our BackPocketDriver app, which monitors key facets of driver behaviour: speed and acceleration. We present the app's requirements that were elicited through engagement with stakeholders and end users, and describe how the app has been designed to satisfy the requirements. In addition, we report on a quantitative evaluation of the app and show that in addition to meeting the requirements, a contemporary smartphone has sufficient sensory fidelity for building driver behaviour apps.

Keywords: Youth-driving · Driver-monitoring · Smartphone-app

1 Introduction

Road safety is a significant public health issue internationally, with approximately 1.3m fatalities and up to 50m injuries per year. Youth are particularly vulnerable, being overrepresented in crash statistics, and with road traffic injuries being the leading cause of death among young people [14].

Technology has the potential to be a key ingredient in addressing the youth driver problem. In our work, we are investigating the role of a smartphone app to deliver a behavioural change intervention to youth drivers. We have developed BackPocketDriver [21], an app whose feature-set is informed by behaviour models and behaviour change theory from the field of clinical psychology. The app employs a mix of messaging, goal setting, feedback, achievements, and leaderboards with the aim of improving driver behaviour. We refer the reader to [21] for a detailed discussion of the app's theoretical underpinnings, mapping of features to theory and resulting feature set.

In this paper, we focus on the design and development of BackPocketDriver's sensing platform. Given their ubiquity, embedded sensors and low cost, there has

© Springer Nature Switzerland AG 2019
I. Awan et al. (Eds.): MobiWIS 2019, LNCS 11673, pp. 57–70, 2019.
https://doi.org/10.1007/978-3-030-27192-3_5

been a lot of interest in using smartphones to monitor driver behaviour. Existing work tends to focus on assessing how well drivers make controlled manoeuvres based on processing accelerometer sensor data. BackPocketDriver additionally evaluates a driver's ability to drive within speed limits. In this paper, we explore the design space for sensor processing. Further, using a gold standard device, we determine the extent to which a smartphone offers a sufficiently accurate alternative to relatively expensive and specialised monitoring devices.

The remainder of this paper is structured as follows. In Sect. 2, we state the functional requirements and quality attributes for the BackPocketDriver app. In Sect. 3 we describe fundamental design options for detecting and processing speeding events and working with motion sensors. In Sect. 4, we evaluate the BackPocketDriver implementation. Prior to concluding in Sect. 6, we briefly report on related work in Sect. 5.

2 Requirements

BackPocketDriver has three functional requirements for monitoring:

R1: *Speed.* The app should detect incidents of speeding.
R2: *Acceleration and braking.* The app should identify incidents of harsh acceleration and heavy braking.
R2: *Turning and lane changing.* The app should detect cases of aggressive turning or lane changing.

The rationale for these requirements stems from smooth driving style and an ability to drive within speed limits being key indicators of safe driving behaviour [17]. The app is also subject to three quality attributes that emerged from focus group discussions with the target demographic and relevant stakeholders:

Q1: *Efficiency.* The app should make only necessary use of mobile data because youth drivers often have limited data plans. Power consumption should also be minimised as users rely on their devices for several purposes and would be unlikely to use a driving app that affected operation of their apps.
Q2: *Dependability.* The app must accurately report on driver behaviour. Reporting false positives (e.g. telling a user they have exceeded speed limits when they have not) and false negatives (e.g. failing to detect harsh acceleration) would erode people's willingness to engage in the behavioural change intervention.
Q3: *Usability.* In the context of this app, usability has broad coverage. The app must appeal to young drivers, be easy to learn and use, and retain user interest over time in order for the intervention to be effective.

3 Design Space

In Sect. 3.1, we describe a design that acquires and processes speed data (R1) in real-time. An alternative approach, described in Sect. 3.2, is to defer processing until the end of a journey. In Sect. 3.3 we outline the algorithms for processing a device's accelerometer and gyroscope sensors, in support of R2 and R3.

3.1 Real-Time Detection of Speeding Incidents

Providing real-time feedback requires that speed-limit data be available on demand. One technique is to use a reverse geocoding service that exchanges a GPS location for its road name and speed-limit. We have developed the *Look Ahead algorithm* that is used in conjunction with a reverse geocoding Web service.

Look Ahead Algorithm. For speed-limit data to be useful, it must be acquired sufficiently ahead of time so that it is available to determine whether a vehicle is travelling in excess of the speed limit at a given location.

The Look Ahead algorithm calculates two values concerning the vehicle:

- Angle of orientation (AO). The current direction of travel, represented as the angle from the geographic north pole.
- Projected location (PL). The location at which the vehicle is expected to be, within a given distance, if it continues in its current direction of travel.

In calculating AO, two locations A and B are used as follows:

$$\angle = \frac{111 \times |A.long - B.long| \times \cos(B.lat)}{110 \times (A.lat - B.lat)} \tag{1}$$

The constants 110 and 111 represent, respectively, the number of kilometres between two locations with a difference in latitude of $1°$, and the number of kilometres between two locations with a difference in longitude of $1°$. Equation (1) yields a value in the range 0 to $90°$, which generally needs to be adjusted based on B's location relative to A. For example, Fig. 1 shows that where location B lies anywhere in the south east quadrant of A, the angle is subtracted from $180°$. Following adjustment, the angle of orientation (AO) is found.

To compute PL, three inputs are required:

1. Current location (L) of the vehicle.
2. AO, derived as explained above.
3. Distance to PL $(DtoPL)$, in metres, between L and PL assuming the direction of travel to be AO.

The formula for calculating PL, in terms of a latitude/longitude pair, is as given in Eqs. (2) and (3).

$$PL.lat = L.lat + DtoPL / 1000 \times \cos(AO \times \Pi / 180) / 110 \tag{2}$$

$$PL.long = \frac{L.long + DtoPL / 1000 \times \sin(AO \times \Pi / 180)}{111 \times \cos(L.lat \times \Pi / 180)} \tag{3}$$

In determining the value for parameter $DtoPL$, the vehicles's current speed is used. This is calculated based on the time taken for it to travel between two locations, A and B. Distance travelled is computed using a geo-processing

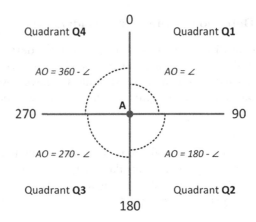

Fig. 1. Deriving a vehicle's angle of orientation

function that assumes a straight-line path between the two locations. Given the distance between A and B, the vehicle's speed $S = D/T$.

Distance to the projected location $DtoPL = S \times T$. An important consideration for specifying a value for T is that it needs to be long enough for the app to make a request of an external reverse geocoding service and to receive the response, such that speed-limit data is available prior to the vehicle reaching PL. However, large values of T reduce the rate at which speed limit data is acquired (meaning that the algorithm is less sensitive to speed limit changes). Furthermore, large values of T provide more opportunity for the vehicle to change direction and not pass through a previously computed PL location. The result in this case is that the app will not have the speed-limit for the vehicle's actual location.

For a vehicle travelling at $100\,\mathrm{Km/h}$, and assuming $3\,\mathrm{s}$ for the remote service call to be made, processed and the result returned, $DtoPL = 27.8\,\mathrm{m/s} \times 3\,\mathrm{s}$, or $83.4\,\mathrm{m}$. For a slower vehicle travelling at $50\,\mathrm{Km/h}$ and with a faster service call time of $1\,\mathrm{s}$, $DtoPL = 13.9\,\mathrm{m/s} \times 1$ ($13.9\,\mathrm{m}$). Thus, the distance between locations L and PL that is necessary to travel in order to make the service call varies significantly given different vehicle speeds and service-call times.

3.2 Post-journey Detection of Speeding Incidents

An alternative approach is to defer processing of journey data until *after* the journey has been completed. With this approach, the app lacks the ability to notify users in real-time of any speeding behaviour; it simply needs to record vehicle location and speed.

During a journey, the necessary data are captured by the device's GPS sensor and stored locally. After the journey, the data are sent to a proxy Web service for processing in a single request. The Web service processes the journey data by invoking the reverse geocoding service to acquire speed limit data.

Compared to the Look Ahead algorithm in which real-time speeding detection is offered, deferred processing offers several benefits. Mobile data usage by the device is greatly reduced (Q1). While the amount of location data sent over the network by the smartphone is comparable to that of the Look Ahead algorithm, the post-processing solution receives only a single response containing a summary of the results, whereas the real-time solution receives a response with speed limit data for every location data point. Furthermore, the app may be configured to upload data only when a Wi-Fi connection is available, thus incurring zero mobile data costs.

Post-processing the data also enables a reduction in the number of reported false positives and negatives (Q2). For a given location, as a vehicle's speed is known at that location, a speeding event can be detected with a single call to the reverse geocoding service, without the need to estimate the vehicle's projected location. Furthermore, heuristics can be applied when it is unclear on which road a vehicle is travelling. Figure 2 shows a specific case involving a flyover. With post processing the vehicle's path from B to C, the speed limit data on the overpass at point A is disregarded, whereas under real-time processing the app would assume the greater speed limit reported for point A and depending on the vehicle's speed report a false negative.

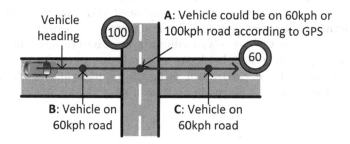

Fig. 2. Flyover road layout that can lead to reporting FP/FN

3.3 Motion Sensor Processing

To determine whether a vehicle has undergone a harsh acceleration, braking, swerving, or lane changing event, the app examines the longitudinal and lateral acceleration of the vehicle. Sufficiently high values for sustained periods of time correspond to harsh driving events.

The most accurate lateral and longitudinal acceleration measurements are gained when sensor data is expressed in the vehicle's coordinate system with gravity subtracted, as shown in Fig. 3. In this case, a vehicle's lateral acceleration, used for the detection of lane-changing and swerving, can be read directly from the sensor's x-axis, x_v. Similarly, the longitudinal acceleration, used to detect

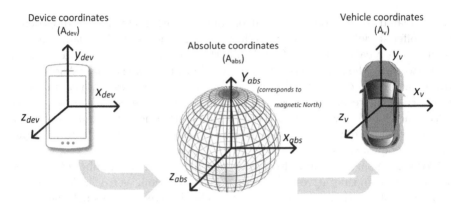

Fig. 3. Device, absolute and vehicle coordinate systems

harsh acceleration and braking, can be read from y_v. Modern smartphones embed sensors to measure lateral and longitudinal acceleration.

Where a smartphone is placed flat and face-up with the top of the device facing towards the vehicle's front windscreen, each axis in the device's coordinate system will directly correspond to an axis in the vehicle's coordinate system. However, having the smartphone positioned in this way is an unrealistic assumption that can be remedied using linear algebra to transform accelerometer measurements taken in the device's coordinate system into those of the vehicle's.

The first step is to rotate the device's coordinate system into an absolute coordinate system. This is carried out using the rotation matrix R_1 from the *Gravity vector* g_{dev} and the magnetic north vector:

$$A_{abs} = R_1^{-1} A_{dev} \tag{4}$$

where A_{dev} is the accelerometer data in device coordinates, R^{-1} is the inverse rotation matrix, and A_{abs} is the data in absolute coordinates.

The final step is to determine the orientation of the device in relation to the vehicle. To obtain this rotation matrix R_2, at least two of the components x_v, y_v, and z_v are required. Assuming that the vehicle starts on horizontal ground, z_v corresponds to z_{abs}. y_v is the vehicle's direction of forward motion and can be measured by a calibration phase in which the driver is asked to drive forward. This approach is taken in [15]. Alternatively, if data is being processed off-line, GPS data for a journey will be available, from which a relatively straight section of road (using root mean squared deviation [8]), is processed to determine the angle between y_{abs} and the vehicle's heading (obtained from GPS data). The advantage of this method is that the user is freed from needing to perform a calibration step at the beginning of each drive.

Once R_2 is obtained, A_v is found using:

$$A_v = R_2^{-1} A_{abs} \tag{5}$$

With A_v, the longitudinal (y_v) and lateral (x_v) acceleration is examined to detect harsh driving events. If longitudinal acceleration of magnitude $>2\,\mathrm{ms}^{-2}$ is detected for more than $0.5\,\mathrm{s}$, a harsh braking or acceleration event is generated. Similarly, where lateral acceleration of $>3\,\mathrm{ms}^{-2}$ for more than $0.2\,\mathrm{s}$ is detected, an abrupt lane changing event is created.

4   Evaluation

In this section, we evaluate the Look Ahead algorithm's accuracy for detecting instances of speeding in real-time. We compare this to our post-processing algorithm. We additionally evaluate our motion sensor processing algorithm in detecting instances of harsh braking, acceleration and swerving. Each algorithm is evaluated with respect to its accuracy, network consumption, and battery power drain.

We employed a gold standard device with which to compare a contemporary smartphone running an implementation of our algorithms. The gold standard device was the Racelogic VBOX data logger with its companion Inertial Measurement Unit (IMU)[1]. The VBOX is widely used in automotive and motorsport applications, and has higher precision hardware than that found in commodity smartphones. The test device used was a Google Pixel smartphone.

In all experiments, data was gathered concurrently using the test and gold standard devices. Data was gathered by performing real-world driving episodes, covering over $600\,\mathrm{Km}$, and recording each device's GPS and accelerometer data during those journeys. To gauge any difference in algorithm performance under different driving conditions, data was gathered in two environments: urban and highway. Intersections, overpasses and speed limit changes are common in urban layouts, and such features might lead to errors in tracking a vehicle's location and recognising speeding events. Conversely highways have few intersections and little variation in speed limit.

4.1   Sensor Accuracy

Location. For each journey, the location data generated by the VBOX was expressed as a function, $f(x)$, mapping a particular timestamp x (in milliseconds) to the vehicle's measured location at that time. Similarly, the test device's location data was expressed as $g(x)$. To find the difference between locations measured by each device at a particular timestamp t, we use $d_t = |distanceTo(f(t), g(t))|$, where $distanceTo$ is the standard function for calculating the distance between two points using the WGS84 ellipsoid[2].

To evaluate the accuracy of the test device's GPS sensor, the average d_t was calculated at $10\,\mathrm{ms}$ intervals, as was the standard deviation. The maximum deviation in meters was also taken for each journey.

---

[1] https://www.vboxautomotive.co.uk/index.php/en/products/modules/inertial-measurement-unit.

[2] https://en.wikipedia.org/wiki/World_Geodetic_System.

Table 1. Deviation of test device GPS sensor from gold standard device

Road layout	Max	Mean	Std Dev.
Urban	26.65 m	5.09 m	2.76 m
Highway	23.80 m	3.96 m	2.55 m

As shown in Table 1, the average discrepancy for the urban and highway environments was relatively small, at 5.09 m and 3.96 m, respectively, and with a standard deviation under 3 m. This indicates that the test device's GPS sensor is reasonably accurate compared with the gold standard. The results also indicate slightly higher discrepancy in urban environments. This is to be expected, due to tall buildings interfering with line-of-sight to GPS satellites.

Motion Sensor. The motion sensor data from the test device was compared with the VBOX data in a similar manner. The VBOX's IMU, used to measure acceleration, was mounted to the vehicle in such a way that the output in the IMU's coordinate system maps directly to the vehicle's. Hence, the IMU's output can be directly compared with that of the algorithm described in Sect. 3.3.

Table 2. Deviation of smartphone motion sensors from gold standard device

Road layout	Type	Max	Mean	Std Dev.
Urban	lat	$15.49\,\mathrm{ms^{-2}}$	$1.34\,\mathrm{ms^{-2}}$	$1.29\,\mathrm{ms^{-2}}$
	lng	$12.43\,\mathrm{ms^{-2}}$	$1.14\,\mathrm{ms^{-2}}$	$1.03\,\mathrm{ms^{-2}}$
Highway	lat	$14.63\,\mathrm{ms^{-2}}$	$1.41\,\mathrm{ms^{-2}}$	$1.33\,\mathrm{ms^{-2}}$
	lng	$15.23\,\mathrm{ms^{-2}}$	$1.17\,\mathrm{ms^{-2}}$	$1.05\,\mathrm{ms^{-2}}$

Table 2 presents the differences between measured lateral (side-to-side) and longitudinal (forward-backward) acceleration from the VBOX and test device. The mean and standard deviations are significant given the maximum values obtained. The results show little difference between lateral and longitudinal accuracy, nor any significant difference based on the road layout. The cause of the difference between the test and gold standard devices is likely due to the coordinate transformation algorithm (Sect. 3.3).

4.2   Speeding Detection Algorithms

The real-time and post-processing algorithms were evaluated for accuracy with respect to data obtained from the gold standard device. Where we discovered that an algorithm determined a user to be speeding when they were not, we recorded a *false positive* (FP) occurrence. Similarly, a *false negative* (FN) was recorded in the event that an algorithm incorrectly determined the vehicle to be obeying the speed limit. Each algorithm's accuracy was evaluated in terms of the proportion of the journey (by distance) considered to be FPs or FNs.

In addition to evaluating the output of each algorithm using location and speed data from the gold standard device, each algorithm was also run with data obtained from the test device to determine whether or not any differences in sensor accuracy resulted in differences in the final output. Since the test device's sensors are of lower fidelity than that of the gold standard device, comparing the algorithms with the two data sources shows whether or not the test device's sensing hardware is sufficiently accurate to identify the driving events of interest to us that were detected by the VBOX.

Accuracy. We found no difference in the accuracy of the algorithms when supplied with VBOX data versus standard smartphone GPS data. Hence, the difference in sensor accuracy does not translate to a noticeable difference in algorithm accuracy. This makes sense due to the small difference in location sensor accuracy as reported in Sect. 4.1.

Under highway conditions, the Look Ahead algorithm has a FP/FN rate of 0.2% as opposed to 2% for urban conditions. The higher FP/FN rate for urban layouts can be explained by highways typically having fewer intersections and longer stretches of road with the same speed limit, presenting fewer opportunities to select the incorrect speed limit or to fail to detect speed limit changes.

No FPs or FNs were detected for the post-processing algorithm. As observed earlier, by deferring processing until after a journey has completed, there is no need to estimate the vehicle's location. Furthermore, post-processing techniques (Sect. 3.2) can be used to determine a vehicle's current road of travel when the reverse geocoding service returns ambiguous results.

Mobile Network Usage. To measure mobile network usage, the total amount of data sent and received by the mobile application was measured, for each algorithm type. This was then divided by the total journey time to give the network bandwidth consumed in bytes per second. Consumption for the real-time Look Ahead algorithm was 6638 bytes/s as opposed to 44 bytes/s for post-processing.

Network usage for the post-processing approach is negligible since the calls to the reverse geocoding service – which return more information than simply the required speed limit data – are handled by our proxy Web service. This is in contrast to the real-time Look Ahead algorithm, which necessarily requires the mobile app to call the reverse geocoding service directly.

Energy Consumption. Little difference was noticed between the different algorithms – a drain of around 0.1 mAh per second was measured regardless of the algorithm used. This can be explained by the fact that the test device's GPS sensor uses significantly more power than processing network traffic, making its use (which is the same for each algorithm) the primary factor in determining energy consumption.

4.3 Motion Sensor Processing Algorithm

To evaluate the motion sensor processing algorithm for detecting harsh braking and lane changing events, we compared the algorithm's output when provided with input data from the smartphone sensor and VBOX IMU. The output of the algorithm is some number of harsh acceleration/braking events (defined to be longitudinal acceleration of more than $2.5\,\mathrm{ms}^{-2}$ for more than $0.5\,\mathrm{s}$) and some number of swerving/harsh lane changing events (defined to be lateral acceleration of more than $3\,\mathrm{ms}^{-2}$ for more than $0.2\,\mathrm{s}$). Table 3 shows the number of each of these events registered per 10 km, for each data source and road type.

Table 3. Detected harsh driving events for motion sensor processing algorithm

		Events per 10 km	
Event type	Data source	Urban	Highway
Acceleration/braking	Smartphone	0.48	0.06
	VBOX	0.65	0.08
Swerving/lane changing	Smartphone	0.16	0.02
	VBOX	0.20	0.04

Based on the results, there are significantly fewer harsh driving events for highway compared to urban conditions. This is because there are fewer traffic lights or intersections from which one may accelerate too quickly, and less traffic which may reduce the perceived need to swerve, change lanes, or brake harshly.

Regarding the accuracy of the algorithm, there is some discrepancy in the number of reported events depending on whether smartphone or VBOX sensor data was supplied. Table 3 summarises the results. The motion sensor processing algorithm reported fewer acceleration/braking and swerving/lane changing events when supplied with smartphone data. As discussed earlier, the combination of the smartphone sensor values and coordinate transformation algorithm supplies different input data to the algorithm than the gold standard data. The effect of this is that when used with the gold standard data, the motion sensor processing algorithm detects a greater number of driving events.

5 Related Work

In recent years, much work has been carried out to develop low-cost sensing platforms using smartphone technology. Today's smartphones embed a range of sensors that typically include an accelerometer, gyroscope, magnetometer and

GPS receiver. The inertial sensors enable smartphone driver support systems (SDSS) to detect driving events, such as acceleration, braking, turning and lane changing. Based on analyzing events, SDSS can make inferences about a driver's skill level, style and safety.

SenseFleet [3], MIROAD [10], DrivingStyles [13] and others [9, 18] are smartphone applications that detect driving events and classify driving behaviour. SenseFleet scores the driver's safety, reporting this as a percentage. Similar work [6] classifies a driver's behaviour as risky or safe.

Concerning SDSS' fitness for purpose to evaluate driver behaviour, SenseFleet detected 90% of driving events that were present in monitored journeys. In other experiments, between 90% and 97% of drivers have been correctly classified as exhibiting aggressive behavior [6,10]. For drink driving detection, recognizing problems with maintaining speed gave rise to a false positive rate of 2.9%, and for detecting abnormal curvilinear movements, 0.5% [5]. In a study concerned with dangerous cornering detection, false negative and false positive rates of 13% were reported [20]. This relatively high rate is attributed to use of only the GPS sensor. In general, other work uses sensor fusion, which involves combining data from multiple sensors to improve performance.

In processing sensor data, use of fixed sensor thresholds, fuzzy logic and machine learning algorithms are widely used. With fixed sensor thresholds, a driving event such as heavy breaking is triggered when an accelerometer value that exceeds some threshold is obtained. Fixed sensor threshold solutions, e.g. [7,12], are simple to implement and minimise processing overhead. Other approaches, e.g. [19,23], can provide better accuracy using pattern matching and machine learning techniques. The Dynamic Time Warping algorithm, which measures similarity between two temporal sequences that vary in speed, has been applied liberally to match sequences of smartphone-sensed driving events with patterns for particular manoeuvres [6,10,16,18]. Ongoing work aims to further improve driver behaviour classification by adapting sensed values to the vehicle, driver and road topology [1,4], and to investigate use of other established machine learning approaches in reasoning about smartphone-sensed data [11].

Beyond a smartphone's inertial sensors, other built-in sensors include cameras and microphones that can be used to detect whether drivers are drowsy or distracted. CarSafe utilizes both the forward and rear-facing cameras to monitor the driver's face and eyes along with the road ahead [22]. Using a combination of machine vision and machine learning techniques, the application offers ADAS (advanced driver assistance system) functionality found in modern high-end cars. DriveSafe [2], similarly to CarSafe, aims to warn drivers when they appear to be distracted or drowsy. In addition to using cameras and inertial sensors to detect sudden movements, suggesting that the driver might be distracted, DriveSafe makes use of the smartphone's microphone, e.g. to identify cases where the driver has turned without using the indicators (which when used emit an audio signal).

6 Conclusions

In this paper, we have described the design and development of a smartphone app to monitor and provide feedback on driver behaviour. While BackPocketDriver is targeted at youth drivers, the work reported in this paper addresses the sensing capabilities of smartphone technology, and has more general applicability.

We have carried out a comparative evaluation of BackPocketDriver using a gold standard device. The results show that today's smartphone has sufficient sensory fidelity to gather driver behaviour data upon which to report meaningful feedback. While the gold standard device offers greater accuracy of vehicle positioning, our speeding-detection algorithms yield identical results when processing data generated by the smartphone and gold standard device. For acceleration, the smartphone-based solution underreports harsh acceleration, braking and lane changing events. It reports around 70% of the events that are detected when using data generated by the gold standard device. The cause of the this difference is attributed to the coordinate transformation algorithm and reduced accuracy of the smartphone's accelerometer.

Beyond assessing fitness for purpose of smartphones to monitor driver behaviour, we have explored the design space for an app that is to monitor and provide feedback on driver behaviour. We have developed real-time and non real-time feedback solutions. The real-time Look Ahead algorithm has the advantage that it can deliver feedback to drivers at the time that they are speeding, whereas the non real-time design defers feedback until after a journey has been completed. The real-time approach consumes significantly more mobile data, by a factor of 150. Furthermore, the non real-time approach offers the opportunity to validate speed limit data, thereby dropping to zero the false positive/negative rates of around 2% for speeding events reported by real-time processing.

The work reported in this paper forms part of a larger project concerned with youth driving. Development of BackPocketDriver has been informed by behaviour models and behaviour change theory in an attempt to produce an intervention that changes youth driving behaviour positively. We are currently running a pilot study using BackPocketDriver to validate the potential of the app to effect behaviour change and to guide further development of the app. We will report on the results of the pilot study in the near future.

References

1. Arroyo, C., Bergasa, L.M., Romera, E.: Adaptive fuzzy classifier to detect driving events from the inertial sensors of a smartphone. In: 2016 IEEE 19th International Conference on Intelligent Transportation Systems (ITSC), pp. 1896–1901, November 2016. https://doi.org/10.1109/ITSC.2016.7795863
2. Bergasa, L.M., Almería, D., Almazán, J., Yebes, J.J., Arroyo, R.: DriveSafe: an app for alerting inattentive drivers and scoring driving behaviors. In: 2014 IEEE Intelligent Vehicles Symposium Proceedings, pp. 240–245, June 2014. https://doi.org/10.1109/IVS.2014.6856461

3. Castignani, G., Derrmann, T., Frank, R., Engel, T.: Driver behavior profiling using smartphones: a low-cost platform for driver monitoring. IEEE Intell. Transp. Syst. Mag. **7**(1), 91–102 (2015). https://doi.org/10.1109/MITS.2014.2328673

4. Castignani, G., Derrmann, T., Frank, R., Engel, T.: Smartphone-based adaptive driving maneuver detection: a large-scale evaluation study. IEEE Trans. Intell. Transp. Syst. **18**(9), 2330–2339 (2017). https://doi.org/10.1109/TITS.2016.2646760

5. Dai, J., Teng, J., Bai, X., Shen, Z., Xuan, D.: Mobile phone based drunk driving detection. In: 2010 4th International Conference on Pervasive Computing Technologies for Healthcare, pp. 1–8, March 2010. https://doi.org/10.4108/ICST.PERVASIVEHEALTH2010.8901

6. Eren, H., Makinist, S., Akin, E., Yilmaz, A.: Estimating driving behavior by a smartphone. In: 2012 IEEE Intelligent Vehicles Symposium, pp. 234–239, June 2012. https://doi.org/10.1109/IVS.2012.6232298

7. Fazeen, M., Gozick, B., Dantu, R., Bhukhiya, M., González, M.C.: Safe driving using mobile phones. IEEE Trans. Intell. Transp. Syst. **13**(3), 1462–1468 (2012). https://doi.org/10.1109/TITS.2012.2187640

8. Pearson K.: LIII. On lines and planes of closest fit to systems of points in space. Lond. Edinb. Dublin Philos. Mag. J. Sci. **2**(11), 559–572 (2010). https://doi.org/10.1080/14786440109462720

9. Hong, J.H., Margines, B., Dey, A.K.: A smartphone-based sensing platform to model aggressive driving behaviors. In: Proceedings of the 32nd Annual ACM Conference on Human Factors in Computing Systems, CHI 2014, pp. 4047–4056. ACM, New York (2014). https://doi.org/10.1145/2556288.2557321

10. Johnson, D.A., Trivedi, M.M.: Driving style recognition using a smartphone as a sensor platform. In: 2011 14th International IEEE Conference on Intelligent Transportation Systems (ITSC), pp. 1609–1615, October 2011. https://doi.org/10.1109/ITSC.2011.6083078

11. Junior, F., Carvalho, E., Ferreira, B., de Souza, C., Suhara, Y., Pentland, A.: Driver behavior profiling: an investigation with different smartphone sensors and machine learning. PLoS ONE **12**(4) (2017). https://doi.org/10.1371/journal.pone.0174959

12. Klauer, S.G., Sayer, T.B., Baynes, P., Ankem, G.: Using real-time and post hoc feedback to improve driving safety for novice drivers. In: Proceedings of the Human Factors and Ergonomics Society Annual Meeting, vol. 60, no. 1, pp. 1936–1940 (2016). https://doi.org/10.1177/1541931213601441

13. Meseguer, J.E., Calafate, C.T., Cano, J.C., Manzoni, P.: DrivingStyles: a smartphone application to assess driver behavior. In: 2013 IEEE Symposium on Computers and Communications (ISCC), pp. 000535–000540, July 2013. https://doi.org/10.1109/ISCC.2013.6755001

14. Organisation, W.H.: Road traffic injuries, December 2018. https://www.who.int/en/news-room/fact-sheets/detail/road-traffic-injuries, archived at http://www.webcitation.org/6vcTntGDI

15. Paefgen, J., Kehr, F., Zhai, Y., Michahelles, F.: Driving behavior analysis with smartphones: insights from a controlled field study. In: Proceedings of the 11th International Conference on Mobile and Ubiquitous Multimedia, MUM 2012, pp. 36:1–36:8. ACM, New York (2012). https://doi.org/10.1145/2406367.2406412

16. Pholprasit, T., Choochaiwattana, W., Saiprasert, C.: A comparison of driving behaviour prediction algorithm using multi-sensory data on a smartphone. In: 2015 IEEE/ACIS 16th International Conference on Software Engineering, Artificial Intelligence, Networking and Parallel/Distributed Computing (SNPD), pp. 1–6, June 2015. https://doi.org/10.1109/SNPD.2015.7176249

17. Sagberg, F., Selpi, Piccinini, G.F.B., Engström, J.: A review of research on driving styles and road safety. Hum. Factors **57**(7), 1248–1275 (2015). https://doi.org/10.1177/0018720815591313, pMID: 26130678

18. Saiprasert, C., Thajchayapong, S., Pholprasit, T., Tanprasert, C.: Driver behaviour profiling using smartphone sensory data in a V2I environment. In: 2014 International Conference on Connected Vehicles and Expo (ICCVE), pp. 552–557, November 2014. https://doi.org/10.1109/ICCVE.2014.7297609

19. Saiprasert, C., Pholprasit, T., Thajchayapong, S.: Detection of driving events using sensory data on smartphone. International Journal of Intelligent Transportation Systems Research **15**(1), 17–28 (2017). https://doi.org/10.1007/s13177-015-0116-5

20. Wahlstrom, J., Skog, I., Händel, P.: Detection of dangerous cornering in GNSS-data-driven insurance telematics. IEEE Trans. Intell. Transp. Syst. **16**(6), 3073–3083 (2015). https://doi.org/10.1109/TITS.2015.2431293

21. Warren, I., Meads, A., Whittaker, R., Dobson, R., Ameratunga, S.: Behavior change for youth drivers: design and development of a smartphone-based app (BackPocketDriver). JMIR Formativ. Res. **2**(2), e25 (2018). https://doi.org/10.2196/formative.9660, http://formative.jmir.org/2018/2/e25/

22. You, C.W., et al.: CarSafe: a driver safety app that detects dangerous driving behavior using dual-cameras on smartphones. In: Proceedings of the 2012 ACM Conference on Ubiquitous Computing, UbiComp 2012, pp. 671–672. ACM, New York (2012). https://doi.org/10.1145/2370216.2370360

23. Zhang, Y., Lin, W.C., Chin, Y.K.S.: A pattern-recognition approach for driving skill characterization. IEEE Trans. Intell. Transp. Syst. **11**(4), 905–916 (2010). https://doi.org/10.1109/TITS.2010.2055239

Color Marker Detection with WebGL
for Mobile Augmented Reality Systems

Milan Košťák$^{(\boxtimes)}$ ⬤, Bruno Ježek ⬤, and Antonín Slabý ⬤

Faculty of Informatics and Management, University of Hradec Králové,
Rokitanského 62, 50003 Hradec Králové, Czech Republic
{milan.kostak,bruno.jezek,antonin.slaby}@uhk.cz

Abstract. This paper presents a real-time tracking method based on a color marker detection. The goal is to develop an algorithm that can find the marker in the input image with preference to speed, precision and flexibility. The paper firstly presents related works in the field of marker detection and their advantages and limitations are summarized. The main advantage of the new proposed solution is that it can be easily parallelized and therefore be implemented on GPU which offers a massive performance for this kind of problems. The designed solution is implemented in WebGL as a two-step algorithm which outputs the image coordinates of the center of the detected marker. Using WebGL technology allows the algorithm to be easily used on all platforms including mobile phones. Testing proves that this implementation of the proposed solution is robust and fast enough for real-time video processing, for example in augmented reality applications. There are also discussed possible improvements in the paper.

Keywords: Marker detection · Mobile web · WebGL · Augmented reality · GPGPU

1 Introduction

Augmented reality (AR) is a technology that combines real world with artificial elements. These elements are usually visual, but the augmentation does not have to be limited to that. For example, it is easy to imagine audio augmentation (e.g. [1] and [2]). AR can be well combined with mobile phones. The fact that mobile phones are ubiquitous devices having a lot of computational power and many different sensors including camera can make a good combined use (e.g. [3] and [4]).

Typical AR system uses camera and associated display to capture information about the real world. This obtained information is then used to perform augmentation of the image. AR systems always need to have some information about the real world in order to provide its function and marker detection is one of the possible approaches (e.g. [5] and [6]). Marker detection has been a widely researched topic in the past as there are many possible uses for it. It also gained a wide spread attention with the advent of AR in the last years.

But there is also an effort to make marker-less tracking (e.g. [7] and [8]). Marker-less based methods extract information from the real scene only. This is usually more

© Springer Nature Switzerland AG 2019
I. Awan et al. (Eds.): MobiWIS 2019, LNCS 11673, pp. 71–84, 2019.
https://doi.org/10.1007/978-3-030-27192-3_6

difficult and requires more computational time. Marker-based tracking registers artificial markers placed in the real scene. Hence the marker is known upfront and it is easily recognized.

Our goal is to create a marker-based detection algorithm that would be fast, precise and flexible. Fast algorithm leaves more time for the actual application that is using the result of the detection. Our solution should be able to detect change in the position of the camera and at the same time should be able to work with any possible shape of the marker, inducing shapes with holes. It also shouldn't be limited to one color because different scenes might require different colors in order to make the marker less obtrusive.

2 Related Work

There are many papers focused on a marker detection in a raster image. Belghit et al. [5] developed a technique that used color marker detection in order to estimate the perspective transformation matrix for the current view of the camera. They used four markers of different colors. Their detection was achieved by repeating application of gaussian filter and morphological operators of closing and opening. Their solution has but certain limitations. Mainly, it is required that no other objects of given colors are present in the scene as it may influence the detection. As the authors used blue, red, green and yellow colors, the limitations proved to be quite significant.

Liu et al. [9] present a color marker-based method for tracking objects in real time. The method is based on contours patterns that are extracted by using adaptive threshold. Each marker in the image is recognized by the template pattern. They claim that their method can work in environment with various illumination conditions.

Saaidon et al. [10] developed a solution for optical tracking using color marker that is meant to be used for detection and tracking of a medical navigation system. The detection algorithm is designed using OpenCV library.

Liu et al. [11] proposed a color marker algorithm that is supposed to be robust to occlusion of the marker which sometimes happens in dynamic scenes. They used Hamming check codes to restore parts of the occluded squares in the marker.

System for marker detection called ARTag is designed in [6]. The solution is meant to encode information inside the marker and read that information with camera. The goal was to provide algorithm that would be precise, reliable and have low false positive rates.

ARToolKit [12] is a system similar to ARTag. The user has to setup the system by capturing all markers that are going to be used in the scene. ARToolKit is then able to recognize these markers. The processing time is increasing as the number of possible markers raises. This marker detection system is widely used for other AR applications, because it is easy to use and freely available. Authors of ARTag system consider as the main problem of this solution the fact that it can often falsely detect areas without any marker [6]. Updated versions of the system ARToolKit Plus was developed as a reaction and enabled to resolve some problems with the previous version of the system.

Paper [13] is devoted solely to comparing these three systems (ARToolKit, ARTag, ARToolKit Plus). Comparison based on immunity to occlusion and lighting variation, on inter-marker confusion rates and on false negative rates is performed.

Zhang et al. [14] did an evaluation of several marker systems – namely ARToolKit, IGD, HOM and SCR. They focused on usability, efficiency, accuracy and reliability. Presented tests included processing time, recognition of multiple markers and image position accuracy with respect to distance and angle of the camera.

None of the presented solution solve the marker detection problem from our point of view sufficiently. They either focus on different output like reading more complicated information from the marker or solve different problems of the detection itself. Their common limitation is the fact that they require the marker to be of a specific shape.

Our previous work [15] presented a marker detection algorithm and its GPU implementation. The algorithm was also looking for a marker in the input image. The solution provided good results, but we are aware that there was a lot of possibility to improve the actual detection to make it more precise. The paper also contained several prototype applications that demonstrated usage of the detected marker. These applications are also used to test whether the implementation of the proposed marker detection algorithm is precise and fast enough and they give a good preview of how these kinds of applications can work.

3   Marker Detection

As it was explained in the previous part of the contribution, our goal is to design and implement an algorithm for marker detection that would be fast and give precise results. The position of the marker is obtained from the image data and in our use cases it is usually a video feed. Therefore, it might be a good idea to develop a solution for a graphic card because they are significantly optimized for this kind of processing.

3.1   Algorithm Description

The algorithm that we propose consists of two steps (see Fig. 1). At the beginning there is an input image, which represents one frame of the video sequence. Number of selected pixels is calculated for each row and each column in the first step. The pixels of the image are selected by the similarity of their color to the given predefined color of the marker that we are looking for. The color of the pixel can be thresholded by intervals in three RGB channels or by Euclidean distance in RGB space. Other possibility is to transform RGB values to another color model, for example HSV or HLS, and compare these values. The number of these pixels in each row and column create the output of the first step.

The second step takes as its input two one-dimensional arrays of numbers of pixels selected in all rows and columns. All values of these arrays are taken, and weighted mean is calculated. The coordinate of given column or row is weighted by the number of selected pixels. Just two numbers are the output of this step, each holding one of the two coordinates of the marker. The principle is quite simple, but it is necessary to design robust and fast implementation to achieve real-time processing, which is presented in the next chapter.

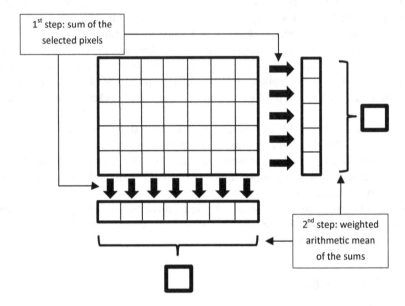

Fig. 1. Illustration of the proposed two-step algorithm

3.2   Improved Versions

The proposed algorithm is robust and can be enhanced in many ways. Probably the most obvious way of obtaining better result is to look at the pixels in a slightly different way. Normally every pixel that meets color requirements is just counted in. Improved version would look at the pixel more closely and calculate how much does it differ from the exact color that we are looking for. This similarity could by defined by Euclidean distance in RGB space. If the pixel has a color that is almost the same as the color of the marker, then this pixel will gain more weight on the resulting coordinate. On the other hand, if the color of the pixel is not very close but it still seems to be the color of the marker, then this pixel will have less weight. False positive detection can be eliminated by using this approach.

Another apparent method of improvement can remove all insignificant rows or columns from the result. These can slightly disrupt the result under some circumstances. The change is done in the second step of the algorithm. When it is reading the number of pixels it would skip all rows and columns whose number is less than a certain threshold. In case the marker is big enough these small disruptions would not have made big impact. Only when scene might contain more pixels of the same color as the marker has then it would make sense to make such enhancement.

Additional improvement comes from the very core of this design. The observed scene can have more markers in it. For instance, if there are two markers in the image then our algorithm will find coordinates of the point that is exactly in between them. The marker can also contain holes in it, and it can even be a circle and our algorithm would still find the center of it as it is shown in the results chapter.

All these mentioned improvements do not have any influence on the rendering speed. Especially first two can have positive impact on the accuracy and stability of the result.

4 Implementation

Our target platform are web browsers. Just a decade ago it would be nearly impossible to implement this kind of algorithm in the environment of a web browser. But WebGL standard changed it all. It provides access to the GPU which is excellent in parallelization and image processing. By using web browsers, our implementation can be easily used not just on the desktop systems but also directly inside mobile phones without the need of installing any additional software. All support is provided by the web browser. Moreover, all mobile phones nowadays have a camera and it can be easily used as an input for applications.

The GPU implementation is designed as a two-pass algorithm. Each pass is processed by the classical visualization pipeline that is composed of vertex and fragment shader or by compute shader in case of newer WebGL version. To obtain appropriate result from each step which uses render to texture method, the size of rendering viewport must be defined.

4.1 First Step of the Algorithm

The first step calculates the number of pixels with the appropriate marker color. This color is defined in the fragment shader file. The rendered output image is a texture with two rows. The number of output columns is determined by a bigger value of the width or the height of the input image. That is to ensure that each row and column have a free cell to write its result sum into. Output size can be determined by

$$2 * max(width, height) \tag{1}$$

Figure 2 illustrates this step with example values. The fragment shader for each pixel in the output texture sums pixels with the correct color for the appropriate column or row. This sum is then written as the output value in the texture. The input image is an ordinary uniform texture sampler. The red zeros mean that there are no available rows for this output pixels – the example image width is bigger than the height.

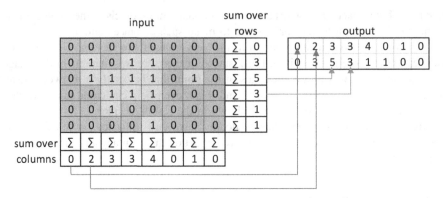

Fig. 2. A figure illustrating the first step of the algorithm, see explanation in the text above (Color figure online)

The first step has a time complexity of $\mathcal{O}(max(width, height))$ which means linear time complexity. The cost of this step – number of cores that the algorithm requires multiplied by the time of the algorithm [16] – is $\mathcal{O}((width + height) * max(width, height))$. This means $\mathcal{O}(n^2)$. It needs to be mentioned that sum of width and height is usually a number that is not higher than a couple of hundreds and modern graphic cards usually have hundreds of cores, which means that if there are enough cores or the image is small, then the cost can be linear – number of cores would be a constant.

4.2   Second Step of the Algorithm

The second step of the algorithm uses output of the first step, and it is illustrated by Fig. 3. Output of the second step is consisting of a texture of just 2 pixels, where each pixel contains one coordinate of the detected marker. This coordinate is calculated as a weighted mean where the coordinate of given column or row is weighted by the count of pixels found. The result of this step are coordinates where the center of the marker is most probably lying.

$$\frac{\sum_{i=0}^{w}(value_i * i)}{\sum_{i=0}^{w} value_i} \qquad (2)$$

Fig. 3. A figure illustrating the second step of the algorithm, see explanation in the text above (Color figure online)

Time complexity is the same as in the first step – $\mathcal{O}(max(width, height))$ which means linear time complexity. This step always requires just two cores and every GPU has always more than two cores. Therefore, the cost of the algorithm is $\mathcal{O}(n)$.

This step can be directly followed by a rendering step that uses the result of the second step. By using this approach, the data do not have to leave the GPU memory which is necessary for fast rendering. The second step can be also be merged with the possible third step into one step and therefore reduce the overhead of another pipeline call.

4.3   Source Code

The source code of the implementation is publicly available in a GitHub repository: https://github.com/milankostak/Marker-detection/tree/v2.0.

5   Results

Implemented algorithm was tested on preset images as well as in the real world. Selected results of this testing are shown in the form of the following screenshots from a mobile phone (Figs. 4, 5, 6 and 7).

Fig. 4. Detected marker in a test environment, basic green shapes of square and hexagon are tested. Detection works well in these situations. (Color figure online)

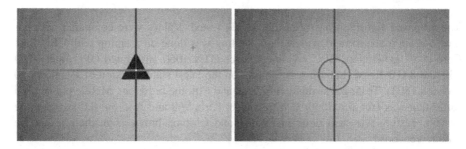

Fig. 5. Detected marker in a test environment with more complicated shapes. On the left is a triangle shape with blue color demonstrating that detection can be set to any color. On the right is a green circle which shows that our solution can even work with shaped that has holes in it. (Color figure online)

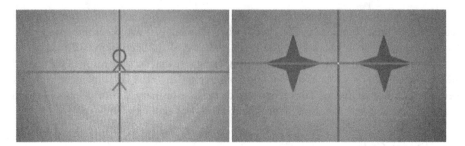

Fig. 6. Detected marker in a test environment. On the left is an icon of a person and our algorithm finds the center of it. On the right are two markers printed on a paper, the algorithm finds the point in-between of them. (Color figure online)

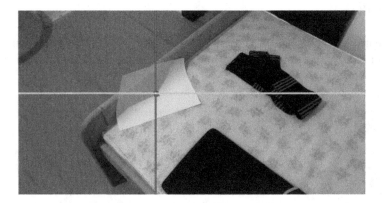

Fig. 7. Presents marker detection in a real-world scene. Marker drawn on the piece of paper was written by hand with an ordinary pen. In addition to it, a half of the marker is covered by a shadow. The algorithm was able to detect clearly the correct marker position even in an image of this difficult scene. (Color figure online)

6   Testing

The proposed algorithm has been thoroughly tested. Values were compared with our previous approach to marker detection. Testing was done on a laptop with CPU Intel Core i5 8th generation, GPU Nvidia GeForce GTX 1060, integrated GPU Intel UHD 630 and 8 GB RAM. Laptop was running on the latest stable version of Windows 10 (version 1803). Testing was done in Firefox and Chrome browsers. Mobile phone used for testing was Huawei Honor 9 with chipset Kirin 960 and Android 8.0 as operating system. Testing was also done in Firefox and Chrome browsers in their respective mobile versions.

6.1 Time Measurement Methodology

Times were recorded with the help of WebGL extensions because default WebGL context does not support direct measurement of rendering time. WebGL 1 extension is called `EXT_disjoint_timer_query` and for WebGL 2 it is `EXT_disjoint_timer_query_webgl2`. They both work in the same way. Appropriate `beginQuery` function is called before the draw (or any other) operation and `endQuery` is called after that operation. Elapsed time in nanosecond is then obtained via `getQueryParameter` function call.

By using this approach, the call is put in the queue and the start time is saved right before starting the rendering operation and the end time is saved right after the rendering ends. Saving is completely in control of GPU and therefore it contains the exact times when GPU started and ended dealing with the rendering operation. It is then necessary to wait until the result of the query is available to the main JavaScript thread that is running on CPU. Once CPU calls draw or query functions, it immediately continues executing the program regardless of what GPU is doing or if it has finished. Therefore, the program must be stalled until GPU makes results of its operations available. For this purpose, `QUERY_RESULT_AVAILABLE_EXT` parameter must be used to check if the result is already available or not.

Unfortunately, these extensions are not widely supported and especially on the mobile phones we were not able to measure it inside any tested browser. These extensions are only supported on the desktop in Chromium browser layout engine. Neither Firefox nor Edge support this extension on the testing device.

Every recorded measurement is an average of one thousand render loops with the first thousand being ignored and the second thousand being used in all experiments. All presented values are rounded to whole microseconds and shown in thousandths of milliseconds for better readability.

6.2 Algorithm Times

Measured times of the basic version of the described algorithm is presented in Table 1. As it was explained earlier, only Chromium layout engine supports the necessary WebGL extensions, so testing was done only in it. Comparison of running the same code with WebGL 1 and 2 contexts can be seen in the same table. First and second steps of the algorithm are measured. Testing was done on both available GPUs – integrated Intel UHD 630 and dedicated NVIDIA GTX 1060 (laptop version). This table shows results for the input image that has 1280 pixels in width and 720 pixels in height, which results in 921,600 pixels in total. Table 1 also shows that there is not any significant difference between using WebGL 1 or WebGL 2. The biggest measured difference is around 5%. Therefore, all other shown values are going to be only for WebGL 2.

Table 1. Times required to finish rendering for given steps in the algorithm, input image: 1280 × 720 pixels

	WebGL 1			WebGL 2		
	1st step	2nd step	Total	1st step	2nd step	Total
Intel UHD 630	1.902 ms	0.965 ms	2.867 ms	1.877 ms	1.019 ms	2.897 ms
NVIDIA GTX 1060 (laptop)	1.035 ms	0.613 ms	1.649 ms	1.035 ms	0.626 ms	1.661 ms

The same measurement is shown in Table 2 for smaller input image. In this case it is 640 pixels in width and 360 pixels in height, which results in 230,400 pixels in total. That is four times less than in the previous case – each dimension size is two times smaller. This measurement was done in order to observe the effect of the input size on the rendering times. Table 3 presents how much faster the rendering is. It can be seen that for the less powerful GPU the times are stably two times smaller. For the more powerful graphic card the rendering for smaller input is much faster.

Table 2. Times required to finish rendering for given steps in the algorithm, input image: 640 × 360 pixels

	WebGL 2		
	1st step	2nd step	Total
Intel UHD 630	0.897 ms	0.506 ms	1.403 ms
NVIDIA GTX 1060 (laptop)	0.186 ms	0.064 ms	0.250 ms

Table 3. Comparison of times for different inputs sizes – width and height are half; the result image is one quarter in the total pixels count

	WebGL 2		
	1st step	2nd step	Total
Intel UHD 630	2.093 times faster	2.015 times faster	2.065 times faster
NVIDIA GTX 1060 (laptop)	5.564 times faster	9.720 times faster	6.634 times faster

6.3 Comparison with Previous Solution

Our previous approach to marker detection was implemented in a different way. The key idea was to divide the picture into small areas of 3 × 3 or 4 × 4 pixels and then counting pixels independently in these areas. These operations were performed multiple times until the reduced image size was small enough. Now we also tried to measure if with the new algorithm we achieved better time of the detection. But our previous approach was measured in a slightly different way and with other devices as it was described earlier and published in [15]. In order to make a good comparison of those approaches, previous solution was measured with the same methodology as the new one.

Comparable times with the new solution for both big and small input image are presented in Table 4 and the measured times are slightly shorter. The reason for this is in the design of the previous solution where every fragment shader is doing less operations and the number of operations for every shader is always constant. Although it requires more cores in order to function properly. But this situation is more an advantage than disadvantage because modern GPUs are counting on that fact. The previous solution but always requires reading data from the GPU because it does not output coordinates directly. They need to be searched in the output of the second step. This was done after reading data from GPU to CPU. And as it is explained later, reading operation is slow. This means that if values do not have to be read from GPU then our new solution would be faster. For more information about fetching information from GPU see the next Sect. 6.4.

This approach also does not provide solution under all circumstances, because it works by dividing the image into areas that are completely independent. If marker is divided between those areas, then found solution may be slightly moved or in some extreme cases not found at all.

Table 4. Measured times of our previous solution with the new methodology of measuring for different resolution of input image

| | WebGL 2 | | | | | |
| | Width = 1280 px, Height = 720 px | | | Width = 640 px, Height = 360 px | | |
	1st step	2nd step	Total	1st step	2nd step	Total
Intel UHD 630	0.610 ms	0.107 ms	0.717 ms	0.160 ms	0.057 ms	0.217 ms
NVIDIA GTX 1060 (laptop)	0.202 ms	0.038 ms	0.240 ms	0.012 ms	0.004 ms	0.017 ms

6.4 CPU Times and Reading from GPU

Reading data from GPU memory is always a slow operation. The reason for this is the fact that it requires synchronization of operating memory and graphics memory. This operation stalls executing of the main program and waits until the data are available.

Reading from GPU does not always have to be needed. If the result is supposed to be worked with on the device that is also doing the marker detection that the information about the found marker does not have to leave the graphics memory and can be directly reused. But it is required to obtain the values and possibly send it to a completely another device in some use cases. That is the approach that we used in our old solution which implemented mobile phone as an interactive device in an augmented reality system with example applications. That is the main reason why the previous approach required the marker coordinates to be searched in the output of its second step. The new solution supports both options. Data can be both kept in the graphics memory or it can be read as a two pixels value from GPU to CPU.

Our old solution always returns number of pixels that is equal to the input number of pixels divided by 144 – each dimension is reduced by 4 and then by 3. That means that both dimensions are reduced by a factor of 12 and for two dimensions it is 144. After that, the obtained data needs to be iterated through to find the information about the marker. On the other hand, the new solution always returns just 2 pixels.

Times required for these operations are presented in the following tables (Tables 5 and 6). Apart from the device that was used for testing performance of the GPU, a mobile phone was also used to test the CPU performance. Dispatching of the algorithm itself is always faster in the new solution. Reading is a trickier operation. It seems that it depends on the used GPU and it looks like it might be hard to predict how the reading will behave on other devices. But it can still be seen that the differences are small, and the overall times are still suitable for smooth rendering in 60 frames per second.

Table 5. CPU times of the new solution for input image with width 1280 px and height 720 px

	WebGL 2			
	1st step	2nd step	Read	Total
Intel UHD 630	0.16 ms	0.07 ms	6.71 ms	6.94 ms
NVIDIA GTX 1060 (laptop)	0.10 ms	0.04 ms	3.21 ms	3.35 ms
Honor 9, Kirin 960	0.53 ms	0.32 ms	3.95 ms	4.80 ms

Table 6. CPU times of the previous solution for input image with width 1280 px and height 720 px

	WebGL 2			
	1st step	2nd step	Read	Total
Intel UHD 630	0.17 ms	0.09 ms	5.02 ms	5.28 ms
NVIDIA GTX 1060 (laptop)	0.11 ms	0.04 ms	3.50 ms	3.65 ms
Honor 9, Kirin 960	0.71 ms	0.47 ms	3.22 ms	4.40 ms

7 Conclusion and Future Work

Proposed algorithm provides a good solution for situations when simple color marker detection is required. The main advantage is in its parallelization. Modern GPUs usually have hundreds of cores that are heavily optimized for fast image and texture rendering. Choosing WebGL for its implementation ensures that the algorithm can be used in all modern browsers and on all devices including mobile phones. Implementation of the algorithm proved that the proposed solution is robust and fast enough for real-time video processing. The correct detected position of different shapes of the marker printed on a paper in a scene with real light conditions demonstrated that the detection is precise even under harder circumstances.

Thorough time measurement of the new algorithm was performed and then compared with our previous approach. Both rendering times and reading times were measured. Rendering times of the new algorithm are slightly longer than for the previous solution. The previous solution but always required reading of the rendered texture on the CPU and that proved to be more than a ten times slower operation. The new algorithm does not require it which makes it over all faster than the old one.

Both versions of WebGL are currently lacking support of other kinds of shaders. They support only vertex and fragment shaders. Just a couple of months back, in December 2018, support for WebGL2 compute shader was presented for the first time. It is still in its early phase of support and is only available in the so-called nightly builds of Chrome browser. As soon as this support stabilizes, our algorithm could be easily implemented with this technology, possibly gaining a better performance.

Acknowledgement. This work and the contribution were supported by a project of Students Grant Agency (SPEV) - FIM, University of Hradec Kralove, Czech Republic.

References

1. Rma, A.H., Jakka, J., Tikander, M., Karjalainen, M., Lokki, T.: Augmented reality audio for mobile and wearable appliances. J. Audio Eng. Soc. **52**, 23 (2004)
2. Bederson, B.B.: Audio augmented reality: a prototype automated tour guide. In: Conference Companion on Human Factors in Computing Systems - CHI 1995, Denver, Colorado, United States, pp. 210–211. ACM Press (1995). https://doi.org/10.1145/223355.223526
3. Kourouthanassis, P.E., Boletsis, C., Lekakos, G.: Demystifying the design of mobile augmented reality applications. Multimedia Tools Appl. **74**, 1045–1066 (2015). https://doi.org/10.1007/s11042-013-1710-7
4. Höllerer, T., Feiner, S.: Mobile augmented reality. In: Telegeoinformatics: Location-Based Computing and Services, vol. 21 (2004)
5. Belghit, H., Zenati-Henda, N., Bellabi, A., Benbelkacem, S., Belhocine, M.: Tracking color marker using projective transformation for augmented reality application. In: 2012 International Conference on Multimedia Computing and Systems, Tangiers, Morocco, pp. 372–377. IEEE (2012). https://doi.org/10.1109/ICMCS.2012.6320245
6. Fiala, M.: ARTag, a fiducial marker system using digital techniques. In: 2005 IEEE Computer Society Conference on Computer Vision and Pattern Recognition (CVPR 2005), San Diego, CA, USA, pp. 590–596. IEEE (2005). https://doi.org/10.1109/CVPR.2005.74
7. Stricker, D., Kettenbach, T.: Real-time and markerless vision-based tracking for outdoor augmented reality applications. In: Proceedings IEEE and ACM International Symposium on Augmented Reality, New York, NY, USA, pp. 189–190. IEEE Computer Society (2001). https://doi.org/10.1109/ISAR.2001.970536
8. Genc, Y., Riedel, S., Souvannavong, F., Akinlar, C., Navab, N.: Marker-less tracking for AR: a learning-based approach. In: Proceedings of International Symposium on Mixed and Augmented Reality, Darmstadt, Germany, pp. 295–304. IEEE Computer Society (2002). https://doi.org/10.1109/ISMAR.2002.1115122
9. Liu, J., Chen, S., Sun, H., Qin, Y., Wang, X.: Real time tracking method by using color markers. In: 2013 International Conference on Virtual Reality and Visualization, pp. 106–111 (2013). https://doi.org/10.1109/ICVRV.2013.25

10. Saaidon, N., Sediono, W., Sophian, A.: Altitude tracking using colour marker based navigation system for image guided surgery. In: 2016 International Conference on Computer and Communication Engineering (ICCCE), Kuala Lumpur, Malaysia, pp. 465–469. IEEE (2016). https://doi.org/10.1109/ICCCE.2016.103
11. Liu, J., Zhang, J., Mei, J., Zhang, X.: CH-Marker: a color marker robust to occlusion for augmented reality. Int. J. Pattern Recognit. Artif. Intell. **32**, 1854004 (2018). https://doi.org/10.1142/S0218001418540046
12. Kato, I.P.H., Billinghurst, M., Poupyrev, I.: ARToolKit user manual, version 2.33, vol. 2. Human Interface Technology Lab, University of Washington (2000)
13. Fiala, M.: Comparing ARTag and ARToolKit Plus fiducial marker systems. In: IEEE International Workshop on Haptic Audio Visual Environments and their Applications, 6 p. (2005). https://doi.org/10.1109/HAVE.2005.1545669
14. Zhang, X., Fronz, S., Navab, N.: Visual marker detection and decoding in AR systems: a comparative study. In: Proceedings of International Symposium on Mixed and Augmented Reality, Darmstadt, Germany, pp. 97–106. IEEE Computer Society (2002). https://doi.org/10.1109/ISMAR.2002.1115078
15. Košťák, M., Ježek, B.: Mobile phone as an interactive device in augmented reality system. In: DIVAI 2018 (2018)
16. McConnell, J.J.: Analysis of Algorithms: An Active Learning Approach. Jones and Bartlett Publishers Inc., Sudbury (2001)

Comparison of the Development of Native Mobile Applications and Applications on Facebook Platform

Michal Macinka[(⊠)] and Filip Maly

Faculty of Informatics and Management,
Department of Informatics and Quantitative Methods,
University of Hradec Kralove, Hradec Kralove, Czech Republic
{Michal.Macinka,Filip.Maly}@uhk.cz

Abstract. Mobile devices are integral tools to facilitate day-to-day activities. These devices have a large variety of sensors, modules and there are a huge number of services which can be used to facilitate human work. This paper deals with the creation of an application for simplified management of notes and tasks using one of the most popular social messaging platforms Facebook Messenger for its distribution. The aim of this work is to create a chatbot application which enables the user to easily create tasks and to notify other users about the changes made and show advantages of application publishing without Google Play store. For comparison with a common solution, a standalone Android application test application will be implemented to use Google Firebase Cloud Messaging for notification. In the end, both solutions will be compared in a matter of testing the speed of notifications and the impact on battery consumption.

Keywords: Facebook Messenger · Chatbot · Natural language processing · Android · Social networking · Development · Application distribution

1 Introduction

Nowadays we use mobile devices not only to communicate with other people, but we use them for everyday tasks. These devices boast a wide range of sensors and modules they can use for a variety of tasks. Along with these devices, their operating systems are developed to allow users to add and remove applications. These applications allow users to perform the same tasks as personal computers with sufficient performance parameters. Depending on the device, there are many operating systems with their own standards, different programming languages, a set of development tools, and portals from which to buy and download applications. Each of these platforms means a large base of potential users.

With an expanding number of different applications, it is difficult to offer something new to the user. The possible solution is to offer users an existing idea, but with a different approach which can be seen with other applications. Speech is about chatbots which can be used, for example, through social networks. In the scientific publication [1] the authors devote a description of the issue, the use of chatbots, the possibilities of creating Messenger bot and description of the implemented architecture.

© Springer Nature Switzerland AG 2019
I. Awan et al. (Eds.): MobiWIS 2019, LNCS 11673, pp. 85–94, 2019.
https://doi.org/10.1007/978-3-030-27192-3_7

Another scientific article dealing with this subject is [2]. This article focuses on the theme of conversational strategies using interactive elements of the user interface because the way the user response is handled plays a key role in the development of effective chatbots. A similar topic is dealt with by authors of scientific publication [3], focusing on the development of more bots and their integration among themselves.

The main goal of this work is to create a chatbot application which will help the user to make work easier and more efficient and save time when making notes, reminders and tasks using social networks, instant messaging and natural language processing. The use of social networks in many sectors of human life is dealt with in a scientific article [4]. The implemented application is based on the idea that despite the huge number of applications of this type, it is still the primary goal of simple control, including a wide range of options available to users without going to settings throughout the application. Scientific publication [5] describe the creation of a similar social media reminder application.

The application will be developed using Node.js technology and Wit.ai services [6], which offers high-quality natural language processing support for a wide range of world languages including Czech.

2 Problem Definition

As mentioned above, the main task of this work is to design and integrate a chatbot application built on the Facebook Messenger platform which will use natural language processing. The main features of the application are to manage user notes and tasks in the easiest way. The user can create, view, mark them as completed, and share them with individual users or groups of users. These groups can be created, joined, and cancelled by users. With Messenger's availability on both the web and mobile Android and iOS mobile applications, the app will be available to every Facebook social network user.

Nowadays, there are a large number of applications for different platforms that handle assigned tasks. This represents enormous competition for new types of such applications. This is because most of these applications offer a wide range of features which can be used to set the note in detail. An example is a time and date for the notification setting, the location with which the note is associated, the users with whom it should be shared, etc. While these settings allow you to configure everything to the slightest detail, the basic idea disappears in the form of simplifying the user's work and saving his time.

The issue of streamlining work and saving time for users is still a topical issue today. There are plenty of applications on the web and in the app stores which try to offer as many functions as possible with modern looks and intuitive controls. It is often difficult for users to decide which application should be installed because what suits one, may not be ideal for another. And this is related to the problem because before the user finds the ideal application, they have to download, install and test them, which means spending some time by selecting them. It is for this reason that this application originated, allowing the user to work without any installation and from any platform.

Competitive apps for appraisal were selected primarily for the existence of an app for both the major Android and iOS mobile platforms. Expected requirements are: notification of changes, alert settings, sharing of notes with other users, simple and intuitive control.

The first competitive application is Wunderlist [7]. The app offers sharing lists with created notes, fast and accurate notifications of changes and set events, links to wearable Android Wear, and web application variants. However, shortcomings include non-intuitive navigation across applications. Another drawback is the need to create an account without which an application cannot be used.

Another selected application is Any.do [8]. This application, in addition to a simple and intuitive user interface, offers the ability to create shared groups for created tasks. Another feature is the ability to connect with the Alexa, smart assistant of Amazon company. Unfortunately, this assistant needs to be downloaded as a standalone application to make this integration possible. Other shortcomings include limited functionality in a free version, representing a limited number of shared lists, the ability to set repeatable tasks, location-based notifications, and more. Similar to Wunderlist, you need to create a user account.

The last evaluated app is TickTick [9]. Instead of previous applications, you can start using the app without creating a user account. The application has an intuitive user interface that is similar to the web version. Like in Any.do app, TickTick in a basic free version lacks a lot of functionality in the form of a monthly task list, task description, removing changes from other users' calendars, or setting the duration of the task. In terms of mobile application development, there is a significant lack of a native user environment for the iOS version of this application. The user interface is the same as for the Android operating system, it can be intuitive and confusing for a regular user of iOS due to the absence of common UI features.

The result of this app testing is that none of the applications meets all the requirements which have been specified. The implemented application will be inspired by the elements from the tested applications in the form of intuitive controls and connection to a service which will simplify the management of notes and tasks. In addition, the test application will be created like a standalone app and will be inspired by these applications to compare with the resulting application (chatbot) in the speed tests of sent/received notifications and battery usage when using individual applications.

3   New Solution

Several solutions have been introduced in the previous chapter, the problem has been defined and will be examined here. This chapter will describe how the application will be implemented.

Our goal will be to create a Facebook Messenger application which will process input information from the user and perform the defined operations on their basis. As mentioned in the scientific publication [10], instant messaging is widely used by many people for various purposes, including recreation with friends or working with colleagues at work. According to [11], instant messaging applications use over 5.8 billion users per month. The Facebook Messenger platform represents 1.3 billion of this total. The Facebook social network has more than 2.23 billion active users per month and 1.15 billion mobile users who are active daily [12]. These values allow us to target the app to as many users as possible. In the event that a user wants to use this platform to communicate with other users, he has a choice of the web client, desktop or mobile applications which are available for most operating systems.

Assuming that a user owns the Facebook account and uses one of the available options, it is very easy to start using our app. The only step is to find the app and press the "Get Started" button. There is no need to download and install the application or create an account for additional functionality compared to the tested applications. These points make it easy for the user to work and save the time he can use to work with the application.

The main implemented application will use Node.js technology and two Wit.ai interfaces [13] for natural language processing. The first is the Wit Message API, which will serve to process the text which the user sends to the chatbot. The second interface is the Wit Speech API for audio recording processing which the user can send as a message attachment. This recording is converted to text using the voice recognition service and is processed in structured JSON data in the same way as a plain text message. Figure 1 describes the processing of input data from the user when communicating with the application.

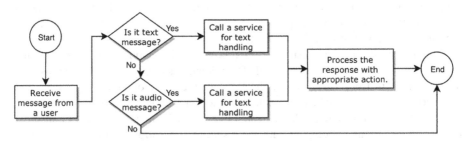

Fig. 1. Flowchart of processing user input.

The text recognition model was trained on 155 records including, for example, variations for adding, viewing, filtering, or completing new tasks. The number of entities has already ensured the model is capable of classifying most of the queries correctly.

The test application will be inspired by the above-mentioned tested applications and will simulate a standalone application which will be compared to the chatbot. This application will be implemented using a React Native cross-platform technology which allows you to write a common code for Android and iOS mobile platforms with a different user interface. This technology also allows you to define a common or platform-specific user interface which acts naturally for each platform. The standalone app will use push notifications using Google Firebase Cloud Messaging [14].

4   Implementation

The technologies of both implemented applications use JavaScript as the main programming language. The chatbot application is represented by a server application implemented using Node.js. The application needs to run its server engine and the Facebook page to which it will be linked and on which the bot will work. With the server engine, the Express module was selected, which, when initialized, verifies the settings of the application configured on the Facebook side. Within initialization, the "Get Started" button is set, which is an important part for the beginning of the conversation. Without an initial user-generated impulse, the application cannot communicate with users on the social network. Every user who starts the conversation with chatbot will acquire a permanent unique key. This key is different for each Facebook page, so it is not possible for other chatbots to start communicating with the user using this key. There are two types of responses which can be sent to the app - text and postback. Text responses are inserted through the text box of the communication window. Postback messages are special types of messages which are represented by the various buttons the Messenger user interface offers. Another element this chatbot uses is the Wit.ai SDK, which serves to send Wit.ai server requests. Sending input data to analyze and get a structured response is handled by *analyzeMessage()* and *analyzeAudio()* functions (Fig. 2).

Fig. 2.   Example of audio message handling.

According to the previously learned natural language processing model, the application analyzes these input data and estimates which of the entities are in the message with a certain probability. For each element of the use case diagram in Fig. 3 exists in the custom entity model.

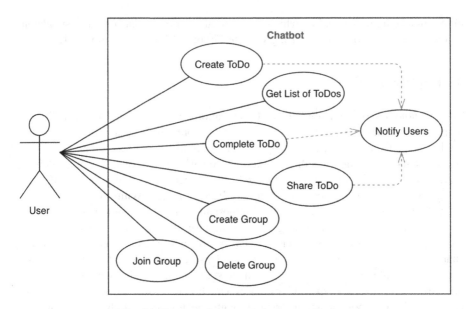

Fig. 3. Use case diagram of chatbot application.

Based on the most likely reaction, the appropriate function is performed. All these features communicate with the Google Firebase Firestore NoSQL database [15]. In this database are stored entities such as users, tasks, and groups.

One of the important functions is adding reminders to individual tasks and sending notifications. Sending notifications is based on a reminder or changes of a task. Changes, in this case, are the creation or completion of a given task. For notifications based on a reminder, each task requires adding a scheduled task which is represented by the cron on the server. The cron is deactivated after user notification. These alerts are sent in the form of messages to individual users, depending on the parameters of the selected task. These parameters are the owner of the task, task sharing, and the group for which the task is created.

The standalone test application is similar to the tested apps mentioned above. It consists of several screens, such as a task list, adding a new task, task details, and group management screens. The main difference to the chatbot is the use of push notifications through Google Firebase Cloud Messaging service. This cloud solution for sending and receiving notifications requires a service which is constantly listening to incoming messages and processing those that belong to the app. Figure 4 shows a class diagram for both implemented applications and their main parameters and functions.

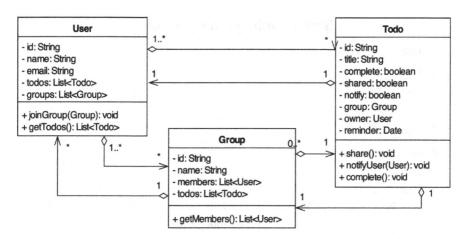

Fig. 4. Class diagram of both implemented applications.

5 Testing of Developed Application

This chapter focuses on defining a variety of scenarios which allow testing and comparison of created applications.

Testing of implemented applications can be taken from different perspectives. The first is to compare the delivery speed of the notifications sent, for example, when creating shared tasks. The second aspect is whether there are significant differences in battery usage for a standalone test application which needs a background service running and the chatbot on the Facebook Messenger application.

The first test deals with the delivery speed of the notifications of the compared applications. Testing is performed by both applications which creates shared tasks and assigned them to a user test group. When the notification is sent to users, the start time is recorded, and the finish time is recorded at delivery. The difference between these values is the time information about the total duration of the delivery. The total number of measured values is 50. T Firebase Cloud Messaging service will has longer delivery times of notifications than the custom implementation.

The second test is to investigate the impact on battery consumption between using a standalone application with background service and the chatbot which uses the Facebook Messenger app. The data of battery consumption will be retrieved within 200 min using the Android Logger application, which includes the current battery status, battery voltage, power status, and more. The result will be a look at the total battery consumption for the 200-min stretch.

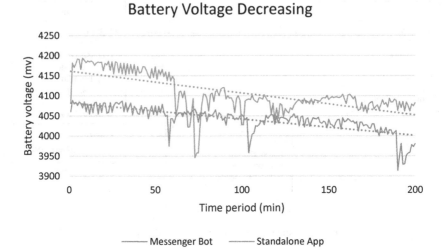

Fig. 5. Battery consumption during the measured time (Color figure online)

Based on the results of measured and tested values the Firebase Cloud Messaging service has longer delivery times of notifications than the custom implementation of notifications in the chatbot application.

From the results of the second test, it can be deduced the standalone test application (orange values) have a higher tendency to use the mobile device's battery than the chatbot application (blue values) which runs within the Messenger application. The comparison of both courses is visible in Fig. 5. This is due to the fact the standalone application requires a constantly running background service for listening to received messages and subsequently handling the notifications received.

Table 1. Testing the delivery speed of notifications for custom implementation in chatbot application.

Number	Start (ms)	Finish (ms)	Diff (ms)
1	1535355401214	1535355401475	261
2	1535355401972	1535355402158	186
3	1535355402737	1535355402939	202
4	1535355403541	1535355403749	208
5	1535355405115	1535355405304	189
46	1535355406059	1535355406258	199
47	1535355406838	1535355407006	168
48	1535355407617	1535355407857	240
49	1535355485315	1535355485561	246
50	1535355486067	1535355486234	167
		Mean	196,96

Table 2. Testing the delivery speed of notifications with Google Firebase Cloud Messaging service.

Number	Start (ms)	Finish (ms)	Diff (ms)
1	1535354699000	1535354699432	432
2	1535354701000	1535354701522	522
3	1535354703000	1535354704081	1106
4	1535354705000	1535354705537	1081
5	1535354706000	1535354706229	964
46	1535354707000	1535354707766	766
47	1535354708000	1535354708700	700
48	1535354709000	1535354709397	397
49	1535354845000	1535354845653	653
50	1535354877000	1535354877657	657
		Mean	599,68

6 Conclusions

The aim of this work was to create and integrate a Messenger Bot application which will allow the user to easily create tasks and notify other users of the changes made. In this application, natural language processing services for text or audio files were implemented and has been created the custom solution for sending notifications to users. For comparison with a usual solution was created the separate test application for Android OS which uses Google Firebase services.

By testing it was found the custom implementation of notification delivery for individual users is much faster than usually used Google Firebase services. These results can be seen in Tables 1 and 2. In addition, because there is no need to install the standalone application for chatbot application, the mobile device resources are spared, and lower battery consumption can be achieved.

Created application due to its targeting all platforms which use Facebook Messenger platform, has a huge number of potential users. In the future, the app could expand on personalized chatbot responses, depending on the user's text, and more to use than just managing tasks.

Acknowledgement. This study is supported by the SPEV project 2019, run at the Faculty of Informatics and Management, University of Hradec Kralove, Czech Republic.

References

1. Lehvä, J., Mäkitalo, N., Mikkonen, T.: Case study: building a serverless messenger chatbot. In: Garrigós, I., Wimmer, M. (eds.) Current Trends in Web Engineering, vol. 10544, pp. 75–86. Springer, Cham (2018). https://doi.org/10.1007/978-3-319-74433-9_6
2. Ikemoto, Y., Asawavetvutt, V., Kuwabara, K., Huang, H.-H.: Conversation strategy of a chatbot for interactive recommendations. In: Nguyen, N.T., Hoang, D.H., Hong, T.-P., Pham, H., Trawiński, B. (eds.) ACIIDS 2018. LNCS (LNAI), vol. 10751, pp. 117–126. Springer, Cham (2018). https://doi.org/10.1007/978-3-319-75417-8_11

3. Memon, Z., Jalbani, A.H., Shaikh, M., Memon, R.N., Ali, A.: Multi-agent communication system with chatbots. Mehran Univ. Res. J. Eng. Technol. **37**, 663–672 (2018)
4. Tsai, W.-H.S., Men, R.L.: Social messengers as the new frontier of organization-public engagement: a WeChat study. Public Relat. Rev. **44**(3), 419–429 (2018)
5. Sinnjakroth, P., Sarasuk, V., Musikasintorn, P., Thumrongsuttipan, T., Hoonlor, A.: Alert Me Please: the implementation of an intelligent-time-management social application. In: 2014 Third ICT International Student Project Conference (ICT-ISPC), Nakhon Pathom, Thailand, pp. 135–138 (2014)
6. Wit.ai. https://wit.ai/. Accessed 31 Aug 2018
7. Wunderlist: Your beautiful and simple online to-do list app. https://www.wunderlist.com/. Accessed 31 Aug 2018
8. To-do List, Calendar & Reminders - Free Task Manager. Any.do. https://www.any.do/. Accessed 31 Aug 2018
9. TickTick. https://ticktick.com/. Accessed 31 Aug 2018
10. Hong, J., Lee, O.-K.(Daniel), Suh, W.: A study of the continuous usage intention of social software in the context of instant messaging. Online Inf. Rev. **37**(5), 692–710 (2013)
11. Most popular messaging apps 2018. Statista. https://www.statista.com/statistics/258749/most-popular-global-mobile-messenger-apps/. Accessed 31 Aug 2018
12. Top 20 Facebook Statistics - Updated July 2018. Zephoria Inc., 29 July 2018
13. Wit—HTTP API. https://wit.ai/docs/http/20170307. Accessed 31 Aug 2018
14. Firebase Cloud Messaging Firebase. https://firebase.google.com/docs/cloud-messaging/. Accessed 31 Aug 2018
15. Get started with Cloud Firestore. Firebase. https://firebase.google.com/docs/firestore/quickstart. Accessed 31 Aug 2018

The Need for Mobile Apps for Maternal and Child Health Care in Center and East Europe

Sebastien Mambou[1], Ondrej Krejcar[1(✉)] ⓘ, Petra Maresova[2] ⓘ,
Ali Selamat[1,3] ⓘ, and Kamil Kuca[1] ⓘ

[1] Faculty of Informatics and Management,
Center for Basic and Applied Research, University of Hradec Kralove,
Rokitanskeho 62, 500 03 Hradec Kralove, Czech Republic
{jean.mambou, ondrej.krejcar, kamil.kuca}@uhk.cz
[2] Department of Economy, Faculty of Informatics and Management,
University of Hradec Kralove, Rokitanskeho 62,
500 03 Hradec Kralove, Czech Republic
petra.maresova@uhk.cz
[3] Malaysia Japan International Institute of Technology (MJIIT),
Universiti Teknologi Malaysia, Jalan Sultan Yahya Petra,
Kuala Lumpur, Malaysia
aselamat@utm.my

Abstract. Mobile health services are booming in the field of maternal and child health in Europe, due to extensions in the area of electronic health and the introduction of the European Policies to increase fertility rate. There are many applications (apps) related to mother and child health in computer stores, but the exact number of mobile apps, their download volume, and the functionality of these applications are not known. the reason of this research was to investigate on the use of mobile health apps (mHealth) in Android and IOS application stores and to describe the key features of the most popular applications that provide information on maternal health and baby. The researchers searched the most popular Android app stores and the iTunes App Store in Center and East Europe. All applications related to family planning (contraception and pregnancy preparedness), pregnancy and perinatal care, neonatal care and health, as well as the development of children under six, were included in the initial analysis. Mobile maternal and child health applications with prominent features in product marketing, children's songs, animation, and games were excluded from the study.

Keywords: Android · IOS · mHealth

1 Introduction

For the past few years, several mobile applications (apps) have flooded the market, especially those with a medical accent or to be more precise those focusing on pregnancy. Consequently, as mentioned by [1], there is a considerable number of

© Springer Nature Switzerland AG 2019
I. Awan et al. (Eds.): MobiWIS 2019, LNCS 11673, pp. 95–108, 2019.
https://doi.org/10.1007/978-3-030-27192-3_8

applications that focus on pregnancy compare to any other medical field. Mobile apps can be a good factor during pregnancy as it may contribute positively during that vital part of women's lives [2]. However, too much information, lifestyle tips, and health care can make anxiety and stress worse during pregnancy. Therefore, efficiency and usability are key aspects to address for the implementation of new applications in maternal health care. Currently people generally have a positive attitude towards acceptance of mobile applications for both medical and non-medical purposes. It points to the potential and meaningfulness of proposing such a solution and its use [3–5]. Furthermore, according to [6], monitoring progress is difficult given the weaknesses of health information systems in some countries. Problems such as under-reporting and differences between official data and estimates made by international agencies are among the contributing factors.

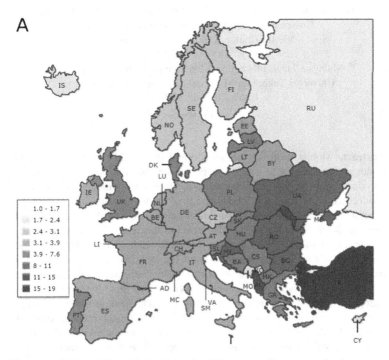

Fig. 1. The map displayed here shows how the infant mortality rate varies by country. The darker the shade, the higher the value [7].

Moreover, in the European Region between 2000 and 2015, the Maternal Mortality Ratio (MMR) almost halved, from 33 to 16 deaths per 100,000 live births respectively. However, in 2015 the highest maternal mortality rate, in the region was 25 times lower and much lower in 2017 (see Fig. 1) and Table 1.

Table 1. Repartition in Europe of the number of Infant mortality per 1,000 births (alive) [7].

Country	Rate	Year	Country	Rate	Year
Turkey	18	2017	Lithuania	4	2017
Moldova	12	2017	Estonia	4	2017
Albania	12	2017	Ireland	4	2017
Romania	9	2017	Belarus	4	2017
Croatia	9	2017	Andorra	4	2017
Bulgaria	8	2017	Netherlands	4	2017
Ukraine	8	2017	Switzerland	4	2017
Macedonia	7	2017	Malta	4	2017
Serbia	6	2017	Luxembourg	3	2017
Bosnia and Herzegovina	6	2017	Austria	3	2017
Latvia	5	2017	Belgium	3	2017
Slovakia	5	2017	Germany	3	2017
Hungary	5	2017	Italy	3	2017
Greece	5	2017	Spain	3	2017
Poland	4	2017	France	3	2017
Portugal	4	2017	Czech Republic	3	2017
San Marino	4	2017	Sweden	3	2017
United Kingdom	4	2017	Norway	3	2017
Liechtenstein	4	2017	Finland	3	2017
Denmark	4	2017	Iceland	2	2017
Slovenia	4	2017	Monaco	2	2017

Besides, the maternal mortality rate for "non-western" women was 60% higher and the infant mortality Rate was higher too. To overcome these issues, several mobile applications are booming in the field of maternal and child health in Europe (see Fig. 2). This research will explore, the use of maternal and child health applications in app-stores (Android and iOS), to provide information about research, future development of mobile apps for maternal and child health. The remaining part of this article is organized as: Sect. 2 will present related works; Sect. 3 will show an in-depth analysis of the method used in this research, and Sect. 4 will open a discussion.

2   Related Work

For the past few years, several studies have been conducted with the goal to find the relationship between the mobile applications (apps) usage and the decrease of complications before, during and after the pregnancy period. In that state of mind, authors [8] revealed that due to the limited number, comparators and outcome measures, no definitive conclusion can be drawn, about the effects of mobile application interventions during pregnancy on maternal knowledge, behavior change, and perinatal health outcomes.

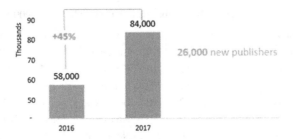

Fig. 2. 45% increase of mHealth apps published between 2016 and 2017 [9, 10]

While millions of women use mobile apps during pregnancy, rigorous studies are essential for health and maternity care providers to design, implement, and evaluate interventions optimally. In addition, Authors [11] concluded by saying that social media and mobile health applications can be widely used to improve maternal well-being. Never the last, Author [12] performed a study which provides essential information on the challenges associated with implementing a pregnancy application in a socially disadvantaged community. In this study, all women were similar in terms of age, race, marital status, and level of education. Of the 94 women, 76% who did not complete the trial, were significantly more anxious, as indicated by the State Anxiety Disorders Inventory (p = 0.001 student's T-test) and more likely to be unemployed (50% vs. 31%, p = 0.012 student test). Data from this trial has been collected and suggests factors such as social and mental health issues, financial constraints, and technological capabilities may affect women's engagement with a mobile phone application. Several parallel studies have also contributed to find better tools to ease diagnosis of some pregnant women [13–15].

In 2014, the European Commission published its Green Paper on Mobile Health previously announced in the 2012–2020 eHealth Action Plan, launching a broad stakeholder consultation on the barriers and issues related to the deployment of mobile health and helping to identify the way forward to unleash the potential of mobile health.

2.1 Maternity Health Medical Applications

Unlike mobile lifestyle health applications, the feasibility and acceptability of medical apps have only been reported in 2 diabetes management studies and are satisfactory [2, 16]. The diabetes treatment evaluation base on five studies during pregnancy can be judge correctly because of objective outcome measures [17]. Despite this, not all studies yielded significant results because of the small sample size; a promising observation can be seen on the effectiveness of mobile medical health applications in improving vaccination rates [18] and asthma management [19–21].

The Authors' study [22] showed that their mobile application of Autonomous Management of Type 2 Diabetes was feasible because of the high response rate. The intervention was considered favorable and significant [22]. For dialysis patients, authors in [23] had a reasonable completion rate after evaluating the feasibility and usability of a self-management assistance system, and most patients appreciated the system and intended to continue the process. [23].

2.2 Strong User Commitment

Authors [24] in their paper observed a strong user commitment with more than 1,730 downloads of their application. Application users had a statistically significant relationship between the use of the application (app) and the completion of a prenatal visit of six months or more ($p = 0.022$). There was a significant association at the boundary between the use of applications and the decrease in the incidence of low birth weight ($p = 0.055$). Maternal age was not a possible confounding factor. With the same idea, authors [11] reported that fifteen randomized controlled trial studies published by June 2018 and meeting the inclusion criteria were included in their meta-analysis. The mobile apps (and website) impacts were visible in promoting maternal physical health, including weight management, gestational diabetes control, and asthma control with a moderate to high effect size ($d = 0.72$). Significant effects were also found to improve maternal mental health ($d = 0.84$) and knowledge of pregnancy ($d = 0.80$).

2.3 Combination of mHealth Lifestyle and Medical Applications

Concerning the general management of diabetes and smoking cessation, authors in [25] reviewed the literature on the combination of mobile health applications involving smoking. The authors reported a low smoking cessation rate, although, in some studies, the intervention groups performed better than the control groups. They showed that mHealth could play an essential role in the management of diabetes. They are considering the SMS results on HbA1c levels, which is consistent with our results [16, 26–28].

3 Selection Process of the Studied Applications

3.1 Selection Criteria

The selected applications include those developed for family planning (contraception and pregnancy preparedness), pregnancy and perinatal care, neonatal care and health, and development of children under six years of age.

Indeed, research was done on two application markets using the following keywords in English: pregnant, pregnancy, childcare, maternity, mother and child, child health, baby health, and maternal health. Based on preliminary research findings, a few other frequently used phrases in maternal and Child Health (MCH) application descriptions were added to keyword searches: menstruation, women, stage of pregnancy, fetus, mother, and child, children's songs, etc. The official websites or App Stores were visited for each of the two app markets, to extract MCH apps using the identified keywords. For each search, a guest account was used so that the search results could not be adapted to an existing account. Also, the name of the app and the number of downloads (Android apps) or the number of reviews (iOS apps) of all apps generated from a search for each keyword in each app market have been saved, after the review by two blind investigators for the name and description of the desired applications. Furthermore, Non-relevant apps for MCH care and product marketing applications were excluded. Besides, the deduplication of apps was done separately for

Android and iOS apps, and search of the application stores was conducted between March 17, 2019, and March 22, 2019.

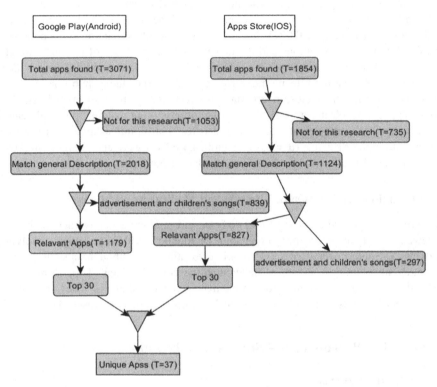

Fig. 3. mHealth application selection. The flow chart describes all steps follow to obtain a list of 37 applications.

3.2   Preprocessing of the Phase

All applications found were sorted by the number of downloads on Android as well as IOS. 3071 mobile apps were identified on Google Play (Android), and 1854 Mobile apps were identified on Apple Store (IOS). Through their descriptions, several presented commercial features (a strong accent on the Pay version or premium Account). As the next step, many applications were found with an interest on one following: relaxation songs, white noise, children's games, focusing on the beginning of pregnancy, or even the baby's sleep. These applications had limited functionalities or were not necessary for this search, but the ranking and the number of downloads were relatively high. For this study, they were excluded, given 2018 and 1124 remaining mobile applications to process (see Fig. 3). Going through their described content, a predominant accent on advertisements such as insurance was detected and those apps where remove according to PRISMA guideline [29], leading to a list of relevant mobile applications to 1179 Android Apps and 827 IOS apps.

Table 2. A list of Thirty-seven mobile apps obtained, by combining 30 most popular searches Android and iOS apps.

Apps	Category	Description
AstroSecret	Medical	Improve chance of pregnancy up to 99%
BaBy+	Medical	Help to track baby development
Baby Breastfeeding Tracker	Medical	Follow your progress as a nurse in real time with our easy-to-use timer and follow the medication your baby is taking
Baby Care	Medical	Baby Diary, Feeding, Baby, Development, Symptoms, Growth, Breast Pumping, etc.
baby Care Tracker	Parenting	Baby Diary, Feeding, Baby, Development, Symptoms, Growth, Breast Pumping, etc.
Baby Care Week	Parenting	Baby development week by week and parenting tips in one baby app
Baby Care-Nature	Health & Fitness	Taking care of babies with natural method
Baby Daybook	Drilly Apps	Baby Care, sleeping and breastfeeding tracker & newborn activity logger
Baby Sleep	Music & Audio	App Music Sleep Baby is free and offers a totally free songs for your Baby
Baby Tracker	Medical	Help to track baby's daily habits, health and exciting
Baby tracker	Parenting	Feeding, Sleep and diaper tracker for your little one
Baby Center-Pregnancy	Health & Fitness	Pregnancy tracker and baby development
Burleigh Creative Pty Ltd	Health & Fitness	Produce White sound that help baby to sleep in a silent environment
Clue Period	Health & Fitness	Help to discover the unique patterns in the menstrual cycle
Contraction Timer & Counter 9 m	Medical	Display average indicators for contraction duration and frequency over the past hour
Feed Baby-Breastfeeding	Medical	Track newborns breastfeeding, diaper changes, pumping and sleeps
Flo health, INC	Health & Fitness	Period & Ovulation & Fertility Calendar
Glow Baby Newborn Tracker	Medical	Breastfeeding Timer Diaper
Headspace	Health & Fitness	Breathe, focus, relax and sleep
Health & Parenting LTd	Medical	Monitor your pregnancy and help to find name of babies
Hello Belly	Medical	Period calendar baby guide
Ipnos Software Inc.	Health & Fitness	Improve sleep with White noise
Life-Period	Health & Fitness	Track period, predict ovulation, schedule cycle

(continued)

Table 2. (*continued*)

Apps	Category	Description
MammaBaby-Breast feeding	Medical	Improve the overall parent experience
Master Internet, s.r.o	Lifestyle	Help to wash kids when they are sleeping. It transforms 2 connected mobile devices as audio and video listener
Mom.life	Medical	Help pregnancy tracker, baby growth calendar, feeding tracker
My Calendar-Period Tracker	Health & Fitness	Help to take control of many aspects of menstrual cycle-from ovulation, fertility period, birth control pills, moods
Ovia Pregnancy tracker	Ovuline	Watch baby grow every day with ovia pregnancy
Precious - Baby	Lifestyle	Help to find baby photos and the phone and organizes them into monthly pictures
Pregnancy+	Health & Parenting	Help to follow pregnancy week by week
Pregnancy Tracker	Parenting	Baby development, growth and pregnancy monitoring week by week for future parents
Pregnancy Tracker and Baby	Medical	Pregnancy calendar and to count pregnancy due to date
Pro Active	Health & Fitness	Menstrual and fertility calendar for women
The Best Baby Tracker	Medical	Help Nursing, Nappies sleep
The Wonder Weeks	Health & Fitness	Personalized weekly calendar of your baby's mental development
WomanLog Pro Calendar	Health & Fitness	Help menstrual cycle and the period ovulation and fertility forecast

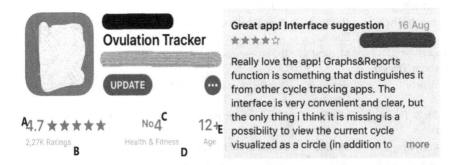

Fig. 4. A maternity health apps presents in IOS apps store. A, B, C, D and E respectively represent: The flow rate of the application; How many people rated this application, the Ranking of the application base on his Category; and how sensible is the content of the application.

The top 30 applications in the Android and iOS markets, respectively, were considered the most used apps and were selected for further analysis in this study. For the applications that used both Android and iOS systems, only the iOS system was used for an in-depth review, with small differences that could be identified between the different versions. Finally, the lists of the 30 most common searches for Android and iOS have been integrated into a combined list containing 37 unique applications (see Table 2). All the selected applications present all the characteristic required for their study, for instance, the number of ratings as well as the presence of several comments (see Fig. 4).

The deep analysis of the 37 mobile applications revealed a similitude in the workflow of the different apps independently of the platform. Also, it is very astonishing to see the number of download associate to these applications. In addition, the reviews prove the use and impact of these mobile applications (see Fig. 4).

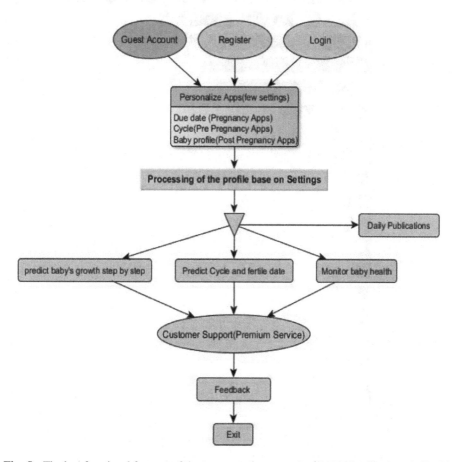

Fig. 5. The key functional features of the most popular maternity Health Applications (mHealth Apps). In this research, the Guest account was used to avoid any related setting link to a specific profile.

3.3 Key Functional Features

Looking closely to each application among the remaining 37, the key functional features of the most popular maternity Health Applications (mHealth Apps) can be extracted. From a guest account the user can have an overview of each application, however preliminary setting (basic profile) is usually required as shown in (see Fig. 5).

On this last, after the processing of a basic profile set before (or basic preference) is completed, several functionalities are presented to the user and the key functional features (button, menu, publications) are highlighted. Along with this feature, it is now possible to ask to be assisted or contact a customer care (Support) in case of any question. However, the Assistance functionality is usually activated when the user is properly registered and has subscribe to a premium account.

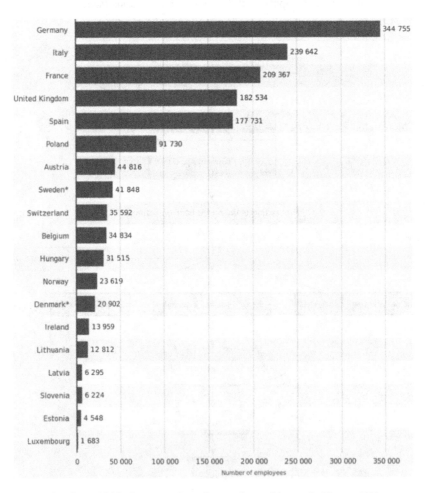

Fig. 6. In 2016, the proportion of general practitioners in Europe [31].

4 Discussion

According to [1], Today's world is characterized by professionals who spend very little time with their families, especially their young children. Working mothers find it difficult to follow the vaccines their babies have received and due to the advance of the technology. It becomes easier for someone to keep a note on his/her phone compare to write in a paper bloc note. Similarly, people because very predisposed to used mobile apps such as mhealth which contribute incredibly to their wellbeing.

Several European countries in particularly from Central and East still struggle to reduce the maternal mortality rate (See Fig. 1), mobile apps can be good support which will permit to increase their awareness on the techniques that will ease their lives and help them to take care of their child. East Europe will certainly beneficiate of the adoption of mHealth as according to [30], more doctors and nurses move from one country to another than any other highly regulated profession in the EU, and flows often go from east to west, from the poorest to the richest. Furthermore, the number of general practitioners is not enough taking into account the growth of the population, new services such as mHealth mobile apps are very necessary. An analysis of European Commission data by POLITICO revealed that the exodus of health professionals was particularly marked in Eastern and Southern Europe. As shown (see Fig. 6), the number of a general practitioner in Center and East Europe is relatively small, also Fig. 1 shows that the interest of mhealth apps keeps increases every year, this can guaranty a development of a better tool that will ensure the safety of the user and the reliability of the mHealth apps services.

5 Conclusion

At the global level, infant mortality rates have been halted in recent decades, which is a development success story. However, progress has been uneven and in past years. Indeed, several applications have been explored with the goal of determining the main features of the most downloaded mHealth apps and providing information on future research and development. In general, these mobile applications can help reduce the disparity or gap between countries in Western and Central and Eastern Europe, with the goal of reducing the infant mortality rate in Europe. Therefore, attention should be placed on evaluating mobile health tools and disseminating results to inform program design and policy development. The field of mobile health should continue to be supported and study as it leads to a positive outcome for women and children in middle-income countries. Further study will reveal the impact of using Intelligent Artificial Agent (AI) as customer support [32–35] or first layer between a real doctor and the patient.

Acknowledgement. The work was supported by the SPEV project "Smart Solutions in Ubiquitous Computing Environments", 2019, University of Hradec Kralove, FIM, Czech Republic.

References

1. Infant mortality, males - European Health Information Gateway. https://gateway.euro.who.int/en/indicators/h2020_37-infant-mortality-males/visualizations/#id=26720
2. Nicholson, W.K., et al.: The gestational diabetes management system (GooDMomS): development, feasibility and lessons learned from a patient-informed, web-based pregnancy and postpartum lifestyle intervention. BMC Pregnancy Childbirth **16** (2016). https://doi.org/10.1186/s12884-016-1064-z
3. Pindeh, N., Suki, N.M., Suki, N.M.: User acceptance on mobile apps as an effective medium to learn Kadazandusun language. Procedia Econ. Finance **37**, 372–378 (2016). https://doi.org/10.1016/S2212-5671(16)30139-3
4. Park, B.-W., Lee, K.C.: A pilot study to analyze the effects of user experience and device characteristics on the customer satisfaction of smartphone users. In: Kim, T.-h., Adeli, H., Robles, R.J., Balitanas, M. (eds.) UCMA 2011. CCIS, vol. 151, pp. 421–427. Springer, Heidelberg (2011). https://doi.org/10.1007/978-3-642-20998-7_50
5. Cheng, L.K., et al.: Usability prioritization using performance metrics and hierarchical agglomerative clustering in MAR-learning application. In: Fujita, H., Selamat, A., Omatu, S. (eds.) New Trends in Intelligent Software Methodologies, Tools and Techniques, pp. 731–744. Ios Press, Amsterdam (2017)
6. Photo gallery - World Statistics Day 2016. http://www.euro.who.int/en/health-topics/Life-stages/maternal-and-newborn-health/data-and-statistics/photo-gallery-world-statistics-day-2016
7. Infant mortality rate by country - Thematic Map – Europe. https://www.indexmundi.com/map/?t=0&v=29&r=eu&l=en
8. The Effect of Mobile App Interventions on Influencing Healthy Maternal Behavior and Improving Perinatal Health Outcomes: Systematic Review. - PubMed – NCBI. https://www.ncbi.nlm.nih.gov/pubmed/30093368
9. The Rise of mHealth Apps: A Market Snapshot - Liquid State. https://liquid-state.com/mhealth-apps-market-snapshot/
10. Pavlas, J., Krejcar, O., Maresova, P., Selamat, A.: Prototypes of user interfaces for mobile applications for patients with diabetes. Computers **8** (2019). https://doi.org/10.3390/computers8010001
11. Chan, K.L., Chen, M.: Effects of social media and mobile health apps on pregnancy care: meta-analysis. JMIR Mhealth Uhealth. **7**, e11836 (2019). https://doi.org/10.2196/11836
12. Dalton, J.A., et al.: The Health-e Babies App for antenatal education: feasibility for socially disadvantaged women. PLoS One **13**, e0194337 (2018). https://doi.org/10.1371/journal.pone.0194337
13. Mambou, S., Krejcar, O., Maresova, P., Selamat, A., Kuca, K.: Novel four stages classification of breast cancer using infrared thermal imaging and a deep learning model. In: Rojas, I., Valenzuela, O., Rojas, F., Ortuño, F. (eds.) IWBBIO 2019. LNCS, vol. 11466, pp. 63–74. Springer, Cham (2019). https://doi.org/10.1007/978-3-030-17935-9_7
14. Mambou, S.J., Maresova, P., Krejcar, O., Selamat, A., Kuca, K.: Breast cancer detection using infrared thermal imaging and a deep learning model. Sensors (Basel) **18** (2018). https://doi.org/10.3390/s18092799
15. Mambou, S., Maresova, P., Krejcar, O., Selamat, A., Kuca, K.: Breast cancer detection using modern visual IT techniques. In: Sieminski, A., Kozierkiewicz, A., Nunez, M., Ha, Q.T. (eds.) Modern Approaches for Intelligent Information and Database Systems. Studies in Computational Intelligence, vol. 769, pp. 397–407. Springer, Cham (2018). https://doi.org/10.1007/978-3-319-76081-0_34

16. Hirst, J.E., et al.: Acceptability and user satisfaction of a smartphone-based, interactive blood glucose management system in women with gestational diabetes mellitus. J Diabetes Sci. Technol. **9**, 111–115 (2015). https://doi.org/10.1177/1932296814556506

17. Maresova, P., Klimova, B., Kuca, K.: Legislation, regulation and policies issues of orphan drugs in developed countries from 2010 to 2016. J. Appl. Biomed. **16**, 175–179 (2018). https://doi.org/10.1016/j.jab.2018.04.002

18. Zairina, E., et al.: Telehealth to improve asthma control in pregnancy: a randomized controlled trial. Respirology **21**, 867–874 (2016). https://doi.org/10.1111/resp.12773

19. Stockwell, M.S., et al.: Influenza vaccine text message reminders for urban, low-income pregnant women: a randomized controlled trial. Am. J. Public Health **104**(Suppl. 1), e7–12 (2014). https://doi.org/10.2105/AJPH.2013.301620

20. Jordan, E.T., Bushar, J.A., Kendrick, J.S., Johnson, P., Wang, J.: Encouraging influenza vaccination among Text4baby pregnant women and mothers. Am. J. Prev. Med. **49**, 563–572 (2015). https://doi.org/10.1016/j.amepre.2015.04.029

21. Yudin, M.H., et al.: Text messages for influenza vaccination among pregnant women: a randomized controlled trial. Vaccine **35**, 842–848 (2017). https://doi.org/10.1016/j.vaccine.2016.12.002

22. Nes, A.A.G., et al.: The development and feasibility of a web-based intervention with diaries and situational feedback via smartphone to support self-management in patients with diabetes type 2. Diabetes Res. Clin. Pract. **97**, 385–393 (2012). https://doi.org/10.1016/j.diabres.2012.04.019

23. Hayashi, A., et al.: Testing the feasibility and usability of a novel smartphone-based self-management support system for dialysis patients: a pilot study. JMIR Res. Protoc. **6**, e63 (2017). https://doi.org/10.2196/resprot.7105

24. Bush, J., Barlow, D.E., Echols, J., Wilkerson, J., Bellevin, K.: Impact of a mobile health application on user engagement and pregnancy outcomes among wyoming medicaid members. Telemed. J. E Health **23**, 891–898 (2017). https://doi.org/10.1089/tmj.2016.0242

25. Rehman, H., Kamal, A.K., Sayani, S., Morris, P.B., Merchant, A.T., Virani, S.S.: Using mobile health (mHealth) technology in the management of diabetes mellitus, physical inactivity, and smoking. Curr. Atherosclerosis Rep. **19**, 16 (2017). https://doi.org/10.1007/s11883-017-0650-5

26. Homko, C.J., et al.: Use of an internet-based telemedicine system to manage underserved women with gestational diabetes mellitus. Diabetes Technol. Ther. **9**, 297–306 (2007). https://doi.org/10.1089/dia.2006.0034

27. The Outcomes of Gestational Diabetes Mellitus after a Telecare Approach Are Not Inferior to Traditional Outpatient Clinic Visits. https://www.hindawi.com/journals/ije/2010/386941/

28. Homko, C.J., et al.: Impact of a telemedicine system with automated reminders on outcomes in women with gestational diabetes mellitus. Diabetes Technol. Ther. **14**, 624–629 (2012). https://doi.org/10.1089/dia.2012.0010

29. Klímová, B., Marešová, P.: Economic methods used in health technology assessment. E a M: Ekonomie a Management **21**, 116–126 (2018). https://doi.org/10.15240/tul/001/2018-1-008

30. The EU exodus: When doctors and nurses follow the money – POLITICO. https://www.politico.eu/article/doctors-nurses-migration-health-care-crisis-workers-follow-the-money-european-commission-data/

31. Physicians employed in Europe in 2016. Statistic. https://www.statista.com/statistics/554938/practising-physicians-employed-in-europe/

32. Mambou, S., Krejcar, O., Kuca, K., Selamat, A.: Novel human action recognition in RGB-D videos based on powerful view invariant features technique. In: Sieminski, A., Kozierkiewicz, A., Nunez, M., Ha, Q.T. (eds.) Modern Approaches for Intelligent Information and Database Systems, pp. 343–353. Springer, Cham (2018). https://doi.org/10.1007/978-3-319-76081-0_29

33. Mambou, S., Krejcar, O., Kuca, K., Selamat, A.: Novel cross-view human action model recognition based on the powerful view-invariant features technique. Future Internet **10**, 89 (2018). https://doi.org/10.3390/fi10090089

34. Mambou, S., Krejcar, O., Selamat, A.: Approximate outputs of accelerated turing machines closest to their halting point. In: Nguyen, N.T., Gaol, F.L., Hong, T.-P., Trawiński, B. (eds.) ACIIDS 2019. LNCS (LNAI), vol. 11431, pp. 702–713. Springer, Cham (2019). https://doi.org/10.1007/978-3-030-14799-0_60

35. Jirka, J., Prauzek, M., Krejcar, O., Kuca, K.: Automatic epilepsy detection using fractal dimensions segmentation and GP–SVM classification. Neuropsychiatric Dis. Treat. **14**, 2439–2449 (2018). https://doi.org/10.2147/NDT.S167841

Security and Privacy

Classification Analysis of Intrusion Detection on NSL-KDD Using Machine Learning Algorithms

Yoney Kirsal Ever[1]([✉]) [iD], Boran Sekeroglu[2] [iD], and Kamil Dimililer[3] [iD]

[1] Software Engineering, Near East University,
Near East Boulevard, TRNC, Mersin 10, Turkey
yoneykirsal.ever@neu.edu.tr
[2] Information Systems Engineering, Near East University,
Near East Boulevard, TRNC, Mersin 10, Turkey
boran.sekeroglu@neu.edu.tr
[3] Electrical and Electronic Engineering, Near East University,
Near East Boulevard, TRNC, Mersin 10, Turkey
kamil.dimililer@neu.edu.tr

Abstract. Since three decades, artificial intelligence has been evolved in order to outperform the tasks that human beings are not capable. These tasks can be any problem from our lives and one of these problems is computer networks-related tasks which huge number of privacy data is transferred even a second. Within last two decades, machine learning techniques with capabilities for prediction, optimisation, and as well as classification are developed for using to solve the real-life problems. In this paper, challenging and popular NSL-KDD dataset for intrusion detection is chosen for performed experiments, where classification and three benchmark machine learning techniques are used in order to determine optimum technique for classification domain. Experiments are performed by implementing 3-layered Back-propagation Neural Network, Support Vector Machine and Decision Tree. Thirty percent (30%) of instances of NSL-KDD Dataset were considered that causes 25193 of total instances in experiments. Each experiment is repeated for two times by using 60% and 70% of instances for training and the rest for testing. Increment of training patterns or instances caused little fluctuations on accuracy rates in Decision Tree and Back-propagation but it causes more effect in Support Vector Machine which is about 1% decrement in accuracy rate. It is seen from the performed experiments' results that, increment or degradation of training ratio of instances in dataset does not affect the performance of the techniques directly.

Keywords: Classification · Machine learning ·
Intrusion detection system · NSL-KDD dataset · BPNN · SVM ·
Decision Tree

© Springer Nature Switzerland AG 2019
I. Awan et al. (Eds.): MobiWIS 2019, LNCS 11673, pp. 111–122, 2019.
https://doi.org/10.1007/978-3-030-27192-3_9

1   Introduction

Since last three decades, deployments in computers and computer connected devices have been evolved very rapidly. Especially, when last two decades are considered, it can be seen that the improvements in the artificial intelligence are affecting the multi-disciplinary fields in digital world. As part of these improvements, machine learning techniques with capabilities for prediction, optimisation, and as well as classification are developed for using to solve the real-life problems where many different and interesting frameworks and models are proposed and available in the literature. Especially, many deployments have been increased in different fields such as computer communication networks, healthcare, economics, statistics, agriculture, and many more [1].

Because of the growing popularity and use of computers and network-based devices everyday in every field of our lives, providing privacy and data integrity has become crucial. It is very important to protect data, resources and systems from attacks and unauthorised access. Attack prevention, authentication and access control play a vital role in communication networks security. In literature the basic difference between authentication and access control is defined as the latter deals with rights and privileges of users who have already gained access into networks, where the former deals with identity verification before access is given [2].

As stated in [3] and [4] in order to provide more secure access to communication networks, concept of intrusion detection, and intrusion detection systems have become important, and many researcher focuses on use of machine learning techniques with various datasets to improve system accuracy, and anomaly detection. In these studies weaknesses of signature-based IDSs that detect novel attacks are tried to be overcome. [5] proposed a new dataset named, NSL-KDD. NSL-KDD consists of selected records of the complete KDD data set and does not suffer from any of mentioned shortcomings. In their study [3], a detailed study with selected records of NSL-KDD dataset [5] where a good analysis on various machine learning techniques for intrusion detection is provided. In this research, the NSL-KDD dataset is analysed and it is found out that some issues of KDD cup99 dataset is solved successfully. It is concluded that NSL-KDD dataset would be a good resource for comparing different intrusion detection models [3]. NSL-KDD dataset has 41 features and all these features are used to evaluate the intrusive patterns for time consuming and reducing performance degradation of the system. The performed experiment has been carried out with different classification algorithms. Similarly, as stated above in order to detect anomalies in signature-based IDSs, in [6] KDD cup99 data set is used for the evaluation. A statistical analysis on this data set is conducted, and authors stated that two important issues affecting the systems' performance evaluation and anomaly detection approaches are found and evaluated explicitly.

In addition to existing studies, in [6] the NSL-KDD data set is analysed critically. In this study, authors discussed the effectiveness of the various classification algorithms and they efficiently analysed detection of the anomalies in the network traffic patterns. The analysis is performed by checking anomalous network traffic generated by the intruders based on the relationship of the commonly known authentication protocols available in the network protocol stack and attacks on them. Analysis is performed by using the data mining tool WEKA is done using classification algorithms available in the data mining tool WEKA. However, authors did not consider the prediction methods and effectiveness of the learning algorithms within this concept.

Similarly, in the study [7], an ANN based IDS was implemented on NSL-KDD dataset. Dataset was trained and tested as binary 0 and 1 category for normal or attack respectively, as well as for five class attack categories. Obtained results are evaluated based on ANN standard parameter such as accuracy, detection rate and false positive rate, and they are compared with other existing studies in the literature. The detection rate obtained is 81.2% and 79.9% for intrusion detection and attack type classification task respectively for NSL-KDD dataset. Some categories such as R2L and U2R had less number of patterns, therefore authors randomly selected from other three classes. Levenberg-Marquardt (LM) and BFGS quasi-Newton Back-propagation algorithm are used in the proposed IDS system for learning. Training and testing applied on dataset with full features (i.e. 41) and with reduced feature (i.e. 29) respectively. It was found that proposed technique gave higher accuracy of attack detection than other stated techniques in the literature. It was found that the system has good capability for five class classification to detect the attack in NSL-KDD dataset for particular class.

Moreover, another study presented [8] an intrusion classification model. NSL-KDD cup99 intrusion detection dataset is used. The model is based on the combination of feature selection and SVM classifier. For training data, the proposed method used a reduced set of input features, where it maintained the classification accuracy of the SVM classifier. Authors discussed that NSL-KDD cup99 dataset contains both normal and attack network connections which is defined as a multiple class classification problem. Several feature subsets of NSL-KDD cup99 dataset is applied by SVM classifier. Analysis and discussions on the experimental results are shown that the proposed method achieved 91% classification accuracy using only three input features and 99% classification accuracy using 36 input features, while all 41 input features achieved 99% classification accuracy.

Besides these existing studies in the literature, a practical solution of using unsupervised ANN in hierarchical anomaly intrusion detection system is presented in [9]. The proposed system is employed SOM neural nets for detection and separate normal traffic from the attack traffic.

The proposed system was used to tuning, training, and testing SOM Neural Network in intrusion detection. The results show that SOM with KDD99 is 92.37% able to recognise attack traffic from normal one, while with NSL-KDD is 75.49% able to recognise attack traffic from normal one. Analysis and discussions on experiment results on intrusion dataset showed that due to their high speed and fast conversion rates, SOM are best suited as compared with other learning techniques. Authors discussed that their approach using SOM obtained better performance results in comparison with other existing acclaimed detection methods.

Last but not the least, it can be analysed that all the existing studies for anomaly intrusion detection have considered classification methods rather than prediction. In this paper, NSL-KDD dataset is used for performed experiments in order to determine optimum technique for classification domain.

The rest of the paper is structured as follows: Sect. 2 presents existing machine learning algorithms in the literature. Section 3 explains detailed description of the proposed design evaluation strategy for experiment values in NSL-KDD dataset. Section 4 summarises discussions on experiment results obtained and experimental analyses. The conclusions and future works are summarised in Sect. 5.

2 Machine Learning Algorithms

In this section, three machine learning algorithms; Back-propagation neural networks, Support Vector Machines and Decision Trees, which are considered in this research will be introduced.

2.1 Back-Propagation Neural Networks

Back-propagation neural network is a supervised learning algorithm which propagates back the error signal to update the weight during error minimisation. Simplicity in implementation and efficiency in classification and prediction problems [1,10–12,21] makes it popular for any kind of application that needs flexible human decision making.

During the training of Back-propagation neural networks, error is calculated in output layer by comparing actual and target output and weights are updating according to the Eq. 1.

$$w_j{}^{k+1} = w_j{}^k + lr(y_i - \hat{y}_i^k)x_{ij} \tag{1}$$

where $w_j{}^{k+1}$ and $w_j{}^k$ are updated and old weights respectively, lr is learning rate parameter, y_i and $\hat{y}_i^k$ are actual and target outputs respectively, and x_{ij} is the input instance.

General topology (architecture) of 3-layered (shallow) back-propagation neural network can be seen in Fig. 1.

2.2 Support Vector Machines

Support vector machine (SVM) is another supervised machine learning technique for classification. It assigns support vectors in order to separate features in hyperplane. In different applications, SVMs have produced successful results which include biometrics, image analysis and bioinformatics [13–15,21]. The basic phases of SVM includes training, and the test as in other supervised machine learning techniques. The most preferred kernel of SVM is Radial Basis Function (RBF).

General topology (architecture) of Support Vector Machine can be seen in Fig. 2.

2.3   Decision Tree

Divide-and-conquer strategy is used in Decision Trees in order to classify data until final leaf. Rules are assigned to each leaf and according to these rules, data flows until classified and decision trees have been used successfully in variety of classification problems recently [17–19].

It is a simple classifier in the form of a hierarchical tree structure, which performs supervised classification. It comprises a directed branching structure with a series of questions. Example Decision Tree is shown in Fig. 3.

3   Design of Experiments

In this section, considered dataset, design of experiments and evaluation strategy will be explained in details. The approach used in this work involves classification models based on machine learning algorithms. This section concentrates on selected classification techniques with NSL-KDD dataset with the best feature selections with accurate results in distinguishing "normal" and "anomaly".

3.1   Dataset and Experiments

NSL-KDD dataset [5] is a well known benchmark in the intrusion detection researches. Thus, classification of 41 attributes in the dataset was conducted in several researches as it was mentioned above. The list of the attributes can be seen in Table 1 and the output classes are labeled as "normal" and "anomaly".

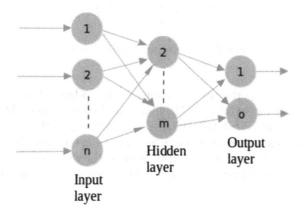

Fig. 1. General n-m-o architecture of back-propagation neural network

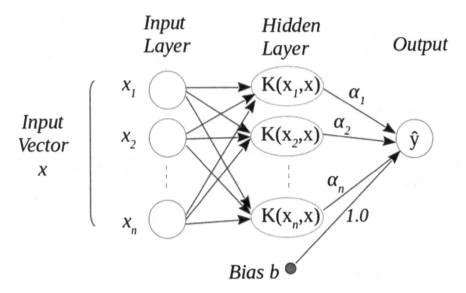

Fig. 2. General architecture of support vector machines [16]

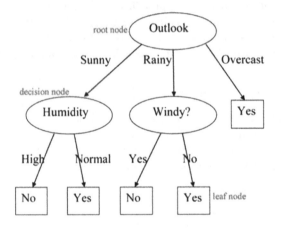

Fig. 3. Example decision tree [20]

Experiments were performed by implementing 3-layered Back-propagation Neural Network, Support Vector Machine and Decision Tree. Thirty percent (30%) of instances of NSL-KDD Dataset were considered that causes 25193 of total instances in experiments. Each experiment was repeated for two times by using 60% and 70% of instances for training and the rest for testing.

Table 2 shows the number of training and testing instances for 60% and 70% ratios.

Table 1. Attributes of NSL-KDD dataset

Attributes 1–11	Attributes 12–21	Attributes 22–31	Attributes 32–41
Duration	logged_in	is_ guest_ login	d_ h count
Protocol type	n_ compromised	count	d_ h_ s_ count
Service	root_ shell	s_ count	d_ h_ same_ s_ rate
flag	su_ attempted	serror_ rate	d_ h_ diff_ s_ rate
src_ bytes	n_ root	s_ serror_ rate	d_ h_ same_ src_ port_ rate
dst_ bytes	n_ file_ creations	rerror_ rate	d_ h_ s_ diff_ host_ rate
land	n_ shells	s_ rerror_ rate	d_ h_ serror_ rate
wrong_ fragment	n_ access_ files	same_ s_ rate	d_ h_ s_ serror_ rate
urgent	n_ outbound_ cmds	diff_ s_ rate	d_ h_ rerror_ rate
hot	is_ host_ login	s_ diff_ host_ rate	d_ h_ s_ rerror_ rate
n_ failed_ logins			

Table 2. Number of training and testing instances for different ratios

Final set	60% Training ratio	Final set	70% Training ratio
Training instances	15115	Training instances	17635
Testing instances	10078	Testing instances	7558

3.2 Evaluation Strategy

Cross-validation is applied in order to obtained more accurate results. Different performance measures such as precision, recall, sensitivity etc. can be used in order to determine the success rates of learning algorithms however in this research accuracy rate which is the basic indicator for two-class problems is determined to be used. Accuracy rates are calculated as shown in Eq. 2.

$$accuracy = \frac{TP + TN}{TP + TN + FP + FN} \tag{2}$$

where TP and TN is the total number of correctly recognised "normal" or "anomaly" labels and FP and FN and incorrectly classified features during the test phase.

4 Results, Discussions and Comparisons

In this section, obtained results, discussions and comparisons will be presented. The goal of this paper is to find the ideal classification algorithm considering achievement of optimal performance on NSL-KDD dataset. The purpose is to analyse the NSL-KDD dataset and notice the performance of different classification algorithms. Thirty percent (30%) of instances of NSL-KDD Dataset were considered that causes 25193 patterns of total instances.

4.1   Results

100 neurons were used in hidden layer of back-propagation neural network and
Sigmoid activation function was used for hidden and output layers. 200 epochs
were used as stopping criteria of training both for 60% and 70% training ratios.
In Support Vector Machine, Radial Basis Function was used as kernel and Gini
criterion was used in Decision Tree.

For the first group of experiments, which only 60% of instances considered
for training, Decision Tree achieved 99.84% of classification result which is the
optimum for all experiments in this research. It is followed by SVM with 98.43%
and Back-propagation 98.06% of classification rates.

By considering 70% of instances for training, Decision Tree achieved 99.81%
of accuracy and it is followed by Back-propagation with 98.05%. Support Vector Machines produced 97.44% of classification rate which is the lowest in this
research.

Table 3 shows all results obtained in this research and Figs. 4 and 5 shows
accuracy graphs for 60% and 70% of training ratios.

Table 3. Accuracy results for all experiments

Method	Accuracy for 60% Training	Accuracy for 70% Training
Decision Tree	99.84%	99.81%
Back-propagation NN	98.06%	98.05%
Support Vector Machine	98.43%	97.44%

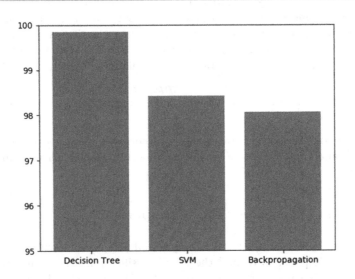

Fig. 4. Classification performance for 60% of training

4.2   Comparisons

As it is mentioned above, several studies were performed on NSL-KDD Dataset for intrusion detection classification by different machine learning algorithms. These studies include different types of Back-propagation Neural Network, unsupervised neural network, modified support vector machines [7–9]. Table 4 presents the summary of the comparison of recent researches and results obtained in this research. In Table 4, Decision Tree outperforms other researches and Machine Learning techniques in intrusion detection classification of NSL-KDD Dataset.

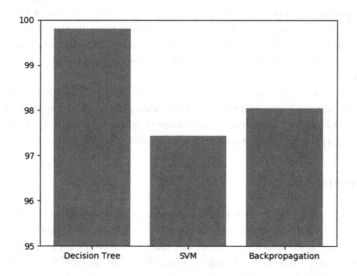

Fig. 5. Classification performance for 70% of training

Table 4. Accuracy results for all experiments

Reference	ML technique	Number of instances in training	Accuracy
[7]	BFGS quasi-Newton BPNN	41	81.2%
[8]	Support Vector Machine	3	91%
[8]	Support Vector Machine	36	99%
[8]	Support Vector Machine	41	99%
[9]	Self Orginizing Maps	41	75.49%
This research	Support Vector Machine	41	98.43%
This research	Backpropagation NN	41	98.06%
This research	Decision Tree	41	99.84%

4.3   Discussions

Considering above obtained results, Decision Tree achieved optimum intrusion detection classification results for all experiments. Back-propagation neural network produced more steady results than Support Vector Machines both for 60% and 70% of training ratios of total instances but Support Vector Machines achieved higher accuracy than Back-propagation in 60% of training ratio but lower in 70% of training ratio.

Increment of training patterns or instances caused little fluctuations on accuracy rates in Decision Tree and Back-propagation but it causes more effect in Support Vector Machine which is about 1% decrement in accuracy rate.

It is a general opinion in machine learning that the increment of training patterns or instances causes the increment of accuracy rates in classification results however, obtained results showed that either the efficiency of machine learning algorithms or the increment of the accuracy rates depend on the characteristics of dataset.

In many two-class applications, Support Vector Machines and Back-propagation Neural Networks produced superior results than Decision Trees but in NSL-KDD Dataset, Decision Tree produced optimum results both for considered training ratios without significant decrementation of accuracy.

5   Conclusions

Artificial Intelligence can be used to solve every problem that especially needs more accurate results in daily lives. One of these problems is network intrusion detection which may provide more secure usage of network and communication.

In this paper, three benchmark machine learning algorithms; decision tree, support vector machine and back-propagation neural network is implemented to 30% of NSL-KDD Dataset in order to observe and analyse the intrusion detection classification performance of considered machine learning techniques.

Obtained results show that machine learning techniques can efficiently classify the anomalies within the dataset and it can be concluded that the features of NSL-KDD dataset are linearly separable and do not need more complicated learning algorithms such as deep learning that increases computational time. It is also obvious that more experiments with different parameters of considered machine learning techniques may increase accuracy rates.

Future work will include the implementation of other machine learning algorithms such as Radial Basis Function Neural Network, Logistic Regression, and Random Forest by considering 100% of instances of NSL-KDD Dataset.

References

1. Kirsal Ever, Y., Dimililer, K., Sekeroglu, B.: Comparison of machine learning techniques for prediction problems. In: Barolli, L., Takizawa, M., Xhafa, F., Enokido, T. (eds.) WAINA 2019. AISC, vol. 927, pp. 713–723. Springer, Cham (2019). https://doi.org/10.1007/978-3-030-15035-8_69

2. Kirsal, Y., Gemikonakli, O.: Improving kerberos security through the combined use of the timed authentication protocol and frequent key renewal. In: 6th IEEE International Conference on Cybernetic Systems 2008, pp. 153–158. Middlesex University, London (2008)

3. Revathi, S., Malathi, A.: A detailed analysis on NSL-KDD dataset using various machine learning techniques for intrusion detection. Int. J. Eng. Res. Technol. (IJERT) **2**(12) (2013). ISSN 2278-0181

4. Dhanabal, L., Shantharajah, S.P.: A study on NSL-KDD dataset for intrusion detection system based on classification algorithms. Int. J. Adv. Res. Comput. Commun. Eng. **4**(6), 446–452 (2015)

5. NSL-KDD Dataset. https://www.unb.ca/cic/datasets/index.html. Accessed 28 Mar 2019

6. Tavallaee, M., Bagheri, E., Lu, W., Ghorbani, A.A.: A detailed analysis of the KDD CUP 99 data set. In: Proceedings of the 2009 IEEE Symposium on Computational Intelligence in Security and Defense Applications (CISDA 2009) (2009)

7. Ingre, B., Yadav, A.: Performance analysis of NSL-KDD dataset using ANN. In: SPACES-2015, Department of ECE, K L University (2015)

8. Pervez, M.S., Farid, D.Md.: Feature selection and intrusion classification in NSL-KDD Cup 99 dataset employing SVMs. In: 8th International Conference on Software, Knowledge, Information Management and Applications (SKIMA 2014), 18–20 December 2014

9. Ibrahim, L.M., Basheer, D.T., Mahmod, M.S.: A comparison study for intrusion database (KDD99, NSL-KDD) based on self organisation map (SOM) artificial neural network. J. Eng. Sci. Technol. **8**(1), 107–119 (2013)

10. Sekeroglu, B., Dimililer, K., Tuncal, K.: Student performance prediction and classification using machine learning algorithms. In: 8th International Conference on Educational and Information Technology (ICEIT 2019), Cambridge, UK (2019)

11. Wu, J., Chang, C.: Classification of landslide features using a LiDAR DEM and back-propagation neural network. In: El-Askary, H., Lee, S., Heggy, E., Pradhan, B. (eds.) Advances in Remote Sensing and Geo Informatics Applications, AG 2019. Advances in Science, Technology & Innovation (ASTI), vol. 927, pp. 155–158. Springer, Heidelberg (2019). https://doi.org/10.1007/978-3-030-01440-7_36

12. Chiba, Z., Abghour, N., Moussaid, K., El omri, A., Rida, M.: A new hybrid framework based on improved genetic algorithm and simulated annealing algorithm for optimization of network IDS based on BP neural network. In: Ben Ahmed, M., Boudhir, A., Younes, A. (eds.) Innovations in Smart Cities Applications. LNITI, vol. 921, 2nd edn, pp. 507–521. Springer, Cham (2019). https://doi.org/10.1007/978-3-030-11196-0_43

13. Sekeroglu, B., Emirzade, E.: A computer aided diagnosis system for lung cancer detection using support vector machine. In: Third International Workshop on Pattern Recognition, vol. 10828, Jinan, China (2018)

14. Kim, C., Park, J., Kim, H.: An actor-critic algorithm for SVM hyperparameters. In: Kim, K.J., Baek, N. (eds.) ICISA 2018. LNEE, vol. 514, pp. 653–661. Springer, Singapore (2019). https://doi.org/10.1007/978-981-13-1056-0_64

15. Xin, M.: An improved support vector machine of intrusion detection system. In: Abawajy, J., Choo, K.-K.R., Islam, R., Xu, Z., Atiquzzaman, M. (eds.) ATCI 2018. AISC, vol. 842, pp. 774–780. Springer, Cham (2019). https://doi.org/10.1007/978-3-319-98776-7_91
16. Aggarwal, P., Sharma, S.K.: Analysis of KDD dataset attributes - class wise for intrusion detection. Procedia Comput. Sci. **57**, 842–851 (2015)
17. Pal, M., Mather, P.M.: Decision tree based classification of remotely sensed data. In: 22nd Asian Conference on Remote Sensing, Singapore (2001)
18. Eissa, M.M., Ali, A.A., Abdel-Latif, K.M., Al-Kady, A.F.: A frequency control technique based on decision tree concept by managing thermostatically controllable loads at smart grids. Int. J. Electr. Power Energy Syst. **108**, 40–51 (2019)
19. Vernuccio, F., Rosenberg, M.D., Meyer, M., Choudhury, K.R., Nelson, R.C., Marin, D.: Negative biopsy of focal hepatic lesions: decision tree model for patient management. Am. J. Roentgenol. **212**(3), 677–685 (2019)
20. Dougherty, G.: Pattern Recognition and Classification: An Introduction. Springer, Berlin (2012). https://doi.org/10.1007/978-1-4614-5323-9
21. Ogidan, E.T., Dimililer, K., Ever, Y.K.: Machine learning for expert systems in data analysis. In: 2nd International Symposium on Multidisciplinary Studies and Innovative Technologies, ISMSIT 2018 (2018)

Infrastructure Authentication, Authorization and Accounting Solutions for an OpenStack Platform

Lubos Mercl$^{(\boxtimes)}$, Vladimir Sobeslav, Peter Mikulecky, and Michal Macinka

Faculty of Informatics and Management, University of Hradec Králové,
Rokitanského 62, 50003 Hradec Králové, Czech Republic
`lubos.mercl@uhk.cz`

Abstract. The security of open-source clouds is important, and there are many challenges in the area of user access which can be resolved using various implementations. OpenStack-based clouds must implement some identity solution based on a built-in Keystone project. In addition, it is important to secure the lower layer of this cloud and its infrastructure, where there is some potential vulnerability. This area can be mistakenly underestimated. The approach based on an authentication, authorization and accounting (AAA) solution offers some possibilities for extending Keystone by expanding it to other services, which will help to integrate it into the existing environment. Furthermore, it will enhance security features and thus secure the entire environment. This article discusses the authentication, authorization and accounting principles for an OpenStack platform and offers a simplified description of their implementation and testing.

Keywords: Cloud computing · Infrastructure · Security ·
Authentication · Authorization

1 Introduction

The cloud has become a standard in today's IT infrastructure. The implementation of cloud technologies offers many benefits, but with centralization and the shifting of work to data centers, new security challenges are arising. These security issues mainly concern private clouds. Private clouds have many ways of approaching security, and therefore users must set their own authentication, authorization and accounting (AAA) principles in the infrastructure.

Open-source clouds take a modular approach. The advantage of this approach is that it covers a wide range of applications. To secure the infrastructure, it is necessary to understand the whole environment, rather than only parts of it.

Therefore, security and complex AAA solutions must be addressed by cloud platform system administrators. This article discusses the AAA principles for open cloud platforms, mainly based on the OpenStack platform. An OpenStack platform is not just one application but is a platform consisting of several mutually interconnected projects, such as Keystone, Nova and Swift. This division into individual components results in faster development.

© Springer Nature Switzerland AG 2019
I. Awan et al. (Eds.): MobiWIS 2019, LNCS 11673, pp. 123–135, 2019.
https://doi.org/10.1007/978-3-030-27192-3_10

2   Problem Definition

Authorization and authentication have a crucial role in security, so these issues must be resolved before the cloud infrastructure is installed. It is important that all the configuration approaches are as automated as possible with respect to scale. This is important for cloud technology growth.

Authorization and authentication have two different roles. The first role concerns access to the cloud for end users. The second role is mainly directed at administrators of entire cloud platforms that configure cloud services and monitor running hardware. There are a few challenges which should be resolved in cloud infrastructures to ensure the security of the OpenStack cloud environment and also the underlying Linux-based operating systems.

2.1   Authentication, Authorization and Accounting

Authentication, authorization and accounting principles help with security in systems and help resolve issues of user access to services or systems and how the user can use them. If users are accessing some particular service, there are three issues that the user and the system must resolve:

1. The user must input credentials into the system (authentication),
2. The system must decide whether the user can access the system (authorization),
3. All activities must be logged (accounting).

Authentication. To access any service or resource, the user should be authenticated. There should not be any services, applications or systems which are not secured, and if there are, there should be a reason for this and it should not be possible for them to be used to compromise the system or for purposes of harm or malfeasance. Users (or services) should use credentials for access, and the system should compare these credentials in a database, to identify the user. This means that the user must input valid credentials, e.g., a login name and password, in order to use the system.

Authorization. After a user is authenticated, the system should evaluate how it can be used by the user. This means defining what the user can do within the system. At this point, it is important to define which resources can be used and how they can be used. For example, in the cloud, there are many resources, but the user should not be able to consume all these resources. Quotas should be implemented. Another example is where some users can only read data, whereas other users can change them.

Accounting. If a user is logged on to the system and can use it, his or her activities should be monitored. A service should be implemented which will keep data about user activity over time. Logged data should consist of the times when the user signed into the system or logged off from the system, all used resources and all user changes in the system, among other things. This is important for all systems, because it helps to keep the system secure. All the changes and activities are recorded and can be analyzed if needed.

2.2   OpenStack and Cloud Infrastructures

OpenStack is a system which helps to operate and control large amounts of computing, storage and networking services in data centers in the cloud environment [4,5,11,17]. OpenStack is an open-source system, consisting of many projects which are interconnected and address many areas. For example, the project Nova helps with computing, Neutron with networking, Cinder and Swift with storage and Horizon with dashboards and visualization. There are also many other projects.

In the area addressed by this paper, there is also the Keystone project for providing the identity service which helps with the user's OpenStack usage. In the Fig. 1, the main elements of the OpenStack architecture are shown.

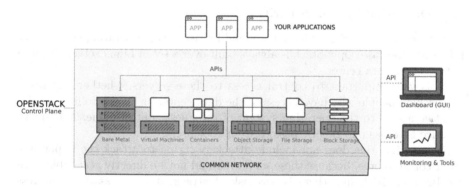

Fig. 1. OpenStack-based architecture. Source: OpenStack [11]

OpenStack is used by many companies. These companies can use its services according to their needs, in order to obtain help with their processes and increase the importance of their business in society. However, OpenStack is not for every company. Many companies do not need OpenStack, because it is large solution for large deployments. OpenStack has many advantages, such as scalability, automation and a largely open platform which can be adjusted according to the needs of the company or end user.

2.3   Keystone

Keystone is the main authentication and authorization service in OpenStack. Using the Keystone API, users can access the cloud. Keystone also monitors and sets the rights of users [9,11].

This service is the default identity provider, and it stores all of its service data in an SQL database. Users can therefore authenticate directly against Keystone. Keystone also serves as an authentication tool for OpenStack components. Keystone defines a few elements that help with authentication, authorization and accounting principles, including:

- User, which represents one cloud consumer,
- Group, which represents a user collection,
- Project, which represents a unit in OpenStack with allocated resources,
- Domain, which is a group of OpenStack elements (Users, Groups, Projects) where elements in this domain are separated from other domains,
- Roles, which is a connection between the identity service and the resource service, and defines the identity authorization for access to resources.

Elements representing the identity service are User and Group, and those representing the resource service are Project and Domain.

2.4   Operating System Security

OpenStack is often referred to as the cloud infrastructure operating system, but this is not the case. OpenStack is always built over a set of Linux servers located in the server data center.

It is very important to control access to these servers, whether physically by checking people who have access to the data center or by controlling administrative access to the operating system of the guest control plane. A frequent practice is to use one generic password for root users.

In practice, this does not include attackers trying to attack the hypervisor guest control plane, because these servers should not be directly accessible from the Internet. Although there is less risk of attack, it is necessary to address this approach in operating systems. These servers are primarily accessed by administrators, and changes made to the servers have the greatest impact on the performance of systems and services operating in the cloud.

2.5   Plain-Text Passwords

The database is used to link services and to provide information in OpenStack. All services must have a written configuration file on how to connect to the database. Each service has a connection string configuration file that contains the login data and database address.

The implementation of this mechanism is problematic. The connection string, in basic settings, is without encryption. An example of the nova.conf configuration file can be seen below.

```
idle_timeout = 180
max_overflow = 100
retry_interval = 5
max_retries = -1
db_max_retries = 3
db_retry_interval = 1
connection_debug = 10
pool_timeout = 120
connection = mysql+pymysql://nova:F6Ka5daCqlCcazuQ@172.17.45.50
/nova_api?charset=utf8
```

If the password is leaked, an attacker might be able to affect the cloud through database changes. These data are not encrypted, primarily because the network, as the communication between the database and the service, is not available from the Internet. For example, the distribution of configuration files between administrators can be problematic during debugging, and the password can get into the wrong hands.

3   Related Work

There are a number of studies based on the security of the OpenStack platform and on resolving authentication, authorization and accounting issues.

Srinivasan [18] analyzes basic security challenges in cloud computing which are related to the technical resources used, as well as other aspects. Elia [3] examines general vulnerabilities in the OpenStack platform. This work globally analyzes the entire platform. It is found that OpenStack is a very open platform and has many vulnerabilities that may be hidden. Luo [7] analyzes and describes security and cloud system access control mechanisms, mainly based on OpenStack. A framework is introduced, called the OpenStack Security Modules (OSM) project, which improves the flexibility and security of policy management. Majumdar [8] deals with user-level security auditing in cloud environments. This work includes access control and authentication mechanisms, e.g., RBAC, ABAC and SSO, and it implements and evaluates a framework based on the OpenStack platform. Perez [12] combines authentication-, authorization- and accounting based techniques to integrate identities from different organizations. Details of the implementation are described in the GANT CLASSe project.

Sette [15] describes the architecture and implementation of a system and tests the system prototype on the OpenStack cloud and the Amazon Web Services (AWS) cloud. This work presents homogeneous authorization policies across multiple heterogeneous infrastructures as service clouds. Shamugam's [16] work consists of implementing the Kerberos authentication method on the OpenStack platform, considering the possibilities of Kerberos and its implementation. Ruiu [13] analyzes the use of cloud systems via biometric authentication and integrates fingerprints with a cloud computing platform. Senk's [14] work also concerns the use of biometric authentication in enterprise environments.

Dinesha [2] introduces the security of cloud services based on multilevel authentication techniques, which are based on textual, graphical, biometric, 3D password and third-party authentication. Liu [6] proposes digital forensic analysis as part of security systems.

Benjamin [1] describes several security features in OpenStack which support security control and analyzes some of the vulnerabilities of the OpenStack workload layer and how to mitigate them. In addition, Nithya [10] analyzes document protection on OpenStack clouds. This work is mainly relevant to workloads running on the OpenStack cloud, and the paper discusses how to protect documents on OpenStack.

4   Keystone Integration Possibilities

The advantage of Keystone is its ability to expand, using various plug-ins which can be used for authorization via all available modern protocols. There are two main ways of implementing authentication and authorization in Keystone:

1. Direct Keystone integration, where Keystone is connected directly to some authentication, authorization and accounting solution,
2. The Keystone identity provider federation, where Keystone is federated with other solutions via other solution software.

4.1   Direct Keystone Integration

Built-In SQL. The SQL database is used for basic authorization and authentication in OpenStack, via MySQL, MariaDB, etc. These databases can be used to store all the Keystone data. The database contains user accounts, roles, domains and passwords. Passwords are then hashed in the database. This type is especially suitable for testing purposes.

Keystone Token. The second built-in method of authentication and authorization is the so-called Keystone token. The token is a randomly generated string of characters. Originally, UUID tokens were used, but now Fernet tokens are used. This Fernet token format was added to OpenStack in the Kilo release. Fernet tokens originated as a replacement for the existing UUID tokens. A big advantage over UUID tokens is the ability to validate tokens across servers. AES256 is used for encryption, and integrity is verified via SHA256 signature.

Using this solution, it is necessary to have a properly configured token rotation, which allows an attacker only temporary access in an attack. Unfortunately, this functionality is not part of the Keystone configuration, so this operation must be performed using an automated periodic task, e.g., via cron.

Lightweight Directory Access Protocol (LDAP). Further Keystone integration can be achieved with LDAP. The identity providers may be existing IdP solutions, e.g., FreeIPA or Microsoft Active Directory, which can be integrated with Keystone in many ways. The simplest integration type is a direct connection between the IdP server and Keystone. Only user data and mapping are required for this operation. Keystone also offers a more secure version of LDAP, encrypting communications using SSL.

4.2 Keystone Identity Provider Federation

The Keystone identity provider federation is a way to store user information in a separate database, and then to use this as an authentication mechanism for users to obtain a token. The federation still uses LDAP, but only as an identity backend. LDAP is only used as a database for user information, so that authentication requires an external service.

In Keystone, we distinguish two basic roles. The first identity provider (IdP) role is a service that contains user information and handles user authentication. Keystone can also play this role. The second role is the service provider (SP). This is for services requested by users. There must be a trusted connection between SP and IdP components. Keystone supports two basic federation protocols: Security Assertion Markup Language (SAML) and OpenID Connect. The advantage of using the federation is primarily the separation of SP and IdP, giving a separate and independently managed database of users.

Security Assertion Markup Language (SAML). Security Assertion Markup Language (SAML) is one of the basic authentication and authorization standards for domains (such as ADFS). SAML is an XML-based protocol. Nowadays, it is best to use the second version. In general, SAML can specify SSO (single sign-on). Using SSO, it is easy to convert accesses and roles. Above all, SAML can only accept the user password once. Two different Shibboleth and Mellon protocols can be used for SAML.

X.509 TLS Mutual. X.509 is based on issuing certificates. Certificates are issued by certain CA authorities ad must be credible to the server used for authentication by the user. In the case of OpenStack, these are servers with Keystone roles. The attributes of the certificate are then mapped onto the existing Keystone user. If the Keystone certificate is accepted and there is a user with the given attributes, Keystone adds a role to the user and allows the user into the cloud environment. The main advantage of this solution is that the user does not need a password to access OpenStack. The same certificate that was used for authentication can also be used for secure communication. Another advantage is the scalability of X.509. X.509 can be easily extended, using other authentication mechanisms such as Kerberos. This can be done simply by adding a new provider ID and mapping correctly.

Kerberos. Kerberos is another protocol from a series of SSO protocols. Kerberos is built using a client-server architecture. Kerberos technology is very simple to integrate with existing IPA tools such as Active Directory. If AD is used as an IPA, then the domain controller acts as a key distribution center (KDC).

The user then asks the domain controller for access. If the user has access rights, the domain controller returns the token. This token is only valid for a certain time and can be authenticated against Keystone.

4.3 Comparison of Security Features

In the following Table 1, plug-ins and solutions can be found which can expand Keystone and can be used as part of an AAA solution for OpenStack. The table shows a few of the basic categories that have been reviewed.

Table 1. Comparison of Keystone plug-ins

Plug-in name	Clear-text passwords	Credentials via network	Man-in-the-middle attack	Mutual authentication	Password policy enforcement
SQL built-in	Yes	Yes	No[a]	No	Yes
Keystone token	N/a	No	No[a]	No	Yes[b]
LDAP	Yes	Yes	No[a]	No	Yes[c]
SAML	Yes	No	No[a]	No	Yes[c]
X.509 TLS Mutual	No	No	Yes	Yes	Yes[d]
Kerberos	No	No	Yes	Yes	Yes[d]

[a]By default no, but can be expandable.
[b]Depends on LDAP or SQL backing store configuration.
[c]Depends on LDAP backing store configuration.
[d]Depends on X.509 CA LDAP backing store configuration.

Clear-Text Passwords. This criterion identifies whether clear-text passwords are stored somewhere in the infrastructure. This is very dangerous and can be used to hack into the environment if attacker can find the password.

Credentials via Network. This criterion takes into account whether credentials are transferred via the network and can be intercepted and decrypted.

Man-in-the-Middle Attack. This criterion examines whether a solution is susceptible to a man-in-the-middle type of attack. A man-in-the-middle attack is where the communication between the user and the end service is realized through an attacker's system, so that the attacker can maliciously intercept and change the communication.

Mutual Authentication. Mutual authentication means authentication of two parts at the same time. This means that the user or client is requested to use two-factor authentication, (e.g., password and certificate) and both of them must be valid.

Password Policy Enforcement. The password policy enforcement criterion is where it is possible to enforce on the user some policy requiring specific password criteria for every password. For example, criteria may include password length, retention, character policy, etc.

5 Implementation and Testing

For testing and comparing the authorization options from the previous section, an OpenStack solution in a high-availability setup was used, to test how Open-Stack deals with Keystone outages on individual controllers.

The control plane was installed in virtual machines using SaltStack config-uration management and Salt Formulas. The OpenStack distribution used the Ocata release, and packages from upstream repositories were used for testing. The software-defined network solution used Open vSwitch in non-DVR mode. Ubuntu Xenial was chosen as the operating system. For the LDAP solution, an Active Directory (AD) solution was used in all cases, placed on a separate server where Windows Server 2012 R2 was installed.

The test scenario was a Heat stack containing three virtual machines with a simple web application with a MySQL database. The Heat project is an orches-tration tool for OpenStack clouds. Keystone implementation and testing was performed using the following procedure:

1. Configure certificates and users on the Active Directory side,
2. Install the Keystone add-on,
3. Edit the Keystone configuration files,
4. Configure certificates,
5. Implement simple Heat stack provisioning,
6. Test the availability of the web application.

From the selected solutions for complex integration, it was easiest to imple-ment a direct Keystone connection to Active Directory. This integration did not require any external Keystone extension.

The safest and most complicated integration was the combination of Kerberos and X.509, which is the best solution for security in all communications.

The most common solution is SAML integration through the Shibboleth protocol. For this type of integration, it is necessary to install a libapache2-mod-shib2 package that provides communication between the Shibboleth and Apache services (Keystone is run under Apache), and then to set all parameters using the XML file located in /etc/shibboleth/shibboleth2.xml. In this file, it is necessary to have a correct configuration.

```
<SSO entityID="<ID provider location>" ECP="true"> SAML2 SAML1
</SSO>
<ApplicationDefaults entityID="https://Keystone IP address:5000">
```

The Shibboleth integration also includes setting the correct mapping to Active Directory. This is done using the following JSON file in the mapping example shown below. The file is then mapped to a Keystone service. This authorization type is mainly used to log in to the Horizon component, which is a graphical user interface for OpenStack. In the following example, mapping takes place where two attributes are expected from Active Directory: login and email. These attributes are mapped to a domain named "default" and to the Keystone local user with the matching login name and email address.

```
{   "rules": [
        {   "local": [
                {   "user": {
                        "name": "{0}"',
                        "email": "{1}",
                        "domain": { "id": "default" },
                        "type": "local"
                    }
                }
            ],
            "remote": [
                {   "type": "login"
                },
                {   "type": "email"
                }
            ]
        }
    ]
}
```

Another tested scenario was deployed with SAML and X.509 in one environment. This setup seems to be the best solution, for several reasons. The first is its simplicity. Keystone has the ability to use multiple authentication backends simultaneously. These backends exist and are used independently of each other. This also applies largely to Keystone federations, such as SAML, LDAP and OIDC. Multiple backend implementation can be seen in the following code.

```
[auth]
methods = password,token,saml2,x509
saml2 = keystone.auth.plugins.saml2.Saml2 x509 = keystone.auth.
plugins.mapped.Mapped
```

This implementation is especially suited to end users. They can log in to the cloud using SSO via SAML, or using a certificate imported from an Internet browser. This solution eliminates the problem of weak user passwords in the cloud that could be used to attack the cloud. Another advantage of using this solution is its simple user management, as shown in the diagram below. Ideally, X.509 should be used as follows. The cloud manager group should have its own certification authority, based on Active Directory. This authority will then issue certificates to users. The advantage of this approach is a simple user message. For example, if you need to block the user, you only need to revoke (invalidate) the certificate. All these changes would be made by the administrator, and the access would be purely controlled by X.509.

6   Conclusion

In this article, the most common problems of open cloud infrastructures have been mentioned and analyzed. In the experimental section, authentication plugins for Keystone were tested, and a simple web application was launched above the set add-ons.

Based on this research, it is possible to select the optimal solution for Keystone authorization, as well as to mitigate the problem of unencrypted passwords and access to hypervisor operating systems. Each authorization plug-in has its advantages and disadvantages.

For testing and development environments that do not contain any production workload, a built-in solution can be used, where Keystone and passwords are stored in a database as the identity provider. For enterprise deployment, when many users with different roles access the system, it is necessary to use a Keystone federation and user information, in order to have some stored IPA. For environments that use the OpenStack cloud as part of their software, it is important to consider an SSO solution, so that users can use one password to access all systems.

Security Assertion Markup Language (SAML) and Kerberos are the only systems in the test to handle SSO. In the last scenario, it is worth considering whether it is appropriate to implement X.509 with a Keystone federation alone. Users using X.509 can use the cloud in a secure way without having to use passwords.

Acknowledgment. The research has been partially supported by the Faculty of Informatics and Management, UHK, Specific Research Project 2107: Computer Networks for Cloud, Distributed Computing and Internet of Things II.

References

1. Benjamin, B., Coffman, J., Esiely-Barrera, H. et al.: Data protection in OpenStack. In: 10th IEEE International Conference on Cloud Computing, CLOUD 2017. IEEE Computer Society, pp. 560–567 (2017)
2. Dinesha, H.A., Agrawal, V.K.: Multi-level authentication technique for accessing cloud services. In: 2012 International Conference on Computing, Communication and Applications, ICCCA 2012 (2012)
3. Elia, I.A., Antunes, N., Laranjeiro, N., Vieira, M.: An analysis of OpenStack vulnerabilities. In: Proceedings – 2017 13th European Dependable Computing Conference, EDCC 2017. Institute of Electrical and Electronics Engineers Inc., pp. 129–134 (2017)
4. Khedher, O., Chowdhury, C.D.: Mastering OpenStack, 2nd edn. Packt, Birmingham (2017)
5. Jackson, K., Bunch, C., Sigler, E., Denton, J.: OpenStack Cloud Computing Cookbook, 4th edn. Packt, Birmingham (2018)
6. Liu, C., Singhal, A., Wijesekera, D.: Identifying evidence for cloud forensic analysis. Advances in Digital Forensics XIII. IAICT, vol. 511, pp. 111–130. Springer, Cham (2017). https://doi.org/10.1007/978-3-319-67208-3_7
7. Luo, Y., Luo, W., Puyang, T., et al.: OpenStack security modules: a least-invasive access control framework for the cloud. In: 9th International Conference on Cloud Computing, CLOUD 2016. IEEE Computer Society, pp. 51–58 (2017)
8. Majumdar, S., Madi, T., Wang, Y., et al.: User-level runtime security auditing for the cloud. IEEE Trans. Inf. Forensics Secur. 13(5), 1185–1199 (2018)
9. Martinelli, S., Nash, H., Topol, B.: Identity, Authentication, and Access Management in OpenStack: Implementing and Deploying Keystone, 1st edn. O'Reilly Media, Sebastopol (2015)
10. Nithya, A.K., Dhannya, A.K.: Privacy protected documents on OpenStack cloud. In: Proceedings of the 29th International Teletraffic Congress, ITC 2017. Institute of Electrical and Electronics Engineers Inc. (2017)
11. OpenStack project web page. http://openstack.org. Accessed 20 Mar 2019
12. Perez, M.A., Lopez, M.G., Marin, L.R., Chadwick, D.W., Schechtman, S.I.: Integrating an AAA-based federation mechanism for OpenStack the CLASSe view. Concurrency Comput. 29(12), e4148 (2017)
13. Ruiu, P., Caragnano, G., Masala, G.L., Grosso, E.: Accessing cloud services through biometrics authentication. In: Proceedings – 2016 10th International Conference on Complex, Intelligent, and Software Intensive Systems, CISIS 2016. Institute of Electrical and Electronics Engineers Inc., pp. 38–43 (2016)
14. Senk, C., Dotzler, F.: Biometric authentication as a service for enterprise identity management deployment: a data protection perspective. In: Proceedings of the 2011 6th International Conference on Availability, Reliability and Security, ARES 2011, pp. 43–50 (2011)
15. Sette, I.S., Chadwick, D.W., Ferraz, C.A.G.: Authorization policy federation in heterogeneous multicloud environments. Trade J. 4(4), 38–47 (2017)
16. Shamugam, V., Murray, I., Sidhu, A.S.: Elliptical curve cryptography-kerberos authentication model for keystone in open stack. In: Mohamed Ali, M.S., Wahid, H., Mohd Subha, N.A., Sahlan, S., Md. Yunus, M.A., Wahap, A.R. (eds.) AsiaSim 2017. CCIS, vol. 752, pp. 633–644. Springer, Singapore (2017). https://doi.org/10.1007/978-981-10-6502-6_54

17. Solberg, M., Silverman, B.: OpenStack for Architects. Packt, Birmingham (2017)
18. Srinivasan, M.K., Sarukesi, K., Rodrigues, P., Manoj, M.S., Revathy, P.: State-of-the-art cloud computing security taxonomies – A classification of security challenges in the present cloud computing environment. In: Proceedings of 2012 International Conference on Advances in Computing, Communications and Informatics, ICACCI 2012, pp. 470–476 (2012)

Security Measures in the Vehicular Ad-Hoc Networks – Man in the Middle Attack

Krzysztof Stepień and Aneta Poniszewska-Marańda[(✉)] [iD]

Institute of Information Technology, Lodz University of Technology, Łódź, Poland
krzysztof.stepien@edu.p.lodz.pl, aneta.poniszewska-maranda@p.lodz.pl

Abstract. Vehicular Ad-Hoc Network (VANET) is an indispensable part of Intelligent Transportation Systems (ITS). It depends on correspondence between progressively associated vehicles and static Road Side Units (RSU). It could offer different applications such as crash shirking cautions, soak bend admonitions and infotainment. VANET has a huge potential to improve traffic effectiveness, and street well-being by trading basic data between hubs (vehicles and RSU). However, this communication between nodes is liable to an assortment of assaults, such as Man-In-The-Middle (MITM) attacks which represent a major risk in VANET. The paper presents MITM impact on VANET network and strategies that hackers might adopt to launch the attacks that could cause delay, drop or tamper of sent messages between the cars.

Keywords: Vehicular Ad-Hoc network · Man-In-The-Middle attack · Smart cities · Intelligent Transportation System · Internet-of-Things

1 Introduction

Internet of Things (IoT) is not only the conception of connectivity but the real computing paradigm that connects multiple devices with Internet capabilities. Those devices could connect to the Internet using different communication technologies such as Long Term Evolution (LTE), Bluetooth, WiFi and in the future 5G. Therefore, it provides a wide scope of applications such as smart-phones, smart-grid, smart health, smart vehicles.

Vehicular Ad-Hoc Network (VANET) is one of those applications that provide a network to a huge number of vehicles over the globe with the plan to improve traffic effectiveness. In VANET, the smart vehicles equipped with various sensors intelligently exchange messages with one another between each other (*Vehicle-To-Vehicle, V2V*) or with infrastructure (*Vehicle-To-Infrastructure, V2I*).

VANET network has an extremely tense nature due to its dynamic environment. Therefore, it is crucial to provide a secure, reliable and attack-free setting for message propagation. Every critical data (such as an accident on the road) propagated through VANET must be assured that is produced by authentic vehicles. Besides, the network is ought to be capable of satisfying traditional

© Springer Nature Switzerland AG 2019
I. Awan et al. (Eds.): MobiWIS 2019, LNCS 11673, pp. 136–147, 2019.
https://doi.org/10.1007/978-3-030-27192-3_11

security requirements, i.e., availability, authenticity, privacy, confidentiality, non-repudiation and integrity.

Nevertheless, these conditions could be extremely challenging to fulfill. There are various attacks that could interrupt data flow inside VANET network and even destroy the whole infrastructure. One of those attacks is *Man-In-The-Middle (MITM)*. Here, malicious node (MITM) either listen in or modify the messages traded between two legitimate cars. Exchanged messages could contain sensitive information about the current situation on the road, private driver messages, etc. VANET network should protect human life, therefore any MITM node inside the network can have a severe impact (Fig. 1).

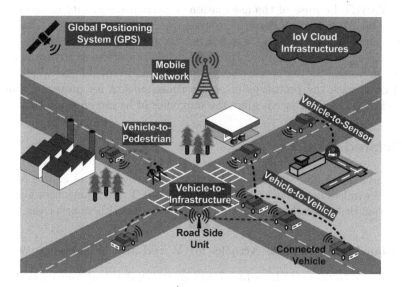

Fig. 1. Illustration of VANET in smart cities [4]

The MITM attack is an attack where the hacker can modify, drop or defer valuable data in the system. There are two ways that the hacker can dispatch the attack: passive and active.

Passive attack refers to the situation when the attacker silently eavesdrops the communication channel between legitimate vehicles. One of the possible situations is when the MITM attacker intercepts law-enforcement vehicles channel and forward this information around for their own advantages.

In case of *active assault*, the hacker can drop, delay or change the content of received information in the system. One of the possible situations is when the hacker intercepts messages about an accident on the road and then changes/delay/drop the content of the message. This could have a critical impact on the network as other legitimate nodes will receive the compromised/delayed messages.

Every strategy of the attack could have different significant impact on the VANET network performance. The independent attacks could have a different impact regardless of attack performed in the collaboration. Therefore, both attack could affect the performance of the network in a diverse way.

As it was mentioned before, human life is straightforwardly associated with VANET. Therefore the system should share only accurate and authentic data. MITM attacks could interrupt authentic information sharing. Therefore, many researchers come with conclusions, what is the general effect of these MITM assaults in a sensitive system like VANET? It is important also to maintain information about system reliability according to the various strategies of the MITM aggressor. As a consequence, it is fundamental to concentrate such aggressors in VANET because of the association of extremely delicate messages (e.g. accident, black-ice warnings) in the system.

The paper is structured as follows: Sect. 2 presents the related works concerning the mean-in-the-middle attacks for wired and wireless networks and fo VANET networks. Section 3 describe the idea of man in the middle attacks while Sect. 4 deals with the prototype of security mechanisms for preventing among others the MITM attacks – it gives the outcomes of he methods analysis.

2   Related Works

The Man-in-the-middle attacks are identified and described of course both for wired and wireless networks and of course for VANET and many other networks. This section describes the overview of MITM attacks in these two cases.

2.1   Man-In-The-Middle Attacks for Wired and Wireless Networks

Man-In-The-Middle (MITM) attack is not an attack that had risen exceptionally for VANET network. It was well-known for cryptography and computer security before in wired and wireless networks. Stricot-Tarboton et al. [16] presented a taxonomy of MITM on *Hypertext Transfer Protocol Secure (HTTPS)* by classifying the hackers into four tiers: state, target, conduct and defenselessness. On the other hand, Chen et al. [1] focused on the mathematical model for MITM attacks on *Secure-Sockets Layer (SSL)* conventions of wired networks.

Conti et al. [15] presented a survey about MITM attacks on *Open Systems Interconnection (OSI)* layers of two mobile communication technologies. Those technologies were Global System for Mobile communications (GSM) and Universal Mobile Telecommunications System (UMTS), where MITM attacks were outlined in respect to their OSI layer.

Glass et al. [2] studied how much the MITM attacks could affect the Medium Access Control (MAC) layer in terms of wireless mesh and mobile ad-hoc networks. The authors successfully received positive results achieving high detection rates and no false positives. Kaplanis [7] studied MITM attacks that could pass over WiFi networks. It was concluded that MITM attacks are likely to happen in case of lack of encryption over the data link layer (Fig. 2).

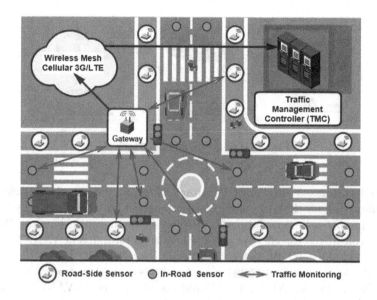

Fig. 2. Communications chain of data feeds in smart transportation [10]

2.2 Man-In-The-Middle Attacks for VANET

During recent years, a significant research effort is being taken to accomplish security and privacy in VANET. One of the pioneers in this field were Raya et al. [17]. They featured a few security challenges in VANET. They come into conclusion that privacy preservation during a highly mobile environment is critical. The most important factors in this field are authentication, integrity, availability, confidentiality, and non-repudiation [8].

The attacks could be distinguished into two groups: high and low level, however, those models are restricted in range and there could be many different strategies applied. A few assaults were identified and classified according to security requirements. For example, DoS and MITM attacks are classified as the major ones. On the other hand, Ahmad et al. [5] created different classification where attacks long with their risk in VANET could be ordered by three classes, i.e. critical, major and minor. According to this study, MITM attacks are critical and have a serious effect on VANET (Fig. 3).

Afdhal et al. [12] during their research analysed the black hole attack impact on two routing protocols: *Ad Hoc On-Demand Multi-path Distance Vector (AOMDV)* and *Ad Hoc On-Demand Distance Vector (AODV)*. They conclude that MITM attacker affects the routing protocols performance. Other researches like Dhyani et al. [11] in answer to those problems proposed the idea of broadcasting unicast packages and integrating trust within AOMDV [5].

Grimaldo et al. [13] studied the performance of a wide range of routing protocols in VANET under black hole attacks. They appraised AODV, Optimized Link State Routing (OLSR), Dynamic Source Routing (DSR) and Destination-

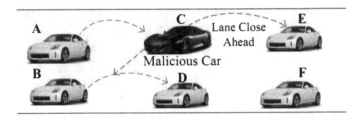

Fig. 3. Man in the middle attack [6]

Sequenced Distance-Vector (DSDV) protocols for MITM attackers performing black hole attack for the real system, concluding that the black hole attacks have a critical impact on successful packet delivery in the network. Further, Purohit et al. [14] considered the effect of black hole attacks for different VANET routing protocols including AODV and Zone Routing Protocol (ZRP).

Nevertheless, considered routing protocols were used in traditional Mobile Ad-Hoc Networks (MANET). They could not be utilized in VANET networks, because of substantial scale and high portability of the vehicles. Almutairi et al. [18] handled the black hole attack using a different approach. Every vehicle maintains a trust routing table for its neighbours. Even in the case when no neighbour is available close to the real vehicle, then the messages are exchanged with RSU to avoid any miscommunication inside the system. Even this solution has some drawbacks like RSU requirement when not every place could fulfil this condition.

Cherkaouia et al. [19] presented the solution in continuously monitoring the network where every abnormal activity could be instantly identified. This is an efficient technique to distinguish MITM attacks performing black-hole as the system is persistently checked in a real-time environment.

Rawat et al. [21] considered the data falsification attack in VANET where the MITM aggressor propagates false information within the system. They suggested a contention window and hash in order to avoid publishing wrong data throughout the network. Further, Leinmuller et al. [20] distinguished different message producing attacks in VANET. They focus on the attacker that might be connected to the RSU with message forging ability. The main drawback of this investigation is that the hacker is always stationary which is not practical in a genuine VANET environment.

Grover et al. [9] studied attacks based on creating the illusion of a non-existent situation in the VANET network. They studied attack effect basing on the vehicle speed, collisions in the network, channel utilization. Authors present the solution that bases on using RSUs to identify attackers posing attacks. However, it has some drawbacks such as RSUs might not be always present in the network.

3   Man in the Middle Attacks

The origin of the phrase "Man-In-The-Middle" was taken from the basketball sport, where a player in the center tries to capture the ball while the other two attempt to pass it [5]. A similar idea could appear in VANET network where MITM hacker jeopardizes the communication channel among authentic vehicles. The attack could pose severe outcomes as the content of the message contains well-being related data. In order to perform the MITM attack, two conditions must be satisfied: the message must be intercepted by the hacker node and the hacker must be able to decipher the content of the message. MITM attacks in VANET can be launched in two ways:

1. Passive Mode – the hacker eavesdrops transmission channel between specific vehicles, such as police vehicles or ambulances.
2. Active Mode – the attacker can drop, delay or change the content of intercepted message.

Every event or transmitted bundle (MG) in VANET network contain at least three information:

- data about the event,
- location of the event generation,
- time of the event occurrence,
- any other information such as protocol versions, message ID.

The message produced from the vehicle will contain the following three data and could be presented as a simple equation:

$$MG = data, location, time \tag{1}$$

where:

- data – holds the information generated by the vehicle,
- location – holds the coordinates of the event generation vehicle in terms of x, y, z, which can be gained from vehicle's GPS,
- time – message generation time (t_{send})

The attacker can compromise the content of above equation in terms of data, location or time. Intercepting crucial and confidential information could create a disaster in the network. The similar chaos could appear if the location of the message has tampered. As the messages in VANET network must be delivered on time, delayed messages might be disregarded by the receiver. Effectively, the attacker can dispatch MITM in following three habits:

1. delay the legitimate message,
2. drop the legitimate message,
3. tamper the legitimate message.

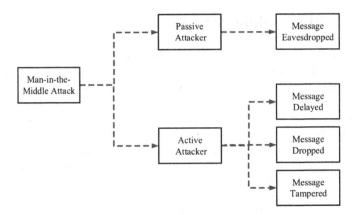

Fig. 4. Man-In-The-Middle attacks in VANET [5]

Figure 4 shows the idea of both passive and active MITM attacks in VANET. Passive attack refers to the eavesdropping transmission channel between legitimate vehicles. On the other hand, the actively MITM attacker can drop, delay or alter the authentic transmitted messages which are delivered through the system.

MITM as Message Delayed

VANET communication relies on the successful transmission of messages between every authorized medium. In this sort of assault the malicious nodes intentionally postpone the messages, i.e. the messages are sent to neighbour nodes with a factor of "delay".

VANET having very sensitive nature could not be exposed to such attacks. This could cause big failures in the system. Consider, the situation where all other genuine vehicles are sharing data about the accident during the night. Those messages should be delivered on schedule, therefore deferring such message by a malicious node can result in an exceptional circumstance. Therefore, such vehicles need to make stride progressively to maintain a strategic distance from a mishap situation. Further, this circumstance can likewise put human life in threat.

MITM as Message Dropped

This attack refers to the "black hole" attacks in VANET, where an attacker intentionally drops the received legitimate message (MG) suppressing the further distribution of MG. Therefore, any genuine vehicles could not get any sort of messages as the messages never reach their goal. Abandoning the security-related messages can have a noteworthy effect on the system as it contains sensitive data, for example, accident avoidance. Dropping data about traffic accident or hard situation on the road can put the life of vehicular clients in risk as they are denied from prohibited from receiving delicate data by the attacker.

MITM as Message Tampered

The message tampered attack bases on targeting a particular received message by the attacker. Once a message is received, it is modified by the attacker. It could pose a severe impact on the network as the content may contain delicate data. As an example, the genuine vehicle broadcast a message about hard traffic conditions. Then those messages could be altered by the attacked where he adds additional information that contradicts previously established statement. Then, new messages could be misleading for the authorized vehicles and it can create a real accident in the network.

As it was mentioned before, every transmitted information in VANET contains three essential data: information, time, location. In this specific assault, the assailant can change:

- *transmission time* into compromised transmission time by changing it with garbage time t_g
- *data* into misleading *compromised data*
- coordinates of sender location into an unknown location

4   The Prototype of Security Mechanisms – Outcomes of Methods Analysis

The prototyped VANET network was created in order to develop the solution which could prevent Man-In-The-Middle attacks but also Bogus and Timing attacks. The project was realized using Java language.

Vehicle Identification Number, VIN was used to preserve the vehicle unique identification. The VIN number was emitted once the vehicle is produced, and can never be changed, in contrary to license plates. Furthermore, the license plates can be used to identify the owner, which violates the privacy standpoint. To ensure that VIN number really derives from the vehicle it claims, the Certificate Authority, CA signature is used. It solves the problem with messages integrity and non-repudiation of the sender. Prototype network mocks multiple intersections where vehicles can drive. Visualization of the prototype of VANET network is presented in Fig. 5 where all valid cars are marked as the green rectangles, while the hacker (i.e. infected) nodes are marked red dots [3].

In the case of MITM attack, malicious vehicle listen to the communications between two vehicles. Then pretends to be each of them to reply the other and inject false information between vehicles. In order to bargain with this kind of attacks, reasonable solutions are confidential communications (using powerful cryptography) to avoid the fact that an attacker can eavesdrop the communication channel among the other vehicles, and a secure authentication and data integrity verification (using hash functions) to prevent messages modifications.

The presented solution requires identification in order to uniquely identify a vehicle. It uses VIN number as the unique id of every car connected to the network. Every vehicle has its own Vehicle Identification Number (VIN) since it is emitted once the vehicle is produced, and can never be changed, unlike license plates for example. Moreover, license plates are designed so that they

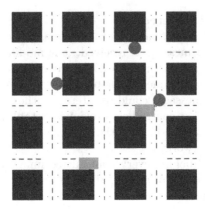

Fig. 5. Visualization of VANET network with valid and infected vehicles (Color figure online)

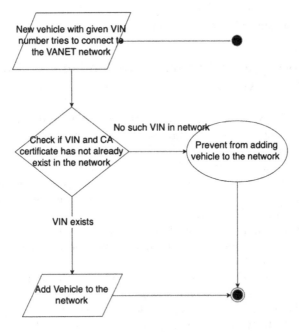

Fig. 6. General approach with adding vehicles to the VANET network

can be used to visually identify a vehicle making it less appealing on the privacy viewpoint (Fig. 6).

The system uses digital signatures, which not only solves the mutual problem that could happen with authentication, message integrity and non-repudiation of the sender (Fig. 7). It also guarantees fresh messages, making them impossible to replay by the attacker. Each message has its own time stamp. In terms of data trust, RSU's gather information from all nodes and revoke the certificates of certain vehicles after a minimum threshold of reports (Fig. 8).

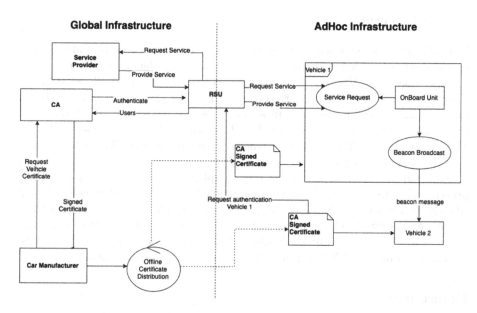

Fig. 7. Global infrastructure schema for created solution – application uses only VIN numbers generated by car makers after manufacturing specific car

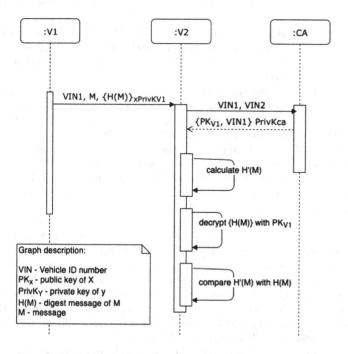

Fig. 8. Sequence diagram presenting the message exchange between the nodes and RSU

5   Conclusions

Vehicular Ad-Hoc Network is the future of ITS where a secure and attack-free environment is needed to reach the desired traffic efficiency. However, due to the open nature of VANET, it is exposed to various attacks, such as Man-In-The-Middle attacks. The main purpose of this kind of network is not only to provide road safety and service but also to preserve the security of all nodes in the network. Therefore, securing the VANET comes as a considerable challenge. The major issues in VANETs are privacy and authentication. Any attack could pose a serious threat to life.

Solution presented in the paper is a complement of the entire system that prevents also from another attack that might happen inside the network [3]. Attacks inside such as Sybil or Bogus are just as important as attacks that might be generated before connecting to the network. As a future work, this research will be extended by evaluating the impact of the MITM attack models for various contexts of VANET networks based on the mobility of nodes.

References

1. Chen, Z., Guo, S., Duan, R., Wang, S.: Security analysis on mutual authentication against man-in-the-middle attack. In: Proceedings of the First International Conference on Information Science and Engineering, Nanjing, China, pp. 1855–1858 (2009)
2. Glass, S.M., Muthukkumarasamy, V., Portmann, M.: Detecting man-in-the-middle and wormhole attacks in wireless mesh networks. In: Proceedings of the International Conference on Advanced Information Networking and Applications, Bradford, UK, pp. 530–538 (2009)
3. Stepień, K., Poniszewska-Marańda, A.: Towards the security measures of the vehicular Ad-Hoc networks. In: Skulimowski, A.M.J., Sheng, Z., Khemiri-Kallel, S., Cérin, C., Hsu, C.-H. (eds.) IOV 2018. LNCS, vol. 11253, pp. 233–248. Springer, Cham (2018). https://doi.org/10.1007/978-3-030-05081-8_17
4. Awais Javed, M., Ben Hamida, E., Znaidi, W.: Security in intelligent transport systems for smart cities: from theory to practice. Sensors **16**, 879 (2016)
5. Ahmad, F., Adnane, A., Franqueira, W.N.L., Kurugollu, F., Liu, L.: Man-in-the-middle attacks in vehicular Ad-Hoc networks: evaluating the impact of attackers' strategies. Sensors **18**(11), 4040 (2018)
6. Al-kahtani, M.S.: Survey on security attacks in vehicular Ad Hoc networks (VANETs). In: Proceedings of 6th International Conference on Signal Processing and Communication Systems (ICSPCS), pp. 1–9 (2012)
7. Kaplanis, C.: Detection and prevention of man in the middle attacks in Wi-Fi technology. Master's thesis, Aalborg University, Aalborg, Denmark (2015)
8. de Fuentes, J.M., Gonzalez-Tablas, A.I., Ribagorda, A.: Overview of security issues in vehicular Ad-Hoc networks. In: Cruz-Cunha, M.M., et al. (eds.) Handbook of Research on Mobility and Computing, Evolving Technologies and Ubiquitous Impact, pp. 894–911. IGI Global, New York (2010)
9. Grover, J., Laxmi, V., Gaur, M.S.: Attack models and infrastructure supported detection mechanisms for position forging attacks in vehicular Ad Hoc networks. CSI Trans. ICT **1**, 261–279 (2013)

10. Masek, P., Masek, J., Frantik, P.: A harmonized perspective on transportation management in smart cities: the novel IoT-driven environment for road traffic modeling (2016)
11. Dhyani, I., Goel, N., Sharma, G., Mallick, B.: A reliable tactic for detecting black hole attack in vehicular Ad Hoc networks. In: Bhatia, S.K., Mishra, K.K., Tiwari, S., Singh, V.K. (eds.) Advances in Computer and Computational Sciences. AISC, vol. 553, pp. 333–343. Springer, Singapore (2017). https://doi.org/10.1007/978-981-10-3770-2_31
12. Afdhal, A., Muchallil, S., Walidainy, H., Yuhardian, Q.: Black hole attacks analysis for AODV and AOMDV routing performance in VANETs. In: Proceedings of the International Conference on Electrical Engineering and Informatics (ICELTICs), Indonesia, pp. 29–34 (2017)
13. Grimaldo, J., Marti, R.: Performance comparison of routing protocols in VANETs under black hole attack in Panama City. In: Proceedings of the International Conference on Electronics, Communications and Computers (CONIELECOMP), Cholula, Mexico, pp. 126–132 (2018)
14. Purohit, K.C., Dimri, S.C., Jasola, S.: Mitigation and performance analysis of routing protocols under black-hole attack in vehicular Ad-Hoc network (VANET). Wirel. Pers. Commun. 97, 5099–5114 (2017)
15. Conti, M., Dragoni, N., Lesyk, V.: A survey of man in the middle attacks. IEEE Communications Surv. Tutor. 18, 2027–2051 (2016)
16. Stricot-Tarboton, S., Chaisiri, S., Ko, R.K.L.: Taxonomy of man-in-the-middle attacks on HTTPS. In: Proceedings of the 2016 IEEE Trustcom/BigDataSE/ISPA, Tianjin, China, pp. 527–534 (2016)
17. Raya, M., Papadimitratos, P., Hubaux, J.P.: Securing vehicular communications. IEEE Wirel. Commun. Mag. 13, 8–15 (2006)
18. Almutairi, H., Chelloug, S., Alqarni, H., Aljaber, R., Alshehri, A., Alotaish, D.: A new black hole detection scheme for VANETs. In: Proceedings of the 6th International Conference on Management of Emergent Digital EcoSystems, Buraidah, Saudi Arabia, pp. 133–138. ACM, New York (2014)
19. Cherkaouia, B., Beni-Hssanea, A., Erritali, M.: Quality control chart for detecting the black hole attack in vehicular Ad-Hoc networks. In: Proceedings of the 8th International Conference on Emerging Ubiquitous Systems and Pervasive Networks (EUSPN 2017), Lund, Sweden, pp. 170–177 (2017)
20. Leinmuller nad, T., Schmidt, R.K., Schoch, E., Held, A., Schafer, G.: Modeling roadside attacker behavior in VANETs. In: Proceedings of the IEEE GLOBECOM Workshops, New Orleans, USA, pp. 1–10 (2008)
21. Rawat, D.B., Bista, B.B., Yan, G.: Securing vehicular Ad-Hoc networks from data falsification attacks. In: Proceedings of the IEEE Region 10 Conference (TENCON), Singapore, pp. 99–102 (2016)

A Framework for Secure and Trustworthy Data Management in Supply Chain

Shinsaku Kiyomoto[1(✉)], Yuto Nakano[1], Atsushi Waseda[1], Toru Nakamura[2], Masahito Ishizaka[1], and Yasuaki Kobayashi[1]

[1] KDDI Research Inc., Fujimino, Saitama 356-8502, Japan
[2] Advanced Telecommunications Research Institute International, Sorakugun, Kyoto 619-0288, Japan
kiyomoto@kddi-research.jp

Abstract. In this paper, we consider a trustworthy framework for data management in a supply chain. The framework provides verifiable evidence for secure data management in each organization involved in a supply chain. It consists of three main components: black box systems that securely store digital evidence, verification services that verify the digital evidence and publish a guarantee document for data management, and a trusted directory service that manages the guarantee document. Furthermore, future directions for research are discussed in this paper. We believe the framework will improve security and trustworthiness of supply chains.

Keywords: Supply chain · Cyber-physical system · Security · Trustworthiness · Data management · Digital evidence

1 Introduction

A supply chain of products consists of a huge number of organizations and has a multilayer hierarchical structure. Supply chains are typical cyber-physical systems that combine physical environments with data handling in cyber spaces and on ICT systems, and both physical and cyber-space risks need to be considered, even though current research activities are aimed primarily at the physical components [6,27]. Supply-chain traceability is a common way to identify an invalid organization or person, where backdoors or vulnerabilities are embedded in a product [12]; for example, traceability in food supply chain and supply chain of medicines is requested in order to confirm whether a product is valid and secure.

Security management of the whole supply chain in cyber space becomes a key element to ensure system security [18,24], especially critical systems such as electric power supply and communication networks; however, it is complicated due to the lack of a framework that can be used to verify security management in each organization. In this paper, we especially focus on digital data management in a supply chain. Critical digital data used in supply chains should be securely managed in accordance with security requirements. Examples of critical data in

© Springer Nature Switzerland AG 2019
I. Awan et al. (Eds.): MobiWIS 2019, LNCS 11673, pp. 148–159, 2019.
https://doi.org/10.1007/978-3-030-27192-3_12

supply chains are blueprints, printed circuit board data, source codes, inspection reports, and benchmark results.

On the other hand, the data economy has been discussed as a new economic trend and this market is expected to expand into a global one; data exchange is regarded as another type of supply chain in the data economy. This trend creates a new supply chain for data transfer or sharing [15]. In the data economy, security management for exchanged data is an essential requirement to build trust in the data supply chain between organizations as well. Examples of data supply chain cases are privacy sensitive data, source codes, and learning models for AI algorithms.

NIST published NIST Special publication 800-171, "Protecting Controlled Unclassified Information in Non-federal Systems and Organizations" [23]. This provides a set of recommended security requirements for protecting the confidentiality of controlled unclassified information (CUI) in organizations. In a supply chain, CUI or other confidential data are exchanged between organizations. CUI is confidential and critical information needed to build a product or service. Once an organization's CUI is disclosed in a supply chain, the thread can have a deleterious effect on the organization's products or services. However, no framework for verification of security management for the CUI in other organizations has been provided to the organization that initially created such confidential information or the organization that has a responsibility for managing the information.

In this paper, we design a trustworthy framework for management of CUI or other important data in a supply chain process. The framework provides a functionality for storing digital evidences about data management and verifying data management processes in each organization. The rest of the paper is organized as follows; Sect. 2 introduces research activities related to supply chain issues. An overview of the framework is provided in Sect. 3, and the various components of the framework are presented in Sect. 4. We discuss some research issues in Sect. 5 and conclude this paper in Sect. 6.

2   Related Work

There are several research articles about physical risks, such as disasters, in global supply chains [6,27]. Meixell and Norbis proposed a method [19] for physical security risk assessment in global supply chains. A framework to integrate the dimensions of risk, categorization of the risk driver, and performance in a supply chain have been presented by Ritchie and Brindley [7] Barron et al. discussed cyber security risks [4]: malevolent use of a 3D printer. Issues affecting information security in supply chains were discussed in [18,24]. Ellison and Woody considered risks in a global supply chain for software development and evaluated their impacts [12]. Christopher and Peck [9] highlighted the risks of complex supply chain and addressed the importance of resilience. More recently, Ponomarov et al. [21] and Ali et al. [2] also considered this issue. Wang et al. [29] conducted a survey and gave classification of supply chain networks, then proposed their definition and description of resilient system. Adaptivity and agility are also important factor in supply chain, and some researches have been conducted [8,10,13,30]. Ivanov *et al.* [14] introduced a conceptual framework of adaptive supply chains and later its new metrics for performance measurement was proposed by Leończuk *et al.* [17].

There are technical approaches designed to improve the information security of supply chains. Atallah *et al.* [3] proposed secure supply-chain collaboration protocols which enable all members in the supply chain to achieve common goals without revealing private information. Bhargava *et al.* presented auditable and secure data sharing in digital supply chains [5]. Zage *et al.* [31] proposed a robust detection method for deceptive behavior in supply chain. Applying a blockchain technology to supply chain is getting a lot of interests, for example, Tian [28] proposed a food supply chain traceability system, and Abeyratne and Monfared [1] considered application to manufacturing supply chain in order to increase the transparency and visibility.

Some issues on digital evidences collection and analysis such as integrity and scalability are highlighted in [26]; in particular, some solutions have been applied for digital forensics [11]. Richter *et al.* proposed a TPM-based approach [22] for securing digital evidences. a high-level architecture for collection of digital evidences was presented in [16]. Shidong *et al.* presented a digital evidence protection scheme [25] using a security notary service as well.

3   Overview of Framework

In this section, we present an overview of our framework. In our framework, each organization publishes a data management certificate that serves as evidence for data management satisfying the security requirements for the data, and registers the certificate in a trusted directory service. All organizations can access the directory service and confirm certificates related to the data; thus it is possible to confirm the data are securely managed in organizations involved in the same data supply chain. The certificates includes link information for corresponding digital evidence; digital evidence is provided if verification is required. Figure 1 shows the framework for data management in a supply chain.

3.1   System Architecture in Each Organization

System architecture of our trustworthy framework for data management in a supply chain is shown in Fig. 2. The framework consists of three components as follows:

- Storage services as "Black Box": the black box is a form of secure storage that stores digital evidence and it provides such evidence to verification services. This component is installed as a local system and it is constructed as a hierarchical and distributed system. Details will be provided in 4.2.
- Verification Service: the verification service verifies all digital evidence corresponding to the data and generates a data management certificate. This component uploads the generated certificate to the trusted directory service. Details will be provided in 4.4.

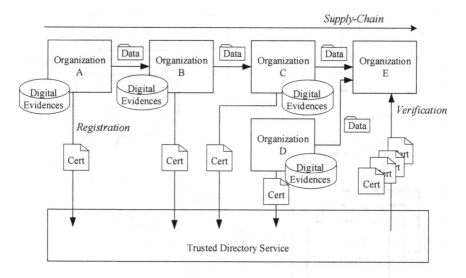

Fig. 1. Overview of framework

- Trusted Directory Service: the trusted directory service manages data management certificates and provides them to authorized entities. Details will be provided in 4.6.

Each organization manages a verification service and black box storage. The trusted directory service is managed by a trusted third party or managed as a trusted service. The service connects to a notary service based on a time-stamp service or block chain technologies [20], in order to ensure validity of time stamp information of the directory storing certificates.

3.2 Procedure

Data used in a supply chain have to be securely managed in each organization involved in the supply chain. Data management in each organization can be verified by using a trusted directory service. The overall procedure from registration of a certificate and its verification in the framework is described in the following:

1. Each terminal that uses the target data has a function for recording digital evidence and recorded digital evidence is stored in the local storage of the black box system.
2. When a data management certificate is published, the verification service obtains the corresponding digital evidence from the black box system; then verifies the digital evidence according to the conditions of data management which are defined as the data security requirements.
3. If all the digital evidence meets the conditions, the verification server publishes a data management certificate for the data and registers it in the trusted directory service.

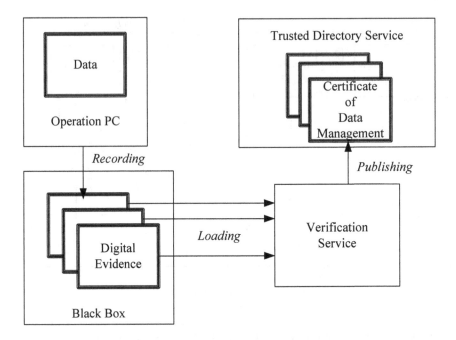

Fig. 2. System architecture

4. The trusted directory service manages certificates registered by organizations, and provides certificates to organizations that wish to confirm the data management processes of the data in its supply chain.
5. An organization that wishes to confirm all the data management processes of the data in a supply chain obtains all the corresponding data management certificates and verifies them. The organization requests digital evidence which links information that is included in the certificates and verifies them, if necessary.

4   Components

Our framework consists of three main components: a black box system for storing digital evidence, a verification service that publishes a data management certificate, and a trusted directory service that manages certificates and supports verification of the certificates. In this section, components in the framework are described. Furthermore, we explain digital evidence, data management certificates, and the conditions for data management.

4.1   Digital Evidence

Data management processes can be verified using digital evidence. Digital evidence is a digital data record in an operation process designed to protect data and environmental information of data management. An example of digital evidence is shown in Table 1.

Table 1. Example of digital evidence

Target	Digital evidence
Restriction of data access	Access control log
	Records of operated terminals and operating data
Secure environment	Virus check records
	System update records
Controlled environment	List of installed software
	List of connected devices
	Network connection status
	Communication log
Restriction on functions	Security scan logs
	Software/driver installation logs
	List of running processes
Restriction on users	Log-in/log-off log
	Account/user role

Each piece of digital evidence has header information. The header information consists of information for searching digital evidence: an operation ID that identifies an operated terminal and operators for data, transaction time (or period), and classification of digital evidence.

4.2 Black Box System

The black box consists of two components: a storage device that records digital evidence and a database located on a server. Storage devices are installed in each local system and they periodically upload digital evidence to the database server. The database server provides a search function for stored digital evidence and a verification service using the search function and obtains the corresponding digital evidence from the database server. Digital evidence header information is used for searching digital evidence. The database server generates link information for each piece of digital evidence and provides it along with the digital evidence to the verification server when the verification server requests digital evidence.

4.3 Certificate of Data Management

A data management certificate is published by the organization that manages the data and it includes link information for the digital evidence that has been

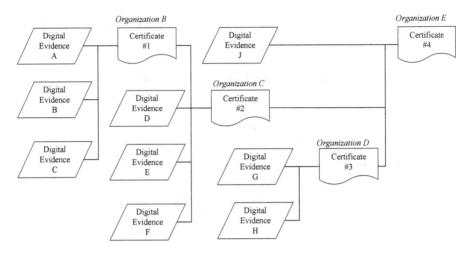

Fig. 3. Logical structure of certificates and digital evidences

verified by the organization. The certificate is a document guaranteeing that the data is securely managed according to predefined conditions as security requirements. The data management certificate consists of the following components:

- Publisher information: this field denotes the publisher of the certificate, i.e., the organization managing the data
- Data IDs: this field indicates IDs of data which are the object of data management.
- Validation Date: this date denotes the date on which the certificates will expire
- Link information for digital evidence: this information includes all link information to digital evidence that was verified in the process of publishing the certificate.
- Link information for conditions: this information includes link information to conditions for data management, which are defined based on security requirements.
- Digital Signature: this is a digital signature generated by the publisher's private key. The signature ensures the integrity and authenticity of the certificate.

Certificates and digital evidences are referred as a hierarchical logical structure as in Fig. 3. Link information for referred certificates are managed by the trusted directory service.

4.4   Verification Service

A verification service generates a data management certificate for each piece of data. Before generating the certificate, the service verifies the digital evidence corresponding to the data. Thus, the server makes a request to the black box system to search the corresponding digital evidence, and obtains the digital evidence. The process of verification is described as follows:

1. The verification service searches the digital evidence of records of operated terminals and operating data within a certain time span and obtains the corresponding digital evidence.
2. The service checks the digital evidence and identifies the corresponding terminals according to the target data ID.
3. The service searches all digital evidence about the corresponding terminals within the specified time span; then it obtains the digital evidence.
4. The service checks the digital evidence and confirms whether all the digital evidence satisfies the data management conditions.
5. If all digital evidences meets the conditions, the service issues a certificate of data management using a private key of the organization.
6. The service sends the certificate to the trusted directory service and registers it. if the certificate has to refer other certificates, the service send link information for corresponding certificates to the trusted directory service as well.

4.5   Example of Data Management Conditions

Data management conditions have already been defined by the organization that manages the data or requests another organization to manage the data. Conditions should be defined based on security requirements for data management. An example of data management conditions is described in the following:

- *Authorized users can access the data.* The condition has to be verified using digital evidence such as log-in/log-off records and access control status.
- *The system should be updated to the latest version in order to remove vulnerabilities in the system.* The condition has to be verified using digital evidence such as system updating records.
- *Functions not used to manage the data should be deactivated.* The condition has to be verified using digital evidence such as a security scan report, software installation logs, and system configuration files.
- *Anti-virus software has to be installed in the terminal and periodically scanned.* The condition has to be verified using digital evidence such as virus scan logs.
- *Data is encrypted when it is saved to local storage.* The condition has to be verified using digital evidence such as device storage status log.
- *Only permitted software is installed in the system.* The condition has to be verified using digital evidence such as list of installed software.
- *Data should be sent through secure communication channel.* The condition has to be verified using digital evidence such as communication log.
- *Communication should be monitored and controlled.* The condition has to be verified using digital evidence such as communication log.

4.6 Trusted Directory Service

The trusted directory service provides a directory service for data management certificates. The service manages the certificates over their entire lifecycle as well. For example, if a certificate has expired, the certificate is removed from the directory. Furthermore, the service provides information about a trusted chain of the certificates, and the verification records of the certificates. This service might be managed by a trusted third party in an open supply chain. The service has the following sub-components:

- Authentication sub-component: manages access policies to the directory. Access to a certificate might be restricted to just authorized users. A user should be authenticated and authorized; then permitted to access the certificate. An entity that submits a certificate should be authenticated and authorized as well.
- Storage of certificates: this sub-component stores certificates and provides a search function for the certificates. Link information to other certificates is managed in the storage.
- Trustworthiness index: this index denotes the trustworthiness of certificates and the trustworthiness of the organizations that publish the certificates. Each index is calculated based on trusted records such as records on the verification of certificates (how many organizations trust the certificate), and endorsements from other organizations.

5 Consideration

We have designed a trustworthy framework and components for a secure and trustworthy supply chain. The framework can be implemented based on the design; however, it should be improved to make the framework more secure and efficient. Thus, there are some ongoing research topics as follows:

- **Design of a secure black box system.** The integrity of digital evidence is a fundamental requirement for validity of data management in our framework. Digital evidence has to be securely stored in the black box system and its integrity must be ensured. It should be ensured that no entity can alter or erase digital evidence once the digital evidence has been recorded in the system; furthermore, the time the evidence is recorded is mandatory information in its verification. Thus, the digital evidence should be write-once data in the system, and time at which information is recorded should be securely recorded as well. How to design a secure black box system is an ongoing research issue we intend to investigate.
- **Efficient verification of digital evidence.** The most important issue in the process of certificate generation undertaken by a verification service is how to realize efficient verification of digital evidence. There are several types of digital evidence and simple definitions as conditions for secure data management are generally requested. There are two approaches to designing the

verification process; a language to define security conditions that has the ability to define simple and brief conditions only, and a verification algorithm that should be intelligent enough to fill the gap between defined conditions and digital evidence. Each organization can intuitively define the security conditions for data management. Another approach is to use a simple matching engine as a verification algorithm and the ability of a language that defines security conditions is highly expressive; detailed conditions can be defined and matching of any digital evidence can be achieved. We are considering the first approach and will design a more efficient algorithm for verification of digital evidence.

- **Efficient verification of certificates and their lifecycle management.** The trusted directory service manages the data management certificates. The service revokes a certificate if the certificate is invalid or the organization publishing the certificate is invalid. Expired certificates should be removed from the directory service. The relationship between certificates is a chained structure; if a certificate in the chain is invalid, verification of other certificates in the chain is a futile exercise. If an organization verified a certificate in the past, verification of the certificate can be skipped. Thus, an efficient verification scheme should be considered and the management of certificates over their entire lifecycle should be designed as well.

6   Conclusion

In this paper, we presented our framework for building a trustworthy supply chain. Components of the framework were presented and some research issues were discussed. As our future work, we will find solutions for the issues, and then we will implement the system and evaluate feasibility and scalability of the system.

Acknowledgement. A part of this work was supported by the Cabinet Office (CAO), Cross-ministerial Strategic Innovation Promotion Program (SIP), "Cyber Physical Security for IoT Society" (funding agency: NEDO).

References

1. Abeyratne, S.A., Monfared, R.P.: Blockchain ready manufacturing supply chain using distributed ledger. Int. J. Res. Eng. Technol. **05**(09), 1–10 (2016)
2. Ali, A., Mahfouz, A., Arisha, A.: Analysing supply chain resilience: integrating the constructs in a concept mapping framework via a systematic literature review. Suppl. Chain Manag.: Int. J. **22**(1), 16–39 (2017)
3. Atallah, M.J., Elmongui, H.G., Deshpande, V., Schwarz, L.B.: Secure supply-chain protocols. In: EEE International Conference on E-Commerce, 2003, CEC 2003, pp. 293–302, June 2003. https://doi.org/10.1109/COEC.2003.1210264
4. Barron, S., Cho, Y.M., Hua, A., Norcross, W., Voigt, J., Haimes, Y.: Systems-based cyber security in the supply chain. In: 2016 IEEE Systems and Information Engineering Design Symposium (SIEDS), pp. 20–25, April 2016

5. Bhargava, B., Ranchal, R., Ben Othmane, L.: Secure information sharing in digital supply chains. In: 2013 3rd IEEE International Advance Computing Conference (IACC), pp. 1636–1640, February 2013
6. Boin, A., Kelle, P., Clay Whybark, D.: Resilient supply chains for extreme situations: outlining a new field of study. Int. J. Prod. Econ. **126**(1), 1–6 (2010)
7. Brindley, C., Ritchie, B.: Supply chain risk management and performance: a guiding framework for future development. Int. J. Oper. Prod. Manag. **27**(3), 303–322 (2007)
8. Christopher, M.: The agile supply chain: competing in volatile markets. Ind. Mark. Manage. **29**(1), 37–44 (2000)
9. Christopher, M., Peck, H.: Building the resilient supply chain. Int. J. Logistics Manag. **15**(2), 1–14 (2004)
10. Christopher, M., Towill, D.: An integrated model for the design of agile supply chains. Int. J. Phys. Distrib. Logistics Manag. **31**(4), 235–246 (2001)
11. Cosic, J., Baca, M.: Do we have full control over integrity in digital evidence life cycle? In: Proceedings of the ITI 2010, 32nd International Conference on Information Technology Interfaces, pp. 429–434, June 2010
12. Ellison, R.J., Woody, C.: Supply-chain risk management: incorporating security into software development. In: 2010 43rd Hawaii International Conference on System Sciences, pp. 1–10, January 2010
13. Goranson, H.T., Goranson, T.: The Agile Virtual Enterprise: Cases, Metrics, Tools. Greenwood Publishing Group (1999)
14. Ivanov, D., Sokolov, B., Kaeschel, J.: A multi-structural framework for adaptive supply chain planning and operations control with structure dynamics considerations. Eur. J. Oper. Res. **200**(2), 409–420 (2010)
15. Kiyomoto, S., Rahman, M.S., Basu, A.: On blockchain-based anonymized dataset distribution platform. In: 2017 IEEE 15th International Conference on Software Engineering Research, Management and Applications (SERA), pp. 85–92, June 2017
16. Kuntze, N., Rudolph, C.: Secure digital chains of evidence. In: 2011 Sixth IEEE International Workshop on Systematic Approaches to Digital Forensic Engineering, pp. 1–8, May 2011
17. Leończuk, D., Ryciuk, U., Szymczak, M., Nazarko, J.: Measuring performance of adaptive supply chains. In: Kawa, A., Maryniak, A. (eds.) SMART Supply Network. E, pp. 89–110. Springer, Cham (2019). https://doi.org/10.1007/978-3-319-91668-2_5
18. Lu, T., Guo, X., Xu, B., Zhao, L., Peng, Y., Yang, H.: Next big thing in big data: the security of the ICT supply chain. In: 2013 International Conference on Social Computing, pp. 1066–1073, September 2013
19. Meixell, M.J., Norbis, M.: Assessing security risk in global supply chains. In: First International Technology Management Conference, pp. 510–515, June 2011
20. Meneghetti, A., Quintavalle, A.O., Sala, M., Tomasi, A.: Two-tier blockchain timestamped notarization with incremental security. CoRR abs/1902.03136 (2019). http://arxiv.org/abs/1902.03136
21. Ponomarov, S.Y., Holcomb, M.C.: Understanding the concept of supply chain resilience. Int. J. Logistics Manag. **20**(1), 124–143 (2009)
22. Richter, J., Kuntze, N., Rudolph, C.: Security digital evidence. In: 2010 Fifth IEEE International Workshop on Systematic Approaches to Digital Forensic Engineering, pp. 119–130, May 2010

23. Ross, R., Dempsey, K., Viscuso, P., Riddle, M., Guissanie, G.: Protecting controlled unclassified information in nonfederal systems and organizations. NIST Special Publication 800–171 Revision 1 (2018)

24. Roy, A., Gupta, A.D., Deshmukh, S.G.: Information security in supply chains - a process framework. In: 2012 IEEE International Conference on Industrial Engineering and Engineering Management, pp. 1448–1452, December 2012

25. Shidong, Z., Liu, J., Sheng, Y., Xiaorui, Z.: Research and implementation of digital evidence enforcement protection program. In: 2013 6th International Conference on Intelligent Networks and Intelligent Systems (ICINIS), pp. 33–35, November 2013

26. Soltani, S., Seno, S.A.H.: A survey on digital evidence collection and analysis. In: 2017 7th International Conference on Computer and Knowledge Engineering (ICCKE), pp. 247–253, October 2017

27. Tang, C.S.: Perspectives in supply chain risk management. Int. J. Prod. Econ. **103**(2), 451–488 (2006)

28. Tian, F.: A supply chain traceability system for food safety based on HACCP, blockchain & Internet of Things. In: 2017 International Conference on Service Systems and Service Management, pp. 1–6, June 2017

29. Wang, J., et al.: Toward a resilient holistic supply chain network system: concept, review and future direction. IEEE Syst. J. **10**(2), 410–421 (2016)

30. Yusuf, Y.Y., Gunasekaran, A., Adeleye, E., Sivayoganathan, K.: Agile supply chain capabilities: determinants of competitive objectives. Eur. J. Oper. Res. **159**(2), 379–392 (2004)

31. Zage, D., Glass, K., Colbaugh, R.: Improving supply chain security using big data. In: 2013 IEEE International Conference on Intelligence and Security Informatics, pp. 254–259, June 2013. https://doi.org/10.1109/ISI.2013.6578830

Wireless Networks and Cloud Computing

IoT Aboard Coastal Vessels: A Case Study in the Fishing Industry

Andreas Vollen and Moutaz Haddara(✉)

Department of Technology, Kristiania University College,
32 Christian Krohgs Gate, 0186 Oslo, Norway
moutaz.haddara@kristiania.no

Abstract. Internet of Things (IoT) technologies provide promising opportunities to organizations through connecting and enabling collaborations among physical objects, devices, systems, platforms and applications. However, there is a lack of sufficient research exploring IoT in the fishing industry, especially in smaller fishing vessels operating in remote and rural areas. Hence, through a case study, this paper investigates the benefits and challenges of an Internet-based refrigerated sea water (RSW) system aboard the fishing vessel Storegg in Norway. RSW systems ensure keeping the catch cooled in certain temperatures until it is delivered to the consumer. Several factors affect the catch quality and price, and one of them is how the fish was chilled during the whole supply-chain operations. Our findings illustrate how a 450 MHz band can provide an inexpensive and low-latency Internet connection to fishing vessels, which enables IoT technologies in remote areas such as the Norwegian coastline. In addition, the results show that virtual private networks (VPNs) can be used to secure access in IoT, and can improve existing RSW-systems' security. After implementing the RSW-system, Storegg gained timely remote vendor support, which in turn increased the systems' uptime, and dwindled the risk of losing fish quality and revenues, however, also the case study suggests that security is a critical factor for fishery with serious consequences. Our findings also insinuate that there is currently a significant focus on extending Internet connections and coverage at the Norwegian coast, and that digitalization is at the top of the agenda in the Norwegian fishing industry.

Keywords: IoT · Fishery · RSW-systems · Coastal vessels

1 Introduction

Internet of Things (IoT) technologies are changing several industries and providing standards and infrastructures to connect physical objects, applications, machines, and devices [1]. IoT has the potential to make industries more efficient and create new business opportunities. The most prominent areas include; smart homes, energy, healthcare, manufacturing, supply chains, sustainability, among others. Smart Industry or industry 4.0 is the core of IoT and smart manufacturing [2]. New intelligent techniques and models to perform real-time monitoring make IoT an excellent candidate solution for several challenges. When it comes to the Norwegian fishing industry, it is world-renowned for supplying a selection of the best quality fish and seafood to the

© Springer Nature Switzerland AG 2019
I. Awan et al. (Eds.): MobiWIS 2019, LNCS 11673, pp. 163–177, 2019.
https://doi.org/10.1007/978-3-030-27192-3_13

global market [3]. Regarding value, it is the world's second-largest exporter of fish after China and generated an alighted profit of approximately 18 billion NOK in 2017 [4]. The development of fisheries has resulted in fewer but more efficient fishing boats, and boats have been reduced from around 13.000 to 6100 vessels during the period from 2000–2017. Furthermore, with long traditions in ship-construction, Norway has become a leader in building technologically advanced offshore vessels [5]. This study, therefore, set out to investigate IoT-technologies in the fishing industry onboard coastal fishing boats in Norway. Coastal fishing boats are middle-sized and catch fish along the coast, but there are also larger boats like trawlers and purse that go further at sea. This paper investigated two different coastal ships for the case study, Storegg and Runing (25–35 m long). Storegg has already implemented some IoT solution, while Runing did not. It would also be essential to examine bigger boats, but to narrow down the research scope and focus, they none were included in this research.

The contribution by investigating the state of Norway's fishing fleet could help designing smarter systems in the future and to shed light on how IoT can be seamlessly integrated in the fishing industry. The authors were not able to identify any research towards IoT in coastal fishing boats at the time of writing this paper. Before conducting the study, the authors were aware that the Internet is covering the Norwegian coast and is also available on the fishing vessels, however, we were not aware about which Internet technologies are used on these vessels. Internet connection is fundamental to operate IoT devices, so this could be a challenge in rural and remote areas such as the North Sea. Most of the Internet connections today are land-based, and satellite connections are expensive. A fishing vessel is like a small factory at sea, with machinery, valves, and pumps. Furthermore, it is also a living space for those who work there with a living room, kitchen, and bedrooms. Industry 4.0 and smart houses technologies and applications create almost endless possibilities for IoT in a fishing vessel. Since Norway has one of the most modern fishing industries and one of the world-leading countries in the Marine shipping industry, it was expected to find several IoT technologies aboard coastal fishing vessels. However, early in this research, only one smart and Internet-connected system was identified, a Refrigerated Sea Water (RSW) system, which is used to cool down fish to preserve quality and state. Hence, a closer exploration of the RSW-system was chosen to learn more about IoT in the coastal fishing vessels. In this paper, we study the IoT-based RSW-system aboard the fishing vessel "Storegg". In addition, we investigate another shipping vessel "Runing", which did not implement any IoT devices, in order to understand the barriers for adopting IoT technologies in their case. Further, we collect data from other parties and stakeholders involved in the fishing industry and respective research, in order to know more about IoT opportunities and challenges with this sector understudy.

The remainder of the paper is organized as follows. First, we demonstrate the research background and underlying technologies studied in this research in Sect. 2. In Sect. 3, we present our research methodology. In Sect. 4, we provide our main findings and discussions, followed by a conclusion, study implications and recommendations for future research in Sect. 5.

2 Background Literature

2.1 Internet of Things

Internet of Things is an area based on the technological concepts of cyber-physical systems, which enables the emergence of what is called smart factories, smart manufacturing, Industry 4.0, and factory of the future [6]. In this modular structured environment, cyber-physical systems monitor physical processes, replicate a virtual copy of the physical world and make decentralized and autonomous decisions [6]. Via IoT solutions, cyber-physical systems communicate, collaborate, and cooperate with each other with full autonomy, and also collaborate with humans in real-time fashion in order to achieve a certain goal or task [6]. Hence, wireless communication technologies and systems are playing an essential role and are enabling smart objects to be networked [7]. Through IoT, industries can achieve better visibility and gain enhanced insights into their operations and assets through the integration of machine sensors, middleware, software, and back-end cloud computing and storage infrastructure [8]. These layers can provide extensive datasets that may give insights through advanced analytics, which can optimize operational efficiency and potentially accelerate productivity. The analytics' outcomes can be reduced unplanned downtime and more optimized productivity [6]. An interesting fact pointed out by [9], is that the power of 1% relating to the operational cost/inefficiency savings, could make a significant contribution and impact on the return on investment.

By creating an interaction between surrounding systems, higher intelligence can be achieved in the machine performance [1]. These seamless interactions with surrounding systems and devices can turn conventional machines into self-aware and self-learning machines with improved performance and maintenance management in the environment where it operates [10]. IoT depends on standardization to be successful, which would provide interoperability, compatibility, standardization, reliability, and effective operations on a global scale. One of the vital areas for enabling IoT is the middleware that often follows the service-oriented architecture (SOA) approach. Using SOA principles and infrastructures provide access to applications within an ecosystem with defined components and enable machine-to-machine communication. The SOA approach, also enables software and hardware to be reused, as well as providers and requestors to communicate with each other despite the heterogeneous nature of the underlying layers. Scalability, modularity, security, and cross-platform compatibility are among the critical design requirements for IoT [11].

2.2 Big Data Analytics in Fishery

IoT devices worldwide generate massive amount of data in every second [6]. This data has the potential be used and analyzed to create valuable knowledge [12, 13]. [14] researched big data analytics and IoT technologies in the maritime industry in Norway. Their paper describes that most of the existing IoT applications and research focus and directed towards land-based applications. To compensate, they created a novel framework for offshore support vessels that operate in areas that rely mostly on satellite communications, which is very expensive. Thus, they found it to be unrealistic to use cloud-based solutions for big data analytics onboard these vessels. Their framework focuses on real-time analytics onboard the vessels, while historical data is stored at land because of limited computing resources available onboard. The vessels can then send the historical data in batches for maintenance and development in the future [14].

2.3   IoT Enablement in Rural and Remote Areas

The 450 MHz band can deliver extensive coverage, yet the telecom industries have not used this to a significant extent. By using a 450 MHz band, it will be a highly cost-effective coverage for indoor users and rural/remote areas. With broader coverage, this may open the door for new business opportunities like the support of IoT everywhere, not only in urban areas. The 450 MHz band can also be used to off-load the 1800 MHz band and leave more capacity to handle other premium services. Several IoT applications will not need high bandwidth but will depend on connectivity in remote areas [15]. [16] conducted a case study on optimizing coverage and low energy consumption on remote, rural and difficult for access areas. Casual technologies used in urban areas are not available in such remote areas, which make it challenging to install the transportation layer infrastructure to support IoT applications. Hence, they used a long-term evolution (LTE) 4G network, which was based on a sub-1 GHz (450 MHz) bands designed for large packet data applications [16]. While LTE networks are not originally designed for IoT applications, however, they found it to be a useful communication technology to serve as a back-haul for IoT, especially in the transportation layer [16]. The Energy sector in Europe has also emphasized the importance of operating on the 450 MHz band to enable "smart meters" applications. The band is considered as critical communication need as smart grids will require a significant increase in data rates and spectrum access [17]. In general, IoT communications could be classified into two main classes, massive machine-type communication (mMTC) and ultra-reliable low latency communication (URLLC). In mMTC it is a large number of low-cost devices with high requirements on scalability and increased battery lifetime. URLLC are critical applications where an uninterrupted and robust exchange of data is essential. For example, factory automation needs real-time control of machines and systems for fast production. In general, factory automation has considered being challenging in term of latency, and the requirements vary from 250 ms to 10 ms. Process automation applications include monitoring and diagnostics of industrial elements and processes include, among others heating and cooling. Since the values change slowly, the latency required a range from 50 to 100 ms [18].

2.4   Regulations and Development in the Industry

The focus on technology development and adoption in the fishing- and maritime industries is growing in Norway. This is mainly due to the incentives that are provided by the Norwegian government. For instance, companies that pilot and are able to demonstrate their technological developments, can get up to Thirty (30) million NOK in funding from Innovation Norway [19]. However, these new developments and changes in the industry need to keep regulations in mind when designing new smart systems that can meet the standards set by the government. The Norwegian Food

Safety Authority has strict regulations to safeguard the Norwegian seafood and fish products' quality. Quality is essential when exploiting a limited fishery resource and safeguarding value creation in the industry as best as possible. The handling of fish during the catch is of paramount importance to the quality of fishery products. If the fish is not handled well early in the supply chain, the reduced quality will follow the fish to the end consumer. Hence, the immediate cooling after the catch, and the maintained cooling until the product reaches the consumer are of crucial importance [20].

2.5   RSW-Systems

As mentioned earlier, the cooling of a catch during the transportation is one of the fundamental factors of final fish quality. Refrigerated sea water systems are widely used to chill fish haul where the water temperature is maintained on −1 °C. The salt content of seawater allows for low water temperature. By using a refrigeration system, the seawater is cooled down and circulated in large tanks containing both seawater and fish. The RSW system removes the necessity to carry ice from shore, reducing weight under transport. While preparing for hauling fish, the water is pre-cooled, and the fish is dumped into the tanks which increase the temperature [21] in [22].

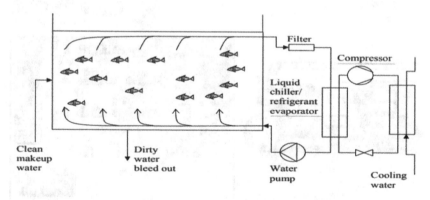

Fig. 1. A simplified overview of an RSW system.

The chilled seawater passes upwards from the tank, keeping the fish suspended and at the same time, cooling it (Fig. 1). The water returns through the top of the tanks and back to the chilling system and repeat the circulation process. The tanks are generally loaded to approximately 80% fish and 20% water. The necessary machinery includes chillers, compressors, receivers, condensers, and pumps [23].

2.6   Tekno-Tronic PLC

Automation and control have, to a large extent, replaced human elements onboard ships. Teknotherm, for instance, uses a programmable logic controller (PLC) system installed in the control cabinet (Fig. 2), which is an industrial computer [24]. The system is developed to help to handle operations, maintenance and troubleshooting the system [25]. Some of the advantages provided are listed below:

- Readout of operating status for the refrigeration system
- Start and stop of the compressor
- Start and stop of pumps
- Entering set-points
- Alarms and alarm history
- Password protection and user access rights
- Runtime equalization
- Backup of settings
- Logging of temperatures, unit pressures and running conditions for trending and reporting
- Export of various data to Excel for support
- Remote control, diagnosis, and troubleshooting via the Internet
- Access through tablets, PCs, etc.
- Communication with IAS system

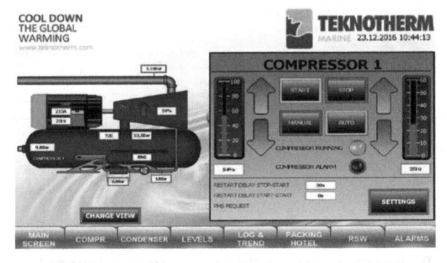

Fig. 2. A compressor control view in the PLC system by Teknotherm [26].

2.7 Security and Tosibox

The ability to secure communications between things and humans is one of the most significant challenges in IoT. Machine-to-machine (M2M) protocols do not address the proper security and privacy needs. A system should have two different requirements to create excellent protection for different devices. Authentication where only specific users to connect to the system. Authorization, access to resources that have been authorized. Virtual Private Networks (VPN) is a means to secure such IoT deployments

[27] in [28]. Security is an area that of chief importance for IoT devices; many devices are often left unguarded in the open with minimal security measures, and attackers could gain access to their data transmissions. The Finnish VPN company Tosibox, provides a versatile encryption solutions that add an encrypted control layer to remote data access mechanisms on devices that lack these functions [29]. Tosibox has won the ISO 9001 certification for the development, manufacturing, licensing and selling of connection solutions, products, and services for the Internet of Things. The company explains that it is an essential step towards its goal to be a global standard for secure remote connections [30]. They have also won the Industrial and Security Category Awards at the IoT/M2M Innovation World Cup in 2017 [31].

Fig. 3. An illustration of the main functionalities of Tosibox [32].

VPNs have been a popular solution for secure remote network connections over the years, but no company has done it correctly, according to Tosibox. The product is described as a plug-and-play, multi-factor, physical VPN connection product based on the concept of "Key" and "Lock". It can control implementations for stand-alone deployments among other PLC displays, and industrial machines (Fig. 3). Tosibox claims that their product has the fastest adoption in M2M deployments in the manufacturing and security sectors. Tosibox replaces the need for a cloud-based connection and can be easily deployed by plug-and-go and is a cost-efficient solution. Tosibox turns an Internet connection between two devices into an encrypted end-to-end connection. It uses the terms "Key" and "lock" for each device. Each "lock" device can be used only with a correct key device, and multiple lock devices can be linked to the same device. Each Tosibox has an assigned unique private IP and is created centrally by the company. Separately both devices connect to the Internet via a server and start to communicate [33].

3   Research Methodology

This research adopted a case study research methodology [34], where qualitative semi-structured interviews [35] and document analysis were the primary sources used for data collection. Document analysis is frequently used in combination with other qualitative methods as a triangulation approach to enable richer understanding and data collection on a topic. As qualitative researchers are expected to draw on multiple sources of evidence, in order to pertain validation through the use of different data sources and methods [36].

Interviews with eleven (11) key-informants from different aspects of the fishing industry with in-depth knowledge about fishery and the systems were conducted over the phone (Table 1). The interviews were recorded and transcribed. Follow-up phone calls were also conducted to get further clarifications and information. The interview questions were directed towards: (a) understanding of the state-of-the-art technologies in the Norwegian fishing vessels, (b) The different IoT systems adopted and used in the industry, (c) the challenges and barriers for adoptions, and finally (d) the future of IoT in the fishing industry. The data from the sources were consolidated and put together to provide a good overview of the data for our analysis.

Table 1. Overview of informants.

Informant	Organization	Industry
Machinist	Storegg	Fishery
Captain	Runing	Fishery
Developer	Tehnotherm	Vendor
Sales manager	Teknotherm	Vendor
Researcher	Norwegian Directorate of Fisheries	Government
Statistic department	Norwegian Directorate of Fisheries	Government
Statistic department	Norwegian Directorate of Fisheries	Government
Customer service	Ice.net	Vendor
Developer	Ice.net	Vendor
Technician	Ice.net	Vendor
Professor	NTNU Ålesund	Researcher

4   Findings and Discussions

The goal of this paper is to investigate an RSW-system connected to the Internet in the fishing industry to show the benefits of IoT. Some of the initial findings were the lack of development towards IoT onboard coastal vessels and the vast research gap in this specific area. As one of the informants in the Norwegian Directorate of fisheries put it: *"One of the reasons can be the result of conservatism in the industry or due to low budgets"*. Coastal vessels do not have large budgets, and invest little towards new development. However, larger fishing vessels invest heavily in new ships, technology and "risk" their investments towards IoT. An existing example of automation in larger vessels, is that the data about the fish is sent directly to the fish factory without human interference. Since this paper has not investigated larger boats, it can only be speculated that they are more technologically advanced towards IoT technologies, which was also confirmed by several of our informants.

4.1   Enablement of IoT in Fishery

In contrast, smaller fishing vessels operating in the coast of Norway have a potential advantage over larger fishing vessels when it comes to IoT. In the study by [14], they found that offshore support vessels in Norway operate in areas, which rely on satellite communications, which is very pricey. In most cases, these are the same areas where large fishing boats operate. On the other hand, coastal fishing boats are not dependent on satellites to get Internet. In our case study onboard "Storegg", we found that they rely on a much cheaper Internet solution from a provider that doesn't rely on satellites. The provider uses a low frequency on the 450 MHz band from base stations along the coastline covering the entire coast up to 120 km at sea (Fig. 4), providing Norway's coastline with a unique Internet connection for IoT devices. In addition, Fig. 4 also demonstrates that the area covered is the most common area for operations during fishery. Furthermore "Bankfiske 1" is marked at 120 nautical kilometers out on the sea, which is the area that smaller fishing vessels under 10,67 m can operate at. In the most common fishing areas, it is possible to receive Internet connection, except for mackerel catching where it is required to go further at sea.

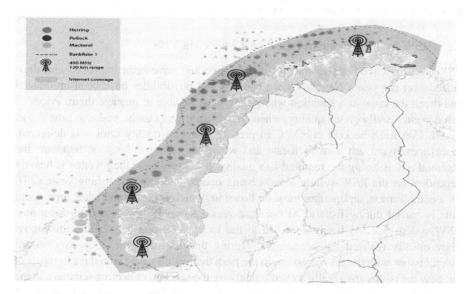

Fig. 4. Internet coverage along the coast of Norway. Compiled based on interviews data from Ice.net (Technician at Ice), Barentswatch [37] and Norwegian Directorate of Fisheries [38].

For Storegg, this Internet coverage provides connectivity to most of their operational areas, and enables existing and potential IoT technologies in small vessels with low budgets. Since the provider Ice.net took over the old 450 MHz band in 2013, they have done massive upgrades, and increased the coverage and speed that can provide speeds between 9–37 MB per second [39]. As one of the informants pointed out: *"The challenge with IoT in the past was slow Internet speeds, but that has changed"* -

(Technician at Teknotherm). Since smaller vessels have such possibilities, more focus should be directed towards smaller ships in developing new IoT solutions. Digitalization is high on the agenda in the industry as seen in the example from Innovation Norway giving 30 million NOK in funding which can be boost companies with innovative ideas in IoT. With the increased focus on digitalization by the government and the industry itself, we only see the start of what to be realized by IoT in the fishery. In the last years, many providers and researchers have seen the opportunity for IoT created by the 450 MHz band (e.g., [16] and [15]). An excellent combination to enable IoT in rural and remote areas like the coast of Norway. For coastal ships, this is unique compared to expensive satellite communications in the transportation layer. In addition, satellites have high latency time that is up to 500–1200 ms, which is considerably high compared to the 450 MHz band that operates with only 40 ms response time (Developer at Ice). For IoT development, this can be a substantial difference when developing new applications as seen in the examples in factory automation and process automation, which requires a range from 10–250 ms [18]. The latency can be a massive challenge for large boats operating with satellite communication. Hence, the 450 MHz band has several advantages compared to satellite communications, and one of the core questions that needs further investigation is: would the 450 MHz band network be able to support thousands of new IoT applications in the fishing industry?

4.2   RSW-Systems Brought into Smart Space via VPN

RSW-systems have been around for a long time and have been improved and digitalized over the years. New advanced controls and possibilities have been introduced and dwell the crew in a situation where they must be able to manage them. Prices of fish depend heavily on the quality, where and when it was caught, and also how it was stored. Fish must be kept at -1 °C to preserve the best quality until it is delivered. Sometimes issues are hard to locate and when something unforeseen happens, the potential risk is losing the required fish quality. In other words, the revenue is heavily dependent on the RSW-system always being operational onboard fishing vessels. To fix a complication, an operator must be flown in, which is costly and takes time – and time is crucial during fishery. At our case vessel Storegg, they started to use a new RSW-system that has been connected to the Internet for one year before this study. They quickly realized the advantages. During the first half-year, they experienced several issues with the RSW-system. In the past, that would have taken days to repair it, but now the issues are usually solved quickly by the vendor connecting remotely to the system. With increased support efficiency, and they gained more uptime and less risk of quality decrease, *"Having the RSW-system connected to the internet has proven to be a huge advantage, it gives us a sense of security, and we have experienced more up-time which helps us to reach our goals more effectively."* - (Machinist at Storegg).

    In fishery downtime can be very costly, as Storegg sometimes spend days searching for fish, and if something goes wrong, they may lose profits and valuable time. With the knowledge that support is remotely available, the crew feels a sense of security in their work. The vendor Teknotherm has been using Tosibox in their systems for around five years. For them, the system has saved a countless number of trips, which cut the cost dramatically and gave them the possibility to support their customers more efficiently.

Furthermore, the system has proven to be a competitive advantage against other RSW vendors. When the technician is connected, s/he can control everything that the PLC is connected to. When connected, the PLC gives access to temperature logs, pressure, alarms and change settings and more, which is basically everything that an operator onboard can do. Tosibox enables them to connect to the PLC system controlling the RSW-system remotely through a VPN connection (see Fig. 1 above). The PLC is programmed to make the RSW-systems keep a steady temperature of the seawater in the tank and measure pressure. The connection between Tosibox and PLC is possible since it is built on the communication bus. The RSW-system and its sensors are not connected to the Internet directly but rather to the Ethernet aboard the vessel. One of the advantages of VPNs is the increased security, but the loss of functionality such as saving data to the cloud for analytics. If the system had sensors to measure how much fish that was caught (as in bigger boats), a connection to the cloud would give huge advantages. For example, the Directorate of Fishery in Norway has decreed that all fishing vessels must report their catch (weight and location) in an electronic log. This is today manually added by the crew themselves. First, the crew put a bearing rod into the tank to calculate approximately how much fish they have caught and type it into the system. This is used to analyze how much fish that have been caught in the ocean to safeguard value creation and sustainability in the industry. When they are ready to sell the fish, they go to a website "sildelaget.no" to auction their catch, in which they use the same information as in the electronic log. When the fish is delivered, a printed temperature-report from the PLC is handed over to the fish factory. This is used to control quality but is also a requirement from the Norwegian Food Safety Authority. If these manual operations were to be automated through IoT technologies, the Tosibox would not be sufficient to support such features, as they it is not using a cloud solution. So, one of the drawbacks with Tosibox is the scalability for connecting different systems and advanced analytics. A higher intelligence could be achieved in the machine performance by creating an interaction between surrounding systems [10]. With an SOA approach, access could be applied to applications in an ecosystem despite the heterogeneous nature of underlying layers. As [11] stated, scalability, modularity, security and cross-platform compatibility are among the critical design requirements for IoT. All data from the PLC is stored locally at ships, and the vendor can only receive a report when they connect to the PLC system. The technician needs an active connection to bring out data from the ships and currently they don't conduct any analytics. This is not an optimal solution and connecting the system to the cloud could bring huge advantages like reduced unplanned downtime and optimized efficiency through analytics [9]. Teknotherm wishes to go over to such cloud-based systems in the future to get some of the more advanced possibilities, but there are no secure options in the current market as they stated. As discussed above, the Internet is enabled for IoT development in the industry, so monitoring and diagnostics should be possible with the right technology [18].

4.3 Security

One of the issues with IoT and remote connections has been the lack of standards and ensuring high data security. Security represents a significant problem when bringing

IoT to ships, as breaches can have devastating consequences, *"You could open the bottom valve and sink the whole ship"* - (Machinist at Storegg). Several informants stated that security and especially hacking was a considerable concern. At the fishing vessel Runing for instance, they know about the benefits of IoT and have a system ready to be connected. However, *"the risk is way too big"* (Captain at Runing). An incident that happened a few years ago could have caused the ship to sink. One of the vendors connected to the system and mistakenly entered wrong valve settings, which caused the boat to take in and accumulate water in one of the tanks on the starboard side. After the incident, the vendor was not allowed to connect to any of their systems without authorization from the vessel. M2M protocols do not address the security and privacy needed in the industry, as stated by [27], there needs to be a level of authentication and authorization. Tosibox provides the security that is lacking in M2M and IoT. In Tosibox the data feed from the devices is secured, as well as, establishing a secure control path to each device, which is a significant capability other IoT platforms generally do not offer, and that was one of the reasons that it received several awards in the IoT area (e.g., ISO 9001 and IOT/M2M Innovation World Cup). Besides providing security, it is also easy to use: "The system is straightforward to use, and we only use a few hours to set it up" – (Developer at Teknotherm). The Tosibox is like a router that needs a key to be operated and a password to establish a secure network tunnel. The box simplifies VPN without compromising security and can secure many IoT end-points. At Storegg, Tosibox secures the data feeds from the device and establish a secure control path to the RSW-system (PLC). The cost for Storegg was a one-time cost in hardware (250 USD), and only a few hours of setup by the vendor. The cost-effective solution saves both the vendor and customer a lot of time and money. The easy setup is maybe one of the reasons why this system has become a success for the vendor. Digitalization is forcing vendors to innovate and was one of the reasons that Teknotherm started connecting their devices to the Internet. As seen at Storegg, connecting an RSW-system to the Internet brings many benefits, so why haven't there been more developments? "In sea fishery, we are lagging behind in the IoT development. Onshore, we already started to provide such solutions since 2007 via cloud solutions" - (Developer at Teknotherm).

5   Conclusions and Future Research Avenues

In this case study, we discussed and showed how IoT is empowered in coastal fishing vessels in Norway through a 450 MHz band. Furthermore, a map of operation in the fishing industry with Internet coverage has been presented. It has also been discussed and proven that smaller vessels should get more attention when developing new IoT solutions. The potential is tremendous in the industry, and the focus on digitalization is rising. After implementation of the RSW-system, Storegg gained increased support from their vendor. This gave them more uptime, and decreased risk of losing quality and revenue. One of the lessons learned is that security is a critical factor and should be taken into account when developing and researching new solutions, as it may have grave consequences if violated. It was also discussed that a VPN could be used for securing access in IoT in order to improve RSW-systems. This study has two main implications for research. First, it proves that the current Internet connectivity at the coast of Norway enables IoT adoptions aboard fishing vessels. This can, in turn, help research to develop new smart solutions for the fishing industry in the future. Second, by demonstrating the finding of the RSW-system connected to the Internet on Storegg, we exhibit the benefits and drawbacks of the current state-the-art technologies, and we open the door for more research on this subject. For practice, this research sheds light on the fishing industry in order to get a better understanding of the existing IoT applications, and what potential benefits they may achieve by looking into the new possibilities of this technology. For vendors and suppliers, there is a vast market that has not been filled and largely untapped.

For future research, it would be beneficial for the industry to investigate larger boats like Trawlers and to study other vendors and key players in the industry like Rolls Royce. It would also be valuable to explore how the 450 MHz band can tackle and support thousands of potential new applications, and if the low latency will be affected and increased. Finally, more research is essential to unearth suitable scalable solutions for the fishing industry.

References

1. Haddara, M., Staaby, A.: RFID applications and adoptions in healthcare: a review on patient safety. Procedia Comput. Sci. **138**, 80–88 (2018)
2. Uckelmann, D., Harrison, M., Michahelles, F.: Architecting the Internet of Things. Springer, Heidelberg (2011). https://doi.org/10.1007/978-3-642-19157-2
3. Food and Agriculture Organization of the United Nations: Fishery and Aquaculture Country Profiles The Kingdom of Norway. http://www.fao.org/fishery/facp/NOR/en. Accessed 2019
4. Statistisk sentralbyrå - Statistics Norway: Fisheries. https://www.ssb.no/en/fiskeri. Accessed 2019
5. Blue Maritime Cluster: Blue Maritime Cluster. http://www.bluemaritimecluster.no/gce/the-cluster/about-us/. Accessed 2019
6. Haddara, M., Elragal, A.: The readiness of ERP systems for the factory of the future. Procedia Comput. Sci. **64**, 721–728 (2015)
7. Helgesen, T., Haddara, M.: Wireless power transfer solutions for 'things' in the internet of things. In: Arai, K., Bhatia, R., Kapoor, S. (eds.) Proceedings of the Future Technologies Conference (FTC) 2018. Advances in Intelligent Systems and Computing, vol. 880. Springer, Cham (2019). https://doi.org/10.1007/978-3-030-02686-8_8
8. Sajid, O., Haddara, M.: NFC mobile payments: are we ready for them? In: 2016 SAI Computing Conference (SAI), London, vol. 960–967 (2016)
9. Gilchrist, A.: Industry 4.0: The Industrial Internet of Things (edited by Pepper, J.), p. 18. Apress, Nonthaburi (2016)
10. Lee, J., Kao, H.-A., Yang, S.: Service innovation and smart analytics for industry 4.0 and big data environment. Procedia Cirp **6**, 3–8 (2014)
11. Bandyopadhyay, D., Sen, J.: Internet of things: applications and challenges in technology and standardization. Wirel. Pers. Commun. **58**, 49–69 (2011)
12. Elragal, A., Haddara, M.: Design science research: evaluation in the lens of big data analytics. Systems **7**, 27 (2019)

13. Elragal, A., Haddara, M.: Big data analytics: a text mining-based literature analysis. In: NOKOBIT-Norsk konferanse for organisasjoners bruk av informasjonsteknologi, Fredrikstad, Norway, vol. 22, no. 1, pp. 17–19, November 2014

14. Wang, H., Osen, O., Li, G., Li, W., Dai, H.-N., Zeng, W.: Big data and industrial internet of things for the maritime industry in northwestern Norway. In: TENCON 2015–2015 IEEE Region 10 Conference, pp. 1–5. IEEE (2015)

15. Kuosa, H.: Nokia - Use 90% fewer base stations and double capacity by leveraging the 450 MHz band. https://www.nokia.com/en_int/blog/use-fewer-base-stations-double-capacity. Accessed 2015

16. Carrillo, D., Seki, J.: Rural area deployment of internet of things connectivity: LTE and LoRaWAN case study. In: 2017 IEEE XXIV International Conference Electronics, Electrical Engineering and Computing (INTERCON), pp. 1–4 (2017)

17. European Commission: A Spectrum Roadmap for IoT Opinion on the Spectrum Aspects of the Internet-of-things (IoT) including M2M, November 2016

18. Schulz, P.: Latency critical IoT applications in 5G: perspective on the design of radio interface and network architecture. IEEE Commun. Mag. 55(2), 70–78 (2017)

19. Bjånesøy, R.: Norges Sildesalgslag. https://www.sildelaget.no/no/media/nyhetsarkiv/arkiv/2018/mars/stoetter-ny-teknologi-og-nye-loesninger/. Accessed 2019

20. Norwegian Food Safety Authority: Norwegian Food Safety Authority. In: Kvalitet på fisk og fiskevarer. https://www.mattilsynet.no/mat_og_vann/produksjon_av_mat/fisk_og_sjomat/mottak_tilvirking_fisk/kvalitet_paa_fisk_og_fiskevarer.9953. Accessed 2019

21. Wang, S.G., Wang, R.Z.: Recent developments of refrigeration technology in fishing vessels. Renew. Energy 30(4), 589–600 (2005)

22. Sætrang, S.: RSW systems with CO2 as refrigerant - testing of new system solutions for sea water coolers. NTNU - Norwegian University of Science and Technology (2009)

23. Teknotherm: RSW system. https://www.teknotherm.no/product/rsw-system/. Accessed 2019

24. Wikipedia: Programmable logic controller. https://en.wikipedia.org/wiki/Programmable_logic_controller. Accessed 2019

25. Teknotherm: AUTOMATION. https://www.teknotherm.no/service-spare-parts/automation/. Accessed 2019

26. Teknoterm: Tekno-Tronic. https://www.teknotherm.no/wp-content/uploads/2017/05/Tekno-Tronic.pdf. Accessed 2019

27. Medaglia, C.M., Serbanati, A.: An overview of privacy and security issues in the Internet of Things. In: Giusto, D., Iera, A., Morabito, G., Atzori, L. (eds.) the Internet of Things, pp. 389–395. Springer, New York (2010). https://doi.org/10.1007/978-1-4419-1674-7_38

28. Collina, M., Corazza, G.E., Vanelli-Coralli, A.: Introducing the QEST broker: scaling the IoT by bridging MQTT and REST. In: 23rd Annual IEEE International Symposium on Personal, Indoor and Mobile Radio Communications, pp. 36–41 (2012)

29. Dickson, B.: Techcrunch - Solving the persistent security threats for the internet of things. https://techcrunch.com/2015/11/28/solving-the-persistent-security-threats-for-the-internet-of-things/?guccounter=1. Accessed 2019

30. Tosibox: Tosibox - Tosibox Awarded ISO 9001 Certification. https://www.tosibox.com/tosibox-awarded-iso-9001-certification-2/. Accessed 2019

31. Adotas: Tosibox Wins Two Categories At IOT/M2M Innovation World Cup. http://www.adotas.com/2017/03/tosibox-wins-two-categories-at-iot-m2m-innovation-world-cup/. Accessed 2019

32. Tosibox: https://www.tosibox.com/product/lock500/. Accessed 2019

33. Tosibox: Whitepaper: TOSIBOX – Your Private Highway Through The Internet Of Things, no. 3 (2016)

34. Yin, R.: Case Study Research and Applications: Design and Methods, 6th edn. Sage Publications, Thousand Oaks (2017)
35. Bell, E.: Business Research Methods. Oxford University Press, Oxford (2018)
36. Bowen, G.: Document analysis as a qualitative research method. Qual. Res. J. **9**(2), 27–40 (2009)
37. Barentswatch: https://www.barentswatch.no/fiskinfo/40. Accessed 2019
38. Fiskeridirektoratet: Fiskeriaktiviteten i Norskehavet (2006)
39. Valmot, O.: Digi.no - Det nye tredje nettet. https://www.digi.no/artikler/det-nye-tredje-nettet/320666. Accessed 2019

Load Balancing in Multi-cellular
4G Using Cloud Computing

Ravyar Jasim Hamd[1], Tara Ali Yahiya[1], and Pinar Kirci[2(✉)]

[1] University of Kurdistan Hewler, Erbil, Iraq
t.ibrahiml@ukh.edu.krd
[2] Istanbul University-Cerrahpaşa, Istanbul, Turkey
pkirci@istanbul.edu.tr

Abstract. In this paper, some load balancing algorithms were used in order to solve the problem of congestions in the networks through a load balancer. In order to investigate the performance of these algorithms, Riverbed network simulator is used. Some performance parameters were studied such as CPU utilization on the server, user equipments and end-to-end delay to the servers. As well as the case of failure of the servers in cloud computing is studied especially its effect on the ongoing applications represented by http application is analyzed.

Keywords: 4G · LTE · Load balancing · Cloud computing

1 Introduction

Cloud computing is a technology which enables the sharing of hardware and software resources. Service models of the cloud computing are Software as a Service, Platform as a service and Infrastructure as a Service. Cloud computing is evolving with the system of telecommunication in parallel. The integration of mobile and wireless networks with cloud computing will offer ubiquitous services anytime and anywhere to the users. However, since the number of mobile devices are increasing, the demand for services located on servers in the cloud computing will increase too. In order to deal with such situation, load balancing is a prominent solution to distribute the load equally to the servers through the use of different types of load balancing algorithms.

In the work, the system of telecommunication used to be integrated with cloud computing is the LTE or 4G. This system is widely deployed and its integration with cloud computing will raise so many challenges, one of the most important one is "how to load balance the traffic generated in multi-cellular LTE on the servers located in the cloud.

Increasing growth of user demands and the emergence of new technologies in the mobile communications have triggered researchers and industries to come up with comprehensive manifestations of the upcoming fourth generation (4G) wireless communications in mobile technology. The main concept in fourth generation for the transition to the All-IP is to have a common platform for all the technologies that have to develop so far and to harmonize with user expectations of the many service to be provided" [1]. Nowadays, 4G or LTE technology is very popular and it is the latest

© Springer Nature Switzerland AG 2019
I. Awan et al. (Eds.): MobiWIS 2019, LNCS 11673, pp. 178–187, 2019.
https://doi.org/10.1007/978-3-030-27192-3_14

available wireless technology to use which has new advancements including better bandwidth and services comparing to other earlier wireless technologies.

Demand for bandwidth is increasing at a rapid pace due to popular use of Smartphone, tablets and other high-end web enabled devices. Mobile users and the resulting data usage are random, time varying, and often unbalanced" [2]. this makes the server may be overloaded, which overloaded servers can face resource shortage, and this affects access of new users and impacts the QoS of active users. Thus, imbalanced load seriously deteriorates the overall network performance due to inefficient resource utilization. This problem will be solved by deploying a load balancer and use load balancing techniques. On the Internet, companies whose Web sites have a great amount of traffic usually use load balancing. These companies can have contract with cloud provider in order to provide them many functionalities including load balancing.

2   Comparison of Different Load Balancing Algorithms

LTE (Long Term Evolution) is quite new and at the same time complex technology, wireless operators are trying to expand their LTE networks day after day, in order to take advantage of additional overall efficiency, lower latency and the ability to handle increased different data traffics [3].

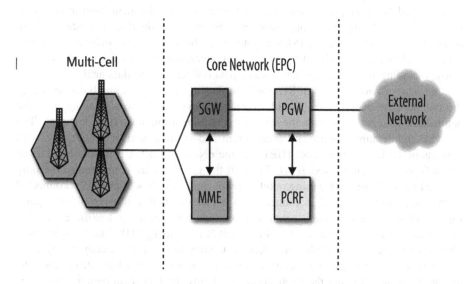

Fig. 1. Multi-cell 4G LTE architecture [4, 5]

In this paper, it is focused on multi-cell 4G LTE rather that single-cell 4G LTE. Figure 1 shows an example of simple multi-cell 4G LTE architecture.

The core network of LTE architecture is composed of the following components: Home Subscriber Service (HSS): HSS is basically a central database that contains information about all the network operator's subscribers. Mobility Management Entity

(MME): MME is the main control entity for the E-UTRAN. Serving Gateway (S-GW): S-GW acts like a router and forwards data between the eNodeBs and PDN gateway. Packet Data Network Gateway (PDN/P-GW): P-GW is the point of communication to the outside world using SG1 interface [5].

Merely, cloud computing is an on-demand service in which shared information, resources, software and other devices will be provided per clients' requirements at specific period of time. Generally, it's a term which is used in case of Internet and the whole Internet can be observed as a cloud [6–9].

The core problematic in this work is how to combine LTE with cloud computing in order that the latter offers the service of load balancing to the operators of 4G. Load balancer can be represented by an algorithm that should be executed on cloud computing to balance load. In the work, some static load balancing algorithms in 4G LTE using cloud computing is studied in order to show and analyze how a load balancer affects the overall network performance compared to the case when there is no load balancer. The parameters of performance studied in the work are represented by CPU Utilization, Processing Delay, Traffic Dropped, Load and Task Processing Time. We will also show and analyze the comparison of different load balancing algorithms on how they affect the network performance and the servers. Then, we will study the case when there is a failure recovery in the cloud, and study its effects on the performance of the network and its availability. Finally, UE end-to-end delay comparison will be shown between the case of having load balancer and no load balancer.

Riverbed Modeler [10] provides a comprehensive development environment supporting the modeling of communication networks and distributed systems. Both behavior and performance of modeled systems can be analyzed by performing discrete event simulations. The Modeler environment incorporates tools for all phases of a study, including model design, simulation, data collection, and data analysis [11].

Our network architecture in Riverbed consists of many nodes and links, including the components of 4G LTE, Cloud Computing and Load balancer along with the application servers that provide the service to the users through Cloud Computing. The network architecture is multi-cell architecture and is composed of 7 cells, each cell consists of 10 User Equipments (UE) and one eNodeB. Each UE is connected to an eNodeB using Serving eNodeB ID. Then all the eNodeBs are connected to the only Evolved Packet Core (EPC) using point-to-point (ppp_adv) link. The EPC is connected to the cloud and the cloud is connected to a gateway both are using point-to-point (ppp_adv) link. The gateway is connected to a load balancer using 1000BaseX duplex link, while the latter is connected to 4 Ethernet Servers using 1000BaseX duplex link. The architecture also includes Application Configuration for defining the type of application used for traffic generation, Profile Configuration which determines the profile of the nodes using the application and finally the LTE Configuration which is used to specify the characteristics of LTE network especially the link layer and PHY layer. Next section will detail the characteristics of the nodes and links deployed in the network architecture.

3 Results

3.1 CPU Utilization of Servers

In this part, we will show the simulation results for all the 5 scenarios that we have, and the scenarios are Random Algorithm, Round Robin Algorithm, Number of Connections Algorithm, Failure Recover in Round Robin and lastly no load balancing case. We will show the results of all the scenarios in different simulation times, they are 10, 20, 30, 40 and 50 min simulation time, and we will have them as figures. Generally, we will divide the simulation results into two main sections. In the first section, we will show the comparison of different load balancing algorithms. In the second section, we will compare the failure recovery case in Round Robin algorithm with the original Round Robin algorithm, to show how failure affects the results. In this part, we will show CPU utilization results of different servers each for different load balancing algorithms in different simulation times.

As it is shown in Fig. 2a, the CPU utilization average of server1 in no_load_balancing case is much higher in all the different simulation times comparing to the other load balancing algorithms because all the loads that come from the load balancer will be directly forwarded to the server1 only. So generally, no_load_balancing case is having more processing delay and zero traffic drop for the load balancer. As for the servers, we have more requests to forward, high load and high CPU utilization for the server1 only which all the traffic is forwarding to and nothing for the other servers. As for the Round_Robin algorithm, we can see that it has the highest CPU utilization among the three algorithms, this is because of the natural behavior of the algorithm which is distributing the load equally between all the servers so this causes less processing delay and less traffic drop in the load balancer. Indeed, this means more requests forwarded to the servers along with high load and high CPU utilization in the servers. But as for the Number_of_Connections algorithm, we can see that it has nearly the second highest CPU utilization after Round_Robin and this is because of the algorithm behavior. The Number_of_Connections algorithm works in such a way that before forwarding any request to the servers, the load balancer tracks the number of connections that it has with each server, then after checking, the load balancer will forward the request to the server that has least number of connections with it. Consequently, this results in having more processing delay and more traffic drop in the load balancer. This means less requests forwarded to the servers, so along with less load and less CPU utilization in the servers. As for the Random algorithm, which is clear from the name itself, this algorithm behaves randomly and uses underlying random number generator, which means that in some cases it sends more requests to one server than another or for the same server in different times, as we can see in Fig. 2b, the CPU utilization for the last three simulation times for server1 has quit much difference from the first two simulation times which is higher. We will see those different random behaviors in the next figures for the rest of the servers also. Figure 2b depicts the CPU utilization average of server2 in different load balancing algorithms with different simulation times.

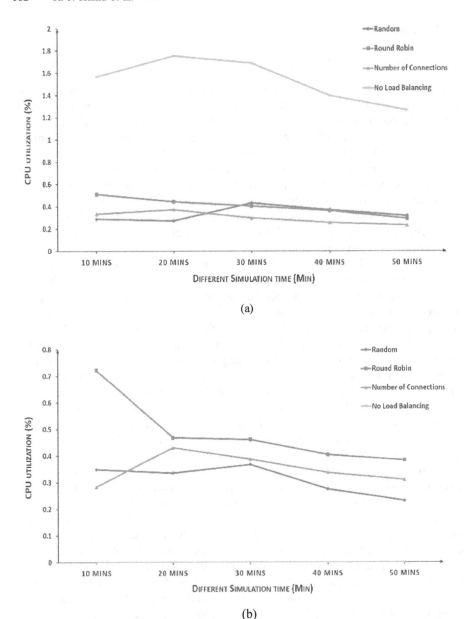

Fig. 2. (a) Server1 CPU utilization for different load balancing algorithms. (b) Server2 CPU utilization for different load balancing algorithms

The Fig. 3a shows that in no_load_balancing case there is zero CPU utilization on server2 in all the simulation times and that is because all the requests are being forwarded to server1, so there is no load on server2. Then we can see that server2 in Round_Robin algorithm has the highest CPU utilization in all the simulated times. Then comes the second highest CPU utilization algorithm which is Number_of_Connections algorithm in all the simulated times except 10-minute simulation time which Random algorithm has higher CPU utilization and this is because of its random behavior that is explained previously in Fig. 2b. Then it is followed by Random algorithm which in this server nearly has the lowest CPU utilization among the other algorithms.

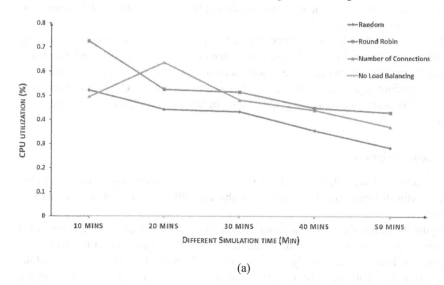

(a)

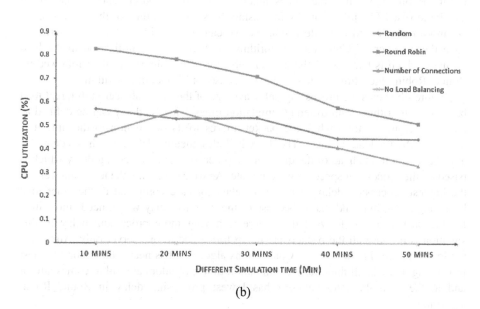

(b)

Fig. 3. (a) Server3 CPU utilization for different load balancing algorithms. (b) Server4 CPU utilization for different load balancing algorithms

Server3 in Round_Robin algorithm has the highest CPU utilization in all the simulated times except 20-minute simulation time which Number_of_Connections algorithm has higher CPU utilization and this is because of having heavy load along with many number of cells and UEs in the scenario, so this causes having less realistic and less accurate results in the first two simulation times, 10-minute and 20-minute, as they are not long enough.

By increasing the simulation time, we get higher chance of having more accurate and realistic results, as Fig. 3b shows, we can see that in the last three simulation times we had more realistic and accurate results according to the algorithm behaviours. At last, the Random algorithm comes which has nearly the lowest CPU utilization comparing to the other load balancing algorithms in all the simulation times except 10-minute.

3.2   Load Balancer

Some results of load balancer such as CPU utilization, processing delay and traffic dropped with different load balancing algorithms in different simulation times will be presented.

Figure 4a shows the CPU utilization average of the load balancer in different load balancing algorithms with different simulation times. As we can see in the 10-minute scenario, the load balancer nearly uses the same CPU percentage in all the algorithms and in no_load_balancing case also. But within increasing the simulation time in the scenarios, we can see that the load balancer is getting different CPU usage statistics, for example, in 30-minute scenario it is shown that the CPU utilization of load balancer in Round_Robin algorithm is the highest among all the others and in Random algorithm it has the lowest CPU utilization. by increasing the simulation time of the scenarios, we get more realistic and accurate results, so we can see that in 50-minute scenario we have the Number_of_Connection algorithm has highest CPU utilization in the load balancer which is because of the natural behavior of the algorithm, then followed by Round_Robin algorithm, no_load_balancing case and Random algorithm.

Figure 4b shows the processing delay average of the load balancer in different load balancing algorithms with different simulation times. Simply, delay can be defined as the delay from the time when the packet arrives to its destination to the time it is dispatched by the load balancer. The delay includes queuing delay, which is a delay for a packet to get to the head of the queue to be processed, and processing delay which is based on the processing speed/forwarding rate. As we can see that the load balancer has the highest processing delay in no_load_balancing case compared to the other load balancing algorithms and that is because of the queuing delay which needs more time for the packets to be forwarded to server1, having more processing delay in this situation is because all the packets are being forwarded to one server only. After that, the load balancer in Number_of_Connections algorithm has nearly the second highest processing delay in all the different simulation times, Random algorithm comes after it and at the end, the load balancer has lowest processing delay in Round_Robin algorithm.

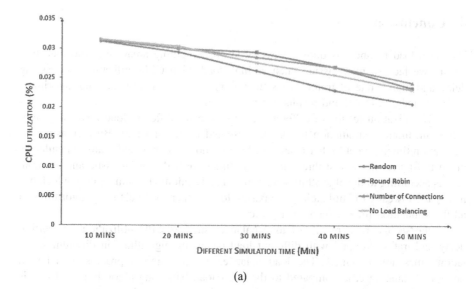

(a)

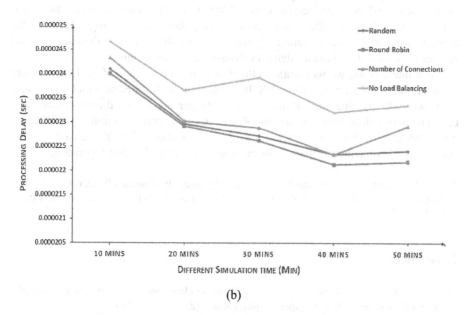

(b)

Fig. 4. (a) Load Balancer CPU utilization for different load balancing algorithms (b) Load Balancer Processing Delay for different load balancing algorithms.

4 Conclusion

Having a load balancer is quite necessary in all computing areas. With no load balancing we face so many issues such as high load, high CPU utilization, processing delay and higher rate of traffic drops. In this paper, some load balancing algorithms were studied and tested and results were collected.

CPU utilization results of different servers each for different load balancing algorithms in different simulation times are presented in the first part. By increasing the simulation time, we get higher chance of having more accurate and realistic results, as given in figures, in the last three simulation times we had more realistic and accurate results according to the algorithm behaviours. The Random algorithm works which has nearly the lowest CPU utilization comparing to the other load balancing algorithms in all the simulation times except 10-minute.

In the second part, results of load balancer such as CPU utilization, processing delay and traffic dropped with different load balancing algorithms in different simulation times are presented. The load balancer has the highest processing delay in no_load_balancing case compared to the other load balancing algorithms and that is because of the queuing delay which needs more time for the packets to be forwarded to server1, having more processing delay in this situation is because all the packets are being forwarded to one server only. After that, the load balancer in Number_of_Connections algorithm has nearly the second highest processing delay in all the different simulation times, Random algorithm comes after it and at the end, the load balancer has lowest processing delay in Round_Robin algorithm.

As a future work, we will work on the traffic dropped average of the load balancer in failure recovery case and Round Robin algorithm with different simulation times. And, we will examine load results in requests per second of different servers in comparison of failure recovery case and Round Robin algorithm in different simulation times. Also, we will see how having a load balancer affects the UE end-to-end delay comparing with having no load balancer, with using Round Robin algorithm.

Acknowledgment. This work has been supported by Scientific Research Projects Coordination Unit of Istanbul University-Cerrahpasa within the IU-Cerrahpasa BAP with project number BYP-2019-33855.

References

1. Ramya, G., Jothilakshmi, M.: Latest trends in wireless mobile communication (4G–5G) technologies. Int. J. Res. Comput. Appli. Robot. **4**(2), 19–23 (2016)
2. Mishra, S., Mathur, N.: Load balancing optimization in LTE/LTE-A cellular networks: a review. Computing Research Repository, abs/1412.7273, December 2014
3. Kumar Singh, R., Singh, R.: 4G LTE cellular technology: network architecture and mobile standards. Int. J. Emerg. Res. Manag. Technol. **5**(12), 10–16 (2016)
4. Abed, G.A.: Queue size comparison for standard transmission control protocol variants over high-speed traffics in long term evolution advanced (LTE-A) network. Sci. Res. Essays – Acad. J. **9**(23), 984–987 (2014)

5. Hicham, M., Abghour, N., Ouzzif, M.: 4G system: network architecture and performance. Int. J. Innov. Res. Adv. Eng. **4**(2), 215–220 (2015)
6. Pawade, P.A., Wasukar, A.R.: Use of cloud computing system for load balancing. Int. J. Res. Sci. Eng. **16**, 481–487 (2016)
7. Rajeshkannan, R., Aramudhan, M.: Comparative study of load balancing algorithms in cloud computing environment. Indian J. Sci. Technol. **9**(20), 1–7 (2016)
8. Swami, C., Anand, N.: Architecture of mobile cloud computing and middleware. Int. J. Emerg. Trends Technol. Comput. Sci. (IJETTCS) **4**(6), 142–144 (2015)
9. Sharma, O., Das, P., Kumar Chawda, R.: Hybrid cloud computing with security aspect. Int. J. Innov. Adv. Comput. Sci. **4**(1), 76–80 (2015)
10. Riverbed's Modeler. https://cms-api.riverbed.com/portal/community_home. Accessed 21 June 2016
11. SteelCentral Riverbed Modeler: Riverbed (2017). https://www.riverbed.com/gb/products/steelcentral/steelcentral-riverbed-modeler.html. Accessed 08 July 2017

A Lightweight Data Transfer Mechanism for Mobile Device over Poor Wi-Fi Signal

Nor Shahniza Kamal Bashah[1(✉)], Siti Zubaidah Idris[2],
Noor Habibah Hj Arshad[1], Norjansalika Janom[1],
and Syaripah Ruzaini Syed Aris[1]

[1] Faculty of Computer and Mathematical Sciences,
Universiti Teknologi MARA, 40450 Shah Alam, Selangor, Malaysia
{Shahniza,habibah,norjan,ruzaini}@tmsk.uitm.edu.my
[2] Industrial Training Institute of Kuala Luumpur, Human Resources Department,
Human Resources Ministry, Jalan Kuchai Lama, 58200 Kuala Lumpur, Malaysia
sitizubaidahidris@yahoo.com

Abstract. Wi-Fi technology is one of the alternative ways for electronic devices to connect to a wireless LAN (WLAN). With BYOD technology, it is common to bring our mobile devices especially smartphone everywhere we go. Surfing the Internet is not the only thing you can do with Wi-Fi, as wireless transfer file between devices is one of the example. Wireless signal strength is essential when we want to transfer a file. The problem is when we face poor signal, especially when the signal bar is only one level remaining in certain areas. Hence, not many task can be done, which usually only messaging service is available such as WhatsApp Messenger. Moreover, activities done while signal is poor will cause to mobile device's battery drain quickly. Therefore, poor signal strength will affect data transferring activities. Hence, this research proposed a new mechanism for data transferring over poor Wi-Fi signal with enhanced data chunk model. Data chunk applies searching technique using hash table for data structure and combine with bloom filter. Thus, it will not only chunk the data into several parts but the transferring process will be faster. This mechanism should be able to cater the above mentioned problem which results to data such as text and mp3 can be transferred even over poor Wi-Fi signal.

1 Introduction

There are two popular wireless connectivity's for mobile devices namely, cellular and Wi-Fi. According to statistical data by The Huffington Post in 2014, 71% of people prefer Wi-Fi rather than cellular network. The main reason is monthly cellular bill can be saved if using Wi-Fi connection. A WLAN technology or usually called as Wi-Fi has been widely used around us whether we realize it or not. It provides connection between mobile devices to transmit data using radio waves. In the old days, data transferred using wired infrastructure. Access point (AP) is a network device that allows mobile devices to connect to a wired network. Usually an AP and a user's mobile device using single antenna in data transmission that speed up to 54Mbit/s [1]. Using multiple antennas in MIMO technology can increase WLAN signal rate but not

© Springer Nature Switzerland AG 2019
I. Awan et al. (Eds.): MobiWIS 2019, LNCS 11673, pp. 188–201, 2019.
https://doi.org/10.1007/978-3-030-27192-3_15

all mobile devices support MIMO since it has the limitation of MIMO that needs to be used at both ends. Using 802.11 a/b/g/n protocols without MIMO prevent the capability of reducing error codes mechanism and data transmission's speed. Signal strength is really important for a user as the stronger the signal, the more data can be transferred. Issue arises when mobile device is use in an area that only received poor wireless signal strength. Hence, data transmission is limited to text messages only and other data type such as audio, animation, video or others cannot pass through it. In order to support data transfer over poor Wi-Fi signal and to improve the transferring process this paper proposes a lightweight data transfer mechanism for mobile device that will not limit the type of data that can be transferred. Hence enables other types of data such as text and mp3 to be transferred even over poor Wi-Fi signal. The paper starts with an explanation of the motivations of the proposed mechanism. Next, the related works are briefly reviewed. The main part of the paper is the elaboration of the lightweight data transfer mechanism. The proof-of-concept implementation is described thoroughly. Further works are given in the conclusion.

2 Motivation

2.1 Poor Wi-Fi Signal Strength in Certain Area

Wireless strength is measured in decibels (dB). It is power measured in referenced to one milliwatt. The range of signal strength is between 0 to −100. The closer signal strength to 0 means it receive strong signal. Poor Wi-Fi signal is when the signal strength is measured less than −70 dB. There are several factors that affect signal strength [2]. Some of them are physical obstruction such as buildings, hills or thick wall that harder for signal to penetrate through it. Other than that, is network range and distances between transmitter and receiver. If the distance is far apart, the weaker the signal strength. Thus, it is very important to pick location for an AP and its antenna orientation accordingly to unleash its full performance. A researcher [3] had introduced top-down AP placement algorithm for placing an AP. This method uses combination of calculation and tree graph to represents several AP states. Wireless band is also one of the factors that affect signal strength. Wireless signal transmission uses IEEE 802.11 standard that transmit data through radio waves. This standard uses 2.4 GHz or 5 GHz unlicensed band. Consequently, other devices use those same bands too. If there are several devices such as microwave oven or mobile phones using the same range, interference might happen. Wireless network interference can cause signal strength weaker. Last but not least network sharing also contributes to the poor wireless signal strength. However, in wireless network, more than one user can communicate through the same network. If those users use same AP simultaneously, so the AP needs to delegate specific resources for each user. Consequently, if the AP is half- duplex, users will face signal drop. According to a study done by collaboration of Purdue and Cambridge University [4] stated that user tends to spend 23% of their time under poor Wi-Fi signal.

2.2   Battery Drain Quickly Due to Data Transfer over Poor Wi-Fi Signal

Transmit data using wireless causes data transmission increased. A comparison study had been done that proofed Wi-Fi technology is the dominant environment used in data transmission compared to LTE, HSPA, UMTS, EDGE and GPRS [4]. When transmitting data over wireless signal, device's battery decreased quickly. Other factor that affects battery is the total energy consumption. It refers to consumption of WNI and resources used such as memory and CPU during the transmission [5]. Lufei [6] stated that screen brightness also consumed more battery power. Any application or device that requires high screen resolution will experience impact of battery drain. It is very important to apply a good power model to sustain battery life [7] because more energy is consumed over poor signal.

2.3   Current Data Transferring Mechanism Only Send Text Data over Poor Wi-Fi Signal Strength

In most cases when a user experience poor signal strength, he or she only managed to send text data through the link. Network games, web surfing, file sharing applications or any related high consuming energy application is almost unlikely possible. It is because the poor signal strength had lengthened packet transmission time and also increases retransmission of a packet.

3   Related Works

Battery consumption of a mobile phone is the main issue when poor signal strength is in the picture. It drains battery power faster than normal as it tries to look out for wireless signal and continues transferring data. The poor Wi-Fi signal strength certainly gives an impact on mobile phone battery and also the network performance, according to Chen et al. [4]. Jayashree et al. [8] stated that mobile phone's battery consists of electro-chemical cells that can be classified by its voltage and capacity. Traditional design when using MAC protocols does not consider the battery state. Their protocol had extended battery life when it consumes up to 96%. However, it can only calculate number of cycles of the remaining battery if only time state for battery discharge and recovery had been supplied. According to Simunic [9] because of 90% of the time WLAN occupied its time by listening. The researcher claimed if merely higher bandwidth raised and battery lifetime is a constraint then only will be a need for power management saving in wireless technology. But nowadays the need of power reduction techniques is a necessity. Other researchers such as Balasubramanian et al. [10], Pathak et al. [11] and Qian et al. [12] conclude that using various applications that are interactive and services that run in the background via Wi-Fi make energy consumption of a mobile phone is a major necessity. A good technique of power control must be applying to reduce the energy spend on that activity. There are many power reduction techniques that had been developed by other researchers specifically for mobile phones. According to Li et al. [13], those techniques are divided into four main categories: network, operating system, application design and computer architecture. Each technique differs to one another based on those categories. As an example, for network category such as hibernation of idle nodes and using remaining energy in nodes for routing. Qian's et al. [12] team developed a tool call ARO an application resource optimizer to solve the issue of energy harvesting in cross layer interaction from user input till protocol layer involving HTTP, transport and radio resource. The team run their tool on Android phone and runs six free applications then the result indicated plenty of inefficient resource usage on the phone. Hence many methods can be developed by researchers to fill the gaps. However, their tool developed over cellular technology in mind. Mobile OS also contributes to energy consumption and several techniques had been introduced by researchers. One of them is a model to predict energy consumed while in different activity states of a mobile phone, developed by Shih et al. [14]. Their model had eliminated power consumed when 802.11b is in idle state. However, they focus only the idle state to reduce the energy. Besides the above model, Zeng et al. [15] and Flinn et al. [16] had developed a method to handle design issues in mobile OS. Heng Zeng's team had identified OS with two roles. The first role is to deal with hardware used by application programs and the second role is to distribute available system resources mainly the battery energy between applications. Their approach based on energy aware power reduction such as eliminates overhead of disk spin don policy that will only use lesser power when in idle mode. Rice et al. [17] had developed a technique on how to measure energy intake on mobile phone that will benefit the application's designers when they want to apply their power model. The researchers had found that 2G technology consume more power consumption than 3G and Wi-Fi technology. Though their experiment did not apply if the mobile phone is on the move and at different location for both transmitter and receiver. The last category is computer architecture to reduce power consumption. The basis is to perform from instruction level. An example is by shutting off parts of processor that is not being used. From all related works listed above, none had explored on network category and this research will try to close the gap. To reduce the transmission time, an energy aware compression scheme is needed to be able to handle the transmission as stated by Barr [18]. The researcher believed a single bit wireless transmission need 1000 times extra energy than 32-bit computation. Chakrabarti [19] had designed searching paradigm that is feature based for database systems. It maps elements as points but the difference is it is used for high indexing database. However, it does not support hybrid tree efficiently. MPPT algorithm based on binary search technique by Shiota et al. [20] makes the searching time shorter. However, the researcher only focusing on power point application.

4 Methodology

Before designing chunk model, an Android application is developed to detect poor signal strength. It is to ensure the transferring process will be operating under poor wireless signal. Then the chunk model is designed. This model has several components. It is based on data structure searching technique using hash table as its core. The hash table combined with bloom filter method to ensure all chunk parts available ready to be send to the receiver. After the new model is designed then a mobile application is developed using Android Studio software. This application transformed the chunk model into a working state. The process flow is illustrates in Fig. 1. As illustrated In Fig. 1, a new mechanism for wireless data transmission over poor Wi-Fi signal strength was proposed. There are several main components in the process. Starting from detecting signal strength, use access point to connect between mobile devices, establish searching technique, filtering the chunk data, receive request from the other party and transfer the data.

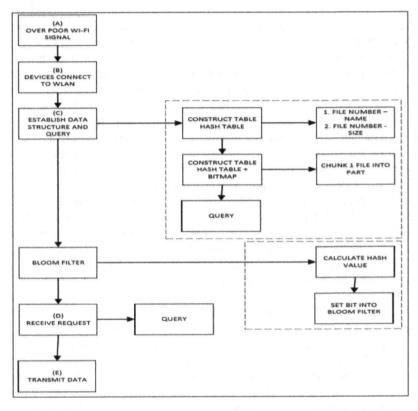

Fig. 1. Process flow for wireless data transmission over poor Wi-Fi signal strength.

(A) Over Poor Wi-Fi signal

In this phase wireless signal strength on the mobile phone received from nearby access point will be recorded. The Android application developed will scan and detect list of wireless network transmitted by access points around the area. The selected access point will display several features of the wireless network:

- SSID - name of wireless network
- BSSID - MAC address of the wireless access point (WAP)

- AP capabilities - security features such as WPA, WPA2, PSK, CCMP and its architecture: ESS
- Signal strength level - indicated by dB unit ranging from 0 to -100 dB• Wireless frequency - WLAN frequency bands between 2.4 GHz to 5 GHz bands
- Timestamp - It is a current time of an event. Timestamp is one of the feature in beacon frame sent by an AP
- Distance – range in cm between access point and its user

This main feature is the wireless signal strength. It will detect wireless signal. So, users will know the condition of the environment whether excellent, good, fair or poor strength. Researcher focuses on transfer data over poor signal strength that ranges between −70 dB to −100 dB. Once condition is met, next phase is ready to be carried out.

(B) Devices Connect to WLAN

Wireless AP is an electronic device that allows wireless devices such as mobile phone to connect to a wired network using Wi-Fi. Usually the AP connects to a router as a standalone device but also can be integral component of the router itself. It is an open network without any security. The connection consists of several steps:

- Scan

In case of an active scan, the client would send out a probe request broadcast frame and receive a probe response from the AP. In case of a passive scan, the client would find the AP by listening to the beacon.

- Authentication

Authentication types are tied to SSID that are configured for the AP. Before a client can communicates on the WLAN, it must authenticate to the AP by using open or shared-key authentication if the AP applied security. If it is an open network, client can authenticate to the network and the AP will send ACK frame and the authentication is established when client return sending back the ACK frame.

- Association

Once authentication is complete the client can associate or register with the AP to receive full access to the network by sending association request to AP. The AP will send ACK frame and association response to the client. Finally, the client will accept by sending ACK frame to the AP.

Generally, to join the wireless network, both devices need to connect to the same SSID. In this phase, mobile phones are connected using Wi-Fi under same access point. This enables those devices to be under same WLAN. The Android application need to be installed on both mobile phones then next step is to establish data transfer mechanism process.

(C) Establish data structure and Query

This is where the transferring data mechanism begins. It involves two data structures. The first data structure using hash table and BitMap and the second data structure is Bloom Filter.

Hash Table

The information needed for the first data structure is file number, file name and file size. The hash table will create two tables that will map file number to name and file number to number of chunks in that file. Each chunk part is 100 KB in size. Examples of those tables are indicates by Tables 1 and 2.

Table 1. Map file number to file name.

1	text.txt
2	song.mp3
3	video.mp4
...	...

Table 2. Map file number to number of chunks in the file.

1	1
2	50
3	300
...	...

Hash Table and BitMap

After the above table is built, the hash table needs to merge with BitMap to create another table that contains all the files and chunk parts. BitMap filters are in memory structure used to enhance performance during query execution. This method maps 1 bit for a chunk part (hash value) in a file to each row, illustrates in Fig. 2. So, a file will be assigned with several bits in the array at least one row. If the bit arrived, then bit 1 will set to it.

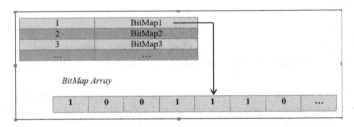

Fig. 2. BitMap filter

After that, query process will check if the chunk is available or not by checking the bit one. If there is no bit 1, it is automatically known that the row is not suitable to be transmit and will be drop.

Bloom Filter

The second data structure is the bloom filter. Bloom filter is a method to check the chunk data is available or not and gave true or false state. The filter works with hash function. For example, we have file number 16 with chunk number 17. We will have hash value of 16–17. This hash value will be calculated using hash function, presents in Fig. 3. The calculated result will be set into bloom filter array and be mapped. Value 1 means data is available.

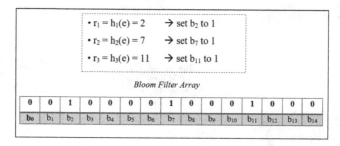

Fig. 3. Bloom filter

(D) Receive Request

Once the Wi-Fi connection is set up and both mobile phones connect to the same SSID, the IP addresses for both devices are available. This IP address is use to establish server socket connection for both devices to communicate. The Internet function is required by the Android platform and it is running at the background. The Asyctask and Handler will handle this task.

Both server and client communicate through a protocol that consists of three message types: request, data and control. The message type has its own format:

- Message Type
- File Number
- Chunk Number
- Data

The process flow of sending request message to server is describes as in Fig. 4. After sending out message to server, the client will wait for reply. On the other hand, when the server receives the request, it uses query process to get the available chunk data.

Query process begins when server receive request from client. The message content will tell query process which file and chunk data is needed to be transmit. So, server will check whether it has those files and chunks using query.

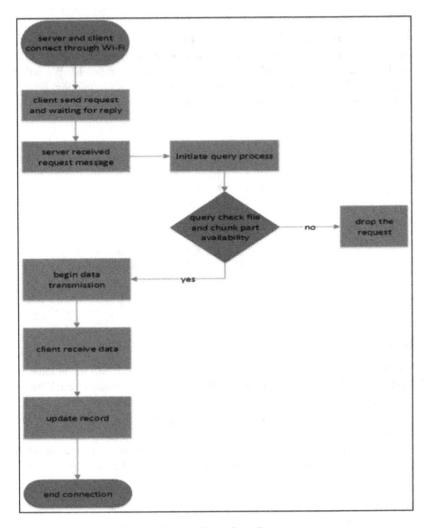

Fig. 4. Process flow of sending request

(E) Transmit Data

If all requested files and chunks available, then data transmission will begin between server and client. The data will be transfer over poor Wi-Fi signal strength. Once the data received at client side, the client will update its status specifying the transmission is success. Then the connection between server and client will be terminated.

5   Result and Analysis

The analysis of the results is divided according to several categories such as data type and processing time.

Data Type

The chunk model was tested under poor Wi-Fi signal strength on three file types: text, mp3 and mp4. Each file type's transmission has different file size: 20 KB, 200 KB and more than 200 KB. Result of the experiment has been recorded as in Table 3. All text files even have different file size has been transmitted and received with a success by the other mobile phone.

Table 3. Types of file that had been transferred

File type	Size (KB)	Status
Text	20	SUCCESS
	200	SUCCESS
	>200	SUCCESS
Mp3	20	SUCCESS
	200	SUCCESS
	>200	FAIL
Mp4	20	FAIL
	200	FAIL
	>200	FAIL

Referring to line graph illustrates in Fig. 5, for mp3 data, if the file is more than 200 KB, it cannot be transferred even after several retransmissions attempted. The transmission process will terminate halfway and returned error status. This is due to file size and signal strength that is not too strong to carry the large file.

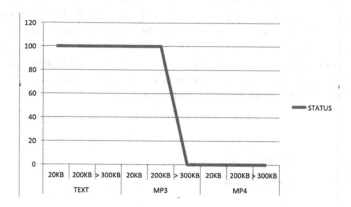

Fig. 5. Files transfer according to file type and size

The last file type that had been tested was mp4 files. The Android application cannot transmit the mp4 file even that file is 20 KB in size. It is due to the signal strength is limited, and cannot carries chunk data. If the signal strength is higher, the file can be transfer without disturbance. The chunk model has been programmed to chunk 100 KB for each chunk part. mp4 data with the size of 300 KB transferred successfully when signal strength is fair with the signal strength ranges between −60 dB to −70 dB.

Impact on Mobile Device

When transfer files over poor Wi-Fi signal strength, there are several impacts than can be seen on hardware, the mobile phone itself or on the mobile phone's system. It has significantly impact on the battery level where the level decreased, the application crashed frequently, mobile phone became hot because of overheating and longer time consumed while transferring file. Impact on the mobile devices has been recorded in Table 4. The value on the table is the percentage level of each impact.

Table 4. Statistics of device impact

More than 20 KB				More than 200 KB		
	Text	Mp3	Mp4	Text	Mp3	Mp4
Battery level decrease	3	15	45	5	30	50
Application crashed	1	20	50	4	45	60
Device heat	0	10	30	1	50	80
Time consuming	0	35	60	3	50	100

Analysis had been done through testing made on file sizes more than 20 KB and 200 KB. The only file type that did not show major significant effect is text file. Refer to Fig. 6 for graphical view. Battery level decrease quite rapidly when transferring mp4 file. Both mobile devices also noticeably hot when touched with bare hand. It is because heat increased when the mobile phone's screen needed to be lit up all the time in order to ensure connection to access point permanently throughout the process. When the screen goes out, the application regularly crashed. Both phones need to be reconnected and the process starts all over again. Mp3 file only shows significant effect when transfer more than 200 KB under poor signal strength. The application also crashed most of the time. On the other hand, the application stability also contributes to the effect on those devices. The application was tested on several platforms and the most stable between platforms tested is Android 4.4.

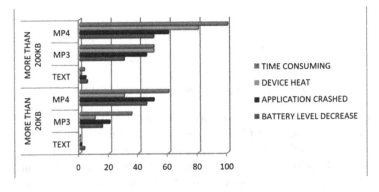

Fig. 6. Impact on device

System Usability Evaluation Survey

Every survey respondent has been given the Android application. They tested the system by transferring file from their own mobile devices. After they have tested the system, a set of five questions was given for them to answer. Each question has a scale from 1–5 which indicates 1 to be Very Dissatisfied, while score 5 is Very Satisfied. Table 5 shows the average score of the survey that was answered by total of five respondents. The average score is calculated by summing all scores according to each question and dividing by 25.

Table 5. Average score for system usability evaluation

Questions	Average score
1. Do you like to use this application again?	1.4
2. Is this application is easy to use?	2.6
3. Does this application has various functions?	1.6
4. Do you think this application is stable?	2.4
5. Do you feel this application needs improvement?	3.6

From the pie chart as illustrates in Fig. 7, we can see that 31% of the respondents thought that the application need improvement. Mainly because some of them facing problem of retransmission when they are in the process of transferring data. 22% of respondent stated this application is easy to use. This application is quite simple as it has only four screen interfaces and can be manage easily. Only 21% thought this application is stable. This percentage is quite low and one of the reasons because the application crashed several times when some of them tried to transfer larger mp3 file size. Because of the main purpose is only to detect signal strength and transferring file, only 14% of respondent believed this application has various functions. The function is limited. And lastly only 12% of the respondents want to use this application again. So some major changes need to be done to improve especially the stability of this application.

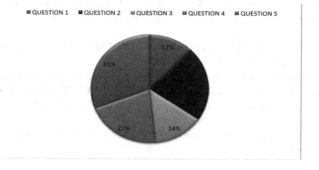

Fig. 7. System usability evaluation percentage

6   Conclusion

This research is conducted in order to address problems in data transferring namely facing poor signal strength, battery drained when transmitting data over poor signal and current data mechanism only support sending text data. Based on the problems, the research has come out with three objectives and the main focus are to detect signal strength and when the condition is detected, data will be transferred using data chunk model. By using data chunk model, users are capable to send mp3 data other than text messages through the Wi-Fi link. This model will chunk file into smaller part and using bloom filter to ensure all chunks parts are available to be transmitted to receiver. After receiver requested file to be transferred, the query process will take over checking if all requested parts are available. If not available, the request will be drop. Otherwise, transmission will occur by transmitting chunked data to the other end even through poor Wi-Fi signal. Result of successfully transmitted files depends on the file type and its size. Several future works have been outline to improve this application and there are some components that can be enhanced to improve the application to be more stable. One of them is by upgrading the version of the application. It is because the application usually crashed when working even with file size between 20 KB to 200 KB. Other than that, the poor Wi-Fi signal strength limitation contribute to failure of transferring file more than 20 KB for mp3, so as an alternative, the Wi-Fi direct or Bluetooth technology can be used. Lastly, if the application is stable it is best to test for other type of files other than text and mp3.

Acknowledgement. This research is supported by the Research Management Institute, Universiti Teknologi Mara registered under the BESTARI Grant Scheme (FRGS) #600-IRMI/PERDANA 5/3 BESTARI (098/2018). The authors would like to thank to Research Management Institute, Universiti Teknologi MARA, Malaysia for their funding support and also acknowledged the support given by Crowd Business and Innovation Research Interest Group, Faculty of Computer and Mathematical Sciences, UiTM Shah Alam.

References

1. Huawei, T.: WLAN MIMO. Huawei technologies Co., Ltd., China (2012)
2. Solutions 4.: 4Gon Solutions. Retrieved from Factors Affecting Wireless Networking Performance (2015). http://www.4gon.co.uk/solutions/technical_factors_affecting_wireless_performance.php
3. Farkas, K., Huszák, Á., Gódor, G.: Optimization of Wi-Fi access point placement for indoor localization. J. IIT (Inf. IT Today) 1(1), 28–33 (2013)
4. Ding, N., Wagner, D., Chen, X., Pathak, A., Hu, Y.C, Rice, A.: Characterizing and modeling the impact of wireless signal. In: ACM SIGMETRICS International Conference on Measurement and Modeling of Computer Systems, New York, NY, USA, pp. 29–40. ACM (2013)
5. Yu, X., et al.: Modeling energy consumption of data. IEEE Trans. Mob. Comput. 13(8), 1760–1773 (2014)

6. Lufei, H.: e-QoS: energy-aware QoS for application sessions across multiple protocol domains in mobile computing. In: Proceedings of the 3rd International Conference on Quality of Service in Heterogeneous Wired/Wireless Networks, Detroit, MI. ACM (2006)
7. Sharafeddine, S., Maddah, R.: A lightweight adaptive compression scheme for energy-efficient. J. Netw. Comput. Appl. 1(34), 52–61 (2010)
8. Jayashree, S., Manoj, B.S., Murthy, C.: On using battery state for medium access control in ad hoc wireless networks. In: Proceedings of the 10th Annual International Conference on Mobile Computing and Networking, pp. 360–373. ACM, USA (2004)
9. Simunic, T.: Power saving techniques for wireless LANs. In: Proceedings of the Design, Automation and Test in Europe Conference and Exhibition, pp. 96–97. IEEE, USA (2005)
10. Balasubramanian, N., Balasubramanian, A., Venkataramani, A.: Energy consumption in mobile phones: a measurement study and implications for network applications. In: Proceedings of the 9th ACM SIGCOMM Conference on Internet Measurement Conference, pp. 280–293. ACM, USA (2009)
11. Pathak, A., Hu, Y.C., Zhang, M.: Where is the energy spent inside my app?: fine grained energy accounting on smartphones with Eprof. In: Proceedings of the 7th ACM European Conference on Computer Systems, pp. 29–42. ACM, USA (2012)
12. Qian, F., Wang, Z., Gerber, A., Mao, Z., Sen, S., Spatscheck, O.: Profiling resource usage for mobile applications: a cross- layer approach. In: Proceedings of the 9th International Conference on Mobile Systems, Applications, and Services, pp. 321–334. ACM, USA (2011)
13. Li, K., Nanya, T., Qu, W.: Energy efficient methods and techniques for mobile computing. In: Third International Conference on semantics, Knowledge and Grid, pp. 212–217. IEEE (2007)
14. Shih, E., Bahl, P., Sinclair, M.J.: Wake on wireless: an event driven energy saving strategy for battery operated devices. In: Proceedings of the 8th Annual International Conference on Mobile Computing and Networking, pp. 160–171. ACM, USA (2002)
15. Zeng, H., Ellis, C.S., Lebeck, A.R., Vahdat, A.: ECOSystem: managing energy as a first class. In: Proceedings of the 10th International Conference on Architectural Support for Programming Languages and Operating Systems, pp. 123–132. ACM, USA (2002)
16. Flinn, J., Satyanarayanan, M.: Energy-aware adaptation for mobile applications. In: 17th ACM Symposium on Operating Systems Principles, pp. 48–63. ACM, USA (1999)
17. Rice, A., Hay, S.: Measuring mobile phone energy consumption for 802.11 wireless. Pervasive Mob. Comput. 6(6), 593–606 (2010)
18. Barr, K.C., Asanović, K.: Energy-aware lossless data compression. ACM Trans. 24(3), 250–291 (2006)
19. Chakrabarti, K., Mehrotra, S.: The hybrid tree: an index structure for high dimensional feature spaces. In: Proceedings of the 15th International Conference on Data Engineering 1999, pp. 440–447 (2009)
20. Shiota, N., Phimmasone, V., Abe, T., Miyatake, M.: A MPPT algorithm based on the binary-search technique with ripples from a converter. In: 2013 International Conference on Electrical Machines and Systems (ICEMS), pp. 1718–1721 (2013)

Secure 5G Network Slicing for Elderly Care

Boning Feng[1(⊠)], Van Thuan Do[1,2], Niels Jacot[2], Bernardo Santos[1],
Bruno Dzogovic[1], Ewout Brandsma[3], and Thanh van Do[1,4]

[1] Oslo Metropolitan University, Pilestredet 35, 0167 Oslo, Norway
{boning.feng,bersan,bruno.dzogovic}@oslomet.no,
vt.do@wolffia.no
[2] Wolffia AS, Haugerudvn. 40, 0673 Oslo, Norway
{vt.do,n.jacot}@wolffia.net
[3] Philips Research, High Tech Campus 34,
5656 AE Eindhoven, The Netherlands
ewout.brandsma@philips.com
[4] Telenor ASA, Snarøyveien 30, 1331 Fornebu, Norway

Abstract. In the time of an ageing world, aging at home is both an economically and socially viable and sustainable solution which may also improve the elderly's well-being. There are currently a few Home-based Elderly Care systems which although operational are not yet optimal in terms of efficiency and security. The paper propose a Home-based Elderly Care solution which makes use of the 5G mobile network slicing with two secure and isolated slices, namely the Health Care slice and the Smart Home slice to provide an inherent secure connection. Further, the solution includes an efficient and secure Emergency Call which ensures that the appropriate caregivers can dispatched and provide help in shorter times. A proof-of-concept implementation is described thoroughly.

Keywords: 5G mobile networks · 5G network slicing · Assisted living ·
Elderly Care · Home based Elderly Care

1 Introduction

Europe and actually the whole world are facing an ageing population [1]. Although there are multiple advantages with an ageing population such as positive contributions to the community through their volunteer services, lower crime rate, familial assistance, etc. an ageing population brings significant challenges like decreased participation rates, increased dependency rates, overload of the healthcare systems, lack of elderly homes, etc. Probably, one of the best solutions to meet these problems is to enable elderly people to live at home as long as possible. Such a solution puts less pressure on the current healthcare systems and is by far more cost efficient than retirement homes while the well-being and happiness of seniors is better preserved. However, to enable aging at home it is essential that elderly people can have a safe, secure and comfortable life at home. For that, it is important to be able to monitor the senior citizen's well-being and to provide appropriate guidance and assistance.

There are currently a few total solutions which provide both monitoring and assistance by combining a variety of technologies like sensor technologies, smart

© Springer Nature Switzerland AG 2019
I. Awan et al. (Eds.): MobiWIS 2019, LNCS 11673, pp. 202–213, 2019.
https://doi.org/10.1007/978-3-030-27192-3_16

home, eHealth, remote surveillance, etc. Unfortunately, they make use of wireless LAN as wireless technology and suffer of disadvantages like poor security, complex configuration, restricted portability, dependent on electricity, etc. To remedy these shortcomings, we propose a Home-based Elderly Care solution which makes use the 5G network slicing concept. More specifically, dedicated logical networks aka network slices will be allocated to the Home-based Elderly Care solution and connect in a secure way all the health sensors and devices, all the caregivers to the Health Care application running on the cloud. The proposed solution will ensure higher level of security and privacy while improving the caregiver's assistance. This paper starts with a brief summary of challenges in Home-based Elderly Care. Next, the state-of-the art and related works on Home-based Elderly Care are comprehensively reviewed. To ease the reading of the paper a brief introduction of the 5G mobile network slicing is included before the main part of the paper, which is the thorough explanation of the proposed solution. Last but not least is the description of the proof-of-concept implementation at the Oslo Metropolitan University's Secure 5G4IoT lab. The paper concludes with some suggestions for future works.

2   Challenges in Home-based Elderly Care

The majority of people want to live at home as long as possible because they will have the feeling of independence, comfort, safety, security, joy and happiness. In addition and quite importantly, by living at home, the seniors will put less pressure on the healthcare system at the same time as the incurred costs are by far lower than the ones at the nursing homes. However, in order to be successful a Home-based Elderly Care solution needs to fulfil the following requirements:

- It shall ensure the security and safety of elderly people
- It shall ensure the privacy and dignity of elderly people
- It shall prioritize the well-being and individuality of elderly people
- It shall be affordable to the majority of elderly people

Although reasonable when taken for itself these requirements might be conflicting with others and make the realization of a good Home-based Elderly Care solution quite challenging. For example, to provide adequate security and safety protection might have negative consequences on privacy and well-being. The prioritization of the well-being and individuality of elderly people may raise the costs and make the Home-based Elderly Care solution not affordable to the majority.

3   State of the Art of Home-based Elderly Care

With the advent of the Internet of Things (IoT) more and more IoT devices have been adopted and used by Home-based Elderly Care solutions [2], which become more and more efficient and trustable. As specified in [3], a Home-based Elderly Care consists of the following components:

- **Vital Signs Monitoring System:** allows the monitoring of vital signs such as heart rate (HR) [5], body temperature (BT), respiration rate (RR) and blood pressure (BP), etc. that are used by the medical professionals to get a good overview about the health of the elderly person.
- **Reminding System:** helps elderly citizens remembering to take their medicines as well as meals at correct time and dosage [5].
- **Automated Activity and Fall Detection System:** is able to distinguish between normal and abnormal activities and to detect a fall in order to trigger an alert, which can again result to an emergency with intervention of caregivers [7].
- **Automated Emergency Call System:** locates, contacts and directs the nearby appropriate caregiver who gives assistance to the elderly person in emergency cases [8].

Figure 1 depicts a typical Home-based Elderly Care solution. All sensors, actuators, devices used by the Home-based Elderly Care components are connected the Health-care center and the caregivers through the Internet. The local connectivity to the Internet is done via a Home Gateway with wired connections or mostly wireless ones using the IEEE 802.1 Wireless Local Network Area (WLAN) family [9].

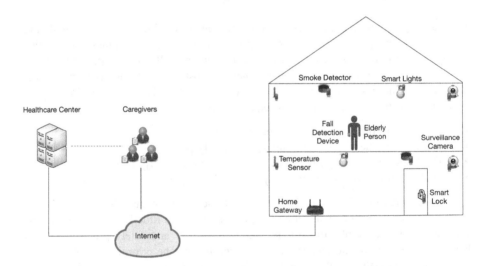

Fig. 1. A typical Home-based Elderly Healthcare solution

Although operational and useful current Home-based Elderly Care systems are subject to severe limitations. First, the connection between the Healthcare Center, caregivers and the Home-based Elderly Care component traversing the open Internet pose serious privacy, security and safety problems that research scientists are struggling to find remedies for [10, 11]. Next, the local connectivity realized by wireless LAN is by default open and hence exposed to malicious attacks. Additional security measures such as encryption and password-based authentication can, of course be used but they will add more complexity in the configuration and management, which is already challenging for non-technical people. Last but not least is the dependency on electricity of Home Gateway and long power outages will paralyze the Home-based Elderly Care system.

There are currently only a few activities aiming at entire Home-based Elderly Care systems [10, 11] but they focus on interoperability, security and privacy and none according to our knowledge, looks for a more secure wireless network or more specifically to make use of 5G network slicing concept in a Home-based Elderly Care as our work described in this paper.

4 Brief Introduction to 5G Network Slicing

The 5th generation mobile network or simply 5G [12] is well known for its superiority compared to 4G in terms of performance, coverage and quality of service and the promise of enhanced mobile broadband (eMBB) with higher data speed and the support of a wide range of services and application ranging from massive machine-type communications (mMTC) to ultra-reliable and low-latency communications (URLLC). Less known but not less important is the fact that 5G is a softwarized and virtualized network. Indeed, a 5G network is not made up of physical network elements as traditional mobile network but of software virtual Network Functions [13].

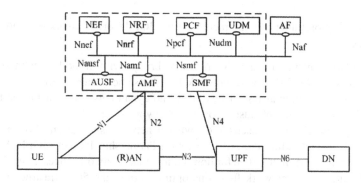

Fig. 2. The 5G Reference Architecture (Courtesy of 3GPP)

As shown in Fig. 2 the 5G Reference Architecture is composed of the following Network Functions:

On the User Plane:

- **UE** (User Equipment): is the user's mobile phone.
- **(R)AN** (Radio Access Network): is the Access Network Function which provides connectivity to the mobile phone.
- **UPF** (User Plane Function): handles the user plane traffic, e.g., traffic routing & forwarding, traffic inspection and usage reporting. It can be deployed in various configurations and locations depending on the service type.

- **DN** (Data Network): represents operator services, Internet access or 3rd party services.

On the Control Plane:

- **AMF** (Access and Mobility Management Function): performs access control, mobility control and transparent proxy for routing SMS (Short Message Service) messages.
- **AUSF** (Authentication Server Function): provides authentication functions.
- **UDM** (Unified Data Management): stores subscriber data and profiles. It has an equivalent role as HSS in 4G but will be used for both fixed and mobile access in 5G core.
- **SMF** (Session Management Function): sets up and manages the PDU session according to network policy.
- **NSSF** (Network Slice Selection Function): selects the *Network Slice Instance* (NSI), determines the allowed *network slice selection assistance information* (NSSAI) and AMF set to serve the UE.
- **NEF** (Network Exposure Function): exposes the services and capabilities provided by the 3GPP network functions.
- **NRF** (NF Repository Function): maintains NF profiles and supports service discovery.
- **PCF** (Policy Control function): provides a policy framework incorporating network slicing, roaming and mobility management and has an equivalent role as PCRF in 4G.
- **AF** (Application Function): interacts with the 3GPP Core Network (CN) to provide services

The software nature of the 5G network brings with it both weaknesses and strengths. Indeed, the 5G mobile network has the same vulnerabilities as any other software at the same time as higher flexibility and dynamicity can be achieved through the logical network segments also known as Network slices.

Currently, there is no consensus on what a network slice is and how it can be realized [14]. In fact, while the 3rd Generation Partnership Project (3GPP) [15] provides a more network-focused definition stating that "network slices may differ for supported features and network functions optimizations" the 5G Infrastructure Public Private Partnership (5G PPP) adopts a business oriented view mandating that "network slice is a composition of adequately configured network functions, network applications, and the underlying cloud infrastructure (physical, virtual or even emulated resources, RAN resources etc.), that are bundled together to meet the requirements of a specific use case, e.g., bandwidth, latency, processing, and resiliency, coupled with a business purpose" [12].

In this paper we use the 5G PPP's definition that allows the support of a variety of devices. To obtain a wireless Home Networking capable of supporting a broad range of devices the 5G network slicing concept is adopted to establish a secure 5G network for Elderly Care.

5 The Proposed 5G Home-based Elderly Care

To improve the elderly people's security and privacy at the same time as to simplify the device management and to reduce the response time of the caregivers we propose to make use of the 5G network to tailor a logical wireless network which as shown in Fig. 3 consists of two network slices:

- **A Healthcare Network slice:** is strictly reserved to the healthcare personnel and caregivers. This network slice is a typical enhanced mobile broadband (eMBB) with high data rates.
- **A SmartHome Network slice**: provides secure connectivity to the elderly home's sensors, actuators and medical devices. This network slice is both massive machine-type communications (mMTC) and ultra-reliable and low-latency communications (URLLC) network slice

Access to these two network slices is granted by the IMSIs (International Mobile Subscriber Identity) hosted in the SIM card carried by the devices. Outsiders are not allowed to access any of these two network slices. By using 5G as wireless technology instead of wireless LAN higher portability and ease of management are achieved since medical devices can be easily moved from one elderly home to the other without the need for re-configuration.

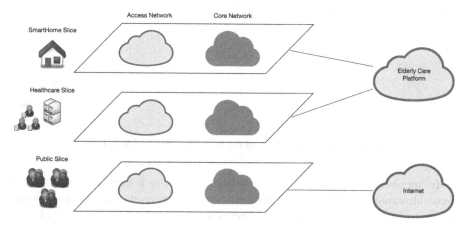

Fig. 3. Network Slicing for Home-based Elderly Care

Another big advantage is the very efficient Emergency Call offered by the proposed solution. Indeed, by providing a dedicated network slice for the Healthcare center and caregivers, it is easier to reach all the actual caregivers in case of emergency by simply broadcasting the alert to the base stations nearby the home of the elderly person in distress.

To demonstrate the security and privacy improvements and the Emergency Call efficiency we propose a 5G Home-based Elderly Care as shown in Fig. 4. All the home sensors, actuators and medical devices are connected to Health Care Center

(HCC) through the Smart Home Network Slice while the caregivers communicate with the HCC using the Health Care Slice. It is worth noting that all the communications happen within dedicated networks without having to go through the open Internet.

The main scenario starts when an elderly person living at home falls. The fall detection will send an alarm to the Health Care which again dispatches appropriate caregivers to help the senior person. Since the focus is on demonstrating the strength of using 5G network slicing the fall detection is not implemented and the fall detection is simulated. To ensure a both flexible and secure physical access to the elderly's home smart locks are installed and connected on the Smart Home Slice to the Health Care Center which can grant access to eligible individuals, e.g. caregivers.

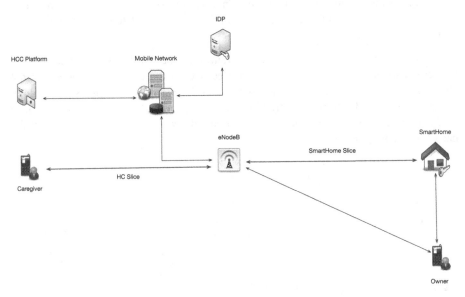

Fig. 4. Overall architecture of the 5G Home-based Elderly Care

To minimize the response time, it is crucial to have a large and wide set of disponible caregivers consisting of different types of caregivers such as professional caregivers, informal caregivers like neighbours, relatives, volunteers, etc. and to locate the available caregivers who are in the vicinity of the elderly home. For that the 5G's ability to broadcast a message to a selected number of base stations gNBs (next Generation eNodeB) will be used. All the available caregivers nearby the elderly home will report themselves to the Health Care Center. The last one will select the most appropriate caregiver according to a variety of criteria such as arrival time, competence, equipment, etc. It will then send a response message to the selected caregiver with the accurate address of the elderly home and necessary instructions to help the senior in need. The caregiver can now proceed to the elderly home, unlock the door, enter and give necessary care to the senior.

It is worth noting that although there can be a large number of authorized caregivers there is only a few selected eligible ones who are granted access to the elderly home and can unlock the door. Security and privacy are ensured at 3 layers. First, only authorized caregiver's mobile phones are allowed to connect to the Health Care network slice and non-authorized persons may not even see the existence of the Health Care (HC) slice. Second, although the Health Care portal is only accessible on the HC slice proper authentication and authorization will still be performed before granting access. As shown in Fig. 4 the authentication is delegated to the Identity Provider (IdP) which may carry out different authentication methods of different strengths such as password, SIM authentication, PKI, etc. Thirdly, only the selected caregivers dispatched for an elderly home can unlock the door.

The sequence of actions upon an elderly fall is as follows:

1. A fall is detected and reported to the Heath Care Center (HCC):
2. The HCC broadcasts an emergency response request to all the caregivers in the vicinity of the elderly home.
3. The available caregivers report themselves to the HCC
4. The HCC selects one or more appropriate caregiver and direct them to the elderly home with necessary instructions.
5. The selected caregivers proceed to the elderly home.
6. Upon arrival at the door the caregivers use their phone camera to take the picture of the QR code[1] and send it back the HCC with a door_open request.
7. The HCC checks the ID of the requesting caregiver and if it matches with the ID of one of the selected caregivers the HCC sends an unlock request to the door.
8. The door unlocks and the caregiver enters the house.

6 Proof-of-Concept Implementation

To provide a network slice for the Home-based Elderly Care, the users associated with the particular resources of the network they can access, have to be isolated from the outside world. Namely, other users from other network slices cannot and should not access the healthcare vertical. If otherwise, then any user in the mobile network can examine the private data of the patients in question.

To prevent illegal access to resources and elderly data the Home-based Elderly Care slice has to be completely isolated from the other slices, especially the public enhanced Mobile Broadband slice for regular smartphones. This means that regular mobile subscribers will be prevented to access the Home-based Elderly Care slice and the resources and services associated to it.

To fulfil the requirement, a specific restricted network policy has to be established in the Cloud Radio Access network aiming at constraining access to specific network resources and allowing only authorised traffic.

---

[1] QR code (abbreviated from Quick Response Code) is the trademark for a type of matrix barcode (or two-dimensional barcode) first designed in 1994 for the automotive industry in Japan.

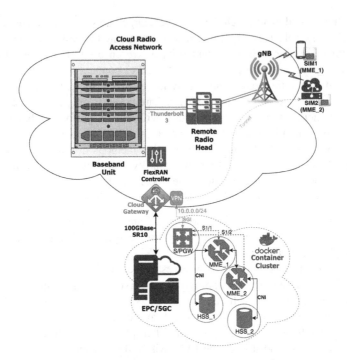

Fig. 5. 5G4IoT Lab Cloud Radio Access Network slicing concept

As shown in Fig. 5, the 5G4IoT lab has established an early 5G network consisting of a Cloud Radio Access Network (C-RAN), connected to a cloudified OpenAirInterface[2] EPC (Evolved Core Network). The infrastructure is deployed using functional split between a Baseband Unit and the Remote Radio Head, with the NGFI (Next Generation Fronthaul Interface). In order to achieve network slicing, the User Equipment with SIM_1 is associated with the Mobility Management Entity MME_1 instance running in the core network, as well as the IoT device with SIM_2 correlated with the MME_2. The both MME instances are virtualized into container environment using the Docker technology. The same applies to the other constituents of the core network, including two instances of HSS (Home Subscriber Server) databases, specifically HSS_1 and HSS_2 related to MME_1 and MME_2 instances correspondingly. The Docker container networking interface (CNI) should thus disallow the two databases to communicate with each other and allow only their corresponding MME instances to perform DIAMETER authentication in their own network domain. By establishing tunnel within a VPN network, the IoT devices with SIM_2 can also securely access their own slice to the SGW (Serving Gateway) and PGW (Packet data

---

[2] The OpenAirInterface Software Alliance (OSA) is a non-profit consortium fostering a community of industrial as well as research contributors for open source software and hardware development for the core network (EPC), access network and user equipment (EUTRAN) of 3GPP cellular networks. https://www.openairinterface.org/.

network Gateway), initiating a route to the corresponding MME_2 with a private network broadcast domain. For the purpose of establishing appropriate routes, the S/PGW are set to create virtual GTP-U (GPRS Tunneling Protocol User data tunneling) tunnels between the virtual interface of the instance to the corresponding virtual interface of the MME_1 and MME_2 subsequently, with different IP domains.

In order to associate an explicit user to the matching database, the FlexRAN controller conjoins the equivalent IMSI values of the device to the ones in the conforming HSS_2 database. This way, the User Equipment (mobile phones) are incapable of reaching the registered devices in the HSS_2 database, since their IMSI values are meticulously canalised into the HSS_1 and their traffic routed explicitly within that route.

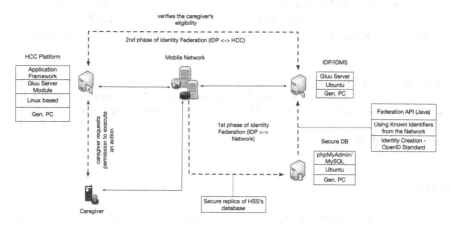

Fig. 6. Implementation of the Identity Management system

Allied to the described network, an identity provisioning and management system (IDMS) [16] has been implemented as shown in Fig. 6, as a way to strengthen as well as simplify the authentication process for users (e.g. caregivers) and devices using the network by offering a single sign-on mechanism across the network and the application layers. More precisely, we inherit existing components from the network that can provide a secure way to identify a device and used it a unified way between layers.

To achieve a consensus on which parameters can be used as identifiers, i.e. identity federation, an API was also developed [17] to bridge between the IDMS and the network. After issuing the identities for the desired caregivers/devices, a module is created and given to the healthcare center, so that when a verification request has to occur, the healthcare center will confirm with the system as if one is eligible to provide support to an elderly person.

This identity management system is created by using an instance of the Gluu Server [18] that provides a combination of the provisioning and management tools, as well the option of deploying OpenID clients for integrations with third-party applications.

7 Conclusion

In this paper we have shown that 5G and its network slicing concept can provide more efficient and secure connectivity to IoT vertical applications such as Home-based Health Care. It is also demonstrated that in addition to the inherent security brought by the isolated nature of the 5G network slice security can be improved further by an Identity Management system, which provides stronger authentication of the caregivers and also paves the way for an efficient and flexible physical access control to the elderly home.

Although the proof-of-concept is working properly only positive testing with use cases as fall detection is carried out. Negative testing must be also performed to ensure that the proposed solution does not carry out actions that are not wanted. The ultimate validation will be a field trial with a limited set of elderly and a number of caregivers in a real 5G mobile network. This trial can be envisaged in the H2020 5G VINNI[3]'s facility pilot in Kongsberg, Norway when it is fully established by the beginning of 2020.

Acknowledgement. This paper is a result of the SCOTT project (www.scott-project.eu) which has received funding from the Electronic Component Systems for European Leadership Joint Undertaking under grant agreement No. 737422. This Joint Undertaking receives support from the EU H2020 research and innovation programme and Austria, Spain, Finland, Ireland, Sweden, Germany, Poland, Portugal, Netherlands, Belgium, Norway.

References

1. United Nations: Department of Economic and Social Affairs, Population Division. World Population Ageing 2017 (ST/ESA/SER.A/408) (2017)
2. Wolf, M. Here's Why Elder Care May be the Next Billion Dollar Technology Opportunity. Forbes. Available online: http://www.forbes.com/sites/michaelwolf/2014/04/24/heres-why-elder-care-may-be-the-nextbillion-dollar-technology-opportunity/#43d7d7f67226. Accessed 11 May 2017
3. Majumder, S., et al.: Smart homes for elderly healthcare—recent advances and research challenges. Sensors **17**(11), 2496 (2017). https://doi.org/10.3390/s17112496. ISSN 1424-8220. PMID 2908812
4. Choudhury, B., Choudhury, T.S., Pramanik, A., Arif, W., Mehedi, J.: Design and implementation of an SMS based home security system. In: Proceedings of the 2015 IEEE International Conference on Electrical, Computer and Communication Technologies (ICECCT), Coimbatore, India, 5–7 March 2015, pp. 1–7 (2015)
5. Park, J.-H., Jang, D.-G., Park, J., Youm, S.-K.: Wearable sensing of in-ear pressure for heart rate monitoring with a piezoelectric sensor. Sensors **15**, 23402–23417 (2015)

---

[3] 5G-VINNI: 5G Verticals INNovation Infrastructure, an European H2020-ICT-2017 research project which aims at accelerating the uptake of 5G in Europe by providing an end-to-end (E2E) facility that validates the performance of new 5G technologies by operating trials of advanced vertical sector services.

6. Zao, J.K., Wang, M.-Y., Tsai, P., Liu, J.W.S.: Smartphone based medicine in-take scheduler, reminder and monitor. In: Proceedings of the 2010 12th IEEE International Conference on e-Health Networking Applications and Services (Healthcom), Lyon, France, 1–3 July 2010, pp. 162–168 (2012)
7. Popescu, M., Li, Y., Skubic, M., Rantz, M.: An acoustic fall detector system that uses sound height information to reduce the false alarm rate. In: Proceedings of the 30th Annual International Conference of the IEEE Engineering in Medicine and Biology Society (EMBS 2008), Vancouver, BC, Canada, 21–24 August 2008, pp. 4628–4631 (2008)
8. Bottazzi, D., Corradi, A., Montanari, R.: Context-aware middleware solutions for anytime and anywhere emergency assistance to elderly people. IEEE Commun. Mag. **44**, 82–90 (2006)
9. Banerji, S., Chowdhury, R.S.: On IEEE 802.11: wireless LAN technology. Int. J. Mob. Netw. Commun. Telematics (IJMNCT) **3**(4) (2013). https://doi.org/10.5121/ijmnct.2013.3405
10. Van Hoof, J., Demiris, G., Wouters, E.J.M.: Handbook of Smart Homes, Health Care and Well-Being. Springer, Basel (2017)
11. Stefanov, D.H., Bien, Z., Bang, W.-C.: The smart house for older persons and persons with physical disabilities: structure, technology arrangements, and perspectives. Neural Syst. Rehabil. Eng. IEEE Trans. **12**, 228–250 (2004)
12. 5G Infrastructure Public Private Partnership (5G PPP): View on 5G Architecture (Version 2.0), 5G PPP Architecture Working Group 18 July 2017
13. ETSI: GS NFV 002 Network Functions Virtualization (NFV), Architectural Framework, v.1.1.1, October 2013
14. Dzogovic, B., Santos, B., Noll, J., Thuan Do, V., T, Feng, B. Van Do, T.: Enabling smart home with 5G network slicing. In: Proceedings of the 2019 IEEE 4th International Conference on Computer and Communication Systems ICCCS 2019, Singapore, 23–25 February 2019, pp. 543–548 (2019). IEEE Catalog Number CFP19D48-USB Conf. Chair Yang Xiao. ISBN 978-1-7281-1321-0
15. 3rd Generation Partnership Project (3GPP): Technical Specification TS 23.501 V1.3.0 (2017-09) Technical Specification Group Services and System Aspects, System Architecture for the 5G System; Stage 2 (Release 15), September 2017
16. Santos, B., Do, V.T., Feng, B., van Do, T.: Identity federation for cellular Internet of Things. In: Proceedings of the 2018 7th International Conference on Software and Computer Applications - ICSCA 2018, pp. 223–228 (2018)
17. Santos, B., Do, V.T., Feng, B., van Do, T.: Towards a standardized identity federation for Internet of Things in 5G networks. In: 2018 Proceedings of the IEEE SmartWorld 2018, pp. 2082–2088 (2018)
18. Gluu Server. https://www.gluu.org/. Accessed May 2019

Intelligent Mobile Applications

Intelligent Mobile Applications

Towards Efficient and Scalable Machine Learning-Based QoS Traffic Classification in Software-Defined Network

M. Z. Fatimah Audah[1], Tan Saw Chin[1(✉)],
Y. Zulfadzli[2], C. K. Lee[2], and K. Rizaluddin[3]

[1] Faculty of Computing and Informatics, Multimedia University,
Cyberjaya, Malaysia
sctan1@mmu.edu.my
[2] Faculty of Engineering, Multimedia University, Cyberjaya, Malaysia
[3] Telekom Malaysia Research & Development, Cyberjaya, Malaysia

Abstract. Internet Service Provider (ISP) has the responsibility to fulfill the Quality of Service (QoS) of various types of applications. The centralized network controller in Software Defined Networking (SDN) provides the chance to instil intelligence in managing network resources based on QoS requirements. A fined-grained QoS Traffic Engineering can be realized by identifying different traffic flow types and categorizing them according to various application/classes. Previous methods include port-based classification and Deep Packet Inspection (DPI), which have been found non-accurate and highly computational. Thus, machine learning (ML) based traffic classifier has gained much attention from the research community, which can be seen from an increase number of works being published. This paper identifies the issues in ML-based traffic classification (TC) in order to devised the best solution; i.e. the TC framework should be scalable to accommodate network expansion, can accurately identify flows according to their source applications/classes, while maintaining an efficient run-time and memory requirement. Therefore, based on these findings, this work proposed a TC engine comprises of Training and Feature Selection Module and Classifier Model, which is placed at the data plane. The training and feature selection will be done offline and regularly to keep the Classifier Model updated. In the proposed solution, the SDN switch forwards the packets the Classifier Model, which classify the packets with accurate applications and send them to the control plane. Finally, the controller will perform resource and queue management according to the labeled packets and updates the flow tables via the switch. The proposed solution will be the starting point in solving efficiency and scalability issues in SDN-ISP TC.

Keywords: Traffic Classification · Software Defined Networking · Machine Learning

1 Introduction

The biggest challenge for an Internet Service Provider (ISP) is to cope with the Quality of Service (QoS) requirements for increasing number and various types of applications. The term QoS refers to a level of assurance for a network element; e.g. router and

© Springer Nature Switzerland AG 2019
I. Awan et al. (Eds.): MobiWIS 2019, LNCS 11673, pp. 217–229, 2019.
https://doi.org/10.1007/978-3-030-27192-3_17

application, that it's traffic and service requirements can be satisfied [1]. Though the same links might be traversed by traffic of different applications, they will not be of the same priority, bandwidth and latency requirements. For example, video traffic may allow packet drops but requires low latency, which is the opposite of bulk transfer traffic. Voice over Internet Protocol (VoIP) traffic demands little bandwidth but sensitive to time delay. Surveillance video requires low latency and large bandwidth to keep it flowing. Heavy usage of multimedia applications such as video on demand or applications such as voice on IP have created a great challenge for ISP to ensure their subscribers have sufficient bandwidth for QoS provisioning. To accommodate the huge increase of internet traffic, ISPs have to provide more facilities to increase network throughput, especially during peak-hours. However, fluctuation of traffic demand between peak and off-peak period usually left a significant percentage of bandwidth unused [2]. Furthermore, solutions with an objective to offer more capacity will eventually fail as it will be used up by the ever increasing traffic.

Software-Defined Networking (SDN) carries new possibilities to provide intelligence in the network. By splitting the data plane and control plane of a network and communicate using the southbound API; i.e. OpenFlow protocol, more flexible infrastructure can be implemented. Therefore, ISPs can control the network more efficiently to provide the best services for their subscribers. The keystone of SDN is centralized and software-based network's control, allowing clear communication with network resources according to the applications requirements. The forwarding decisions in OpenFlow based network devices can be controlled by the software. Therefore, ISPs can improve traffic flows management with respect to their QoS demands.

In this work, we propose a QoS-aware SDN Internet traffic classification framework based on Machine Learning (ML), to classify traffic flows which can improve resources allocation through efficient traffic management. Besides being highly accurate, using ML-based classifier eliminates the need to examine packet content. In order to allocate resources efficiently, SDN controller need a quick and accurate identification of the network traffic flows. However, currently, SDN are unable to provide a detail and refined flow control [3]. Besides the information in Layer 1, 2, 3 and 4 of the Open Systems Interconnection (OSI) model, OpenFlow does not has access to the application layer information. In addition, flow table is being generated only based on the information derived from Ternary Content Addressable Memory (TCAM). TCAM offers fast lookup, thus is a preferred classification method. However, its drawbacks; i.e. limited memory, excessive power usage and complex conversion of rule ternary, will soon make it unreliable [4].

Internet traffic classification has been rigorously studied by researches, where various approaches have been developed and proposed to address issues imposed by the techniques. Traffic classification of internet traffic offers a fined-grained QoS Traffic Engineering by identifying different traffic flow types and categorizing them according to various application/classes [3]. It is also the answer to network management problems for ISPs and their equipment vendors, where the outcome is a more efficient network resources allocation. By implementing traffic classification techniques in ISP, traffic patterns; i.e. the time and endpoints in which packets being exchange, and classes of applications can be identified [5].

In SDN, by having a centralized controller, decision making process is done solely by the controller, while the switches become programmable simple forwarders. This architecture is a perfect platform for improvements in networking as it is highly manageable, adaptable, flexible and simple. By taking advantage of these properties, traffic flows can be managed based on QoS requirements and existing resources. Unlike conventional best effort network service, which lack traffic control, SDN controller can offer guaranteed applications-specific QoS [6]. However, in order to deliver this, efficient and flexible traffic management, routing and flow scheduling are needed to manage packets of various applications. Some works have explored this issue through flow balancing [7], fair queuing scheme [8] and workload merging scheme [9]. In this paper, we intend to address the problem by proposing an ML-based framework for Internet traffic classification, which then can be applied for traffic management, routing and flow scheduling to satisfy QoS requirements.

The remaining of the paper is organized as follows. Related works on ML-based Traffic Classification is presented in Sect. 2, while Sect. 3 described the Overview of SDN Traffic Classification Framework. The future direction of this research is given in Sect. 4. Finally, the paper concludes in Sect. 4.

2 Related Works

2.1 ML-Based Traffic Classification

Traffic classification (TC) techniques commonly inspects packets' content on the network to identify the types of classes or the source application of the packet. Packets with similar 5-tuple; i.e. protocol, source and destination address, source and destination port, belong to the same flow which its application is being identified. The approach used for traffic classification includes port-based [10], Deep Packet Inspection (DPI) [11–13] and statistical-based [14–27]. Port-based classification is among the earliest techniques and is simple and fast. It uses the ports in the TCP/UDP header to map applications with renowned TCP/UDP port numbers. Unfortunately, this approach is no longer accurate since dynamic port numbers being used for many applications or transported via end-to-end encrypted channels [5]. DPI method examines packet contents to search for data that is application-specific. It identifies traffic flow's application by matching its payload with predefined patterns. Though it can accurately classify flows, it has a few disadvantages [15, 16]. First, this technique assumes that packet contents is visible for inspection, which relates to data privacy. Second, the increasing number of applications not only complicates pattern updates, but impractical. Third, DPI is high in computational cost as more patterns need to be compared with increasing applications. Fourth, maintaining a database containing all applications is costly. Finally, encrypted traffic is impossible to be classified by DPI.

On the other hand, statistical-based method can classify traffic flows without the need of deep inspection of packet contents. This technique assumes that the statistical properties of each traffic at the network layer are similar for applications with the same QoS requirements. Thus, different source applications can be distinguished from one another. By recognizing statistical patterns in the flows' features, such as arrival times of inter-packet, the first few packets' size, IP address, packet length, flows' duration, round trip time and source/destination ports [17], the technique can classify them into groups with similar patterns. Apart from some customized algorithms, many researchers are looking at Machine Learning (ML) techniques as an alternative to DPI. ML based traffic classification is seen as the future as it has much lower computational cost and can recognize encrypted traffic.

Traffic classification with ML technique requires a large number of traffic flows to be collected. The flows' features or attributes are then being used as the input data to train ML algorithm and classify them into predefined traffic classes. Finally, the trained model can be used in real-time to classify unknown traffic flows using the learned rules. This work concentrates on the development of ML classifier to classify internet traffic in SDN. Acquiring the traffic flows and analyzing them can be carried out in the control plane because the controller in SDN is centralized and has the overall network view.

ML based traffic classification can be carried out in different perspective; i.e. application-aware [4, 14, 18–20] and QoS-aware [6, 16, 21–26]. The former objective is to classify traffic flows' applications; i.e. Youtube, Facebook, Spotify, Tumblr, Skype, etc., while the latter is to classify traffic flows' classes; i.e. Audio, Browsing, Chat, Mail, Video, etc. In QoS-aware traffic classification, several applications might have the same QoS requirement, hence falls under the same QoS class. Some argues that classifying the flows based on their classes is more effective because it is almost impossible to identify all applications on the Internet as the number is growing exponentially. Nevertheless, by identifying either the application or classes of a traffic flow, an efficient route can be chosen in order to ensure its QoS is met.

In [24], QoS-aware traffic classifications are proposed using DPI and semi-supervised ML. DPI is used to identify the flows and were tagged with their applications, forming a partially labelled dataset. Then, using this dataset, a classifier is trained and different application flows are sorted accordingly into 4 QoS categories; i.e. Voice, Video, Bulk Transfer and interactive data. The frameworks use DPI to maintain a partially labelled database that is dynamically updated to retrain the classifier. Therefore, it will be able to recognize new applications which is rapidly deployed from time to time. However, maintaining a database in the control plane leads to scalability issue in the future.

In [26], both DPI and ML algorithm are used as the classifier. For every flow, ML will be used first as the classifier and its result will be accepted or rejected based on a threshold. The threshold can be dynamically changed according to classifier's accuracy. DPI will be used to classify the flow if the ML result is rejected. The authors intend to use ML as it is fast, but because DPI accuracy in classifying flows are higher, it is used as a check and balance. However, the threshold which determines the acceptance of ML result might be set too low, which leads to many DPI classifications to be done, hence taking longer time and more computing resources. Similar to [26], both DPI and ML algorithm are used as the classifier in [25]. While [26] will use either DPI or ML as the classifier, [25] uses both. Once an elephant flow is detected, the applications will be identified first by DPI, then classified into classes using Support Vector Machine (SVM). Though the accuracy exceeded 90%, the use of both DPI and ML as classifiers incur high computational cost.

The classification scheme proposed in [6] uses decision tree to classify incoming traffic flows based on features such as port number, order index and packet size. Priority number is assigned for each classes; i.e. Voice: High, Video: Medium and Data: Lowest, which will be used for a queuing model that is designed to manage the waiting time of the packets. An experimental SDN setup consisting of four nodes is then used to test the proposed queuing scheme with respect to FIFO. The delay measured in the proposed scheme is 93% better than FIFO scheme, which does not implement traffic classification. This has proved the significant of traffic classification in traffic flow management. The authors of [19] have shown that the collection of traffic data using OpenFlow protocol can be done with a single OpenFlow switch deployed in hybrid-SDN enterprise network. The classifier used Random Forest, Stochastic Gradient Boosting and Extreme Gradient Boosting to classify the network traffic according to 8 applications; i.e Bittorent, Dropbox, Facebook, HTTP, LinkedIn, Skype, Vimeo and Youtube. Results show that classifiers' accuracy in classifying Vimeo and LinkedIn is only 71% to 76%, compared to other applications which exceed 83%. This might be because these applications are similar to other application in their classes; i.e. Vimeo is similar to Youtube and LinkedIn is similar to Facebook, which has similar statistical patterns.

An application-aware classification framework for mobile applications, called Atlas [18], used crowd sourcing to gather training data from mobile devices. A decision tree is trained and the model is used to classify the top 40 applications on Google with over 94% accuracy. Although the proposed framework is simple and produce reliable ground truth data, the actual implementation is very limited as personal mobile devices need to be accessed in order to collect data from them.

The works in [14] developed a traffic classification framework for an SDN home gateway (HGW). Three classifiers are used to classify encrypted traffic according to applications; i.e. multilayer perceptron (MLP), stacked autoencoder (SAE), and convolutional neural networks (CNN). To provide real-time network management for SDN-HGW, the classification must be carried out at the data plane, with limited CPU power and memory. Though the classifiers' accuracy exceeded 95%, CPU usage is more than 60%, leaving little spare capacity for other programs.

The authors in [20] argues that QoS-aware classifications unable to satisfy QoS requirement of multimedia applications. For example, both Netflix and Livestream generate video streaming, but Netflix has larger streaming buffer than Livestream, thus better adaptability to bandwidth fluctuation. In addition, the same mobile application can generate multiple types of flows, e.g. voice, video and file sharing can be done with Skype. Therefore, a more detailed traffic classification that can identify the applications as well as flow types is needed. The proposed framework first gathers ground-truth training data available from mobile devices. Then, the application name is identified by a decision tree classifier, and finally a k-NN classifier will classify the flow type/class. The accuracy of application identifier is 95.5%, while 98% for classes classifier. Combining both application and QoS-aware classification could be the best method for traffic classification in Internet traffic, as it provides fine-grained classification which can lead to better routing and resources management. Table 1 provides the summary of the works discussed above.

Table 1. ML-based traffic classification in SDN

Ref.	Learning model	Accuracy	Advantages	Shortcomings	TC placement
[23]	Semi-supervised learning	>90%	Only require partially labelled training dataset	Maintaining a database in the control plane leads to scalability issue in the future	Control Plane
[26]	ML model	>85%	DPI is used as check and balance	Long run-time and high computational cost	Control Plane
[25]	Semi-supervised learning	>90%	Identifies the applications and classes in elephant flows	The use of both DPI and ML as classifiers incur high computational cost	Control Plane
[19]	Random Forest	86.4%	Ground-truth data obtained from a hybrid-SDN	Focusing only on TCP traffic	Control Plane
[18]	Decision Tree	94%	Crowd sourced ground-truth data from mobile devices	Classify only 40 most popular applications	Control Plane
[20]	Decision Tree	95.5%	Classified the flows according to applications and classes	The proposed framework assumes that end users' devices can receive command from the controller	Control Plane
	k-NN	>90%			
[14]	Deep Neural Network	>95%	Classified encrypted data	Real-time classification will cause high CPU usage	Data Plane

Based on the works described above, a number of issues have been identified. First, a traffic classification framework should be scalable to accommodate network expansion. In [23], although the use of DPI produces accurate ground-truth training data, maintaining a database of the patterns for every application will result to storage problem on the control plane. Hence, there should be an alternative to DPI for supervised and semi-supervised ML algorithm to run effectively.

Second, traffic classification framework should be able to accurately identify flows according to their source applications/classes. The authors of [21] and [22] have shown that the classification accuracy is highly dependent on the volume and dimension of the training datasets. Pre-processing of the training data, which involves feature selection method and the acceptable number of each application/classes data, will determine the overall accuracy of an algorithm, as well as per applications/classes accuracy.

The authors in [18] have taken advantage of device management software agents on enterprises' employees mobile devices to collect ground-truth data, while [19, 27], have collected data on their network campus over a period of time, while [14, 22] used published datasets to train their model. Therefore, it is essential to obtain a dataset which has a balance number of all applications/classes that we intend to classify, and formulate an effective feature selection method to achieve maximum accuracy.

Finally, the run-time and memory requirement for a proposed algorithm should not cause resource exhaustion. As mentioned above, [26] will take longer time to classify the flows if the threshold is set too low. Meanwhile, though deep learning is more effective in classifying high dimensional data, it consumes lots of computing resources as shown in [14] and [16]. Thus, the proposed method should aim for accuracy without neglecting the amount of computing resources that can be used to run traffic classification without crashing the system.

2.2 SDN Traffic Classification Framework

The works in [3, 6, 18–23, 25] and [4] suggested that, since the controller has a global network view, traffic collection and analysis can be carried out in the control plane. For every new flow, its statistics will be extracted and passed from the data plane to the control plane where its application/class will be identified. However, it has been proven in [28] that the performance of a controller degraded with high rates of new flows; i.e. for 125 new flows per second (NFPS), the CPU controller usage reaches 100%. Note that, the first n packets of each new flow need to be sent to the controller for classification process, causing resource exhaustion of the control plane. In addition, as the network size expands, so as the interconnection with network elements, thus increasing the demands on the controller capacity and efficiency. Therefore, placing the classifier in the control plane might cause the controller to eventually fail in delivering its tasks.

In contrast, the works in [14, 16] and [28] locates TC engine in the data plane. Both [16] and [14] used deep learning as their classifier, while [28] does not used ML-based classifier. The accuracy of deep learning is highly dependent on the volume and dimension of the training data. Its potential will be affected if the sampling data are subjected to bandwidth constraints. In SDN, even though packets sampling can be done by the controller, a large amount of sampled data will occupy the limited bandwidth, which might lead to communication problem between controller and the switches. Therefore, the authors in [16] have proposed to use Virtualized Network Function (VNF) to deploy TC using Deep Neural Network (DNN). The VNF runs in virtual machines on top of the hardware infrastructure of the data plane. For data sampling, packets can be forwarded to the VNF without interrupting the control channel. Meanwhile, once packets have been identified by the DNN model, it will be sent to the controller for flow table updates. The benefits of having a VNF to run TC is that the network functions will not be affected if the VNF crashes. However, there is no evaluation on the memory requirement and the run-time of the classifier on the VNF. Hence, no further conclusion can be made on the network performance.

On the other hand, in [14], the deep learning training and model updates are being carried out in the application plane, which has more computing resources than the data plane. Though the authors do not specify the source and procedure of data sampling, decoupling this from the data plane increases the network scalability. In this work, the computational performance analysis for running deep learning classifiers have been reported. The CPU usage of classifying 150,000 packets are between 7%–9% for SAE, 19%–22% for MLP and 58%–65% for CNN classifier. Therefore, it can be concluded that the choice of ML classifier is relatively important towards the scalability of the whole network.

The authors of [28] has prototyped an SDN TC architecture on OpenFlow1.3 in the data plane and have shown improvements on network's performance and scalability. A device called Data Plane Auxiliary Engine (DPAE) has been introduced as a network element to offload TC workload from control plane to data plane. Upon flow classification, relevant information will be sent to controller via a new protocol, namely DPAE to Controller communications (D-CPI). D-CPI is proposed to automate the configuration of DPAE and communicate TC results with the controller. However, note that the classifier used is not ML-based and the accuracy has not been discussed. Two classifiers have been implemented, namely Link Layer Discovery Protocol (LLDP) identity classification and statistical classification. The LLDP identity can be identified by matching against LLDP features defined as a regular expression or using Python's in operator. Meanwhile, the statistical classifier is to match the packets as a flow according to their TCP port numbers and IP addresses. The proposed architecture resulted to a linear increase of DPAE CPU usage and recorded only 50% of CPU usage against 500 NFPS. This has significantly improved over their earlier findings with TC located at the control plane; i.e. 100% CPU usage for 125 NFPS. Therefore, it can be concluded that placing the TC engine on the data plane has higher chance of having a scalable network architecture.

To the best of our knowledge, there is no study that has carried out an experimental evaluation on the scalability of ML-based TC in SDN. However, based on the works of [14, 16] and [28], we can conclude that both the types of algorithm and TC engine placement contributes to the performance and scalability of TC in SDN. Therefore, we intend to focus on these properties in proposing the framework of TC solution. In terms of accuracy, the works by other researchers have proven to produce accurate classifier, but only [26] and [14] evaluate the run-time and memory requirement needed to finish the classification task. However, [26] recorded low throughput with low accuracy of ML classifier, making the need to run DPI increases, while [14] consumes lots of computing resources to run deep learning classifier. Therefore, we will focus on the efficiency of the classifier in terms of its run-time and memory requirement without degrading its accuracy.

3   Scalability-Aware SDN Internet ML-Based QoS-Aware Traffic Classification Framework

According to the issues of ML-based TC in SDN that have been highlighted in Sect. 2, this work outlines two objectives to be achieved. First, to propose a traffic classifier model with high classification accuracy, short run-time and less memory requirement. To achieve this, a quality dataset with balance number of applications/classes should be acquired and an effective feature selection method should be devised.

This work will use Naïve Bayes algorithm as it is possible to be trained with a small training dataset without overfitting. The classifier has faster convergence time than discriminative model, such as logistic regression. Since our focus is on the efficiency and accuracy of the classifier, choosing this algorithm will ensure fast and light computing requirement. The model will be evaluated based on how accurate the model's decisions on previously unseen data. Three evaluation metrics will be used; i.e. Accuracy, Recall and Precision. Accuracy is defined as the percentage of correctly classified flows among all flow, while Recall and Precision are measured on per-class basis. Recall is a measure of the model's ability to identify all classes of interest in the dataset, as below:

$$Recall = \frac{Number\ of\ True\ Positive}{Number\ of\ True\ Positive + Number\ of\ False\ Negative} \tag{1}$$

where True Positive is the number of flows correctly labelled as X, while False Negative is the number of flows belong to X but incorrectly labelled as other than X.

On the other hand, Precision is a measure of the model's ability to correctly identify all flows in the dataset. The formula for Precision is given as below:

$$Precision = \frac{Number\ of\ True\ Positive}{Number\ of\ True\ Positive + Number\ of\ False\ Positive} \tag{2}$$

where False Positive is the number of flows incorrectly labelled as X.

To achieve high percentage of these metrics, redundant and irrelevant features should be removed. Dataset with only the most relevant features not only improves model accuracy, but also reduces model complexity, thus requires less computational cost. There are two types of feature selection; i.e. filter and wrapper method. The filter method has lesser computational cost, but the wrapper method, results in higher learning performance [29]. In this work, forward feature selection with Naïve Bayes learner and predictor will be implemented. Subsets of features will be used to train the model and the decision to add or remove a feature is based on their implications on the trained model. The process begins without a feature in the model and adding ones from the original set in each iteration. Subsequently, the features that improves the model performance will be kept in the list and the process stops once the addition of a new feature does not contribute to the model performance. Finally, only the features in the list will be used as inputs to the classifier.

Naïve Bayes classifier with various feature selection technique has been widely used in research works to classify Internet traffic in traditional network architecture.

However, apart from [15], to the best of our knowledge, there is no other works using this type of classifier in SDN architecture. The work in [15] proposed a classifier based on a modified Naïve Bayes, where the algorithm drops the assumption of attributes' independence. The accuracy of the algorithm is first compared to Naïve Bayes' accuracy which recorded slight difference; i.e. 98.8% for the proposed algorithm and 85.25% for Naïve Bayes. The authors then applied feature selection method on both algorithms which resulted to an improved accuracy of Naïve Bayes; i.e. 90.05%, while no improvement seen on their algorithm. The proposed algorithm also has shorter run-time, both before and after feature selection is done, which is crucial in video streaming. It is well known that the prediction accuracy of Naïve Bayes algorithm suffers from the existence of irrelevant and redundant features. Hence, a feature selection method must be devised to improve the learning performance. However, the method used in [15] was only based on filter method, which depends on the features' scores in several statistical test, without involving any learning algorithm. Realizing the importance of feature selection method, we suggest wrapper methods based on greedy search algorithm, where Naïve Bayes performance will be evaluated for every possible combinations of features. This method tends to find the best features that match the learning algorithm; i.e. Naïve Bayes, resulted to improved learning performance. Furthermore, the works in [15] focused only on classifying video streaming traffic; i.e. NetFlix and YouTube which is far than enough looking at the continuous increment of the number of internet applications. Furthermore, though the run-time has been compared to Naïve Bayes, the memory requirement of the classifier has not been evaluated, which is important to ensure scalable solution. In [15], only 11 features used in the classification, while in our work, more features will be included in the dataset and the importance of each feature will be evaluated by the forward feature selection technique. By doing this, the application types can be narrowed down which can further contribute to network resource management.

The second objective is to propose a scalable TC framework that can accommodate network expansion. Based on the studies in [28], it is evident that the TC engine should be placed in the data plane to avoid performance degradation of the controller. The high-level TC framework is shown in Fig. 1. The whole TC engine will be placed in the data plane, where Feature selection and classifier training is done offline and regularly to update Classifier Model, which runs online. By having the TC engine placed in the data plane, the possibility of overloading control plane's resources can be avoided. Looking at the current network expansion rate, the demands on the controller capacity and efficiency rapidly increases, which can cause controller failure. In our proposed solution, instead of sending the packets directly to the control plane, the switch forwards the packets through the transport network; e.g. Ethernet, to the Classifier Model. Once a packet has been identified, it will be labelled with certain application/class and sent to the controller, which is made possible with the programmability property of the SDN switches. In the control plane, the controller performs resource and queue management according to the labelled packets and updates the flow tables via the switch.

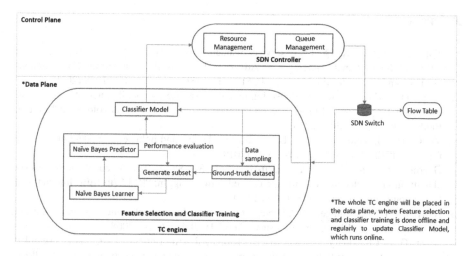

Fig. 1. The proposed software framework of Naïve Bayes Traffic Classification in SDN-ISP

4 Conclusion

SDN architecture has a promising future for a guaranteed application-specific QoS. Unlike conventional best effort network services, SDN improves traffic engineering by taking over the control of the entire network through a centralized controller. However, to realize this, the controller needs a quick and accurate identification of the network traffic flows to enhance traffic routing, resource management and flow scheduling. Current practice in traffic classification requires packet inspection which is not feasible due to privacy issues as well as high power and memory consumption. On the other hand, statistical-based method, particularly ML-based can be trained to formulate accurate traffic classifiers by recognizing statistical patterns in the flows. This work has pointed out the gaps in the previous works on SDN traffic classification; i.e. efficient and scalable TC engine. Hence, an ML-based QoS-aware Internet traffic classification should be devised to equip service providers with enhanced traffic engineering. Realizing the issues, this work proposes a Naïve Bayes traffic classifier which is part of the TC engine placed at the data plane. The proposed solution will be the starting point in solving efficiency and scalable issue in SDN-ISP TC.

Acknowledgments. This research work is fully supported by the research grant of TM R&D and Multimedia. University, Cyberjaya, Malaysia. We are very thankful to the team of TM R&D and Multimedia University for providing the support to our research studies.

References

1. Nina, K., Anastasia, K.: Quality of services evaluation method in next generation networks. In: 2018 14th International Conference on Advanced Trends in Radioelecrtronics, Telecommunications and Computer Engineering (TCSET), Lviv-Slavske, pp. 1055–1058 (2018)
2. Budiman, E., Wicaksono, O.: Measuring quality of service for mobile internet services. In: 2016 2nd International Conference on Science in Information Technology (ICSITech), Balikpapan, pp. 300–305 (2016)
3. Yu, C., Lan, J., Guo, Z., Hu, Y., Baker, T.: An adaptive and lightweight update mechanism for SDN. IEEE Access **7**, 12914–12927 (2019)
4. Guerra Perez, K., Yang, X., Scott-Hayward, S., Sezer, S.: A configurable packet classification architecture for software-defined networking. In: 2014 27th IEEE International System-on-Chip Conference (SOCC) (2014)
5. Nguyen, T.T.T., Armitage, G.: A survey of techniques for internet traffic classification using machine learning. IEEE Commun. Surv. Tutorials **10**(4), 56–76 (2008)
6. Aujla, G.S., Chaudhary, R., Kumar, N., Kumar, R., Rodrigues, J.J.P.C.: An ensembled scheme for QoS-aware traffic flow management in software defined networks. In: 2018 IEEE International Conference on Communications (ICC), Kansas City, MO, pp. 1–7 (2018)
7. Sood, K., Yu, S., Xiang, Y., Cheng, H.: A general QoS aware flow-balancing and resource management scheme in distributed software-defined networks. IEEE Access **4**, 7176–7185 (2016)
8. Vasiliadis, D., Rizos, G., Vassilakis, C.: Class-based weighted fair queuing scheduling on dual-priority delta networks. J. Comput. Netw. Commun. **27**(5), 435–457 (2012)
9. Tajiki, M.M., Akbari, B., Shojafar, M., Mokari, N.: Joint QoS and congestion control based on traffic prediction in SDN. Appl. Sci. **7**(12), 1265 (2017)
10. Madhukar, A., Williamson, C.: A longitudinal study of P2P traffic classification. In: Proceedings of the 14th IEEE International Symposium on the Modeling, Analysis, Simulation, pp. 179–188, September 2006
11. Jeong, S., Lee, D., Choi, J., Li, J., Hong, J.W.: Application-aware traffic management for OpenFlow networks. In: 2016 18th Asia-Pacific Network Operations and Management Symposium (APNOMS), Kanazawa, pp. 1–5 (2016)
12. Sanvito, D., Moro, D., Capone, A.: Towards traffic classification offloading to stateful SDN data planes. In: 2017 IEEE Conference on Network Softwarization (NetSoft), Bologna, pp. 1–4 (2017)
13. Lee, S., Park, J., Yoon, S., Kim, M.: High performance payload signature-based Internet traffic classification system. In: 2015 17th Asia-Pacific Network Operations and Management Symposium (APNOMS), Busan, pp. 491–494 (2015)
14. Wang, P., Ye, F., Chen, X., Qian, Y.: Datanet: deep learning based encrypted network traffic classification in SDN home gateway. IEEE Access **6**, 55380–55391 (2018)
15. Dias, K.L., Pongelupe, M.A., Caminhas, W.M., de Errico, L.: An innovative approach for real-time network traffic classification. Comput. Netw. **158**, 143–157 (2019). https://doi.org/10.1016/j.comnet.2019.04.004
16. Xu, J., Wang, J., Qi, Q., Sun, H., He, B.: Deep neural networks for application awareness in SDN-based network. In: 2018 IEEE 28th International Workshop on Machine Learning for Signal Processing (MLSP), Aalborg, pp. 1–6 (2018)
17. Ibrahim, H.A.H., Aqeel Al Zuobi, O.R., Al-Namari, M.A., MohamedAli, G., Abdalla, A.A.A.: Internet traffic classification using machine learning approach: datasets validation issues. In: 2016 Conference of Basic Sciences and Engineering Studies (SGCAC), Khartoum, pp. 158–166 (2016)

18. Qazi, Z.A., Lee, J., Jin, T., Bellala, G., Arndt, M., Noubir, G.: Application-awareness in SDN. In: Proceedings of the ACM SIGCOMM 2013, Hong Kong, China, pp. 487–488 (2013)
19. Amaral, P., Dinis, J., Pinto, P., Bernardo, L., Tavares, J., Mamede, H.S.: Machine learning in software defined networks: data collection and traffic classification. In: Proceedings of the IEEE ICNP 2016, Singapore, November 2016, pp. 1–5 (2016)
20. Uddin, M., Nadeem, T., TrafficVision: a case for pushing software defined networks to wireless edges. In: Proceedings of the IEEE MASS 2016, Brasilia, Brazil, October 2016, pp. 37–46 (2016)
21. Lashkari, A.H., Draper Gil, G., Mamun, M., Ghorbani, A.: Characterization of tor traffic using time based features. In: Proceedings of the 3rd International Conference on Information Systems Security and Privacy, ICISSP, vol. 1, pp. 253–262 (2017). ISBN 978-989-758-209-7
22. Fan, Z., Liu, R.: Investigation of machine learning based network traffic classification. In: 2017 International Symposium on Wireless Communication Systems (ISWCS), Bologna, pp. 1–6 (2017)
23. Yu, C., Lan, J., Xie, J., Hu, Y.: QoS-aware traffic classification architecture using machine learning and deep packet inspection in SDNs. Proc. Comput. Sci. 131, 1209–1216 (2018)
24. Yu, C., Lan, J., Guo, Z., Hu, Y., Baker, T.: QoS-aware traffic mechanism for SDN. IEEE Access 7, 12914–12927 (2019)
25. Wang, P., Lin, S.C., Luo, M.: A framework for QoS-aware traffic classification using semi-supervised machine learning in SDNs. In: Proceedings of the IEEE SCC 2016, San Francisco, CA, USA, June 2016, pp. 760–765 (2016)
26. Li, Y., Li, J.: MultiClassifier: a combination of DPI and ML for application-layer classification in SDN. In: The 2014 2nd International Conference on Systems and Informatics (ICSAI 2014), Shanghai, pp. 682–686 (2014)
27. Lashkari, A.H., Draper-Gil, G., Mamun, M.S.I., Ghorbani, A.A.: Characterization of encrypted and VPN traffic using time-related features. In: Proceedings of the International Conference on Information Systems Security and Privacy (ICISSP), pp. 407–414, February 2016
28. Hayes, M., Ng, B., Pekar, A., Seah, W.K.G.: Scalable architecture for SDN traffic classification. IEEE Syst. J. 12(4), 3203–3214 (2018)
29. Tsamardinos, I., Borboudakis, G., Katsogridakis, P., et al.: A greedy feature selection algorithm for big data of high dimensionality. Mach. Learn. 108, 149 (2019). https://doi.org/10.1007/s10994-018-5748-7

An Expert System Approach for the Diagnosis and Rectification of Yarn Faults

Dawit Teklu Weldeslasie[1], Gebremariam Mesfin[1,2(✉)],
Tor-Morten Gronli[3], Muhammad Younas[4], and Gheorghita Ghinea[2]

[1] Aksum University, Tigray, Ethiopia
dawit.tekulu@gmail.com
[2] Brunel University, London, UK
{gebremariam.assres,george.ghinea}@brunel.ac.uk
[3] Westerdals Oslo ACT, Oslo, Norway
Tor-Morten.Gronli@kristiania.no
[4] Oxford Brookes University, Oxford, UK
m.younas@brookes.ac.uk

Abstract. Previous research indicate that expert system has been in use for automating operations in the textile and garment industry. However, its application on yarn faults diagnosis and rectification is inadequately explored which left the troubleshooting of yarn faults operated manually by human experts. This paper aims to explore the implementation of expert system for diagnosis and rectification of yarn faults. Accordingly, experts were interviewed at textile and garment factories, and a model of the domain knowledge is developed using decision tree. Moreover, a prototype system of the knowledge base of yarn faults is developed and evaluated. Results showed that the overall performance of the prototype system is generally higher than the results in previous expert system research, and introducing multi-lingual facility and performing small scale prototyping in expert system is a promising approach for yarn fault diagnosis and rectification.

Keywords: Diagnosis · Rectification · Yarn faults · Textile ·
Garment industry · Expert system · Performance · Domain knowledge

1 Introduction

Yarn constitutes a long interconnected fiber used in the production of textile and garment industries. The manufacturing of yarn, however, introduces yarn faults (defects) in various characteristics [7, 10, 18]. Yisihak et al. [8] also presents that the textile and garment industries in Ethiopia faces such defects during the spinning processes of yarns.

Yarn faults directly affect quality of the textile/garment during the yarn manufacturing thereby it decreases profit margin of each product. Although, the use of appropriate diagnostic and rectification method can reduce faults, the insufficiency of availability of human experts in textile and garment is a challenge [8].

© Springer Nature Switzerland AG 2019
I. Awan et al. (Eds.): MobiWIS 2019, LNCS 11673, pp. 230–242, 2019.
https://doi.org/10.1007/978-3-030-27192-3_18

In the context of Ethiopia, the textile and garment industry has been recognized as the second priority economic sector [6]. Nevertheless, the industry lacks international competitiveness the and low performance owing to the lack of trained manpower [4, 8, 9]. Thus, it is characterized by considerable shortcomings in production channel such as the manifestations of several defects during the spinning of yarns [3].

In a production line, defects are transferable. That is, each decision made in later stages in the production depends on the combination of decisions made in the preceding stages [19]. Moreover, a satisfactory diagnosis and rectification entails experience, complete understanding on the processing stages, interaction between process variables and the structural features determining properties of the material, as well as problem solving skills. Accordingly, the process is expertise and time demanding which makes it expensive to diagnose and rectify yarn faults. However, previous research such as in [20] showed that automating the knowledge base in the context of expert systems can actually take the place of the human expertise.

The basic idea behind expert system is that the expertise, which is the vast body of task specific knowledge, can be transferred from human to computer. That is, the knowledge of a typical expert can be stored inside the computer which users can call upon the computer for specific advice, help, diagnosis and rectification as required [21]. Therefore, the expert system can be used to help inexperienced workers to attain a level of performance closer to that of a domain expert.

The potential of expert systems for providing expertise advice which can leverage for the efficient diagnosis and rectification process is also evident for the textile and garment industries in Ethiopia. However, the process of troubleshooting yarn faults has been traditionally carried out by human experts and the use of computerized systems exhibiting expert system is not practiced yet. Therefore, our paper concentrates on the possibility of applying expert system in the textile and garment industry in Ethiopia so as to address the challenges associated with lack of competitiveness more effectively and economically [22].

The paper is organized as follows. Related work is presented in Sect. 2; and research methodology, system prototype and evaluation are provided in Sects. 3, 4 and 5, respectively. Finally, Sect. 6 provides the conclusion.

2   Related Work

Literature shows that the diagnosis of yarn fault through expert system has received considerable attention in the textile and garment industry where a few attempts have been made to automate the process. For example, Song [12] describes a prototype expert system for yarn spinning process planning for the textile industry. However, the authors have neither evaluated performance of the prototype system nor included the concept of yarn faults.

Hussain and Shamey [13] have also designed and developed an expert system for diagnosing the defects during cotton dyeing. The performance of the system has been tested and evaluated by human experts resulting in 80% accuracy. As the authors did not show the optimal alternative for representing the human expert, it still requires further improvement so that an effective approach can be drawn from the analysis of multiple experts' opinion responses.

Another attempt for yarn fault diagnosis is the hybrid expert system architecture provided in [10]. However, the study was not based on the development and evaluation of a prototype system and lacks in sensing the real environment of textile and garment industry. Moreover, although further research to develop a prototype system for yarn faults diagnosis is indicated, the authors did not address the concept of yarn faults rectification procedures and the proposed architecture lacks to integrate local language.

Overall, our review in [10, 12, 13] indicate that the global research attempts relating to expert systems and yarn faults has a potential to encourage the textile and garment industry towards implementing expert systems. Predominantly, it shows a research gap in integrating expert system for diagnosis and rectification of yarn faults.

In Ethiopia, the textile and garment industry is characterized by considerable shortcomings in production lines. According to Amare [3], the major shortcomings in the supply chain are the yarn faults found during the spinning (see Fig. 1). Therefore, in context of Ethiopia, yarn fault diagnosis and rectification is a potential intervention area where expert system can play significant role in automating the spinning processes.

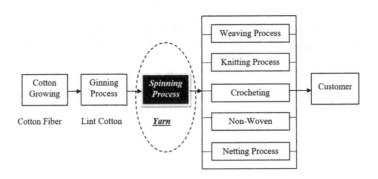

Fig. 1. Supply chain of textile and garment industries [3]

Similar expert system based research has been conducted on other domains (in the context of Ethiopia) with the aim to incorporate reasoning and providing solutions for certain socio economic challenges. For example, there has been research attempts to address the challenges relating to information technology and health with the help of expert system [14–17] as presented in Table 1. Each of the studies have employed similar research methodology- survey of the literature, data collection using purposive sampling, implementation of production rules and evaluation.

Table 1. Summary of related work on expert system research

Author	Title	Sector	Language support	Prototype performance
Tagel [14]	Knowledge based system for pre-medical triage treatment at Adama University Asella hospital	Health	English	82.71%
Solomon [15]	A self-learning knowledge based system for diagnosis and treatment of diabetes	Health	English	84.2%
Amanuel [16]	Developing an expert system for computer and network troubleshooting	ICT	English	79.25%
Adane [17]	Localized Knowledge based System for Human Disease Diagnosis	Health	Amharic	81.50%

However, to the best of our knowledge, the yarn faults diagnosis and rectification did not get emphasis yet, and most of the studies conducted are implemented in English language. Moreover, the existing research (in the context of Ethiopia) have limitation in applying reputable research methodology (e.g., like design science) which would encourage to apply performance evaluation of the prototype systems for further improvement.

In general, our review of the related literature indicated research gap in that (1) the application of expert system in the diagnosis and rectification of yarn faults is not much explored, and (2) its implementation in textile and garment industry in the context of Ethiopia (e.g., language and environment) has paramount importance. Accordingly, the rest of the paper presents about this research problem.

3   Methodology

This study is performed based on the principles described in design science research methodology. Hence, adaptation of the design science research into our research context, and the research procedure, instrument/software, and demography of participants employed are presented next.

3.1   Research Framework

Our research framework is adapted from the design science method which involves the application, testing, modification and extension of existing theories through experience, creativity, intuition, and problem solving skill (see Fig. 2). In Fig. 2, the research environment for yarn manufacturing is composed of employees, textile and garment industries, and their existing technologies. The constructed artifact, embodies the knowledge base concerning the diagnosis and rectification of yarn faults.

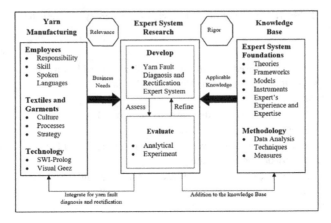

Fig. 2. An adapted design science research framework [2]

Accordingly, a prototype system was developed for the purpose of providing a deeper insight into the context of the problem in which the developed artifact itself is used as a research object. In our prototype, production rule is used to generate instruction for the diagnosis and rectification of yarn faults.

3.2 Procedure

In this study, we have applied the following procedure which is developed based on the guiding principles in the design science research [2].

- Firstly, literature review was performed focusing on setting up the motivational aspects relating to the study domain. Accordingly, we have identified major challenge in yarn fault in the textile and garment industries where the lack of domain expertise (in Tigrai-Ethiopia) can be complemented with expert systems.
- Next, a survey of existing knowledge base in expert systems is performed from primary as well as secondary sources. Current theories, frameworks, models, tools, and domain expertise are identified through survey of the literature, questionnaires, expert's interviews, and physical observation.
- Then, a prototype expert system for the diagnosis and rectification of yarn faults is designed and developed.
- An evaluation of the prototype system is performed concentrating on the degree with which the artifact can address the requirements for the diagnosis and rectification of yarn faults. The develop/evaluate loop continues until a satisfactory condition is fulfilled.
- Finally, the findings are communicated to the public through this paper.

3.3   Instruments and Software

SWI-Prolog [11] and Visual Geez font are used to develop the prototype system and both provide multilingual support (for English, Amharic and Tigrigna). These software enable end-users to communicate with the prototype system easily in local languages.

Table 2. User acceptance evaluation questionnaire

No	Question description
1	How do you rate the simplicity and interactivity of the prototype system in your native language?
2	How do you rate the ability of the prototype system in explaining yarn faults?
3	How do you found the helpfulness of the prototype system in remembering previously encountered faults?
4	How do you rate the speed or time saving of the prototype system?
5	How do you measure the accuracy of the prototype system in diagnosing and rectifying yarn faults?
6	How do you rate the training utility of the prototype system?
7	How do you rate the completeness of yarn fault knowledge in the prototype system?
8	How do you rate the contribution of the prototype system for yarn fault diagnosis and rectification?

A questionnaire with 5-point Likert scale is employed as a data collection instrument from the end users (see Table 2). The corresponding attribute (value) pairs are the following- Excellent (5), Very Good (4), Good (3), Fair (2), and Poor (1).

3.4   Participants

A total of 10 (8 male and 2 female) domain experts who are involved in the yarn manufacturing of a spinning section at ALTEX and MAA Garment factories were randomly selected to participate in the system acceptance evaluation. The participants' profiles were a mix of various job titles (operators, technicians, and managers), education level (diploma, bachelor degree, and master degree), work experience (1–12 years), and speak Tigrigna, Amharic and English languages. Similar to the study in [1], we used both purposive sampling and single population proportion formula to determine our sample.

Each of the 10 domain experts have sufficiently tried the prototype system and they were asked to respond (give their opinion score) to the questionnaire in Table 2. Additionally, 3 domain experts were purposively selected from ALTEX and evaluated the performance of the prototype system using 17 test cases relating to yarn faults. The evaluators have categorized the cases into 6 classes of faults, namely, "class A", "class B", "class C", "class D", variable length and packing.

4 The Prototype System

4.1 Conceptual Modeling

The expert system foundations is one critical component of the adapted (design science) research framework in Fig. 2. Thus, we used the following expert system techniques for the diagnosis and rectification of yarn faults as part of this component.

Manual inspection is a loop-based technique which involves inspection, early defect detection, reporting to personnel, determining causes, and correcting the defects. For a manual inspection to be effective, the entire inspection loop must be completed [7]. This scenario is also used to specify the requirements of prototype system.

Decision tree structure is another technique which is used to model the process of yarn fault diagnosis and rectification. It provides a procedural and shows the levels of decisions that a domain expert uses during diagnosis and rectification of yarn faults. The required knowledge was extracted from domain experts and secondary sources [10] for building a tree consisting of 20 class labels.

We have also used forward chaining (as opposed to backward chaining) as an inference technique. The forward chaining is selected because it is simple, interactive, and suitable for problems driven by primary data. Figure 3 shows a model of the inference engine for the prototype system which works in a cycle.

The cycle begins the inference by launching the "main.pl" prolog program using the known data and proceeds forward; only a topmost rule is executed at a time; when fired, the rule adds a new fact to the knowledge base; but, a rule can be executed only once; Finally, the match-fire cycle stops when the rule got the command "halt" which tells the system that no further rules can be fired.

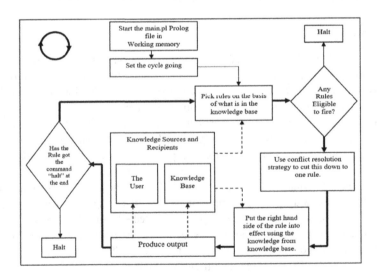

Fig. 3. Forward chaining inference mechanism of the developed prototype

The other technique is the use of learning and memorization component which enables the prototype system to learn and remember from experience (based on the existing data). This component performs the storing and memorization of the knowledge about yarn faults. That is, a user enters his/her name through the user interface; the inference engine finds previous faults from learning and memorization component; next, the user is get remembered his/her previous fault history.

When new fault is detected, the inference engine creates link with learning and memorization component; and then user completes the diagnosis and rectification activity. Finally, the learning and memorization component stores these faults permanently.

Code List 1. A pseudo code of rules for the diagnosis and rectification of yarn faults

```
Rule 1:

IF the fault is occurred at production stage,
          AND the fault has characteristic length,
          AND fault length = ">0 AND <=4 mm",
          AND the diameter of the fault is known,
          AND fault diameter ">1 AND <=5 mm",
          AND local count ">=2 AND <=5 mm".
THEN the fault is NEP,
          AND give image of NEP fault,
          AND give description of NEP fault,
          AND give root cause for NEP fault,
          AND recommend appropriate rectification to solve NEP fault.
... [Up to Rule 20]
```

The last technique which we employed in the prototype system is extraction of rules from decision tree using natural language. These rules represent the knowledge base of instructions for yarn fault diagnosis and rectification. The sample rules in Code List 1 are from class 'A' fault characteristics which is later used in the knowledge-base of the prototype system. Twenty similar rules have been developed for the prototype system constituting the "english.pl" program.

4.2 Implementation

Prototype implementation of the above mentioned expert system techniques for yarn fault diagnosis and rectification is presented next. Figure 4 illustrates architecture of the prototype system showing components and their interactions.

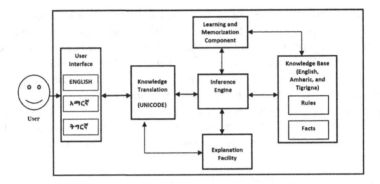

Fig. 4. Architecture of the prototype system

As can be seen in Fig. 4, the inference engine component uses forward chaining technique to accept user data until the premises match the pre-set goal as shown in Fig. 3. It also interacts with the knowledge base component to compose rules and facts for the diagnosis and rectification yarn faults. Sources of the rules and facts include domain expertise, and various documents (e.g., manuals). Similarly, the inference engine interacts with the knowledge translation component to translate English terminologies related to yarn fault diagnosis and rectification into Amharic and Tigrigna.

The learning and memorization component is used for remembering fault history encountered by end users. It interacts with the inference engine to store new knowledge of faults encountered by each user in their respective accounts and when the user wants to leave the system, the component merges with short-term and long-term memory for permanent storage using the "userfacts.pl" program.

When a user makes a request for history, the system acquires all necessary resources from long-term memory and put them into short-term memory. The prototype system learns itself only when a user encounters new faults. The command "assertz(tell (user_facts.pl))" manages the learning process inside the inference engine. Thus, the system requests a user to enter his/her name in Tigrigna language and the user gets reminded about the faults he/she has had previously.

When the user requires clarification the specific fault he/she encountered, the explanation facility interacts with the inference engine to enables to get more help using a "what" command. It also provides "why" and "how" commands which give reasons for the yarn fault incidence and recommend actions for best outcomes respectively.

The user interface component enables the user to interact with the prototype system in the three languages. It provides constraints on the terminology, procedures and concepts that are expressed in English, Amharic and Tigrigna.

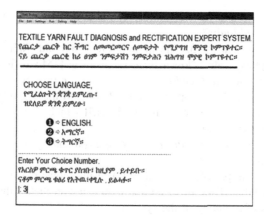

Fig. 5. Screenshot of the user interface output by the main module code

In Fig. 5, a screenshot of user interface is provided. The main module code ("main. pl") loads a user interface for menu window (in English, Amharic and Tigrigna languages). It enables the user to follow the instructions prompted by the prototype system.

5   Results

The study reported in this paper concentrates on the evaluation of a prototype system that diagnose and rectify yarn faults. The evaluation is performed based on end-user and domain expert opinions as presented next.

5.1   System Evaluation

The end-user acceptance evaluation was performed as followes. First the domain experts interacted with the system and then they responded to the questionnaire. The resulting mean opinion scores and percentage performance for each of the respective questions in Table 2 are presented next.

Q1. How do you rate the simplicity and interactivity of the prototype system in your native language?

In the case of Q1, the mean opinion score is **4.7** and the acceptance rate is **94%**. This shows an improvement over the results in [17] which is only **83.2%** in terms of simplicity and understandability of the system. This result is obtained due to the incorporation of multilingual support provided in the prototype system as opposed to the single Amharic interface in [17].

Q2. How do you rate the ability of the prototype system in explaining yarn faults?

The mean opinion score for Q2 is **4.3** and the acceptance rate is **86%**. This shows an improvement comparing with the result in [13] which is **80%**. This is due to the fact that the prototype system has incorporates images of yarn faults in the explanation facility.

Q3. How do you found the helpfulness of the prototype system in remembering previously encountered faults?

The result for Q3 shows **3.9** mean opinion score and **78%** acceptance rate. However, the acceptance rate is lower than the result in [15] which is **96.6%**.

Q4. How do you rate the speed or time saving of the prototype system?

In the case of Q4, the mean opinion score is **4.6** and the acceptance rate is **92%**. This shows an improvement over the results in [15] which is only **90%** in terms of processing speed of the system.

Q5. How do you measure the accuracy of the prototype system in diagnosing and rectifying yarn faults?

The accuracy of the prototype system (Q5) result shows mean opinion score **4.5** and acceptance rate **90%**. This shows an improvement over the results in [13] which is only **84%** in terms of accuracy of the system.

Q6. How do you rate the training utility of the prototype system?

In the case of Q6, the mean opinion score is **4.6** and the acceptance rate is **92%**. This shows an improvement over the results in [13] which is only **90%** in terms of training utility of the system.

Q7. How do you rate the completeness of yarn fault knowledge in the prototype system?

The result for Q3 shows **3.9** mean opinion score and **78%** acceptance rate. However, the acceptance rate is lower than the result in [16] which is **88%**.

Q8. How do you rate the contribution of the prototype system for yarn fault diagnosis and rectification?

The mean opinion score for Q2 is **4.9** and the acceptance rate is **98%**. This shows an improvement comparing with the result in [15] which is **96.6%**. This implies that majority of the evaluators are positive on the overall contribution of the prototype system.

Accordingly, an aggregate mean opinion score **4.425** was obtained and **88.5%** of the respondents rated the prototype system as excellent. Our prototype system showed improvements on 6 quality attributes compared to the results in previous studies. This indicates that majority of the evaluators are positive on the need for integrating expert systems at the industries.

5.2   Evaluation of the Knowledge Base

Among the domain experts, 3 were purposively selected to perform exhaustive evaluation on the prototype system. The task was focused on the use of the test cases to evaluate the performance of the knowledge base component. The domain experts selected 17 test cases relating to yarn faults and each one validated 2 categories of faults of the prototype system by counting its correct and incorrect decisions.

As shown in Table 3, the domain experts have evaluated the prototype system 88.2% correct in diagnosing and rectifying yarn faults. Moreover, most of the evaluators have provided positive overall feedback relating to the performance of the prototype system.

Table 3. Category of faults and performance of the prototype using test cases

No.	Description	Diagnosed faults using prototype			
		Number of cases	Correct	Incorrect	Performance
1	Class 'A' faults	3	2	1	66.7%
2	Class 'B' faults	3	3	0	100%
3	Class 'C' faults	3	2	1	66.7%
4	Class 'D' faults	3	3	0	100%
5	Variable faults	3	3	0	100%
6	Package faults	2	2	0	100%
Total		17	15	2	88.2%

Therefore, the mean evaluation result (acceptance and knowledge base) of the prototype system is 88.4% which encourages for further research to fully integrate expert systems into the diagnoses and rectification of yarn faults. Additionally, as stated by Wielemaker [11], our results on this small scale expert system implementation demonstrates the practicability of using SWI-Prolog for building large scale system.

The implication of this results is that yarn fault which is one of the major defects caused by lack of expertise in textile and garment industries (particularly in Ethiopia) can be complemented by such technological solutions. That is, the expert system offers advice on how to solve the yarn faults (in place of the human experts) whenever there is shortage of expertise in the area. The performance of the prototype is also enhanced compared to previous studies [12–16] which indicates the effectiveness of applying design science research methodology in the development and evaluation of expert system artifacts.

Additionally, providing yarn fault information in native languages by implementing multilingual facility (e.g., English, Amharic and Tigrigna) in user interfaces enables end-users to better understand the diagnosis and rectification process. The prototype system can also serve as on-the-job training utility.

6 Conclusions

The study reported in this paper concentrated on the development and evaluation of an expert system for diagnosing and rectifying yarn faults. Domain experts were selected to evaluate the overall utility of the system and the performance the knowledge base component. Results showed that integrating expert systems into the diagnoses and rectification of yarn faults is a promising endeavor for future large scale implementations. The importance of such technological solutions is evident particularly, in the textile and garment industries in Ethiopia, where the major cause for yarn faults is lack of expertise in the area. Our future research will concentrate on enhancing the performance of the prototype system by incorporating more evaluators, adding local languages, and using new models. Moreover, similar studies will be performed considering the weaving, knitting, crocheting, and netting process of the textile and garment industries.

References

1. Asferi, B.: Exploring pest management practices and development of knowledge base system for pepper disease diagnosis, Dissertation, AAU (2010)
2. Hevner, A.R., March, S.T., Park, J.: Design science in information systems research. MIS Q. **28**(1), 75–105 (2004)
3. Matebu, A.: Model development of quality management system for ethiopian textile industries (2006)
4. Kitaw, D., Matebu, A., Competitiveness for ethiopian textile and garment industries: a way forward (2010)
5. Davis, F.D., Bagozzi, R.P., Warshaw, P.R.: User acceptance of computer technology: a comparison of two theoretical models. Manag. Sci. **35**(8), 982–1003 (1989)
6. Ethiopia TVET Agency: Guideline for Value Chain Development (2014)
7. Kalayu, G.: Identifying defect causes of weft greige knitted fabric: the Case of MAA-Garment & Textiles Factory. Dissertation, Mekelle University (2014)
8. Yisihak, N., Begna, T., Solomon, T.: Technological capibalities of ethiopian textile and garment industries, December 2011
9. Sorri, R.: Performance measurement and improvement of ethiopian garment industries, Dissertation AAU (2010)
10. Dlodlo, N., Hunter, L., Cele, C., Metelerkamp, R., Botha, A.F.: A hybrid expert systems architecture for yarn fault diagnosis. Fibres Text. Eastern Eur. **2**(61), 43–49 (2007)
11. Wielemaker, J., Schrijvers, T., Triska, M., Lager, T.: SWI-Prolog. Theory Pract. Log. Program. **12**(1–2), 67–96 (2012)
12. Song, S.: An expert system for yarn spinning process planning and quality characteristics control in textile industry. J. Korean Soc. Qual. Manag. **20**(1), 147–157 (1992)
13. Hussain, T., Shamey, R.: A knowledge-based expert system for dyeing of cotton, part 2: testing and evaluation. Color. Technol. **121**(2), 59–63 (2005)
14. Aboneh, T.: Knowledge based system for pre-medical triage treatment at Adama University Asella Hospital (2013)
15. Solomon, G.: A self-learning knowledge based system for diagnosis and treatment of diabetes (2013)
16. Amanuel, A.: Developing an expert system for computer and network troubleshooting, Dissertation, AAU (2014)
17. Tarekegn, A.N.: Localized knowledge based system for human disease diagnosis. Int. J. Inf. Technol. Comput. Sci. (IJITCS) **8**(3), 43 (2016)
18. Gupta, N.: Analysis on the defects in yarn manufacturing process & its prevention in textile industry. Int. J. Eng. Inventions **2**(7), 45–67 (2013)
19. Ford, F.N.: Expert system support in the textile industry: end product production planning decisions. Expert Syst. Appl. **9**(2), 237–246 (2000)
20. Akerkar, R., Sajja. P.: Knowledge-Based Systems. Jones & Bartlett Publishers (2010)
21. Kahraman, C., Bozbura, F.T., Kerre, E.E.: Uncertainty modeling in knowledge engineering and decision making (2012)
22. Shamey, R., Shim, W.S., Joines, J.A.: Development and application of expert systems in the textile industry (2009)

Mobile AR Solution for Deaf People

Correlation Between Face Detection and Speech Recognition

Ales Berger[✉], Milan Kostak, and Filip Maly

Faculty of Informatics and Management, University of Hradec Kralove,
Hradec Kralove, Czech Republic
{ales.berger, milan.kostak, filip.maly}@uhk.cz

Abstract. In the last two years, the authors' research has been focused on designing a smart solution to compensate for hearing or visual deficiencies using the Google Glass hardware device and its own software architecture. This paper presents a solution aimed on deaf people or people with hearing impairment. At the beginning of this paper there is a brief explanation of the architecture of the designed solution, a description of the user interface through Google Glass. Related work to face detection, visual activity detection and speech recognition is presented with many possible approaches to these research areas. The principle of the solution lies in the combination of face detection and subsequent assignment of the recognized speech to the mouth of the correct face in the image. The aim of the solution is to digitally capture the ambient sound and based on its evaluation using neural networks, to present detected speech in a text form assigned to detected face from camera stream. The testing has shown that the solution is beneficial, and it is working as expected. Machine Learning Kit provides good results in face detection and communication with Google Cloud Speech API is fast enough for smooth user experience.

Keywords: Google Glass · Augmented reality · Deaf people · Face detection · Speech recognition

1 Introduction

Nowadays, in general, the results of image processing and sound recognition are very good. Systems can distinguish objects, faces, text, tone of voice, and language that a particular person speaks. The authors have been dealing with this topic for three years. It began with the processing of the image in 2016. In 2017, a new branch of research was added where the authors focused on the detection of speech. Functional test prototypes have been developed for both research branches. Both prototypes are still not optimal, but the authors are trying to optimize the solution. Based on initial research, Google Glass (GG) has been selected as the flagship. It is a device that is not common but due to its design is ideal for users with visual or hearing impairment. Research specializes in helping people these impairments.

During the development of separate prototypes for both cases, the authors encountered a correlation in speech detection and face detection. This article focuses on

© Springer Nature Switzerland AG 2019
I. Awan et al. (Eds.): MobiWIS 2019, LNCS 11673, pp. 243–254, 2019.
https://doi.org/10.1007/978-3-030-27192-3_19

this correlation, and the authors want to find out whether facial detection can also involve spoken recognition to link face detection information with speech recognition information.

On this topic, the authors want to implement the extension of the original prototypes and test whether they are at least able to use this added value in practice - to help people with hearing impairment.

2 Problem Definition

Hearing loss is a situation when people cannot detect conversational or loud noises in one or both ears. According to the World Health Organization (WHO) light hearing results when the better ear has a threshold of 25 to 40 decibels (dB), 41–60 dB is moderate impairment, 61–80 dB is heavily damaged hearing and plus 80 dB is totally deaf. Mild to hard hearing damage is referred to as, "hard hearing". People with 'hard hearing' are difficult to talk to which limits the impaired person to use sign language. However, it can be corrected by equipping them with a hearing aid [1].

Nowadays (in 2019) there are approximately 466 million (over 5% of global population) people who are at least partially deaf [2]. Of this proposition, 432 million adults have a hearing loss of over 40 dB while 34 million are children with a hearing loss of over 30 dB. Most of these people live in low and middle-income countries in sub-Saharan Africa, South Asia, and Asia Pacific. A third of the deaf around the world are over 65 years old. Since sign language is not very common among the global population, the authors' solution compensates for the malfunction of the ear using the various functions of GG.

The Deafness in the Czech Republic
In 1992, a report estimated there are three percent of the population (300,000 people) experienced hearing impairment [3]. By 1998 the number rose to 500,000 people (5%) [4] and a follow-up study a decade later put the proportion at 10% (1 million people) [5]. The elderly were the most affected strata of the population.

2.1 Smart Phone Users Worldwide

To the present day, world has embraced the smartphone and the internet to a large degree. Smart solutions are software constructed in a way that they can interact dynamically with a detected signal and produce an appropriate feedback. For the year 2019, the number of mobile phone users was forecasted to reach 4.68 billion. Most of the mobile market growth can be attributed to the increasing popularity of smartphones [6].

The number of mobile phone users in the world is expected to pass the five billion mark by 2019. In 2016, an estimated 62.9% of the population worldwide already owned a mobile phone [7]. The mobile phone penetration is forecasted to continue to grow, rounding up to 67% by 2019. China was predicted to have just over 1.4 billion mobile connections in 2017, while India was forecast to reach over one billion [8]. By 2019, China is expected to reach almost 1.5 billion mobile connections and India almost 1.1 billion.

3   Related Work

Face detection and speech recognition are topics that receive considerable attention among researchers. In the past years, devices did not have enough computational power to perform these operations in real time, but this has all changed. These days even smart phones can do these operations in real time to some extent. This paper mainly focuses on combination of face detection and lip activity detection with speech recognition.

3.1   Face Detection

Face detection is a problem of computer vision that is trying to solve localizing and extracting of a person's face from the image input. This input can be a video file or a real time camera feed. Face detection is used in many everyday applications – from person recognition systems to automatically focusing on a face in a camera. Therefore, many papers have been written on this topic describing several possible approaches to it. Techniques that try to solve face detection problem range from simple edge-based algorithms to complex convolutional neural networks.

Hjelmås and Low [9] present a detailed survey of face detection algorithms. They divide possible methods into two groups – feature based, and image based. Feature based method typically works with feature searching or edge detection. But it has its limitations due to the unpredictability of face appearance. Image based method of detection uses face patterns as examples. These approaches are divided into linear subspace methods, neural networks and statistical approaches.

Li et al. [10] present a modern approach to face detection that includes usage of neural networks that are vastly used for image recognition these days. They propose a convolutional neural network cascade that operates at multiple resolutions. The key is in quick rejecting image regions in the fast low-resolution stage and then evaluate small number of candidates in high-resolution stage.

3.2   Visual Lip Activity Detection

In order to recognize if a person in the image is speaking, lip activity detection must be performed. This allows to assign the recognized speech to the correct person.

Siatras et al. [11] in their paper introduced a solution for lip activity detection using solely information from the input image. Their method is based on variability of intensity values of the mouth region in the image when the person speaks. Open mouth exposes part of the interior of the mouth which is usually darker. And pronunciation of many phenomes involves open mouth and therefore big increase in the number of mouth pixels with low intensity is produced. On the other hand when a person is not speaking then the mouth is closed which leads to very low variability of the intensity values. The authors claim that their solution was successfully tested for simultaneous speech of multiple people.

Other methods try to use only audio information to determine speaker and his location. For example, authors of [12] use microphone array processing to estimate the direction of arrival form audio sources.

3.3   Human Speech Recognition

Speech recognition is a process of translation of spoken language into text. This process as well as face detection can be solved using neural networks. They are usually used in combination with Hidden Markov models (e.g. [13]). Its form called deep recurrent neural network is investigated in [14].

For our application we need to be able to assign the speech to the correct person if there are multiple people speaking in the image. For this purpose, it is necessary to get also the tone of the speech of the speaking person in order to correctly assign it.

Ways of identifying speaking person can be divided into high-level and low-level. High-level include information like dialect, style of speech etc. These are valuable for humans but are harder to recognize automatically. Low-level features include for instance signal amplitudes and voice frequency [15].

3.4   Authors Solution

In 2017 the authors presented a specialized smart solution developed specially to help blind and visually impaired people [16]. This solution was really successful, and in 2018 authors opened a new branch of the research. They used the same hardware and platform, but different sensor: a microphone. Authors presented a prototype solution for deaf and hearing-impaired people [17]. Compared to conventional compensating aids, the developed solution connects modern technologies and originality. The aim of the solution is to digitally capture the ambient sound and based on its evaluation using neural networks present the needed information in a text form to the user. This aim was successfully accomplished, and Google Glass was a well-chosen device for this purpose.

The Google Cloud is the primary storage for the GG devices besides providing a host of other services such as computing and running application developments [18]. One of the most critical services used by GG is the Vision API whose purpose is to interpret the content of an image [19]. To achieve this powerful machine learning models are used to classify the images and to detect objects within the image. The API also integrates the image with Google Cloud storage. The analyzed data is then downloaded to the smartphone which then sends keywords to GG. The GG then plays the sounds in the ear of the blind person to help them navigate their immediate environment such as walking in the open area.

GG employs several technologies to achieve its goal of helping the blind or deaf person to perceive their environment.

4   Solution Design

The solution uses the GG hardware to detect the ambient sounds which are then streamed to the Cloud via an Android smartphone. The response from the Cloud is then pushed (via smartphone) to the GG which then displays the visual feedback.

4.1 Architecture of Prototype

Architecture presented in 2017 and 2018 defines tree parts. Server, Mediator (Android Smartphone) and Client (Google Glass).

Server

From the very beginning of the client-server technology, the server is in charge of computationally demanding tasks, long-term data persistence, or logic storage in one place. The general architecture server is not introduced by a particular hardware computer, but by a set of independent services that can be communicated through a single public interface.

Modern cloud services offer tremendous performance, so it is effective to transfer all the more challenging tasks to this place. Computing performance and data storage are virtually unlimited and affordable thanks to cloud services.

Mediator

The Mediator designation was used due to the position between the client and the server. The mediator has two roles. At one point, the mediator acts as a server and the other as a client. Thanks to the high performance of today's smart mobile phones, it is possible to implement logic in this place of general architecture. In some cases, the mediator can evaluate a request from a client without having to query the server. Part of the application logic can also be placed on an intermediary. At the same time, it is possible to assign the client's behavior to the mediator.

Client

Client (Google Glass) works with camera, microphone and display. In general architecture, the client can be any device that can be interconnected, for example, via Bluetooth with an intermediary. The client's task is to collect and transmit data efficiently. There is no complicated computing power or load. The most important element of this section is the user interface, sensors, and communication with the mediator. The client does not know about the server or other services in this architecture. It refers only to the mediator.

4.2 Google Glass

Google Glass is a smart head-mounted gadget that is coupled with a smartphone for internet connectivity and access to the Android Operating System (Android OS). The connected smartphone also allows for customization of GG. The hardware of GG comprises several components which perform various functions, that is; a camera, display, touchpad (mounted on the right arm), microphone and speaker. These components are all mounted on a pair of glasses which rest on the nose and ears. The display is projected into the right eye through a prism, while the microphone plays sounds into the eardrum. However, its uniqueness lies in the fact that GG allows the user to use android technology without using their hands [20].

Technologies incorporated in the device include Wi-Fi, Bluetooth and Android OS. It is equivalent to a wearable version of a software package offered on a smartphone such as communicating on social media [21] (Fig. 1).

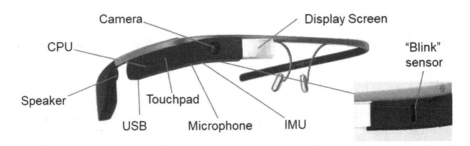

Fig. 1. Google Glass device [22]

The product cycle of GG began in April 2012 when Google proposed a product that incorporated wearable technology into an optical head-mounted display (OHMD). The first generation focused mainly on the use of the camera and was sold for a limited period beginning on 15th of April 2013. The second generation replaced Texas instruments with an Intel processor while the third generation featured a display over both eyes. The latest generation has incorporated more modifications and was the version used by the authors in testing the smart solution (a mobile application) [23]. Google has stopped mass production making it difficult to find in retail shops around the world.

Technology

The Android OS is the software backbone of the GG system as it holds middleware and key applications. The Android OS allows developers to write code in the Java or Kotlin programing language. The Android framework allows GG to access various openwork libraries such as, SQLite and OpenSSL as well as providing access to UNIX security file system permissions. The GG also boasts of Bluetooth and Wi-Fi technologies which allow short-range wireless communication within the 2.4 GHz frequency band. These are the main form connection between the GG and the mobile gadget (Smartphone, Laptop, or Tablet).

The more complex technologies include eye tap, smart grid, and wearable technology. The components of the eye tap device display computer information to the user and allow the computer to process what the user is seeing. The latter components can also alter the observation when it is necessary to create a computer-mediated reality. Therefore, it allows the eye to function as the camera and the display. The wearable computer is strapped or carried on the user's body to ensure the constant connection between the gadget and the computer. It also eases the burden of hardware coded logics by providing process support in close proximity.

Conditions Addressed and Advantages of GG

The GG can be used to mediate health conditions that cause blindness through cognitive disability (inability to focus on large amounts of information, intellectual, and reading) and visual incapacitation. This is achieved through assistive technology (GG) whose products allow the user to actualize vision, dexterity, learning, and communication. The advantages of GG are: ease of wearing and handling, useful for a wide variety of people, quick access to pictures and maps, speedy feedback, can be used with a smartphone, it has a natural command language for communicating to the user.

Projector

The Fig. 2 shows an eye view that will focus on the Google Glass prism display. The extended layer appears to the user at the top right or center of the field of view over right eye. Since the glass prism is semi-transparent, the user can see a sharp layer directly in front of the eyes without moving the device.

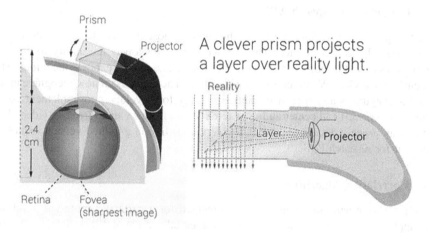

Fig. 2. Clever prism projector [24]

5   Implementation

The development of a mediator and client application was in Android Studio IDE. The programming language used is Java over the Android Operating System. The server part is written in the Go language – this part is only a web interface that makes cloud services more accessible. Communication with the server is via WebSocket protocol. Client and mediator use Bluetooth for communication. The ML Kit Face Detection from the Firebase package is used to detect the face on the mediator. The resulting converted text is then assigned to a face that shows activity signs. These results are projected to the user via Google Glass.

5.1   Face Detection – Machine Learning Kit

Face detection is the process of automatically locating human faces in visual media (digital images or video). A face that is detected is reported at a position with an associated size and orientation. Once a face is detected, it can be searched for landmarks such as the eyes and nose [25]. It is important to define some of used terms.

- **Face tracking** extends face detection to video sequences. Any face appearing in a video can be tracked. Faces that are detected in consecutive video frames can be identified as being the same person.

- **A landmark** is a point of interest within a face. For example, left eye, right eye, and base of the nose. ML Kit provides good ability to find landmarks on a face.
- **A contour** is a set of points that follow the shape of a facial feature.
- **Classification** is determining whether a certain facial characteristic is present. For example, a face can be classified as smiling or not.

5.2   Google Cloud Speech API

Based on previous research experience, the authors chose the Google Cloud Speech-to-Text Speech Detection Service. This service offers developers the ability to convert audio tracks to text through robust neural networks. The service exposes the public API and enables REST or WebSocket communication. The service can now recognize more than 120 languages and speech variants. It is easy for developers to implement voice commands, convert call center audio, or retrieve text from an audio track or video. The service can process data in real time. The service is free in a limited version, which is sufficient for research [26].

5.3   Correlation Algorithm

A simple assignment algorithm was implemented for a particular prototype solution. The application collects information from the cloud service and face detector. In the event that information from both mentioned services is obtained in a similar time, it is assumed that the transcript belongs to the given face. In case the server returns information about the tone of the voice and there are two faces on the screen, the algorithm is able to assign the transcript to the given face and keeps track of the tone of voice for specific instances of the face. Then you simply assign specific text to your face.

6   Testing of Developed Solution

After implementation, testing was performed. Testing was mainly attended by authors and the aim of the testing was to find out if the used technology and the principles really work. If the implemented prototype appears to be beneficial, subsequent optimizations will take place in all parts of the solution.

6.1   Face Detection

Image processing is performed directly on the mobile device. There is no need to communicate with the server. Therefore, the speed of image processing and facial recognition is dependent on the mobile device's performance (Fig. 3).

Fig. 3. Face detection example

6.2 Mouth Activity

The next step is to implement mouth activity detection. Since face detection offers a complete description of the facial contours, including the lips, it is possible to obtain information about the difference in lip position depending on the time. In the event of none or minimal change, mouth activity is inactive. As Fig. 4 shows, the mouth is drawn with the same color as the rest of the face.

Fig. 4. Mouth activity - inactive (Color figure online)

In the latter case, when the points in the image change their distance from each other, the mouth activity is referred to as active and is drawn in a different color. The color indicates how much mouth activity it exhibits (Fig. 5).

Fig. 5. Mouth activity - active (Color figure online)

The figures also show the value written in red. This is a confidence score. This value is very important for every detection and machine recognition. Image recognition systems predict whether a face with an appropriate level of confidence in the prediction is being drawn in the image. Application developers who use these services should consider a limit of reliability (threshold value) in their solutions when the result is still applicable [27]. For example, when designing an application to identify family members, a threshold should be set to return results that have a confidence level of at least 85%. The application will return only those matches that exceed the set value and will return more accurate results than if the confidence level was set lower. The threshold is set individually in each case, some applications require a higher threshold and some lower. In author's solution there is used a threshold of 75%. If the value is lower, the face object is not used anymore.

Data	Length	Time
↑Binary Message (Opcode 2, mask)	10924	21:05:33.244
↑Binary Message (Opcode 2, mask)	10924	21:05:33.337
↓{"text": "Hello.", "isFinal": false}	36	21:05:33.342
↑Binary Message (Opcode 2, mask)	10924	21:05:33.430
↓{"text": "hello", "isFinal": false}	35	21:05:33.473
↓{"text": " my", "isFinal": false}	33	21:05:33.473
↑Binary Message (Opcode 2, mask)	10924	21:05:33.522
↓{"text": "Hello,", "isFinal": false}	36	21:05:33.608
↑Binary Message (Opcode 2, mask)	10924	21:05:33.615
↑Binary Message (Opcode 2, mask)	10924	21:05:33.708
↓{"text": " my name.", "isFinal": false}	39	21:05:33.745
↑Binary Message (Opcode 2, mask)	10924	21:05:33.801
↓{"text": "hello,", "isFinal": false}	36	21:05:33.871
↓{"text": " my name is", "isFinal": false}	41	21:05:33.871
↑Binary Message (Opcode 2, mask)	10924	21:05:33.894
↑Binary Message (Opcode 2, mask)	10924	21:05:33.987
↓{"text": "hello, my", "isFinal": false}	39	21:05:33.997
↓{"text": " name is", "isFinal": false}	38	21:05:33.997
↑Binary Message (Opcode 2, mask)	10924	21:05:34.080

Fig. 6. WebSocket stream – human speech detection

6.3   Human Speech Recognition

This section requires an Internet connection to communicate with the cloud service. Here the prototype is limited by the connection speed. However, the WebSocket protocol used to communicate with Google Cloud Speech-to-Text cloud service can transfer binary data from the microphone very quickly, and in the case of a quiet environment, the user can get the answer in the form of a translated text in tenths of seconds. The figure below shows the speed and principle of communication (Fig. 6).

7   Conclusions

In this paper, the authors describe modern technologies based on neural networks and real-time WebSocket communication. During their research from previous years, they encountered a correlation between face detection and human speech recognition. The paper describes how faces are commonly detected today and what options exist for human speech recognition. The paper also describes a simple and fast algorithm for mouth activity detection. The authors have used the ready-made ML Kit Face Detection solution. This library offers to developers very important facial points. Based on these points, it is possible to recognize the mouth and with the presented algorithm to determine whether the mouth is active or not. Face detection is processed on the mobile device and no internet connection is required. Google's cloud-based solution is used for speech recognition, which is very effective and offers excellent real-time results. The paper also describes how the solution was implemented. Architecture describes each of the three parts. Server, Mediator, and Client. Each part has its own specific role to perform and to achieve the best results. Subsequently, the authors tested implemented solution. Testing proved that the proposed solution is functional and brings the possibility of further development for the help of hearing-impaired people, to whom the whole research is aimed. The chosen technologies are proven and still very usable. Another challenge that authors need to solve will be performance improvement and testing for more faces and more voice tones.

Acknowledgment. This work and the contribution were supported by the project of Students Grant Agency – FIM, University of Hradec Kralove, Czech Republic.

References

1. Shearer, A.E., Hildebrand, M.S., Smith, R.J.: Hereditary hearing loss and deafness overview. In: Adam, M.P., et al. (eds.) GeneReviews®. University of Washington, Seattle (1993)
2. Deafness and hearing loss. https://www.who.int/news-room/fact-sheets/detail/deafness-and-hearing-loss
3. Národní plán opatření pro snížení negativních důsledků zdravotního postižení. https://www.knihkm.cz/handy/texty/narplan93.htm
4. Hrubý, J.: Kolik je u nás sluchově postižených (1998)
5. Hrubý, J.: Tak kolik těch sluchově postižených u nás vlastně je? (2009)

6. Forecast number of mobile users worldwide 2019–2023—Statistic. https://www.statista.com/statistics/218984/number-of-global-mobile-users-since-2010/

7. Mobile phone penetration worldwide 2013–2019—Statistic. https://www.statista.com/statistics/470018/mobile-phone-user-penetration-worldwide/

8. Mobile connections worldwide by country 2013–2019—Statistic. https://www.statista.com/statistics/203636/mobile-connections-worldwide-by-country/

9. Hjelmås, E., Low, B.K.: Face detection: a survey. Comput. Vis. Image Underst. **83**, 236–274 (2001). https://doi.org/10.1006/cviu.2001.0921

10. Li, H., Lin, Z., Shen, X., Brandt, J., Hua, G.: A convolutional neural network cascade for face detection. In: 2015 IEEE Conference on Computer Vision and Pattern Recognition (CVPR), pp. 5325–5334. IEEE, Boston (2015). https://doi.org/10.1109/CVPR.2015.7299170

11. Siatras, S., Nikolaidis, N., Krinidis, M., Pitas, I.: Visual lip activity detection and speaker detection using mouth region intensities. IEEE Trans. Circ. Syst. Video Technol. **19**, 133–137 (2009). https://doi.org/10.1109/TCSVT.2008.2009262

12. Johnson, D.H., Dudgeon, D.E.: Array Signal Processing: Concepts and Techniques. PTR Prentice Hall, Englewood Cliffs (1993)

13. Bourlard, H.A., Morgan, N.: Connectionist Speech Recognition. Springer, Boston (1994). https://doi.org/10.1007/978-1-4615-3210-1

14. Graves, A., Mohamed, A., Hinton, G.: Speech Recognition with Deep Recurrent Neural Networks. arXiv:1303.5778 [cs] (2013)

15. Doddington, G.R.: Speaker recognition—identifying people by their voices. Proc. IEEE **73**, 1651–1664 (1985). https://doi.org/10.1109/PROC.1985.13345

16. Berger, A., Vokalova, A., Maly, F., Poulova, P.: Google glass used as assistive technology its utilization for blind and visually impaired people. In: Younas, M., Awan, I., Holubova, I. (eds.) MobiWIS 2017. LNCS, vol. 10486, pp. 70–82. Springer, Cham (2017). https://doi.org/10.1007/978-3-319-65515-4_6

17. Berger, A., Maly, F.: Prototype of a smart google glass solution for deaf (and hearing impaired) people. In: Younas, M., Awan, I., Ghinea, G., Catalan Cid, M. (eds.) MobiWIS 2018. LNCS, vol. 10995, pp. 38–47. Springer, Cham (2018). https://doi.org/10.1007/978-3-319-97163-6_4

18. Google Cloud including GCP & G Suite—Try Free. https://cloud.google.com/

19. Cloud Vision API Documentation—Cloud Vision API Documentation. https://cloud.google.com/vision/docs/

20. Holey, P.N., Gaikwad, V.T.: Google glass technology. Int. J. **2** (2014)

21. Exploiting a Bug in Google's Glass - Jay Freeman (saurik). http://www.saurik.com/id/16

22. Vahabzadeh, A., Keshav, N.U., Salisbury, J.P., Sahin, N.T.: Improvement of attention-deficit/hyperactivity disorder symptoms in school-aged children, adolescents, and young adults with autism via a digital smartglasses-based socioemotional coaching aid: short-term, uncontrolled pilot study. JMIR Ment Health **5** (2018). https://doi.org/10.2196/mental.9631

23. Deshpande, S., Uplenchwar, G., Chaudhari, D.N.: Google glass. Int. J. Sci. Eng. Res. **4**, 0–4 (2013)

24. How does Google glass work? (Infographic). https://www.varifocals.net/google-glass/

25. Face Detection. https://firebase.google.com/docs/ml-kit/detect-faces

26. Cloud Speech-to-Text - Speech Recognition—Cloud Speech-to-Text API. https://cloud.google.com/speech-to-text/

27. Overview of Face Detection and Face Recognition - Amazon Rekognition. https://docs.aws.amazon.com/rekognition/latest/dg/face-feature-differences.html

VR-Fit: Walking-in-Place Locomotion with Real Time Step Detection for VR-Enabled Exercise

Sercan Sari[1(✉)] and Ayse Kucukyilmaz[2]

[1] Yeditepe University, Kayisdagi, 34755 Istanbul, Turkey
ssari@cse.yeditepe.edu.tr
[2] University of Lincoln, Brayford Pool, Lincoln LN6 7TS, UK
akucukyilmaz@lincoln.ac.uk

Abstract. With recent advances in mobile and wearable technologies, virtual reality (VR) found many applications in daily use. Today, a mobile device can be converted into a low-cost immersive VR kit thanks to the availability of do-it-yourself viewers in the shape of simple cardboards and compatible software for 3D rendering. These applications involve interacting with stationary scenes or moving in between spaces within a VR environment. VR locomotion can be enabled through a variety of methods, such as head movement tracking, joystick-triggered motion and through mapping natural movements to translate to virtual locomotion. In this study, we implemented a walk-in-place (WIP) locomotion method for a VR-enabled exercise application. We investigate the utility of WIP for exercise purposes, and compare it with joystick-based locomotion in terms of step performance and subjective qualities of the activity, such as enjoyment, encouragement for exercise and ease of use. Our technique uses vertical accelerometer data to estimate steps taken during walking or running, and locomotes the user's avatar accordingly in virtual space. We evaluated our technique in a controlled experimental study with 12 people. Results indicate that the way users control the simulated locomotion affects how they interact with the VR simulation, and influence the subjective sense of immersion and the perceived quality of the interaction. In particular, WIP encourages users to move further, and creates a more enjoyable and interesting experience in comparison to joystick-based navigation.

Keywords: Virtual reality · Locomotion · Walking-in-place ·
Virtual velocity · Head-mounted display · Motion analysis ·
Position tracking · Mobile VR

1 Introduction

In recent years, due to technological advances, virtual reality (VR) applications have become exceedingly popular. The introduction of low-cost smart phone adapters, such as the Google Cardboard [1], also played an important role to

© Springer Nature Switzerland AG 2019
I. Awan et al. (Eds.): MobiWIS 2019, LNCS 11673, pp. 255–266, 2019.
https://doi.org/10.1007/978-3-030-27192-3_20

boost the popularity and utility of VR in everyday applications. This is manifested in a huge rise in the number of mobile VR users worldwide, which increased from approximately 2 millions in 2015, to an expected 135 millions by 2020 [2].

In VR, users sense and react to rapidly changing 3D information made available through the use of appropriate software and hardware. Creating a realistic VR experience is closely linked to *immersion*, which creates an altered mental state by engaging the user's senses. However, unlike expensive head mounted displays (HMDs), mobile VR kits only are capable of limited levels of immersion. This is partially caused by the physical capabilities of mobile adapters and displays, which are much inferior to those provided by expensive HMDs. This creates a need for better design techniques to enable a smooth and realistic interaction between the user and the virtual world. We hypothesize that the way users interact with the environment is an effective force to increase the immersion and improve the user experience.

In contrast to *passive* VR applications, such as watching 360 videos, interactive applications impose the users to have an active interplay within the environment. One such interaction is to allow users to gain mobility in the simulated space, i.e. virtual locomotion, through virtual walking or running. While using HMDs, controlling the locomotion is not straightforward due to limited workspace and lack of visibility of the real world. Traditional locomotion methods using computer mice or gamepad interactions are typically insufficient to provide a realistic sensation of walking. The most common approach for virtual locomotion in VR is to use a hand-held controller for inputting motion commands. However this method is not realistic and introduces a cognitive process, meanwhile continuously reminding the user that he is in a VR simulation, negatively affecting immersion [3]. On the other extreme, omnidirectional treadmills (ODTs) are used to allow the user to walk on in all directions. However, ODTs require complicated design mechanisms, and are cumbersome and costly for personal use [4].

To allow users to wander around in virtual space, while still staying in affordable ranges, walk-in-place (WIP) approach for locomotion control was proposed [3]. In WIP, as the name implies, the user walks or runs in place, and steps are captured using sensor data. In this study, we compare the effects locomotion control on user experience by comparing joystick navigation to WIP. We investigate these effects within an exercise application, and investigate how the control technique would affect user behaviour when reaching the goals of the application, i.e. activity boosting, and user satisfaction.

2   Background

There are many different approaches for virtual locomotion. The simplest and most widespread approach, commonly used in computer games, is to use a joystick, which might come in the form of a game pad. Step commands are given as affine transformations (rotation and translation) defined by the looking direction of the avatar and position advancement, all inputted through joystick input.

However, controlling both rotation and translation through a joystick turns out to be confusing when using a HMD, hence is problematic as a motion control technique, and typically not used in such VR settings. An alternative way is to handle rotations with physical body rotations and controlling translations with the joystick [3].

In [3,5], it is argued that a real walking approach, where the user can actually walk during interaction, is remarkably better in terms of naturalness and simplicity for virtual locomotion. An optical tracking system can be used while implementing the real walking approach [3], however this approach is also limited since the tracked space and the virtual space are required to be of the same size. This problem can be solved using omnidirectional treadmills [4]. However, this solution is often expensive and bulky, which limits its use with a mobile platform.

In [6], it is proposed that using the walk-in-place (WIP) approach is a favorable alternative over the joystick and treadmill approaches. It was suggested that locomotion can be controlled using WIP as easily as using a joystick [7]. In addition to this, WIP has also been observed to be as practical as real walking [5]. In this study, we propose that the way users control the simulated locomotion affects how they interact with the VR simulation. We present VR-Fit as a VR-enabled exercise application, and evaluate how task performance and the perceived quality of the activity, such as enjoyment, encouragement for exercise, interest, ease of use, and exercise intensity is affected by the use of WIP.

WIP relies on sensor information to detect user steps. The location and type of the sensor, step detection algorithm implementation, and noise reduction in sensor readings can result in a latency between action and reaction. In [4], Darken et al. argue that starting and stopping latency is a significant challenge while implementing WIP. The starting latency is the delay between the moment a step is recognized and converted into virtual motion, whereas the stopping latency relates to how long it takes the virtual motion to stop once the user stops taking any steps. In case latency is high, navigation quality will drop [7]. Different algorithms have been developed to deal with latency. Step detection methods can be divided into the following three categories:

2.1 Peak Detection

This method uses successive peak and valley acceleration values to detect steps [8–11]. Mock et al. [10] use acceleration values and implement a step counter method which finds *hills* of consistently perceived acceleration values. When a hill is detected, one step is registered. In [9], it is observed that while walking, the measured vertical and horizontal acceleration values can be modeled as sinusoidal waves. Therefore, when a sinusoidal pattern is identified, a step can be detected. In [8], local maximums among a series of sensing measurements are identified. When a local maximum is identified, one step will be registered. [11] regards the local maximum between two different local minima to capture steps. This work implement an initial low-pass filtering on data to clean the noise in acceleration measurement. After that, they define a threshold to see if the difference between two adjacent local minimum and local maximum values is large enough. If this difference is greater than the predefined threshold, one step will be counted. Although peak detection is simple to implement, it is shown that this method may not consistently provide accurate results, especially when used with mobile phones, due to irregularities in the ways that the users are handling these devices [12].

2.2 Gait Analysis

Gait is defined as the pattern of walking, which is typically modeled through footfall patterns. At the moment of a footfall, the lower leg is perpendicular to the horizontal plane, i.e. the floor, and walking velocity is zero. In order to detect steps, zero velocity update method is used in [11,13,14]. In [15], gyroscopes are tied to users' shoes to gather scalar values determining the foot speed. If this speed is smaller than a given threshold, one step is registered. In [13], a pressure sensor is installed in the soles of the users' shoes to detect zero velocity update while walking. In [14], the authors place inertial sensors to users' calves. Although these can effectively detect the user's steps [13–15], the dependency on external sensors, and the need for good sensor placement induce a difficulty in using the approach for everyday use.

As discussed above, even though a gait analysis provides accurate step counts, it requires external sensors located on the body. In mobile VR, the use of smart phones allow us to use the sensors that are already built on board for step counting. However, since these sensors cannot be fixed to the lower extremities, e.g. legs, ankles, calves, as commonly practiced in gait analysis, extracting gait patterns through mobile sensing is not feasible.

2.3 Threshold Setting

In threshold setting [16–18], sensory data is compared to some threshold, and a step is registered if the reading is higher than the threshold. In [17], an inertial sensor is placed on the user's ankle. When the measured data exceed a predefined threshold, a step is detected. Alternatively, in [18], the authors apply a similar approach to detect steps, in which they tie an inertial sensor on the user's leg. In [16], Alzantot et al. suggest to use a finite state machine (FSM) in addition to setting thresholds to count steps. They define different states in the FSM as *regular walking*, *walking briskly*, and *running*, which exhibit different regular variations in motions. These regular variations are automatically classified into the states using threshold values. When detecting steps, the proposed scheme first identifies the state of a user, and then triggers a state transition if sensory values exceeds the threshold assigned for that particular state.

Due to relative simplicity of implementation, threshold setting is a viable alternative for step detection and step calculation in literature [17,19]. The threshold method may fail to be effective when used with mobile devices in case of hand-held applications. In such applications, the unconstrained motion of the mobile device cause the data range to change abruptly, affecting the utility of the thresholds [19,20]. However, in our study, the VR headset is worn in the head, hence ensures a good frame of reference for sensors on the smart phone. Hence, in our setting, we assume that these problems can be neglected without loss of generality.

In this study, we used the threshold setting method to implement virtual locomotion in a mobile VR application due to minimal sensor requirements and simplicity of implementation. One challenge in threshold setting method is the choice of thresholds, which can be affected by the movement patterns of users, and the properties of surface and shoes [19]. In order to investigate how our implementation is affected by such differences, we conducted a small-scale pilot study with 3 users as summarised in Sect. 5. The users freely walked in place on different surfaces, and we investigated how the detected step counts change across users and surface types. We verified that user and surface types do not radically affect the WIP performance in our application.

3   Methodology

3.1   Task Description

Fig. 1. Game screen for VR-Fit

In order to compare WIP and joystick-based locomotion interface, we implemented a fitness application, named VR-Fit. In VR-Fit, the user is placed in a forest setting, where he/she acts as a runner, fleeing from a fire (See Fig. 1). En-route to his/her escape, a firewall chases the user. The aim of VR-Fit is to motivate exercise, hence the user enters his/her daily step target, and is provided with the current number of steps while walking/running. In case the fire reaches the user, or the user exits the game, exercise records, e.g. current walking distance and steps remaining to achieve the daily goal, are updated. To make the fitness application complete, a profile review was added into the system. In the profile, the user is given options to review his/her profile, e.g. weight, height and age specifications, and set new daily goals. VR-Fit is implemented for iOS. Unity 3D and Xcode platforms are used to develop the software and the 3D environment.

3.2   Virtual Locomotion: WIP and Joystick Locomotion Algorithms

There are many virtual locomotion techniques, such as using joysticks for navigation, omnidirectional treadmills for real walking, and walking-in-place. In order to present the benefits and utility of WIP, we compare it with joystick-based navigation. We hypothesize that WIP is beneficial as it would encourage the user to do exercise.

The locomotion in VR-Fit is enabled through a threshold setting WIP technique. Once a step is detected, physical movement is translated into virtual movement to enable virtual locomotion. For this purpose, we use the data coming from the accelerometer and the gyroscope located on the mobile device. When a user starts walking/running in place, acceleration values in y-$axis$ (perpendicular to the ground plane) are recorded and compared to predefined thresholds. If the acceleration exceeds the predefined threshold, a step is registered and motion is generated. Algorithm 1 shows how steps are detected and used in WIP to generate motion. Note that the HMD orientation is used to determine the moving direction of the generated motion in the virtual space.

Algorithm 1 Walking-in-Place Algorithm

$stepCount \leftarrow 0$
$checkMovYdir \leftarrow Input.gyro.userAcceleration.y$
$predefinedThreshold \leftarrow 0.012$
if $checkMovYdir > predefinedThreshold$ **then**
    $stepCount \leftarrow stepCount + 1$
    virtualMovement()
end if=0

Joystick-based locomotion uses gaze direction and and joystick input to generate the motion. In particular, the user's head direction is used to set the virtual heading, whereas the velocity is set based on joystick input. Algorithm 2 details the joystick-based locomotion technique we used in the experiments.

4   Pilot Study: Evaluation of WIP Implementation

In order to evaluate the utility of WIP to generate consistent motion, we tested our step count detection algorithm. In particular, we were interested in seeing

Algorithm 2 VirtualMovement Method

$rb \leftarrow GetComponent(RigidBody)$
$head \leftarrow GameObject.FindObjectOfType(CardBoardHead)$
$headDirection \leftarrow head.Gaze.direction$
$virtualSpeed \leftarrow rb.velocity$
$virtualSpeed \leftarrow headDirection \times 12 = 0$

whether the threshold setting approach we adopted is able to estimate the step counts consistently without regard to user and environment differences. In order to validate this, we conducted a small-scale user study with 3 participants and observed the outcome of the step counting algorithm on a granite floor and a carpet.

The pilot study was conducted with two male and one female volunteers, whose ages ranged between 19–23. All three participants used the application on both types of floor (granite and carpet). The participants were asked to walk in place three times for each floor type and take 100 steps. The experimenter counted the steps and terminated the trials when 100 steps were reached.

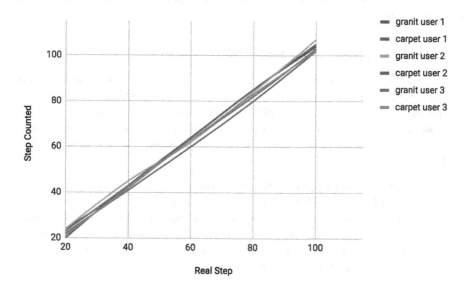

Fig. 2. Estimated vs. actual step counts for all users on granite vs. carpet floor types

After the trials, number of estimated steps was recorded to validate step counting algorithm. As shown in Fig. 2, the step count algorithm achieved consistent performance across users and different types of floors.

5   Experiment: WIP vs. Joystick-Based Locomotion

In order to provide a comparison of alternative locomotion methods, we conducted an experimental study with 12 subjects. A within-groups factorial design was used for this comparative study. The participant pool consisted of 5 female and 7 male volunteers, whose ages ranged from 22 to 29.

5.1   Procedure and Experimental Design

We designed a controlled user study to compare between two different interaction techniques, WIP and joystick-based locomotion interface. The participants were randomly assigned to two equal-sized groups. The first group used the application firstly using WIP, followed by joystick-based locomotion. The second group firstly used the joystick-based technique and then the WIP interface. This design eliminated any ordering and learning effects. The participants were instructed about how to navigate using both methods prior to starting the experiment and all participants gave informed consent before participating in the study. The participants were explicitly told that the purpose of the application is to promote exercising, hence they were asked to walk in place regardless of the applied locomotion method.

5.2   Data Acquisition and Evaluation Measures

The estimated step counts are recorded during the experiment to indicate the actual activity level of the users. After the trials, a questionnaire was given to the participants to evaluate their experience under each navigation method. The participants were asked to indicate their level of agreement or disagreement on a 5-pt Likert scale (1 = Totally Disagree, 5 = Totally Agree) for a series of statements:

1. Activity: I got tired from exercise while using the application.
2. Enjoyment: I had fun while using the application.
3. Encouragement for exercise: The application encouraged me to do exercise.
4. Interest: I would be interested in using a similar application in the future.
5. Ease of use: I was able to easily wander around within the virtual environment.
6. Intensity: I felt like I was exercising intensely.

6   Results and Discussion

This section presents the results of the experiment in terms of the quantitative and qualitative measures defined in Sect. 5. Statistically significant differences between conditions are investigated using Wilcoxon signed-rank test in the case of questionnaire results. The differences between conditions in terms of step counts is investigated using one-way repeated measures ANOVA. Since there is

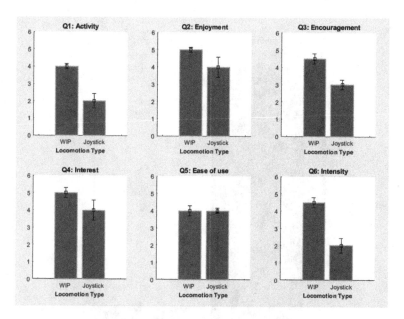

Fig. 3. Means scores and the standard errors of the means for subjective evaluation measures

only a single factor (locomotion technique) with two levels, no multiple comparisons are performed.

Mean scores and standard errors of the means of the questionnaire responses are shown in Fig. 3 (questions 1–6). The results indicate that the locomotion technique has a statistically significant effect on the activity level, manifested as increased fatigue (Q1) ($p < 0.001$), exercise intensity (Q6) ($p < 0.001$) and encouragement for exercise ($p < 0.01$). Even though the participants stated that they felt more tired due to exercise and thought that the exercise was more intense, they were significantly more encouraged to do exercise ($p = 0.005$) when using the WIP interface.

Looking at the estimated step counts, we observe consistent activity levels to those that were perceived by the subjects. As seen in Fig. 4, the subjects walked more the WIP interface than they did with the joystick ($p < 0.001$). These results support the hypothesis that WIP was successful to get the users to move more when compared to joystick-based locomotion.

Qualitative results shown in Fig. 3 also indicate that there is a statistically significant difference between WIP and Joystick interfaces for Q4 ($p < 0.01$), expressing an increased interest for the subjects to use WIP in other applications. The participants reported increased enjoyment when interacting with the WIP locomotion technique, as indicated by their responses to Q2 ($p < 0.05$), The responses to Q5 indicate that the participants were comfortable while using both interfaces, however, there was no statistical difference between two interfaces ($p = 0.25$).

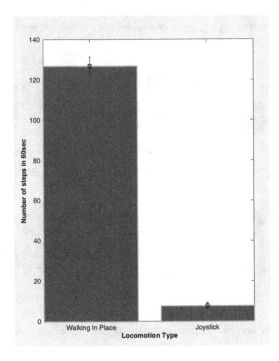

Fig. 4. Number of steps at the end of each trial

7 Conclusions

This study investigated perceptual differences and variations in activity levels between WIP locomotion interface and joystick-based navigation when using a VR-enabled mobile fitness application. We designed and implemented a real-time step detection technique in a VR-setup to enable WIP locomotion in a virtual environment.

We validated our WIP locomotion technique in a pilot study, and verified that the proposed technique eliminates differences between users and the type of floors while detecting steps. Our results indicate that the way users control the simulated locomotion affects how they interact with the VR simulation, influence the subjective sense of enjoyment and attracts more interest while increasing physical activity levels, when compared to more traditional joystick-based locomotion.

In particular, WIP allows users to move further, and let them have a more immersive experience. Significant differences between qualitative survey results clearly indicate the potential of WIP as a viable technique that can be used in mobile VR settings.

References

1. Google Cardboard. https://vr.google.com/cardboard/
2. Mobile VR users worldwide 2015–2020—Statistic. http://www.statista.com/statistics/650834/mobile-vr-users-worldwide/. Accessed 11 Dec 2018
3. Riecke, B.E., Bodenheimer, B., McNamara, T.P., Williams, B., Peng, P., Feuereissen, D.: Do we need to walk for effective virtual reality navigation? Physical rotations alone may suffice. In: Hölscher, C., Shipley, T.F., Olivetti Belardinelli, M., Bateman, J.A., Newcombe, N.S. (eds.) Spatial Cognition 2010. LNCS (LNAI), vol. 6222, pp. 234–247. Springer, Heidelberg (2010). https://doi.org/10.1007/978-3-642-14749-4_21
4. Darken, R.P., Cockayne, W.R., Carmein, D.: The omni-directional treadmill. In: Proceedings of the 10th Annual ACM Symposium on User Interface Software and Technology - UIST 1997 (1997)
5. Usoh, M., et al.: Walking > walking-in-place > flying, in virtual environments. In: Proceedings of the 26th Annual Conference on Computer Graphics and Interactive Techniques - SIGGRAPH 1999 (1999)
6. Péruch, P., Belingard, L., Thinus-Blanc, C.: Transfer of spatial knowledge from virtual to real environments. In: Freksa, C., Habel, C., Brauer, W., Wender, K.F. (eds.) Spatial Cognition II. LNCS (LNAI), vol. 1849, pp. 253–264. Springer, Heidelberg (2000). https://doi.org/10.1007/3-540-45460-8_19
7. Feasel, J., Whitton, M.C., Wendt, J.D.: LLCM-WIP: low-latency, continuous-motion walking-in-place. In: 2008 IEEE Symposium on 3D User Interfaces (2008)
8. Chon, J., Cha, H.: LifeMap: a smartphone-based context provider for location-based services. IEEE Pervasive Comput. **10**, 58–67 (2011)
9. Jang, H.-J., Kim, J., Hwang, D.-H.: Robust step detection method for pedestrian navigation systems. Electron. Lett. **43**, 749 (2007)
10. Mladenov, M., Mock, M.: A step counter service for Java-enabled devices using a built-in accelerometer. In: Proceedings of the 1st International Workshop on Context-Aware Middleware and Services affiliated with the 4th International Conference on Communication System Software and Middleware (COMSWARE 2009) - CAMS 2009 (2009)
11. Wang, H., Sen, S., Elgohary, A., Farid, M., Youssef, M., Choudhury, R.R.: No need to war-drive. In: Proceedings of the 10th International Conference on Mobile Systems, Applications, and Services - MobiSys 2012 (2012)
12. Pan, M.-S., Lin, H.-W.: A step counting algorithm for smartphone users: design and implementation. IEEE Sens. J. **15**, 2296–2305 (2015)
13. Bebek, O., et al.: Personal navigation via shoe mounted inertial measurement units. In: 2010 IEEE/RSJ International Conference on Intelligent Robots and Systems (2010)
14. Lo, C.-C., Chiu, C.-P., Tseng, Y.-C., Chang, S.-A., Kuo, L.-C.: A walking velocity update technique for pedestrian dead-reckoning applications. In: 2011 IEEE 22nd International Symposium on Personal, Indoor and Mobile Radio Communications (2011)
15. Ojeda, L., Borenstein, J.: Non-GPS navigation with the personal dead-reckoning system. In: Unmanned Systems Technology IX (2007)
16. Alzantot, M., Youssef, M.: UPTIME: ubiquitous pedestrian tracking using mobile phones. In: 2012 IEEE Wireless Communications and Networking Conference (WCNC) (2012)

17. Hu, W.-Y., Lu, J.-L., Jiang, S., Shu, W., Wu, M.-Y.: WiBEST: a hybrid personal indoor positioning system. In: 2013 IEEE Wireless Communications and Networking Conference (WCNC) (2013)
18. Zhang, R., Bannoura, A., Hoflinger, F., Reindl, L.M., Schindelhauer, C.: Indoor localization using a smart phone. In: 2013 IEEE Sensors Applications Symposium Proceedings (2013)
19. Brajdic, A., Harle, R.: Walk detection and step counting on unconstrained smartphones. In: Proceedings of the 2013 ACM International Joint Conference on Pervasive and Ubiquitous Computing - UbiComp 2013 (2013)
20. Lee, H.-H., Choi, S., Lee, M.-J.: Step detection robust against the dynamics of smartphones. Sensors 15, 27230–27250 (2015)

Committee of the Combined RBF-SGTM Neural-Like Structures for Prediction Tasks

Roman Tkachenko[1], Pavlo Tkachenko[2], Ivan Izonin[1(✉)],
Pavlo Vitynskyi[1], Natalia Kryvinska[3,4], and Yurii Tsymbal[1]

[1] Lviv Polytechnic National University, Lviv, Ukraine
`roman.tkachenko@gmail.com, ivanizonin@gmail.com,`
`pavlo.vitynsky@gmail.com, yurij.tsymbal@gmail.com`
[2] IT STEP University, Lviv, Ukraine
`pavlo.tkachenko@gmail.com`
[3] University of Vienna, Vienna, Austria
`natalia.kryvinska@univie.ac.at`
[4] Comenius University in Bratislava, Bratislava, Slovakia
`Natalia.Kryvinska@fm.uniba.sk`

Abstract. The paper describes the committee of non-iterative artificial intelligence tools for solving the regression task. It is based on the use of high-speed neural-like structures with extended inputs. Such an extension involves the combined use of primary inputs and extended inputs, via RBF. The resulting combination of inputs allows increasing the extrapolation properties of each element of the committee. This ensures a decreasing of the prediction errors for the solution of the regression tasks in cases of large volumes of data processing. The developed committee is used to solve the task of prediction of insurance costs. It is experimentally found that the proposed committee decreases training and test errors compared with the use of one neural-like structure of this type. The comparison of the committee's effectiveness with existing iterative and non-iterative computational intelligence methods has confirmed the highest accuracy of its work with a small increase of the time of the training procedure. The developed committee in software or hardware variants can be used to solve regression and classification tasks in the condition of large volumes of data for different application areas.

Keywords: Committee · Neural-like structure · Inputs enlargement · SGTM · RBF · Large volumes of data · Prediction task

1 Introduction and Problem Statement

The task of efficiently processing large volumes of data, that is, the search of methods and tools for automatic and fast analysis of large volumes of data, is important in many areas of the industry. Among the effective approaches to its solution is the use of machine learning methods. These methods allow finding initially unknown, complex interdependencies and regularities in data sets [1].

One of the tasks that quite often arise in various application areas is the regression. The regression task or training based on precedents is to construct and training a model

© Springer Nature Switzerland AG 2019
I. Awan et al. (Eds.): MobiWIS 2019, LNCS 11673, pp. 267–277, 2019.
https://doi.org/10.1007/978-3-030-27192-3_21

that will predict the value of the target variable based on the set of input data. Existing methods of machine learning are not always provide [2]:

- the accurate results;
- the sufficient generalization properties;
- the fast processing of large volumes of data.

That is why there is a need to develop new methods for processing large data sets, which will reduce the shortcomings described above.

There are many approaches to the processing the large volumes of data based on committees [3]. According [4] it can be divided into two groups: sequential and parallel. An example of the first one might be the AdaBoost method, the example of the other - Random Forest [5].

Construction of the committee can take place under different algorithms [6]. In this paper, we use the idea of the cooperation between elements of the committee. To do this, it needed to split a large sample into smaller components (sub-samples). The processing of individual sub-samples can improve the accuracy of the method as a whole.

2   Previous Findings

In [7] a new non-iterative artificial intelligence tool for solving regression tasks is described. This tool, based on the new paradigm for artificial neural networks design (Successive Geometric Transformations Model - SGTM), uses a greedy training algorithm. The neural-like structures that are constructed using this model, provide high-speed training procedures with high rates of accuracy [8]. The main advantages of this model in front of the existing feed forward neural networks, as well as the details of its training and application algorithms, are described in [9].

In [10], two hybrid structures of the common SGTM neural-like structure are proposed in order to increase the accuracy of the solution of the regression task:

- SGTM neural-like structure with RBF kernel;
- Combined RBF-SGTM neural-like structure.

The main idea of hybridization for both is to extend primary inputs using RBF. The purpose of such an extension is to increase the dimension of the inputs data's space of the task to obtain a more accurate result. Given the non-iterative nature of the work of the chosen tool (SGTM), this expansion is useful in terms of the speed of work. A detailed algorithmic implementation of the extension of inputs using RBF is given in [10].

In the first of the two hybrids described above, the primary inputs are completely replaced by the extended ones (based on the RBF). The size of the input after the extension depends on the number of RBF centers, which are selected by the user. Such a neural-like structure does not possess sufficient extrapolation properties for the efficient solution of regression tasks.

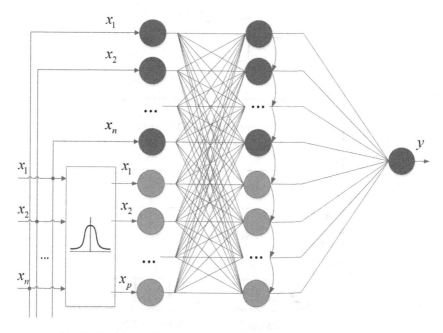

Fig. 1. Topology of the combined RBF-SGTM neural-like structure

The main difference of the second hybrid is that it combines both primary inputs of the task and extensions based on RBF. This combination allows increase the extrapolation properties of the hybrid structure, and as result, to increase the accuracy of the solution of the classification [8] and regression tasks. The topology of this tool is shown in Fig. 1. In the Fig. 1, it can be seen that the input layer is formed from the number of neurons, which is equal to the sum of the primary inputs of the task and the extended ones, using the RBF generator.

3 Proposed Approach

In this paper, we describe new committee of non-iterative structures based on the second hybrid (Fig. 1). The purpose of such design is to increase the accuracy for solving tasks in conditions of large amounts of data processing with satisfactory characteristics regarding to the speed of such processing.

In order to build the committee, we divide the existing dataset into parts according to the proposed algorithm. Each such sub-sample is processed by a separate neural-like structure of the committee. The flowchart of the algorithm for dividing the training sample into two sub-samples is presented in Fig. 2.

The main steps of the algorithm for constructing the committee of the Combined RBF-SGTM Neural-Like Structures are as follows:

270   R. Tkachenko et al.

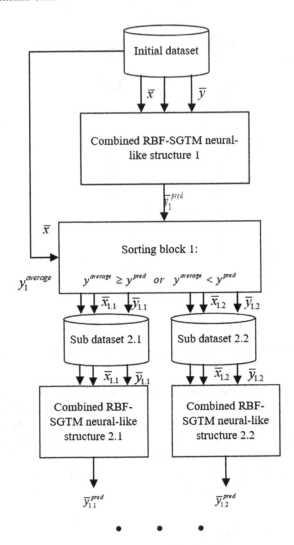

Fig. 2. Flowchart of the algorithm

- to divide the dataset into a training and test sample;
- to calculate the average value $y^{average}$ of the output variable in both samples;
- to train the hybrid neural-like structure from Fig. 1;
- to apply both training and test samples in test mode to get the response surface y^{pred} for each sample;
- to divide both the training and the test sample into two sub-samples. The first will include data vectors for which $y^{average} \geq y^{pred}$, and to the second - all others;
- the repeating the algorithm from the first step with each of the two obtained in previous step sub-samples. The algorithm is repeated until specified stopping criteria.

In the same way, the division of the test sample into a sub-samples occurs. As a result of the execution of, for example, one step of the described algorithm, we obtain two sub-samples for two neural-like structures from Fig. 1. For the two dividing steps we get 4 neural-like structures, and so on. As the results, we will obtain k neural-like structures, each of which will process a certain unique part of the total sample of data. Therefore, we called it committee.

The application of the committee of such structures will decrease prediction errors [11] and increase the generalizing properties of neural-like structures. Usage of parallel computing, in particular on a multiprocessor computer, will reduce the time for processing of large amounts of data [12]. In addition, an effective hardware implementation of such an approach is possible [13].

4 Modelling

The simulation of the method took place in 1338 surveys on insurance payments in four areas of the United States. This prediction task using real data was taken from [14]. It contained 6 factor variables, some of which acquired text values. For the purpose of modelling, the dataset was modified as follows: instead of 6 factor variables, 11 numeric independent variables were created [6], which are visualized using [15] in Fig. 3. Smokers (blue figures) and non-smokers (red figures) are singled out by color. Different figures denote men and women, and the size of the figure determines the size of insurance payments.

The data is divided in the ratio of 1070 to 268 vectors respectively for the training and test samples. The main parameters of the method are one division into two sub-samples (for two structure of the committee), 100 RBF centers. According to the selected parameters, each of the combined RBF-SGTM neural-like structures from the committee contained 111 neurons in the input and hidden layers, 100 of which are extensions of inputs using RBF, and the remaining 11 are the primary inputs of the dataset.

The prediction errors using the neural-like structures of the committee for each sub-sample of data, as well as their weighted value, are given in Table 1. It should be noted that the results of the committee's work are presented for both modes of its work (training and testing).

Table 2 shows the duration of training procedures for: the entire dataset, the two sub-samples that were created as a result of one division step and the total time of training of the proposed method (for one step of division). The last (training time for the proposed method) was defined as the sum of the training time of the entire sample and the greatest time of training one of two sub-samples. Such a formula was chosen due to the possibility of using parallel processing of both sub-samples (in the one step), since the last ones are unique.

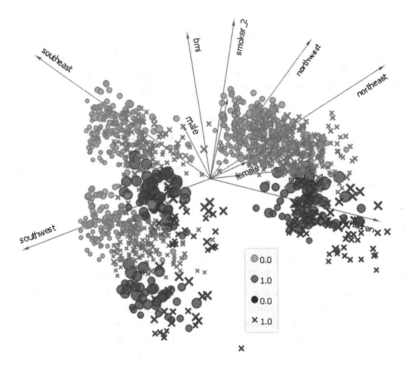

Fig. 3. Dataset (Color figure online)

Table 1. Obtained results.

Sub-sample	Dimensionality, vectors	Indicators		
		MAPE, %	RMSE	SMAPE
Training mode				
Subsample 1	729	30,859413	4904,61659	0,117006
Subsample 2	341	32,294283	4940,75105	0,116870
Weighted value	1070	31,316694	4916,13235	0,116963
Test mode				
Subsample 1	186	35,190399	4404,82332	0,173066
Subsample 2	82	18,765715	7063,32974	0,094458
Weighted value	268	30,164936	5218,24693	0,149014

Table 2. Results of the training procedure duration

Sample	Training time, seconds
Whole sample	0,0987722873687744
Subsample 1	0,0689921379089355
Subsample 2	0,0533866882324218
Training time for the proposed method (one step)	0,167764425277710

It is precisely the weighted error in the testing mode of the committee from Table 1 and the training time for the proposed method from Table 2 taken into account when comparing the effectiveness of the committee with the existing methods.

5   Comparison

In this section have describe the comparison of the developed approach with existing ones [15–18].

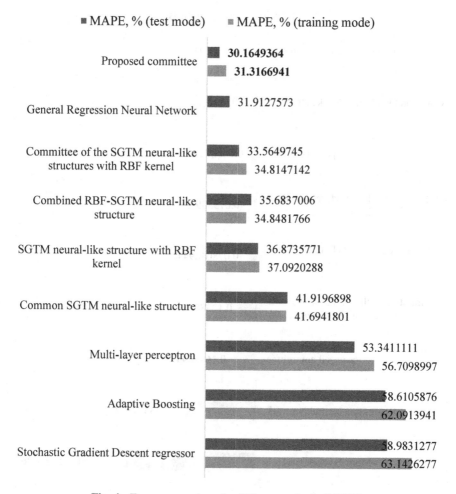

Fig. 4. Errors comparison for different methods (MAPE).

To compare the effectiveness of the developed committee based on combined RBF and primary inputs, traditional regression methods [16–18]: MPL; GRNN; AdaBoost; SGD regressor, as well as existing non-iterative tools:

- Common SGTM neural-like structure;
- SGTM neural-like structure with RBF kernel;
- Combined RBF-SGTM neural-like structure;
- Committee of the SGTM neural-like structures with RBF kernel.

were chosen.

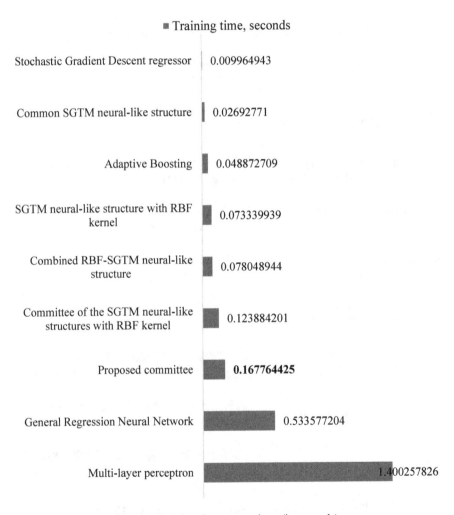

Fig. 5. Training time comparison (in seconds).

In this paper, an experimental comparison of errors (RMSE, MAE, MAPE) in training and application modes for all investigated methods (Fig. 4), as well as the duration of their training (Fig. 5) was conduct.

6 Discussion

As can be seen from Fig. 4 existing methods (MLP, AdaBoost and SGD regressor) shows the accuracy of the solution less than 50%. In addition, MLP shows the lowest speed (Fig. 5). AdaBoost and SGD regressor demonstrated the best results in terms of training time. However, based on the three accuracy indicators, this is an unsatisfactory result. GRNN shows high accuracy but more than 1.5% lower MAPE in comparison of the proposed committee. However, this neural network shows one of the worst indicators of the training time. It takes the penultimate position on this criterion from all investigated methods, and processes the data 3 times slower than the developed committee. In addition, to obtain such a high result in terms of accuracy, the optimal parameter for its operation σ $(\sigma = 0.4)$ was selected experimentally: $(\sigma \epsilon [0.1, 1.5], \Delta = 0.1)$. For each σ from the given interval, approximately the same time ($\approx$0,533577 s) was spent for the implementation of the training procedure. Based on this, the result of GRNN is also not optimal.

If we consider the effectiveness of existing, non-iterative methods, one of the highest performance rates is demonstrated by the SGTM neural-like structure. However, the accuracy of this tool reaches about 59%, which is also not enough to solve this task. The results of two of its hybrids: the SGTM neural-like structure with the RBF kernel and the Combined RBF-SGTM neural-like structure [4] show in 2.7- and 2.9-times lesser speed of the processing respectively. This is due to an increase in the number of inputs of these non-iterative instruments from 11 in the common tool to 100 and 111 in the first and second hybrid, respectively. Nevertheless, both the first and second hybrid neural-like structures show a significant increase in the accuracy of work when solving the task: more than 5% and 6% respectively.

An existing committee constructed on SGTM neural-like structures with RBF kernel, as expected, demonstrates both increased accuracy (3.3% higher precision based on MAPE) and training time (1.68 times longer) compared to the one neural-like structure of this type.

The committee, created by the authors, based on the use of combined RBF-SGTM neural-like structures demonstrates the highest precision values, both in MAPE and RMSE. It shows more than 5% increase in accuracy compared with the one neural-like structure with an increase in the speed of training only by twice.

The proposed committee through the combined use of both primary inputs and their extension with the use of RBF significantly increased the dimensionality of each input data vector (from 11 to 111). However, this contributed to a significant increase in the extrapolation properties of each neural-like structure of the committee. In comparison, an existing committee based on the set of SGTM neural-like structures with RBF kernel used only RBF inputs (it substituted primary inputs (11) on RBF inputs (100)). This did not provide a significant increase in accuracy. In particular, the developed committee provides 3.4% higher prediction accuracy with an increase in training time of 1.34

times compared with the existing committee. This may promote its use for solving practical tasks in the different fields of business [19, 20].

7 Conclusion

The authors developed the committee of non-iterative artificial intelligence tool with increased precision. It is based on the use of a set of combined RBF-SGTM neural-like structures. Each such structure is a hybrid from SGTM neural-like structures. Hybridization was based on the combining of primary inputs and RBF input. As a result of the use of such a combination, the input space has increased substantially. This affected both the accuracy of each individual structure of the committee; its extrapolating properties and the speed of training procedures. Based on the non-iterative nature of the training procedure, a significant extension of space of the input data of the task for increase accuracy makes sense.

Simulation of the method was carried out for solving the task of prediction insurance payments. It is experimentally found a significant decreasing of predictive errors when using the committee in comparison with using only one neural-like structure. The error decreased by 5%, with a slight increase in training time.

The comparison of the developed committee with existing computational intelligence methods of iterative and non-iterative types has confirmed the effectiveness of its use. The developed committee provides the slightest error based on MAPE and RMSE. In addition, it demonstrates satisfactory time characteristics of the training. The developed committee in software or hardware implementation can be used for solving regression and classification tasks on large datasets in various industries.

References

1. Zhernova, P.Y., Deineko, A.O., Bodyanskiy, Y.V., Riepin, V.O.: Adaptive kernel data streams clustering based on neural networks ensembles in conditions of uncertainty about amount and shapes of clusters, pp. 7–12 (2018)
2. Bodyanskiy, Y.V., Tyshchenko, O.K., Kopaliani, D.S.: An evolving connectionist system for data stream fuzzy clustering and its online learning. Neurocomputing **262**, 41–56 (2017). https://doi.org/10.1016/j.neucom.2017.03.081
3. Rokach, L.: Taxonomy for characterizing ensemble methods in classification tasks: a review and annotated bibliography. Comput. Stat. Data Anal. **53**, 4046–4072 (2009). https://doi.org/10.1016/j.csda.2009.07.017
4. Smolyakov, V.: Ensemble learning to improve machine learning results. In: Stats and Bots (2017). https://blog.statsbot.co/ensemble-learning-d1dcd548e936. Accessed 24 Feb 2019
5. Ensemble Methods: Foundations and Algorithms. CRC Press. https://www.crcpress.com/Ensemble-Methods-Foundations-and-Algorithms/Zhou/p/book/9781439830031. Accessed 24 Feb 2019
6. Sharkey, A.J.C.: Types of multinet system. In: Roli, F., Kittler, J. (eds.) MCS 2002. LNCS, vol. 2364, pp. 108–117. Springer, Heidelberg (2002). https://doi.org/10.1007/3-540-45428-4_11

7. Tkachenko, R., Izonin, I., Vitynskyi, P., et al.: Development of the non-iterative supervised learning predictor based on the Ito decomposition and SGTM neural-like structure for managing medical insurance costs. Data **3**, 46 (2018). https://doi.org/10.3390/data3040046

8. Doroshenko, A.: Piecewise-linear approach to classification based on geometrical transformation model for imbalanced dataset. In: 2018 IEEE Second International Conference on Data Stream Mining Processing (DSMP), pp. 231–235 (2018)

9. Tkachenko, R., Tkachenko, P., Tkachenko, O., Schmitz, J.: Geometrikal data modelling. Eupatoria, pp. 279–285

10. Tkachenko, R., Kutucu, H., Izonin, I., et al.: Non-iterative neural-like predictor for solar energy in Libya. In: Ermolayev, V., Suárez-Figueroa, M.C., Lawrynowicz, A., et al. (eds.) Proceedings of the 14th International Conference on ICT in Education, Research and Industrial Applications. Integration, Harmonization and Knowledge Transfer, Main Conference, Kyiv, Ukraine, 14–17 May 2018, vol. 1, pp. 35–45. CEUR-WS.org (2018)

11. Babichev, S., Lytvynenko, V., Gozhyj, A., Korobchynskyi, M., Voronenko, M.: A fuzzy model for gene expression profiles reducing based on the complex use of statistical criteria and Shannon entropy. In: Hu, Z., Petoukhov, S., Dychka, I., He, M. (eds.) ICCSEEA 2018. AISC, vol. 754, pp. 545–554. Springer, Cham (2019). https://doi.org/10.1007/978-3-319-91008-6_55

12. Shakhovska, N.B., Bolubash, Y.J., Veres, O.M.: Big data federated repository model. In: The Experience of Designing and Application of CAD Systems in Microelectronics, pp. 382–384 (2015)

13. Tsmots, I., Skorokhoda, O., Rabyk, V.: Structure and Software Model of a Parallel-Vertical Multi-Input Adder for FPGA Implementation, pp. 158–160 (2016)

14. Medical Cost Personal Datasets. https://www.kaggle.com/mirichoi0218/insurance. Accessed 9 Dec 2018

15. Demšar, J., Curk, T., Erjavec, A., et al.: Orange: data mining toolbox in Python. J. Mach. Learn. Res. **14**, 2349–2353 (2013)

16. Fedushko, S., Ustyianovych, T.: Predicting pupil's successfulness factors using machine learning algorithms and mathematical modelling methods. In: Hu, Z., Petoukhov, S., Dychka, I., He, M. (eds.) ICCSEEA 2019. AISC, vol. 938, pp. 625–636. Springer, Cham (2020). https://doi.org/10.1007/978-3-030-16621-2_58

17. Kazarian, A., Teslyuk, V., Tsmots, I., Mashevska, M.: Units and structure of automated "smart" house control system using machine learning algorithms. In: 2017 14th International Conference the Experience of Designing and Application of CAD Systems in Microelectronics (CADSM), pp. 364–366 (2017)

18. Lytvyn, V., Vysotska, V., Burov, Y., Veres, O., Rishnyak, I.: The contextual search method based on domain thesaurus. In: Shakhovska, N., Stepashko, V. (eds.) CSIT 2017. AISC, vol. 689, pp. 310–319. Springer, Cham (2018). https://doi.org/10.1007/978-3-319-70581-1_22

19. Koryagin, S., Klachek, P., Koryagin, E., Kulakov, A.: The development of hybrid intelligent systems on the basis of neurophysiological methods and methods of multi-agent systems. In: 2016 IEEE First International Conference on Data Stream Mining Processing (DSMP), pp. 23–28 (2016)

20. Kaminskyi, R., Kunanets, N., Rzheuskyi, A., Khudyi, A.: Methods of statistical research for information managers. In: 2018 IEEE 13th International Scientific and Technical Conference on Computer Sciences and Information Technologies (CSIT), pp. 127–131 (2018)

Mobile Web and Practical Applications

Hybrid Distributed Computing System Based on Canvas and Dynamo

Sebastien Mambou[1], Ondrej Krejcar[1][(✉)] [iD], Ali Selamat[1,2] [iD], and Kamil Kuca[1] [iD]

[1] Center for Basic and Applied Research,
Faculty of Informatics and Management, University of Hradec Kralove,
Rokitanskeho 62, 500 03 Hradec Kralove, Czech Republic
{jean.mambou,ondrej.krejcar,kamil.kuca}@uhk.cz
[2] Malaysia Japan International Institute of Technology (MJIIT),
Universiti Teknologi Malaysia,
Jalan Sultan Yahya Petra, Kuala Lumpur, Malaysia
aselamat@utm.my

Abstract. We live in a connected world where billions of smartphones, as well as conventional computers, are used daily, resulting in an exponential growth of data to be shared as quickly as possible. Also, the concept of parallel computing has been addressed for many years, but many researchers have focused on conventional computers. Keeping in mind that it is essential for many distributed databases to retain ACID (Atomicity, Coherence, Isolation, Sustainability) properties despite their low availability, which is a direct consequence of the strict implementation of ACID (academic and industrial observation). We propose a state-of-the-art method based on the parallel calculation of the grid that will use the available computing power of all inactive devices (smartphone and PC) to increase the read operation on hybrid data storages.

Keywords: Atomicity · Consistency · Isolation · Durability

1 Introduction

Many businesses leverage a large amount of user-provided data, so it is essential for the business to provide the best service in terms of availability and at a lower price [1]. However, because of the cost of the infrastructure put in place to meet the exponential need for data storage with fast response time, companies are forced to provide a relatively high price for their services [2, 3]. We propose in this article to use the computing power available, lying on our smartphone and traditional computers once they are in sleep mode (screen saver). We can see in Figs. 1 and 2 that the number of mobile devices smartphone is about 55% of the global connection (All devices), it can be estimated to more than 4 billion devices connected to the Internet. Fortunately for us, these devices have a huge source of computing power and available storage. By the end of 2019, the average storage capacity of the new smartphone will cross 80 GB [4]. Hence, we can assume the constant availability on each smartphone to be 100 MB, and considering a replica of the data segmented on 100 nodes (which will be elaborated in

© Springer Nature Switzerland AG 2019
I. Awan et al. (Eds.): MobiWIS 2019, LNCS 11673, pp. 281–293, 2019.
https://doi.org/10.1007/978-3-030-27192-3_22

this document), we can reach to the theoretical storage of distributed data of a capacity of:

$$\sum_1^{4B} \frac{(100 - Ps)}{r} = C \tag{1}$$

Where 4B is for 4 billion devices; r is the number of nodes having a replica; which is the approximate capacity that we can have in megabytes; Ps is the size of the program responsible for managing the reservation, loading, and management of the 20 MB space allocation in memory, as shown in Fig. 2.

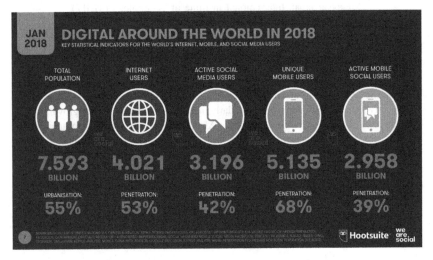

Fig. 1. Estimation of the number of device connected at Jan 2018 [5, 6]

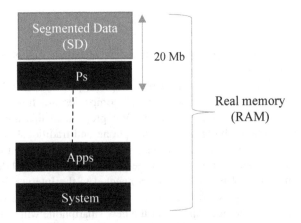

Fig. 2. Reservation of the 20 MB in the RAM

To avoid unnecessary talk on security and writing operations in the database, we will focus our research on the read operation made on the distributed database of our proposed system. This paper will be elaborate as follow: Sect. 1 will present the related work; Sect. 2, we will show the proposed system; Sect. 3 will implement it, and Sect. 4 will give a discussion about the result and will give a conclusion.

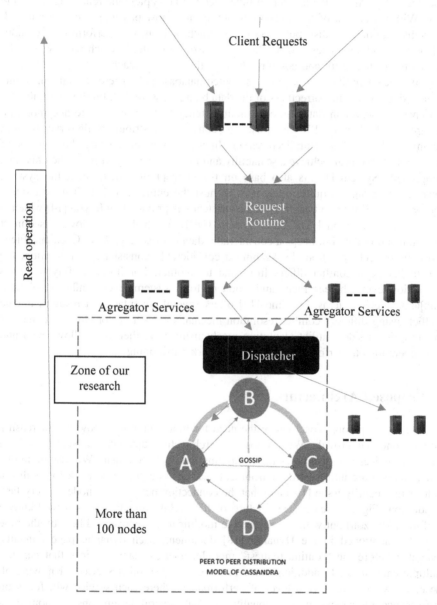

Fig. 3. Get operation performs on our proposed network. Here a client's device makes a get request for a data stored in our network. The request will be assigned to the corresponding aggregator Services which will send it, to the appropriate dispatcher. This last will contact the node in charge to process the read operation across the network as per Cassandra operation [7].

2   Related Work

Distributed computing has attracted several researchers for the past few years due to its unlimited potential [8]. We have seen in the paper [9] that for big computation like rendering a High-Definition (HD) video, it was required to have a supercomputing machine. Furthermore, the amount of time needed to complete the rendering was quite long. With the advent of distributed computing, it is now possible to divide one task and split it among the distributed computer. Each of them will perform their computations [10] and send back [10] to the "supervisor computer", which will oversee the reassembly of the result and combine them so that we can reach to the wanted result. We have seen a similar approach in distributed database [11] where several constraints are added to ensure the correctness of the data being reassembled. Furthermore, the use of Centralize server in database communities tends to be reduce more and more, an example can be Farsite [12] which uses the concept of distributing file server without the involvedness of a centralized server. In addition to that, using the concept of replication, Farsite can achieve a scalability and high availability. It is not the only one, Google File System [13] is also base on the concept of a distributed file system, however, its design is quite different as to host the entire metadata, it uses a single Master server. Similar to Farsite, a data consistency is provided by Bayou [14] which is a Distributed Relational Database System (DRDS) [15–17]. It allows disconnect operation and outage but keeps a considerable data consistency. Also, Coda and Ficus allow disconnect operations by keeping a considerable consistency. In addition, the way to handle a conflict differs from one to another. For instance, Bayou allows application-level whereas Ficus and Coda perform system level conflict resolution. Similar to these systems, Dynamo [18] offers several advantages: it resolves update conflicts using different conflict resolution mechanisms as a vector clock scheme, but prefers a client-side conflict resolution mechanism; Nevertheless, It allows read and write operations to perform even during network partitioning.

3   Proposed Architecture

We live in a populous world where the need for more computing power is increasing with exponential growth. We propose an architecture that takes advantage of the available devices and distributes the computing load between them. We assume in this article that we are in a trusted environment such as a corporate network (we will not address the security issue [19]) and that the connection between the nodes is very fast. In addition, Fig. 3 gives a clear picture of the architecture that uses a well-known platform (Amazon) but with a considerable modification, represented here by the blue area. As mentioned in the Dynamo [18] document, each dynamic page contents, generated before the "routine request" module, queries many services that can use multiple data stores. In addition, some services may use other services. Knowing all these, we want to achieve a level of performance where each service will focus on performance, efficiency, and functionality; for that, several design considerations must be taken.

3.1   Important Points of the Design

To achieve a level of consistency, several systems available on the market perform data replication in a synchronized manner, in order to maintain access to consistent data. This is not done without sacrifice, it is clear that the data replication algorithms used by these systems give priority to the consistency state of the system. Immediately after a failure scenario, the algorithm will keep the system unavailable until it is sure that it reaches the system consistency state.

This is why, in order to increase the availability in a system likely to suffer from a network failure, many optimal replication techniques offer us the possibility to send the copy (replicas) simultaneously and in the background but with some compromises that need to be solved. An important point is when to use the process necessary to resolve the conflict? In other words, do we apply these processes during writing or during the read operation? As mentioned, in clause [20], reading complexity is often low because many systems perform conflict resolution during write operations.

Keeping in mind the need to maintain the scalability property of our proposed architecture, it was necessary to provide a dynamic mechanism that allows us to segment the incoming data on the quorum nodes (here present as the minimum number of nodes involved in the replicate or holding a copy of the segment) of smartphones. This mechanism uses a variant of the "coherent hash" [21] sufficiently adapted to balance the computing load on the available node. Thus, the assignment of the Segmented Data (SD) to a node is done by hashing the SD key to correspond to the positions of the device in the ring of the network, it also passes through the ring (from left to right) for the purpose of meeting the first device with a position larger than its position. Due to some of the challenges that arise when we use the normal "consistent hashing" technique, our variant will repeat the same operation but will consider multiple virtual positions in the ring network of each given quorum node (smartphone available). Thus, each node can be responsible for one or more virtual nodes and this variant gives us another advantage when a failure occurs or when the equipment is no longer available for an unknown reason, in this case, the load, will be transferred to the next available node.

3.2   Description of the Proposed Architecture

Objective: As mentioned before, our world contains an incremental number of a smartphone available with remarkable computing power and very good storage. Our research paper proposes a method to use this storage in the most efficient way Fig. 1, shows that we have about 55% of connected smartphones in the world and most of the time, we do not use them because of our office time or school time or other reasons. During this period of inactivity, we can use these devices to do something else. Our architecture presented in Fig. 2, shows two major players: our dispatcher and all the smartphones present in the ring, acting as in the model Cassandra. Let's take a look at the communication process between these 2 entities. Description of a put operation (Table 1).

Table 1. Degree of importance of the data send (case of an online shopping website).

Level of importance of data	Description
0	System data and application data
1	Most important data (user id, credit card information, ...)
2	Very important data (personal information,...)
3	Important data (wish list, favorites, order details, ...)
4	Data (Vouchers, codes, ...)

We assume that the write(put) operation is performed in our system in a sequential way with a considerable level of consistency. We describe an abstract process - the put operation:

- A client is connected via a platform and send some push request to store some old data (e.g. a picture taken 2 years ago and not accessed since 1.5 year or old vouchers used by the customer) base on his primary key.
- The request is processed and sends to the "Request routine" which sends to one of the aggregator services.
- A dispatcher receives the requestion and make sure of the type of the data to be stored. It recognizes it bases on 5 levels of importance dynamic allocate in the application interface uses by the client.
- Looking at principles presented in [22], we came to the conclusion that few users remember about website's elements such as vouchers (as well as that information of the same level of importance). Thus, when dispatcher receives the data to be stored in the database, the dispatcher segments it so that union **(segments) = original data** and it sends each segment to the readiest node as well as the list of nodes not yet in possession of a copy of the data, i.e., the dispatcher is aware of each node having the segment. Table 2 shows an entry table of the dispatcher.
- the dispatcher will store data of level 4 in our "zone of research" which consists of smartphone devices interconnect at a correct speed (good enough for ensure the appropriate response time set by the admin).
  In fact, the level 4 Data received by the dispatcher will be processed and segmented using multi-agent algorithm call here as Msegmentation() method which returns an array of segmented data of size z initial set and the count of an element in the array. The algorithm will call Msegmentation() as a nested procedure before the assignment of those segmented data to a quorum of nodes (available smartphones).
- Similar to the Cassandra model, the ready node (smartphone having fewer computations) will receive the data and perform the appropriate replica of the data to the neighbor and get back to the dispatcher the node_id having the replica as shown in Fig. 4. It is good to mention that the replica of the information will be done and send to other available nodes till hundred nodes (through experiment, we found 100 as a good number of nodes per replicate), assuming that the replica is well maintained by the global variable total_replicat of the data save in the dispatcher table as shown in Table 2.

Table 2. An entry of a dispatcher

entries		ClientID	Hash Data	Seg 1	Seg 2	...	Seg 100	Node 1	...	Node 100

Throw a gossip method each node will make sure that its neighbor is available and if not report immediately to the dispatcher so that it will not look for it at the time of the push/get request.

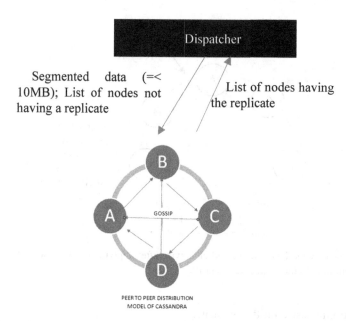

Fig. 4. Shows the put operation. Here the dispatcher interact with the head node which provides the list of nodes containing each replicate of the segment and also get from the head node the data being assembly after combing all the segment so that $\sum segment = original\ data\ stored$.

NB: Simplifying matters, we assume that: *put_request* is a variable which will contain the put (write) request sent by the client; *Extract_data_from_request* is a method able to extract current data that we must save; Call_head_and_save_data gives instruction to the "head" nodes to save the segmented data and replicates it among the "nodes of the preference list".

ALGORITHM

1.	Read put_request;
2.	Data :=Extract_data_from_request(put_request);
3.	If isLevel5(Data) then:
4.	(Array_of_segmented_data, number_of_element):=
5.	Msegmentation(Data);
6.	**While** count< = number_of_elements **do**:
7.	Call_head_and_save_data(Array_of_segmented_data);
8.	Count := count + 1;
	EndWhile;

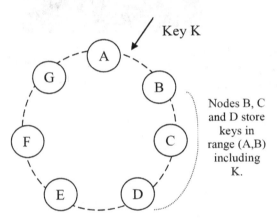

Fig. 5. Shows how the key is replicated clockwise after applying our variant of the "consistent hashing" technique to the segmented data [9].

Discussion: emphasize on the replicate.

Each segmented data is represented here by a key, k, obtained after applying our variant of the "consistent hashing" technique to the segmented data [18]. It is assigned to the "head" node with the responsibility to replicate the Segmented Data (SD) to 100 other nodes. In addition, to save the key locally, the "head" sends a copy to 99 other nodes (called as members of the preference list) clockwise as shown in Fig. 5. The interaction between the head of the node and the dispatcher is essential to maintain an updated list of the preference list so that the copy of the SD is stored in the correct device. It is also good to mention that the preference list, is constructed in such a way that for each position in the ring, we have a unique physical member (device) as the concept of virtual node was introduce before, we skip some positions in the ring to avoid to assign them to virtual nodes hold by the same physical node (or member) Fig. 6.

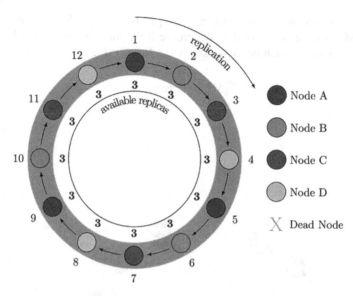

Fig. 6. The preference list is constructed in such a way that for each position in the ring, we have a unique physical member (device) as the concept of virtual node was introduce before, we skip some positions in the ring to avoid to assign them to virtual nodes hold by the same physical node (or member) [14]

3.2.1   The Get Operation

We have discussed the put operation which is an important step as we cannot retrieve something that we don't have. Further, to design a better approach for our get operation, it was also necessary for us, to know how the write operation is done in our system. For the sake of simplicity, we assume that we are in a trusted environment with a failure-free so no need to deal with the security of the transmission and the backup of the data.

Here, in the opposite of Dynamo_amazon, the client will ask the data only to the dispatcher which will make sure that the accurate data is received from nodes through the following process:

- The dispatcher receives the get request sent by the client and base on the ClientID and the hash data, it looks in its table to see to which node the segments have been allocated.
- Like the put operation, the dispatcher will select "head" nodes. In fact, as our dispatcher uses the concept of load balance, it might happen that the request of getting the complete data might be received by a wrong node which is not present in the preference list. In this case, the node in question will send the request to the nearest node which is included in that list through an abstract process. The get operation will be performed by the healthiest and not down nodes in the preference list with an accent on the consistency, at the time of the comparison of those nodes by the dispatcher. It is good to mention that the dispatcher will ensure that the data

reception is accurate or restore the missing part base on the different copies of data received from the nodes of the "preference list" which were selected Fig. 6. The final data must be accurate as shown by the Eq. (2) (Fig. 7).

$$U_{i=0}^{99} SD_i = Original\, Data \tag{2}$$

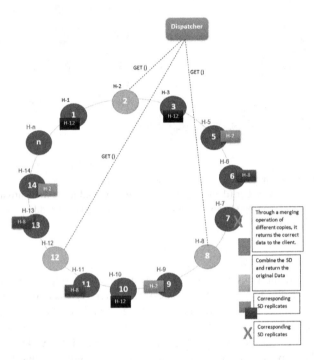

Fig. 7. Get request handled by the Dispatcher, it will ensure that the data reception is accurate or restore the missing part base on the different copies of data received from the nodes of the "preference list" which were selected.

4   Implementation

We performed our experiment on 10 computers interconnected with each other according to the ring topology. Each device interacts with a computer, which plays the role of a dispatcher. This machine receives the put/get request from another machine (client's computer).

For the purposed of the simplicity, we will store and retrieve pictures (no other data) in our network.

4.1 Put Request

In this context, the put request refers to the stored request of an image. Through Fig. 8, we can clearly see that the put request, as well as the image to be stored, will be assigned to the dispatcher. This one will be in charge of the segmentation [23] and will compute the hash key of the segment before sending them to the head node. This last will replicate it across the network and get back to the dispatcher with the ID of each node containing the replicate of the segment.

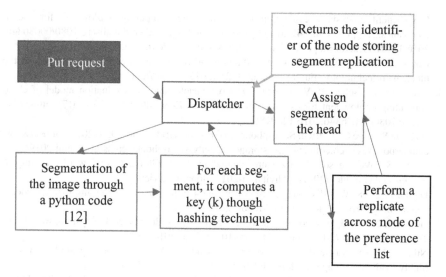

Fig. 8. Shows how the put request is handled in our experiment.

4.2 Get Request

Similar to figure Fig. 8, the get request will be assigned to the Dispatcher and the reverse process will be done. However, we will add a new component responsible to check the heard of the file obtain after the merging of the different segments by the dispatcher.

This component will check if an error occurred in the file and repair the file accordingly [15] before sending it to the dispatcher.

5 Conclusion

Bearing in mind that it is essential for many distributed databases to retain the ACID (Atomicity, Coherence, Isolation, Durability) [24] properties despite their low availability, this document presents a much scalable model that can be used to store a significant amount of data, through the network. It can manage the network partition, data center failures, and server failures. Its scalability, based on the needs of multiple users, makes it a suitable candidate for the architecture of the most efficient data models. As future work, we will further investigate on distributed storage and associate the concept of Machine learning presents in several models [25–30].

Acknowledgement. The work was supported by the SPEV project "Smart Solutions in Ubiquitous Computing Environments", 2019, University of Hradec Kralove, FIM, Czech Republic.

References

1. Cost–benefit analysis – evaluation model of cloud computing deployment for use in companies. Appl. Econ. **49**(6). https://www.tandfonline.com/doi/abs/10.1080/00036846. 2016.1200188?scroll=top&needAccess=true&journalCode=raec20

2. Cocco, L., Pinna, A., Marchesi, M.: Banking on blockchain: costs savings thanks to the blockchain technology. Future Internet **9**, 25 (2017). https://doi.org/10.3390/fi9030025

3. Maresova, P., Sobeslav, V., Krejcar, O.: Cost–benefit analysis–evaluation model of cloud computing deployment for use in companies. Appl. Econ. **49**, 521–533 (2017). https://doi. org/10.1080/00036846.2016.1200188

4. Average Storage Capacity in Smartphones to Cross 80 GB by End-2019 (2019). https://www. counterpointresearch.com/average-storage-capacity-smartphones-cross-80gb-end-2019/

5. Kemp, S., We are social, Hootsuite: Digital in 2017: Global Overview (2017). https:// wearesocial.com/blog/2017/01/digital-in-2017-global-overview

6. Digital in 2018: World's internet users pass the 4 billion mark (2018). https://wearesocial. com/us/blog/2018/01/global-digital-report-2018

7. Gemayel, N.: Analyzing google file system and Hadoop distributed file system. Res. J. Inf. Technol. **8**, 66–74 (2016). https://doi.org/10.3923/rjit.2016.66.74

8. Nikam, P.P., Suryawanshi, R.S.: Microsoft Windows Azure: developing applications for highly available storage of cloud. Int. J. Sci. Res. **4**, 662–665 (2015)

9. Kitamura, M., et al.: Beyond 4 K: 8 K 60p live video streaming to multiple sites. Future Gener. Comput. Syst. **27**, 952–959 (2011). https://doi.org/10.1016/j.future.2010.11.025

10. Pérez-Miguel, C., Mendiburu, A., Miguel-Alonso, J.: Modeling the availability of Cassandra. J. Parallel Distrib. Comput. **86**, 29–44 (2015). https://doi.org/10.1016/j.jpdc. 2015.08.001

11. Lucchese, F.: From P2P to NoSQL: a continuous metric for classifying large-scale storage systems. J. Parallel Distrib. Comput. **113**, 227–249 (2018). https://doi.org/10.1016/j.jpdc. 2017.11.017

12. Adya, A., et al.: FARSITE: federated, available, and reliable storage for an incompletely trusted environment. In: Proceedings of the 5th Symposium on Operating Systems Design and Implementation (OSDI), pp. 1–14 (2002). https://doi.org/10.1145/1060289.1060291

13. Yang, J.: From Google file system to omega: a decade of advancement in big data management at Google. In: Proceedings - 2015 IEEE 1st International Conference on Big Data Computing Service and Applications, BigDataService 2015, pp. 249–255 (2015). https://doi.org/10.1109/BigDataService.2015.47

14. Edwards, W.K., Mynatt, E.D., Petersen, K., Spreitzer, M.J., Terry, D.B., Theimer, M.M.: Designing and implementing asynchronous collaborative applications with Bayou. In: Proceedings of the 10th Annual ACM Symposium on User Interface Software and Technology - UIST 1997, pp. 119–128 (1997). https://doi.org/10.1145/263407.263530

15. Zhang, H., Chen, G., Ooi, B.C., Tan, K.-L., Zhang, M.: In-memory big data management and processing: a survey. IEEE Trans. Knowl. Data Eng. **27**, 1920–1948 (2015). https://doi.org/10.1109/TKDE.2015.2427795

16. Kang, Y.-S., Park, I.-H., Rhee, J., Lee, Y.-H.: MongoDB-Based Repository design for IoT-generated RFID/sensor big data. IEEE Sens. J. **16**, 485–497 (2016). https://doi.org/10.1109/JSEN.2015.2483499

17. Olteanu, D., Zavodny, J.: Size bounds for factorised representations of query results. ACM Trans. Database Syst. **40**, 2 (2015). https://doi.org/10.1145/2656335

18. DeCandia, G., et al.: Dynamo: Amazon's highly available key-value store. In: Proceedings of the Symposium on Operating Systems Principles, pp. 205–220 (2007). https://doi.org/10.1145/1323293.1294281

19. Sobeslav, V., Balik, L., Hornig, O., Horalek, J., Krejcar, O.: Endpoint firewall for local security hardening in academic research environment. J. Intell. Fuzzy Syst. **32**, 1475–1484 (2017). https://doi.org/10.3233/JIFS-169143

20. Gray, J., Helland, P., O'Neil, P., Shasha, D.: The dangers of replication and a solution. ACM SIGMOD Rec. **25**, 173–182 (1996). https://doi.org/10.1145/235968.233330

21. Karger, D., Lehman, E., Leighton, T., Panigrahy, R., Levine, M., Lewin, D.: Consistent hashing and random trees. In: Proceedings of the Twenty-Ninth Annual ACM Symposium on Theory of Computing - STOC 1997, pp. 654–663 (1997). https://doi.org/10.1145/258533.258660

22. Ramachandran, V.: Let's Talk about UX—Principles of User Interface Elements (2019). https://medium.com/nyc-design/lets-talk-about-ux-principles-of-user-interface-elements-125ea165c6d

23. image_slicer@github.com

24. Serrano-Alvarado, P., Roncancio, C., Adiba, M.: A survey of mobile transactions. Distrib. Parallel Databases **16**, 193–230 (2004). https://doi.org/10.1023/B:DAPD.0000028552.69032.f9

25. Mambou, S., Krejcar, O., Kuca, K., Selamat, A.: novel human action recognition in RGB-D videos based on powerful view invariant features technique. In: Sieminski, A., Kozierkiewicz, A., Nunez, M., Ha, Q.T. (eds.) Modern Approaches for Intelligent Information and Database Systems. SCI, vol. 769, pp. 343–353. Springer, Cham (2018). https://doi.org/10.1007/978-3-319-76081-0_29

26. Mambou, S., Krejcar, O., Kuca, K., Selamat, A.: Novel cross-view human action model recognition based on the powerful view-invariant features technique. Future Internet **10**, 89 (2018). https://doi.org/10.3390/fi10090089

27. Mambou, S., Krejcar, O., Selamat, A.: Approximate outputs of accelerated turing machines closest to their halting point. In: Nguyen, N.T., Gaol, F.L., Hong, T.-P., Trawiński, B. (eds.) ACIIDS 2019. LNCS (LNAI), vol. 11431, pp. 702–713. Springer, Cham (2019). https://doi.org/10.1007/978-3-030-14799-0_60

28. Mambou, S., Krejcar, O., Maresova, P., Selamat, A., Kuca, K.: Novel four stages classification of breast cancer using infrared thermal imaging and a deep learning model. In: Rojas, I., Valenzuela, O., Rojas, F., Ortuño, F. (eds.) IWBBIO 2019. LNCS, vol. 11466, pp. 63–74. Springer, Cham (2019). https://doi.org/10.1007/978-3-030-17935-9_7

29. Mambou, S.J., Maresova, P., Krejcar, O., Selamat, A., Kuca, K.: Breast cancer detection using infrared thermal imaging and a deep learning model. Sensors (Basel) **18** (2018). https://doi.org/10.3390/s18092799

30. Mambou, S., Maresova, P., Krejcar, O., Selamat, A., Kuca, K.: Breast cancer detection using modern visual IT techniques. In: Sieminski, A., Kozierkiewicz, A., Nunez, M., Ha, Q.T. (eds.) Modern Approaches for Intelligent Information and Database Systems. SCI, vol. 769, pp. 397–407. Springer, Cham (2018). https://doi.org/10.1007/978-3-319-76081-0_34

Evaluation of Crosshair-Aided Gyroscope Gamepad Controller

Ali Osman Toktaş[✉] and Tacha Serif[✉]

Yeditepe University, Ataşehir, 34755 Istanbul, Turkey
aliosman.toktas@std.yeditepe.edu.tr,
tserif@cse.yeditepe.edu.tr

Abstract. With an ever-increasing number of technological tools and gadgets in our life, people have become familiar with multiple kinds of user interaction interfaces and devices. Day in, day out people interact with various devices that follow different user interaction paradigms, such as when they are using a mobile phone, smart TV or a gaming console. Although these devices have various forms among themselves, the interaction method used to control them can make a significant difference in usability. Gaming consoles have become a huge area of the computer entertainment business in years. With every new generation of gaming consoles, the technologies behind it improve dramatically. Most of the time, the improvements are about the graphics and interaction devices. It can be clearly said that even though the graphics have improved in the last two generations of gaming consoles, the interaction paradigms and approaches were not up to the users' expectations. This is especially the case for a first-person shooter and real-time strategy (RTS) games. Accordingly, bearing in mind the above as a motivation, the aim of this work is to develop a prototype game controller that will improve the usability and gameplay experience of the first-person shooter games.

Keywords: Gamepad · Gyroscope · Controller · Pointing devices · Game input

1 Introduction

In comparison to keyboard and mouse, gamepad controllers do not provide the flexibility that a gamer needs while playing games that a gamer require for precision pointing. One of these genres is the first-person shooter, where using classic gamepad controller makes it unenjoyable. Due to this inconvenience, game developers proposed aim-assist and auto-aim to solve this problem. However, these proposed solutions even though they improve usability, they reduce the game's enjoyment experience. Accordingly, this study aims to benefit from the advantages of the motion sensor to minimize its side effects by combining gamepad controls and sensor motion data as part of a new control scheme. Accordingly, this paper is structured as follows; Sect. 2 reviews and details similar work about game interaction devices. Section 3 elaborates on the technologies and development platforms utilized in the development process and Sect. 4 details the design of the hardware prototype and test game platform. Section 5

© Springer Nature Switzerland AG 2019
I. Awan et al. (Eds.): MobiWIS 2019, LNCS 11673, pp. 294–307, 2019.
https://doi.org/10.1007/978-3-030-27192-3_23

describes the implementation of the prototype device and the test game platform and Sect. 6 details the methods used to conduct the evaluations and discusses the findings. Finally, Sect. 7 draws conclusions and highlights possible future development venues.

2 Background

Despite all the software improvements on classic gamepads, like aim assist and auto aim, gamers preferred keyboard and mouse to gamepads. Both academia and industry tried to develop novel controllers. As a result, over the last decades, many different gamepads were developed and tested with various games. Among the proposed techniques, the most promising controllers were the ones that supported motion sensors like accelerometer and gyroscope.

Accordingly, Alankuş and Eren [1] used a tilt sensor to detect the amount of tilt and use it to increase the sensitivity of the gamepad analog joystick when the gamepad is tilted. In their work, Alankuş and Eren compare their prototype with two other solution candidates - namely the classic gamepad and a tilt-aim enabled gamepad. The results of their experiments show that their proposed solution is statistically better than the tilt-aim approach, and is comparably better than the classical gamepad. On the other hand, Natapov and MacKenzie [2] tweak an existing gamepad and replace the thumbstick with a trackball controller. In this study, they compared their prototype with a standard Xbox gamepad and a PC mouse in a target-tracking scenario. According to their results, the mouse is the best performing controller and the standard Xbox controller is the worst performing one. The trackball controller, however, is the one that is giving a mediocre performance. Similarly, Teather and Ramcharitar [3] evaluate four different controllers - namely mouse, thumbstick, touchpad and a gyrosensor (gyroscope-enabled gamepad) - in a Fitt's law experiment. Fitt's law is a predictive model that considers the time required to move to a target area as a function of the ratio between the distance to the target and the width of the target. Their overall results indicated that the mouse had the best point selection effectiveness, followed by the touchpad, then the gyro-sensor, and finally the thumbstick. With the same motivation, Oshita and Ishikawa [4] make a comparison of action selection interfaces for computer games using gamepad and touchscreen. In their study they use number of actions to make the comparison between the two interaction devices. Their results show that in the overall touchscreen interfaces are relatively better than the gamepad interface. Teather, Roth, and MacKenzie [5] also test input control types tilt and touch with their combinations. Their results indicate that tilt augmented controls are no better than classic touch controls but tilt-and-touch control mode offers a comparable performance.

From a different view, some of the actors in the gaming industry also proposed and produced several interaction devices to improve the gaming experience. As an example, Nintendo released the Wii gaming console, which had the Wii remote controller utilizing accelerometer and an optical sensor, in 2006. The new Wii controller, making use of its sensors, also simplified the pointing task and gesture recognition [6]. Similarly, the Steam controller, which was launched by Valve in 2015, makes use of multiple physical user interfaces - such as thumbstick, gyroscope and touch surface.

The feature that separates the Steam controller from a traditional controller is the introduction of circular haptic touchpads that takes place of the traditional joystick [7].

In recent years, media service providers like Netflix and Amazon Prime become quite popular. Similarly, lately the gaming industry is getting its share from this popular movement. Accordingly, Google has announced it is a new game-streaming platform called Stadia, which is a cloud-based gaming, service where games will be played with a motto of anywhere, anytime and on any device. Popularity of the gaming platforms being in the rise, will only increase the importance of the interaction devices – such as gamepads, touchscreens and sensor-aided controllers [8].

3   Methodology

This section examines possible technologies, development platforms and tools that can be used to develop the prototype gamepad.

3.1   Hardware Used for Controller

In line with today's advancing technologies many game controllers use sensors or get aid from sensors. Along with today's advanced technology, many varieties of game controllers are presented and introduced every day, which. Many of them benefit from motion sensors like gyroscope and accelerometer. Since the aim is to build a customized solution, a wireless gamepad and a sensor to imitate mouse movement will be required. As there are no special expectation form the gamepad, in this case any generic gamepad could be used. Hence, a random wireless gamepad was chosen – in this case a Logitech F710. To compliment the gamepad also an air mouse with 6-axis gyroscope was chosen, specifically Dark DK-AC-KAM02.

3.2   Software Environment

Because of its fast powerful game development framework, Unity was preferred as the development environment. Unity's custom input management feature allows programmed game to work with multiple different input devices. The communication between hardware and the software components of the controller are bridged by nano receiver dongles that work at 2.4 GHz frequencies. Specifically there are two nano dongles that enable communication between gamepad and air mouse, which has a build-in gyroscope embedded inside. Accordingly, the air mouse data received through the dongle is combined with the gamepad to simulate a standard mouse input. The overall integration of the gamepad data and the air mouse's data in undertaken within the Unity's framework. These two devices' activities and their functions are mapped on the Input Management tool of the Unity3D Editor, so that the gamepad can be used shoot and move the characters and the air mouse can be used to target and point a specific location on screen.

3.3 Tilt Input Gamepad

Tilt input gamepad is our proposed method that allows the player to move the character's body and camera view using analog sticks in collaboration with the gyroscope sensor. Using this method, the player makes use of the gamepad with the conventional way and when s/he needs to aim on a target makes use of the gyroscope sensors. The user is notified when there is an opportunity to use sensor-based aiming by the help of a specially designed crosshair.

4 Prototype Design

This section depicts the design of the proposed prototype gamepad using unified modeling language and descriptions.

4.1 Controller Design

The proposed controller will be using the best of both worlds; specifically, it will be using gamepad for the traditional functionality and will be utilizing the motion of the gamepad device by the help of the physically attached gyroscope. The movement data received from the gamepad will be combined with the data collected from the air mouse sensors and processed by the Unity engine's Input Manager.

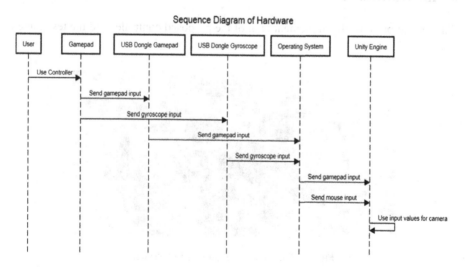

Fig. 1. Sequence diagram of hardware

There are several ways to managing interaction inputs on the Unity Engine. The most efficient way of managing interaction inputs is by using virtual inputs. The advantage with the virtual inputs is the ability to merge the functionality of two separate hardware devices and use them as single controller. This is achieved by mapping some of the functionalities to a one physical device and the rest to another. As a result, the camera view movements can be controlled using both or either the gamepad and the air mouse. Accordingly, shown in the (Fig. 1) when the data retrieved from both devices reach Unity Engine, the buttons on the gamepad and the movement data from the air mouse is then mapped to the relevant action using the Input Manager of the Unity Engine. Using the data received from the gamepad and the air mouse, the player can move the character or rotate view of the camera.

4.2 Test Game Design

Accordingly, a First Person Shooter game is designed and built to test the prototype gamepad. However, this game is specifically designed to test the advantages and disadvantages that could be caused by the newly proposed game controller. Hence, it contains specialized section for evaluation purposes and using its in-built functionalities measures the aiming accuracy, the time needed to aim and the bullet usage. Therefore, the test map includes four different sections of shooting areas. First two sections are only to measure aiming time, which can also be seen as a warm-up for the user to get used to the controller. The third section is test the accuracy of the controllers on both stable and moving targets. The last section is to measure aiming accuracy for only on moving targets.

5 Implementation

This section presents the implementation of the proposed controller and the test game .

Fig. 2. The gyroscope gamepad controller

The proposed controller hardware can work on any game that is run on Unity engine and other game engines such as Source Engine (Fig. 2). Gyroscope gamepad does not disrupt the standard first-person shooter game mechanics. Hence it is backward compatible and can be used with any FPS game. The test game is implemented using Microsoft C# language and entails a virtual 400-m × 400-m gaming ground. The areas are created having in mind the game stage analogy, where each consequent area is more difficult to play and require higher gaming skills.

Fig. 3. Circle crosshair

Accordingly, the aforementioned crosshair is shown when there is a possibility to use sensor-based targeting functionality (Fig. 3). In these cases, the user can infer that s/he can use the air mouse's gyroscope to aim to a target, which can be achieved by pointing the dot in the middle of the circle.

5.1 Implementation of Test Game

The test game makes use of Unity's built-in 3D objects to create walls and targets. Most of the textures are from Unity standard assets, however, some exceptional items such as trees and rocks are form the Unity asset store. To create a more realistic gaming environment, the terrain is enriched with additional items such as tires where a player can shoot through. Also every shooting area has a starting point, where the user needs to start shooting from, in order to calculate the time and shooting precision (Fig. 4).

Fig. 4. Test map

After setting the graphical user interface items, the camera and the character controls, a shooting mechanism is needed to enable the user to shoot within the given test area. Shooting operation is handled with Raycast, which is a mechanism that identifies a collusion between two game objects. Using this mechanism, as soon as the fire button is pressed, a ray is sent from the center of the screen to the first gaming object in front of it. If the object that the ray has hit is a target then the target is destroyed. Each shot fired by user increases the number used bullet counter, which is used to track how many bullets is used and decrease ammo number displayed on screen.

Fig. 5. Circular and square targets (Color figure online)

Overall, there two types of targets used in the game – one with black circles over a red background and one with red, white and blue layers (Fig. 5). Depending to the shooting area – and the type of evaluation aimed – the targets can be static or can be moving within the shooting area. Furthermore, the two targets have different characteristics: Black on red target can be destroyed by shooting at any part of the object, however, the target with three colors can either be destroyed by shooting at the very center red part or by shooting its every layer separately. By doing so, the game calculates the accuracy of the user's shots.

6   Test and Results

This section describes the objective and subjective tests performed using the proposed prototype controller. Furthermore, the shooting areas in which these tests were performed are detailed.

The tests are conducted with 20 participants. All the participants were casual gamers. Three different controllers are used to undertake evaluations; these are keyboard and mouse, classic gamepad and gyroscope gamepad. Two subjective tests are conducted to evaluate the user experience. Namely, these tests were the SUS (System Usability Scale) Questionnaire [9] and the Device Assessment Questionnaire. The SUS Questionnaire is a reliable tool for evaluating the usability of any hardware, software, and application. On the other hand, the Device Assessment Questionnaire from ISO 9241, Part 9 Standard [10] consists of thirteen questions covering issues related to physical operation, fatigue and comfort, speed and accuracy, and overall usability. Participants were asked to respond to each question with a rating from low to high.

Using these three tests and evaluations, tried to evaluate whether the proposed gyroscope-enabled gamepad outperformed the other classic interaction devices – keyboard, mouse and the classic gamepad.

6.1   Test Scenarios

There are 4 different scenarios and each of those scenarios has a different evaluation objective in measuring and comparing the performance of the test devices.

Shooting Range: This scenario has 6 targets, 3 of them placed 40 m away from the player and other 3 are placed 80 m away from the player. Only time and bullet usage were measured in this section (Fig. 6).

Fig. 6. Shooting range

Horizontal Ping Pong: This scenario has 6 targets and they are placed in the left and right hand side of the section's start point. They are 20 to 80 m away from the player. The targets move from left to right and right to left with the speed of 5 m per second until they are all destroyed. Only time and bullet usage were measured from this section (Fig. 7).

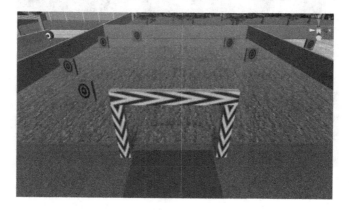

Fig. 7. Horizontal ping pong

Room Breach: This scenario has 13 targets, where 7 of them are stable targets and 6 of them are moving targets. The targets are placed between 10 to 40 m away from the player. Furthermore, moving targets move with the speed of 5 m per second. This scenario is composed of two shooting areas and the game timer stops when the player destroys both areas (Fig. 8).

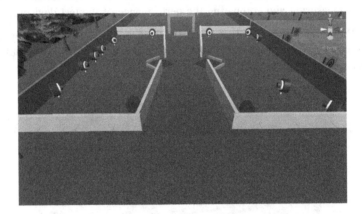

Fig. 8. Room breach

Sloping Range: This scenario has 5 targets where all of them are moving. The targets are placed 70 m away from the player and they move with the speed of 5 m per second with a forward and backwards slope. This section only evaluates moving target scores. This is also the last shooting area of the game where after all targets are destroyed, the results are displayed on the console (Fig. 9).

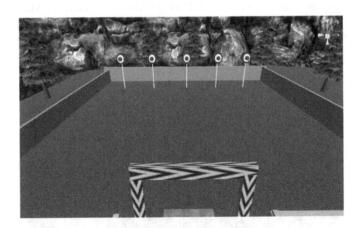

Fig. 9. Sloping range

6.2 Analysis of Test Results

In the analysis of the results IBM's SPSS [11] tool for statistics was used. A MANOVA test is conducted to compare the result using the scores that a user has achieved, time s/he took to finish the game and user's bullet usage.

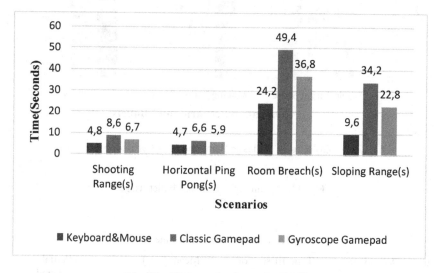

Fig. 10. Time results for each scenario

Figure 10 shows the user's aiming time results in seconds. In this case, lower the results the better. The results indicate that gyroscope gamepad is behind keyboard and mouse but better than the classic gamepad.

Figure 11 presents the scores achieved by the players and the number of bullets that they have used. Accordingly, in this figure, the lower the number of bullets and higher scores mean more accurate shots; hence better user interaction. In this test, gyroscope-enabled gamepad had comparable results to the keyboard and mouse. On the other hand, classic gamepad had the worst results (Tables 1 and 2).

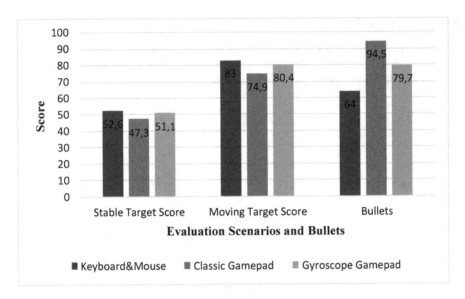

Fig. 11. Results of scores and bullet usage

Table 1. MANOVA between time results

Source	Dependent variable	Type III sum of squares	df	Mean square	F	p	Partial eta squared
Groups	Shooting range	140,175	2	70,088	20,496	0	0,418
	Horizontal ping pong	34,511	2	17,255	4,602	0,014	0,139
	Room breach	6352,687	2	3176,343	63,206	0	0,689
	Sloping range	6357,323	2	3178,661	37,742	0	0,570

The significance value p is smaller than 0.05 (p < 0.05) means there is a significant difference between Time Results.

Table 2. MANOVA between score and bullet usage results

Source	Dependent variable	Type III sum of squares	df	Mean square	F	p	Partial eta squared
Groups	Stable target score	686,100	2	343,050	4,673	0,013	0,141
	Moving target score	298,533	2	149,267	4,607	0,014	0,139
	Bullets	9460,83	2	4730,417	18,36	0	0,392

The significance value p is smaller than 0.05 (p < 0.05) means there is a significant difference between Scores and bullet usage.

6.3 Subjective Tests

As part of the subjective tests, each participant was requested to fill in two question-naires. Accordingly, the implemented prototype gamepad resulted in 80.6 SUS score, where 68 SUS score is considered average. Furthermore, oral feedback received from the participants indicated that using the prototype gamepad was not better than key-board or mouse, usability-wise. However, the participants emphasized that it was much more realistic and entertaining than the traditional interaction tools, because using the gyroscope-enabled controller was like pointing a gun to the screen.

The participants that undertook the Device Assessment Questionnaire were required to respond to thirteen questions related and covering issues of physical operation, fatigue and comfort, speed and accuracy, and overall usability. All the responses were collected using five level Likert-scale. The findings of the Device Assessment Questionnaire is presented in Fig. 12.

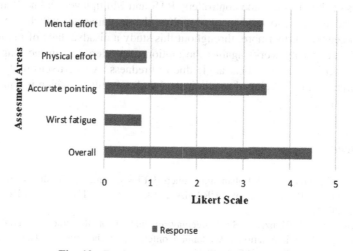

Fig. 12. Device assessment questionnaire results

The collected results show that the prototype gamepad's physical operations are acceptable and no indication of exhaustion were reported, with the exception of a little wrist fatigue. According to the feedback from the participating users, the prototype was easy and comfortable to use; also, on the other hand, very accurate and well fitted for rapid reactions in a fast-paced game.

7 Conclusion

The general purpose of this study is to show that using both gyroscope and gamepad controls together can result with a better game controller. This type of a gamepad would improve the interaction experience and the realistic feeling of first-person shooter games. The proposed solution makes use of the gyroscope and the gamepad on

Unity Engine, which utilizes virtual inputs and cross-platform input manager. By making use of circle crosshair analogy it was possible to combine both controllers' functions at the same time and converge into one controller. Having the 3D environment and angles to command the game, eases any restrictions imposed by a 2D joystick and reduces the workload put the gamer's wrists. Finally, the results show that gyroscope-enabled gamepad is better to use over the classic gamepad on first-person shooter games. Also, it has been highlighted by the testers that the prototype was much more entertaining and realistic. We believe the reason for keyboard and mouse performing better and higher results is due to the experience. Since, the evaluators and gamers at large are people who use mouse and keyboard for years but they interact with gyroscope-based gamepad first time.

As a future work, the gyroscope controller can be tested on different types of games. To handle the controller easier, rather than using circular crosshair, different types of crosshairs can be implemented and tested. In this study, first person shooter games were chosen because they are the most suffering game genre due to the restrictions of the classic game controllers. RTS and Multiplayer Online Battle Arena (MOBA) games are also hard to play with a classic gamepad, which can be good evaluation genres. Furthermore, throughout this study a disadvantage of motion-based controllers, the gravity works against the motion controllers and in the long run it is effects the users aim at a vertical angle due to tiredness. A smart sensitivity management program can be developed to eliminate this disadvantage, which is another topic for investigation.

References

1. Alankuş, G., Eren, A.A.: Enhancing gamepad FPS controls with tilt-driven sensitivity adjustment. In: Proceedings of EURASIA 2014, Paper 13. Hacettepe University Press, Ankara (2014)
2. Natapov, D., MacKenzie, I.S.: Gameplay evaluation of the trackball controller. In: Proceedings of the International Academic Conference on the Future of Game Design and Technology, pp. 167–174. ACM (2010)
3. Ramcharitar, A., Teather, R.J.: A Fitts' law evaluation of video game controllers: thumbstick, touchpad, and gyrosensor. In: Proceedings of the 2017 CHI Conference Extended Abstracts on Human Factors in Computing Systems, pp. 2860–2866. ACM (2017)
4. Oshita, M., Ishikawa, H.: Gamepad vs. touchscreen: a comparison of action selection interfaces in computer games. In: Proceedings of the Workshop at SIGGRAPH Asia, pp. 27–31. ACM (2012)
5. Teather, R.J., Roth, A., MacKenzie, I.S.: Tilt-touch synergy: input control for "dual-analog" style mobile games. Entertainment Comput. **21**, 33–43 (2017)
6. McArthur, V. C. (2009). An empirical comparison of Wiimote gun attachments for pointing tasks. In Proceedings of the 1st ACM SIGCHI symposium on Engineering interactive computing systems (pp. 203–208). ACM
7. Murphy, D.K.: Usability testing of video game controllers: a case study. In: Games User Research. AK Peters/CRC Press, Natick (2016)
8. Google Stadia. https://www.bbc.com/news/technology-47623414. Accessed 31 Mar 2019

9. System Usability Scale. https://www.usability.gov/how-to-and-tools/resources/templates/system-usability-scale-sus.html. Accessed 15 Dec 2018
10. Douglas, S.A.: Testing pointing device performance and user assessment with the ISO 9241, Part 9 standard. In: Proceedings of the SIGCHI Conference on Human Factors in Computing Systems, pp. 215–222. ACM (1999)
11. IBM SPSS Software. https://www.ibm.com/analytics/spss-statistics-software. Accessed 20 June 2019

Prioritizing Use Cases for Development of Mobile Apps Using AHP: A Case Study in To-Do List Apps

Onur Yildirim[1](✉) and Serhat Peker[2]

[1] Atılım University, P.O. Box 06836, İncek, Ankara, Turkey
yildirim.onur@atilim.edu.tr
[2] İzmir Bakırçay University, P.O. Box 35570, Menemen, İzmir, Turkey
serhat.peker@bakircay.edu.tr

Abstract. With the rapid development of communication technologies, the uses of mobile apps have increased in a significant manner over the past few years. Every day many different types of mobile apps are uploaded to mobile application markets. However, it is very difficult for the apps to stay competitive and survive in these marketplaces. Covering the requirements fitting the needs of users is one of significant factors in mobile apps' success in the market. In this regard, this study aims to use Analytic Hierarchy Process (AHP) to evaluate the use cases for the development of mobile apps. The results show that AHP provides an efficient tool which can be used to determine importance of the requirements in mobile apps considering users' preferences.

Keywords: Requirements engineering · Requirements prioritization · Software development · Analytic hierarchy process · Mobile applications

1 Introduction

With the development of mobile and communication technologies, mobile applications (apps) has become an integral part of our daily life. From real-time messaging and communication apps to map apps, and to reminders, many different types of mobile apps are creating significant benefits to their users. With this increasing interest of users in mobile apps, application markets have grown tremendously. In the first quarter of 2019, there were 2.1 million and 1.8 million available apps for download in leading app stores Android Market and Apple Store respectively [1]. By providing variety of mobile apps, these mobile app markets are extremely popular among mobile users.

The application markets are not only a platform for mobile users to download their apps, but they also present a significant revenue potential for mobile app developers. In a recent study reported from Statista [2], in 2020, mobile apps are expected to generate 188.9 billion U.S. dollars in revenues via app stores and in-app advertising. With this revenue opportunity, software developers are now eager to develop mobile apps than ever before.

Many new apps are released to application markets every day. In such a competitive environment, creating value in the software is essential to survive in the market

© Springer Nature Switzerland AG 2019
I. Awan et al. (Eds.): MobiWIS 2019, LNCS 11673, pp. 308–315, 2019.
https://doi.org/10.1007/978-3-030-27192-3_24

place, and developing a product satisfying customer needs plays a key role in this purpose [3, 4]. However, most of the mobile apps in the market fail, because they are built based on a limited set of requirements that do not sufficiently meet the needs of the target user group. Additionally, several applications in the market contain many insignificant functionalities from of user viewpoint. These factors directly affect the users' intention towards the acceptance of mobile apps. Therefore, to resolve these problems, it is necessary to determine the importance of the requirements based on users' preferences.

Determining the importance of the user requirements is a critical process in software development, especially in mobile application development where system releases are more frequent, resources are always limited, and competitiveness is high [5]. This process enables mobile application developers to prioritize and identify the requirements that perfectly fits users' needs. Thus, the value of the product is maximized, and development times and project costs are reduced as well.

Obtaining user preferences is very crucial to prioritize software requirements. Analytic hierarchy process (AHP), which is the most widely used requirement prioritization method, prioritizes requirements according to stakeholder preferences. Therefore, this study aims to evaluate and prioritize use cases for mobile apps development using AHP technique. For this purpose, a case study is conducted in to-do list apps and results are interpreted. The remainder of this study is structured as follows. In Sect. 2, background and related work is provided. Section 3 describes research methodology. In Sect. 4, a case study carried out for to-do list app category is presented. Finally, Sect. 5 presents concluding remark.

2 Background and Related Work

Requirement engineering is one of the important phases in software development. It basically contains the processes of t eliciting, documenting and maintaining requirements [6]. Because of the budget, time and staff constraints, it is very difficult to implement all the requirements desired by the stakeholders [5]. Thus, requirements are implemented with a set of small releases which contains an incremental number of requirements from the whole project requirements.

On the other hand, in today's business software companies are harder to survive due to many challenges (e.g. more and more competitions, new technologies, dynamic market needs, globalization and digitalization). With all of these factors, creating value is essential for software companies in order to achieve sustainable competitive advantage [7, 8]. In this manner, [9] introduced the concept of the value-based approach in software engineering domain. Moreover, [10] addressed the value-based approach in requirements engineering, and the authors in [11, 12] discussed the importance of value-based requirements.

Prioritizing and identifying requirements are crucial in value-based requirements engineering. In this context, requirements prioritization is an important aspect of requirements engineering. It is the value assessment of requirements based on the stakeholders' preferences, and provides software developers the core requirements satisfying stakeholders' most critical needs [13]. There exist numerous requirements prioritization techniques that have been presented by various researchers over the past years. According to a recent a review [14], some of the major techniques for requirements prioritization are analytical hierarchy process (AHP), binary search trees, bubble sort, cost value ranking, planning game, numerical assignment technique, and Wiegers' matrix approach. Many useful models have been also developed to execute this process, including VOP [15], VIRP [13] MDRPM [16], PHandler [17] and DRank [18].

Among the prioritization techniques, AHP [19] is the most widely used and cited technique [14]. Further, Karlsson [20] confirmed that, AHP is one of the few techniques that provide reliable prioritization results. AHP is also used for the evaluations in the mobile domain. One example is [21] in which a fuzzy AHP methodology was used to determine the requirements relative weights in the mobile commerce. In another study [22], AHP approach was used to select the most important mobile service category. Similarly, Nikou et al. [23] employed AHP to identify the most relevant mobile services.

Despite the fact that AHP is the most well-known and widely used technique for requirements prioritization, very few studies have utilized it in the mobile domain. Additionally, no effort has attempted to prioritize requirements of mobile apps using AHP method. To fill this gap, this study prioritizes use cases for mobile apps development by utilizing AHP technique.

3 Methodology

In the present study, a two-stage approach is followed to prioritize use cases for mobile apps. The first stage is determination of use cases for the selected mobile application domain; the second stage uses the Analytic Hierarchy Process (AHP) method to compute of the relative importance weights of the use cases and rank them.

In order to determine the weighting of the identified use cases, a questionnaire is designed. This questionnaire contains the AHP judgment matrix, which enables evaluators to make pairwise comparisons among the use cases. Indeed, the evaluator determines which of the element in a pair is more desirable or preferred compared to the other and performs this for all pairs in the matrix. For the comparison process, this study employed Saaty's nine-point scale [19] as shown in Table 1.

Table 1. Importance levels for AHP

Fundamental scale	Importance
Extremely less important	1/9
	1/8
Very strongly less important	1/7
	1/6
Strongly less important	1/5
	1/4
Moderately less important	1/3
	1/2

(continued)

Table 1. (*continued*)

Fundamental scale	Importance
Equal important	1
	2
Moderately less important	3
	4
Strongly more important	5
	6
Very strongly more important	7
	8
Extremely more important	9

Each evaluator indicated his/her preferences by filling the questionnaire individually. After collecting the questionnaire from the participants, the data were entered to a MS Excel file for getting results.

The relative significance weight is calculated by taking the average of the Eigen vector. The sum of all points of the priority vector is equal to 1. The consistency index (CI) is used to calculate the degree of consistency.

$$CI = (\lambda_{max} - n)/(n - 1) \tag{1}$$

The number of criteria is expressed in n. In the λ_max is equal to the eigenvalue of matrix A. The greatest eigenvalue of matrix A is consistent with λ_max being equal to n [24]. The highest eigenvalue λ_max is calculated as shown below [25].

$$\lambda_{max} = \sum_{i=1}^{n} \frac{(c.v)_i}{n.v_i} \tag{2}$$

In the formula, "c" represents the pairwise comparison matrix, and "v" represents the matrix vector. "CI" is the consistency index value. When this value is obtained, it can be calculated by dividing by "RI" the random index (Table 2) [26].

$$CR = \frac{CI}{RI} \tag{3}$$

The appropriate value of RI is selected depending on the number of criteria, for instance, if the number of criteria is equal to 5, then the appropriate value of RI = 1.12.

Table 2. Values of RI

n	1	2	3	4	5	6	7	8	9
RI	0	0	0.58	0.9	1.12	1.24	1.32	1.41	1.45
n	10	11	12	13	14	15	16	17	18
RI	1.49	1.51	1.54	1.56	1.57	1.58	1.59	1.6	1.61

Before analyzing results, the consistency of each responder was checked. Consistency Ratio (CR) was used for this purpose, and if its value is less than or equal to 0.1 for an evaluator, the responses of him are considered consistent [19]. The weights of the use cases were calculated based on the evaluations of responders passing the consistency test by using AHP method. The aggregate values of relative importance weights were calculated by taking the mean of individual scores of evaluators. The weights calculated for use cases sum up to 1, then they were multiplied by 100 so that their aggregate become 100. Finally, use case prioritization and all the interpretations were performed based on these scores out of 100.

4 Case Study

4.1 Overview of Productivity Apps

To-do list apps are one of the popular mobile app categories and enable the users improve their productivity by organizing their tasks and any type of lists. Since these mobile apps include main CRUD (create, read, update, delete) use cases and are commonly used by mobile users, we have conducted a case study on to-do list app category in order to prioritize use cases for mobile apps.

4.2 Use Case Identification

Based on an extensive review of to-do list apps in the android market, eighteen widely used use cases were identified and they are provided in Table 3.

Table 3. Use cases

Use case ID	Use case name
UC1	Create list
UC2	Read/View list with its items
UC3	Update/Rename list
UC4	Delete list (with its items)
UC5	Clear list
UC6	Add item to list via keyboard
UC7	Add item to list via voice
UC8	Update list item
UC9	Delete list item
UC10	Mark a list item as important
UC11	Set a reminder for a list item
UC12	Set all list items as checked/unchecked
UC13	Set a list item as checked/unchecked
UC14	Move an item from one list to another list
UC15	Share list
UC16	Share a list item
UC17	Add attachment
UC18	Add note to list item

4.3 Evaluators

The evaluators of this study are 54 undergraduate software engineering students who were the participants of requirements engineering course. The questionnaires were given to this sample. This sample was selected since they were all knowledgeable about requirements/use case prioritization and AHP usage in the process. This sample is also important users of mobile apps. In order to ensure that all evaluators have familiarity with the to-do lists apps, the evaluators were requested to actively use Any.do, which is one of the popular mobile apps in this category, over a week prior to data collection.

After data collection, the questionnaires which were not met the consistency ratio (CR) requirement were excluded out and evaluations of 34 respondents were used to obtain the final values of relative importance weights of use cases. Note that our final sample size seems to be small but there were many previous AHP studies based on a small sample. Further, a small sample who have knowledge about the topic is enough for AHP analysis [27].

4.4 AHP Application

After performing the analysis of the received questionnaires, AHP weights and the priority rankings are presented in Fig. 1.

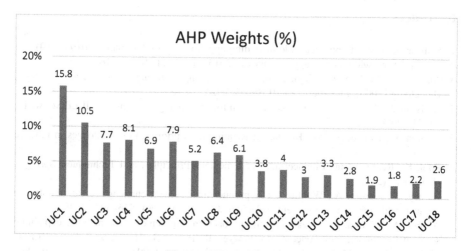

Fig. 1. AHP weights results

As shown in Fig. 1, "Create list" is the most important use case accounting for almost 16% of the total weights followed by "Read/View List with its items" and "Delete list (with its items)" use cases. These use cases are fundamentals of to-do list applications and are considered to be the most important by evaluators. Thus, those use cases should be given priority when building an effective to-do list app. On the other hand, the responders evaluated "Share list" and "Share a list item" use cases as the least important ones for to-do list apps.

5 Conclusion

The present study applies AHP technique to prioritize use cases for mobile apps development and shows its validity in the to-do-list mobile app category. The result indicates that the evaluators view use cases regarding managing lists (e.g. "Create list", "Read/View List with its items", "Delete list") as the most important ones, while they assesses the use cases related to sharing such as "Share list" and "Share a list item" as the least important ones for to-do list apps. These results can be useful to practitioners to understand how to develop the mobile apps fulfilling user' wants, and preferences. Moreover, mobile app developers can use the AHP method to determine which use cases to be implemented and delivered first in the early releases. This study also provides insights for researchers by showing that AHP is applicable to examine the preferences of mobile app users.

Although the AHP method proved to be applicable to prioritize and select the use cases in the mobile app development, it suffers from the scalability problem and more comparisons are needed when the number of requirements increases. Further, the model was only applied in to-do list apps, this approach could be used in a variety of mobile app categories to ascertain its generalizability. Therefore, future research could replicate this study in the development of different mobile app categories.

References

1. Statista: Number of apps available in leading app stores as of 1st quarter 2019 (2019)
2. Statista: Worldwide mobile app revenues in 2015, 2016 and 2020 (2016)
3. Aurum, A., Wohlin, C.: Engineering and Managing Software Requirements. Springer, Heidelberg (2005). https://doi.org/10.1007/3-540-28244-0
4. Karlsson, J., Ryan, K.: A cost-value approach for prioritizing requirements. IEEE Softw. **14**, 67–74 (1997)
5. Lehtola, L., Kauppinen, M., Kujala, S.: Requirements prioritization challenges in practice (2010)
6. Pohl, K.: Requirements Engineering: Fundamentals, Principles, and Techniques. Springer, Heidelberg (2010)
7. Barney, S., Aurum, A., Wohlin, C.: A product management challenge: creating software product value through requirements selection. J. Syst. Arch. **54**, 576–593 (2008)
8. Aurum, A., Wohlin, C.: A value-based approach in requirements engineering: explaining some of the fundamental concepts. In: Sawyer, P., Paech, B., Heymans, P. (eds.) REFSQ 2007. LNCS, vol. 4542, pp. 109–115. Springer, Heidelberg (2007). https://doi.org/10.1007/978-3-540-73031-6_8
9. Faulk, S.R., Harmon, R.R., Raffo, D.M.: Value-based software engineering (VBSE): a value-driven approach to product-line engineering. In: First International Conference on Software Product-Line Engineering, pp. 1–13 (2000)
10. Boehm, B.: Value-based software engineering: reinventing. SIGSOFT Softw. Eng. Notes **28**, 3 (2003)
11. Favaro, J.: Managing requirements for business value. IEEE Softw. **19**, 15–17 (2002)

12. Wohlin, C., Aurum, A.: Criteria for selecting software requirements to create product value: an industrial empirical study. In: Biffl, S., Aurum, A., Boehm, B., Erdogmus, H., Grünbacher, P. (eds.) Value-Based Software Engineering, pp. 179–200. Springer, Heidelberg (2006). https://doi.org/10.1007/3-540-29263-2_9

13. Ramzan, M., Jaffar, M.A., Shahid, A.A.: Value based intelligent requirement prioritization (VIRP): expert driven fuzzy logic based prioritization technique. Int. J. Innov. Comput. Inf. Control. **7**, 1017–1038 (2011)

14. Achimugu, P., Selamat, A., Ibrahim, R., Mahrin, M.N.R.: A systematic literature review of software requirements prioritization research. Inf. Softw. Technol. **56**, 568–585 (2014)

15. Azar, J., Smith, R.K., Cordes, D.: Value-oriented requirements prioritization in a small development organization. IEEE Softw. **24**, 32–37 (2007)

16. Iqbal, M.A., Zaidi, A.M., Murtaza, S.: A new requirement prioritization model for market driven products using analytical hierarchical process. In: DSDE 2010 - International Conference on Data Storage and Data Engineering, pp. 142–149 (2010)

17. Babar, M.I., Ghazali, M., Jawawi, D.N.A., Shamsuddin, S.M., Ibrahim, N.: PHandler: an expert system for a scalable software requirements prioritization process. Knowl.-Based Syst. **84**, 179–202 (2015)

18. Shao, F., Peng, R., Lai, H., Wang, B.: DRank: a semi-automated requirements prioritization method based on preferences and dependencies. J. Syst. Softw. **126**, 141–156 (2017)

19. Saaty, T.L.: Decision making with the analytic hierarchy process. Int. J. Serv. Sci. **1**, 83 (2008)

20. Karlsson, J., Wohlin, C., Regnell, B.: An evaluation of methods for prioritizing software requirements. Inf. Softw. Technol. **39**, 939–947 (1998)

21. Büyüközkan, G.: Determining the mobile commerce user requirements using an analytic approach. Comput. Stand. Interfaces **31**, 144–152 (2009)

22. Nikou, S., Mezei, J., Bouwman, H.: Analytic hierarchy process (AHP) approach for selecting mobile service category: (consumers' preferences). In: Proceedings - 2011 10th International Conference on Mobile Business, ICMB 2011 (2011)

23. Nikou, S., Mezei, J.: Evaluation of mobile services and substantial adoption factors with analytic hierarchy process (AHP). Telecomm. Policy **37**, 915–929 (2013)

24. Saaty, T.L.: How to make a decision: the analytic hierarchy process. Eur. J. Oper. Res. **48**, 9–26 (1990)

25. Franek, J., Kresta, A.: Judgment scales and consistency measure in AHP. Procedia Econ. Financ. **12**, 164–173 (2014)

26. Saaty, T., Vergas, L.G.: Models, Methods, Concepts & Applications of the Analytic Hierarchy Process, 2nd edn (1996)

27. Shrestha, R.K., Alavalapati, J.R.R., Kalmbacher, R.S.: Exploring the potential for silvopasture adoption in south-central Florida: an application of SWOT-AHP method. Agric. Syst. **81**, 185–199 (2004)

Contextual Push Notifications on Mobile Devices: A Pre-study on the Impact of Usage Context on User Response

Stephan Böhm$^{(\boxtimes)}$, Holger Driehaus, and Maximilian Wick

RheinMain University of Applied Sciences, Wiesbaden, Germany
{stephan.boehm,holger.driehaus}@hs-rm.de, m142679@googlemail.com

Abstract. In a time where users are facing increasing amounts of daily push notifications, a variety of research has been conducted to find a more systematic way to deliver content to the user more efficiently. These studies aim to establish scheduled services that are aware of the user's attention or context, and defer the notifications until an opportune moment arises. Thereby, the impact of push notifications should be enhanced, as the user is less disturbed or the situation of the user makes a reception of the content more likely. In this study, the context categories for triggering push notifications on mobile devices are being elaborated and structured. This is followed by an examination of the technical possibilities of the Android platform for determining user activities. Finally, an experimental structure will be presented, with which insights into the reception of push messages and the precision of the activity-related usage context will be acquired. The study is work in progress and describes the structure of the investigation as well as the first results of a small test group of users.

Keywords: Context-aware computing · HCI · Interruptibility · Mobile sensing · Push notification

1 Introduction

In 2003, BlackBerry introduced a feature for their mail client to send new emails to the inbox automatically without the need for the user to refresh it. Six years later, Apple launched the same feature for apps and called it push notifications. Android adopted it shortly afterwards. With the capability of real-time push notifications comes the responsibility for publishers to use these carefully. When dealing with interruptions, people experience stress and frustration [31]. Intelligent, context-aware notification systems have been proposed with different approaches, underlying data, and findings to overcome this problem. The motivation to tap on a notification and engage with the content, for instance, is stronger when the user is bored or in between physical activities. There are also several reasons for being unreachable for push notifications. The user could

© Springer Nature Switzerland AG 2019
I. Awan et al. (Eds.): MobiWIS 2019, LNCS 11673, pp. 316–330, 2019.
https://doi.org/10.1007/978-3-030-27192-3_25

sleep, operate a vehicle, or be in a meeting. On the other hand, certain situations are in favor for the event of a notification. These could include waiting at the bus stop or being at a coffee shop all alone. Previous studies used different approaches to estimate appropriate moments for user interactions. Some findings aimed toward the breakpoints of activities [38, 40, 50], others used specific locations [15] or mental states [43] as indicator for the prediction. Poppinga et al. [45] introduced a sensor-based system to identify opportune moments to trigger notifications. This context-observation approach incorporated six different smartphone sensors to create a decision tree with a data mining software.

Mobile end devices such as smartphones contain a large number of sensors that can be used to determine context information. With the help of this contextual information, a mobile system could proactively decide whether a notification would be successful at a given time. The first step to establish such a system would be to identify all the context information that contributes to the system. The use of contextual information depends on many factors, e.g., how easy it is to obtain or what problems are associated with its exploitation, e.g. an unwanted intrusion into user privacy or restrictions on data protection rules. Therefore it is understandable that the sending of push notifications to mobile devices has so far been primarily date- and time-controlled and that further context information is generally not evaluated. However, the Android platform provides an option for recognizing the current user activity already implemented in the operating system.

Against this background, this paper contains a pre-study on using user activity information for triggering push notifications on mobile devices. The paper is structured as follows: in Sect. 2, related work is discussed and the research objectives are worked out. Section 3 then contains some background on push notifications and context categories relevant on mobile devices. The activity-related usage context and the possibility to determine it with Android smartphones will then be discussed in Sect. 4. An experimental approach for evaluating user activities when sending push notifications and initial findings based on a small test group are then presented in Sect. 5. Section 6 closes with conclusions and an outlook on further research work.

2   Related Work and Research Objectives

A recent survey of the state of the art of intelligent notification systems found numerous studies in the field of understanding the interruptibility for mobile devices [34]. Pejovic and Musolesi [41] predicted receptivity by using context information. Pielot et al. [44] used mobile phone usage features to predict the attentiveness to notifications and Dingler and Pielot [14] did similar studies in 2015. Another study involving Pielot that used the phone's usage activity and contextual information predicted the availability for phone calls [42]. Mehrotra et al. predicted the receptivity by using the notification content and context information [35]. Other Studies focused on the understanding of interruptions in general [7, 16, 27, 30, 33, 36, 37, 48, 51], interruptibility management by using the current activity [25,47], or by using transitions between activities [17,24,39]. There are also findings in filtering irrelevant information [18,32,48]. Another area of studies is about the cost of interruptions, which can be divided into the impact on memory [3,19], the relationship with the ongoing task [5,10–12,19,28], the relationship with the user's emotional state [2,5,29], and the impact on the user experience [28].

While the studies described above are very much aimed at the impact of (contextual) push notifications, the present paper and this pre-study focus more on the achievement of implementation-oriented findings. The implementation-oriented objectives, i.e., the requirements on the test system to be implemented, are to be outlined as follows:

- Development of a test app that enables the triggered sending of push notifications to a defined group of users.
- Recognition of the user activity at the time the push notification is received on the mobile device (based on the standard Android functionality).
- Acquisition of user feedback on actual user activity as well as on reasons on delays on opening the notifications.

In addition, the implemented test system is to be used with a small user group in order to gain initial insights. Essential research questions in this context are for example:

- With which delay times are push notifications opened on the smartphone.
- What are the primary activity states of the users when they open the notifications on the smartphone?
- To what extent do the activity states determined by the Android system and the actual activity state match?

These finding will yet not be generalizable (due to the small user group), but provide first insights that can be used for a later expansion of the tests and an improvement of the system.

3   Research Background

3.1   Push Notifications

The first part of any conversion funnel, like used in the AIDA model, is awareness. As the funnel narrows down gradually, the importance of the first step becomes clear. By neglecting the initial process step, the hierarchical sequence of effects cannot unfold and the whole funnel fails eventually. In mobile computing, push notifications can be an important tool to attract attention. A recent study from Accengage [1], based on the data of 50 billion push notifications, unveils some of the important aspects for push notifications. The use of push notifications alone leads to a doubling of app usage. Due to different operating system regulations, Android users have much higher opt-in rates for push notifications (91%) than users of iOS (44%). The average opt-in rate across both mobile operating systems is about 68%. Since a fifth of the users only launches an app one time only, it is critical to engage the users at an early stage to improve these rates. Publishers face general reaction rates (tap on the notification) of 7.8%, in Germany up to 9.2%. Unsurprisingly, the time of the day is crucial with increases of about 20% in reaction rates when pushed at the right times of the day. The study found that the highest reaction rates are between 10 and 11 p.m. (10.9 to 11.4%) and around noon (7.7 to 8.2% between noon and 2 p.m.). The reaction rates also vary within a week, with a peak at Tuesday at 8.4%, and a base at Wednesday at 7.4%. Aside of the temporal aspect, the content is essential as well. A study from CleverTap [9], with an analysis of 40 billion push notifications found, that even a basic personalization (e.g., name or location) results in a 9% increase in open rates. In addition, the length affects the impact of the push notifications, where the ideal length varies between 20 characters for deals and coupons to up to 90 characters for apps in retail or entertainment. Also, the use of emojis and so called power words (e.g., "deal", "exclusive" or "limited") can lead to an increase in click through rates, as the study suggests.

3.2 Context

With an increase in reaction rates of 20% by just sending the notifications at the proper time, it should be investigated whether these numbers can be pushed further by dynamically addressing different users at their ideal times and not at the mean value of 40 billion notifications. Time implies other contextual factors; it seems obvious that low reaction rates at night are caused by the user's sleep cycle, for instance. Context-aware computing has been discussed long before the use of smartphones. It was first introduced by Schilit et al. [49] in 1995. Since then, many definitions have been proposed to narrow down and operationalize the term. A general definition of context was provided by Dey [13, p. 5]: "Context is any information that can be used to characterize the situation of an entity. An entity is a person, place, or object that is considered relevant to the interaction between the user and the application, including the user and the applications themselves." Zimmermann et al. [52] suggested an operational definition of context, which includes individuality, activity, location, relations, and time. Any entity's context information falls into one of these five categories. By knowing more about these, a given notification should outnumber the outcome of consideration of the time alone in terms of open rates and engagement. The individuality context can be further broken down to natural entity context, human entity context, artificial entity context, and group entity context (cf. Fig. 1). The natural entity context includes the "characteristics of all living and non-living things that occur naturally and are not the result of any human activity or intervention" [52, p. 561]. The human entity context on the other hand comprises the user behavior and basic user properties. A comprehensive view on these characteristics is provided by The General User Model Ontology (GUMO) by Heckmann [23]. The artificial entity context contains anything that results from human actions or technical processes. Lastly, the group entity context covers entities that share characteristics, interact with each other or have certain relationships.

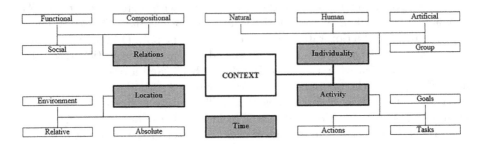

Fig. 1. Context categories and subcategories (based on [52])

The activity context involves explicit goals, tasks and actions. In this context, the actions are the smallest units, followed by the tasks, which are determined by the goal(s) of the user. It can further be distinguished between low- and high-level goals. The latter are more consistent and change less frequently. Tasks are also hierarchic, including subtasks. The location context describes the physical or virtual position of an entity and other spatial information. In addition to the absolute and relative location, the environment has been added by the authors for a more comprehensive view. The location model can also be divided into the quantitative and qualitative location [8]. A quantitative location is measured in coordinative dimensions, like supplied by the Global Positioning System (GPS). Qualitative spatial information allows insights of the location itself, like the building or country the entity is located. The relations context is about the connection the entities have to each other. Social relations are usually about people, the roles they play in certain interpersonal relations and further information about the type of connection they have to other people. A functional relation indicates that one entity makes use of another, like using a tool to achieve something. The compositional relation describes the connection between a whole and its parts (e.g., the human body and its arms). To address these, further research needs to be done, as they are not obtainable by the currently used origins of data. The last context category is time context, which in this approach is both part of the context as a distinct category and wrapping around the other categories to fixate them at a particular point. The time can be expressed as simple representation of a time slot, like morning or evening. In addition, it can be seen more qualitatively when enriched with further information about the entity observed. In this case, working time and leisure time can be differentiated for example. This will be discussed later more in depth.

4 Activity Context and Recognition

4.1 Conceptionalization of User Activity

The activity context contains goals, tasks, and actions. The knowledge of the user's overall goal or current task seems to be an important information to determine the acceptance of being disturbed by a push notification. However, these categories require further study, as they are too complex to understand by evaluating the information given by the sensors or the operating system. As they change frequently, simply asking the user (like achievable for the age or the gender) is inappropriate as well.

The current action of the user, on the other hand, can be understood more easily. The first example would be the significant motion, which already provides high quality information of the user's physical activity. Composite sensors in modern smartphone platforms like Android provide functions for detecting motion types (e.g., walking, running, or cycling) automatically. Because of this, the data complexity and availability can be classified as low. Activities like eating are also possible to recognize, even though the algorithm for detecting these needs to be developed for the specific platform, as they are not part of standard mobile OS implementations yet [6]. Thus, the complexity to detect this class of activities is rated high. The digital activity concerns mainly the smartphone usage when interacting with its user interfaces. Noteworthy are breakpoints (boundaries between user's activities), that result in a lower cognitive load compared to push notification that are sent out with no regard of the user's activity [17,24,26]. Breakpoints are not implemented by the device, but can be detected by analyzing the smartphone usage with a moderate complexity.

Due to the low implementation complexity, the user activity with regard to motion is to be investigated in this study. As mentioned before, the advantage of this type of activity is that a functionality is available on Android smartphones which supports a direct detection of these activity states. This functionality will be described in the following section.

4.2 Activity Recognition with Android

The Android platform provides an `ActivitiyRecognition` Client class that extend the Google API and that can be used to detect the different motion types as listed in Table 1. The activities are measured at periodic intervals (e.g., every second) by reading the device's sensor data in short bursts and then interpreting it. In order to keep energy consumption to a minimum, only low power sensors are evaluated [21]. A typical use is to link the status of an application or the sending of a message to a specific activity. For example, the execution of an application for use in a vehicle can be linked to the detection of the `IN_VEHICLE` activity. The Android activity recognition functionality can also be used to determine transitions between different activities or to determine transitional conditions (enter, exit) of an activity as triggering event.

As a result of an activity detection query, a list of possible user activities with an associated confidence is returned. Additionally, the most probable activity can be queried. The Android platform thus already provides comprehensive technical capabilities that could also be used as triggers for sending push notifications. So far, however, the authors are not aware of any solutions using this functionality. It should be noted that the activity states do not have to be communicated to the push notification provider. It would also be conceivable that the user could configure the activity states in which he wants to receive push notifications. The sender of the push notifications would then only have to know whether the device is ready to receive push notifications or not, depending on the activity (but not what activity the user is currently performing).

Table 1. User activities with android's DetectActivity class [21]

Type of activity	Description
IN_VEHICLE	The device is in a vehicle, such as a car
ON_BICYCLE	The device is on a bicycle
ON_FOOT	The device is on a user who is walking or running
RUNNING	The device is on a user who is running
STILL	The device is still (not moving)
TILTING	The device angle relative to gravity changed significantly
UNKNOWN	Unable to detect the current activity
WALKING	The device is on a user who is walking

In the following, an experimental test system will be described, which makes the activity states available when receiving push notifications, in order to answer the research questions described in Sect. 2. This test system can then serve as a starting point for further research.

5   Experimental Test System and Findings

5.1   Development of the Test System

The following section deals with the technical implementation of the test app. As already described, the app is to be installed at the test users mobile devices in order to be able to evaluate the users' activity status when the notification was received as well as acquiring reasons for a delayed opening of the message. In order to meet these requirements, several individual technical components and systems are required. These components of the test infrastructure are shown in Fig. 2 and described below.

- *Firebase Cloud Messaging (FCM):* FCM [22] is a cloud messaging service from Google. This service sends the push notifications to the end devices.

The first time the app is opened on the smartphone, the device registers with the FCM servers. Via a FCM or third-party web interface, messages can be written, dispatch parameters defined and dispatch dates defined.

- *PushBots:* PushBots [46] offers a web interface with which push notifications can be written, managed and sent. On the one hand, the web interface of PushBots offers a simple management of push notifications. On the other hand, with a plugin for PhoneGap, the company offers an easy way to integrate FCM functionalities into a hybrid app. The plugin enables the registration of the app with the FCM servers and continuous communication.

- *PhoneGap Build:* A hybrid implementation approach was chosen to quickly implement the test app. This is because it is a relatively simple app concept, but a web-based app was out of question due to the necessary access to the Android functionalities for activity determination. With the framework PhoneGap Build [4] applications can be developed platform independent. Instead of device-specific programming languages such as Java and Swift, web technologies such as HTML, CSS and JavaScript are used. The source code is obtained from a Github repository created for the project and compiled and packaged into a hybrid app by the framework. The app can then be installed on the smartphone via a link or by scanning a QR code.

- *Github:* Github [20] was used in the development of the app to manage the different versions of the source code. All changes to the source code are uploaded and stored in a so-called repository. PhoneGap Build also allows access to the source code via the link to the Github repository.

- *Server and Database:* With the help of a MySQL database and a PHP script, the data from the app is stored in a database on a web server. After successful questioning of the user, the app sends a POST request to the URL of the web host. Behind this URL there is a PHP script which extracts the data from the request of the app and stores it in the database for further analysis.

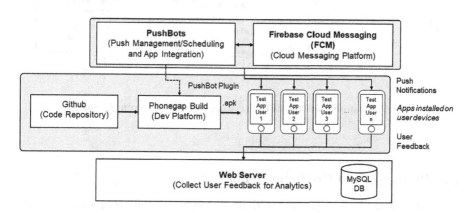

Fig. 2. Simplified test infrastructure components

As a result, the use of the entire system can be described as follows (see Fig. 3): Via the web interface of PushBots, a message can be written by the test administrator and sent to the test persons. The registered devices are notified via the FCM servers. At this point, the app then uses the Activity Recognition API to determine the current activity status of the user and stores this in a local variable together with a time stamp. If the respondent opens the app within five minutes, a query appears as shown in Fig. 3. First, the respondent is asked if the activity state was determined correctly. If the user answers with "YES", the query is finished. If, however, the activity status has not been determined correctly by the system, the respondent can enter the correct status in a dialog box. If the respondent does not respond to the push notification for more than five minutes, the reason for the delay is also queried. This is determined by the difference between the time stamps "Input Push Notification" and "Open App". Finally, the respondent is asked whether the data may be sent to the database server at the university. If the respondent confirms the sending of the data, a POST request is sent to the URL of the database server. The PHP script extracts all the data obtained and stores it in a MYSQL database.

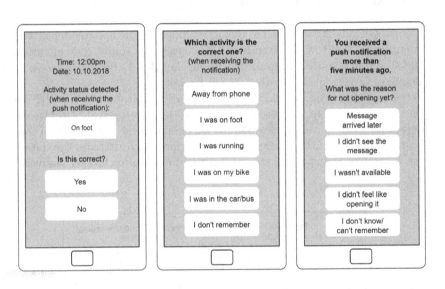

Fig. 3. Example screens of the test app (translated from German)

5.2   Pre-study and Preliminary Findings

The system described above was initially tested in a small group of seven users in a one-week study. The focus was on the analysis of the basic functionality of the system. In the system, a total of 35 push notifications for each user of the sample where scheduled during the test week. The time of push notifications was varied so that different times of the day could be covered. To avoid habituation, different send times were used on each day, but the time sequences were repeated within the week to allow comparisons between weekdays. To receive the push notifications, the participating users had to install an app. This app was also used to collect supplementary user feedback and was equipped with a short user survey that could be answered and transmitted to a server for evaluation. The message itself has no further content. Users were instructed to pay attention to incoming push notifications and to provide corresponding user feedback as soon as they noticed the receipt of a message on their smartphones. The setup of the study is therefore also experimental in the sense that users opened the push notifications as a part of a testing task and not out of curiosity or interest in the content.

After completion of the test phase, a total of 195 recorded user feedbacks on the push notifications were recorded in the log files of the server. The accuracy of the activity determined by the system was very high. For 89.2% of the transmitted push notifications, the users stated that the activity determined was correct. The confidence for the activity with the highest probability was very high as well (91.8%). However, the results as presented in Table 2 show that for 81.5% of the push notifications the activity type was STILL. This could be related to the fact that the test group is a convenience sample consisting of university staff and students. These smartphone users mainly do desk work and thus the probability of addressing them in other activity phases is low if, as in the study, only about five push notifications per day are sent.

Table 2. User activities recognized in pre-test [21]

Type of activity	Cases	Percentage
IN_VEHICLE	7	3.6
ON_BICYCLE	0	0
ON_FOOT	11	5.6
RUNNING	0	0
STILL	159	81.5
TILTING	5	2.6
UNKNOWN	13	6.7
WALKING	0	0
Total	195	100.0

In addition to the user activity information, the test app also captured delay times and the reasons for delayed openings of the push notifications. The average delay time was about 20 min. However, as the distribution of the delay times in Fig. 4 shows, the delay time varied very much across the 195 messages sent. About 48.2% where opened within five minutes after the push notification was sent, 31.8% within half an hour, and only 20% later than this. The most mentioned reason that the push notification was not opened within five minutes after arrival was that the notification was not recognized (77.3%) followed by being not available or not being able to open the message (20.6%).

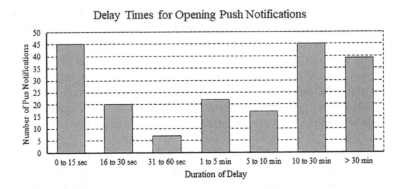

Fig. 4. Delay times for opening the push notifications

The delays cannot be explained by the fact that the users were on the move and were therefore unable to open the push notification, as 85.6% of the delay of more than five minutes was due to STILL activity. In order to achieve a high opening rate, other factors must also be taken into account. If, for example, the dispatch times are considered, it can be seen that many push notifications are published particularly quickly before and after midday (noon, 2 p.m.). Long delays occur especially often at evening respectively at end of working day, i.e., by 6 p.m.

6   Conclusion and Further Research

In this article, an experimental system for sending push notifications was presented, with which the precision of the system-side recognition of user activities was investigated and user feedback on causes of delayed opening of messages was collected. The initial evaluation with a small test group indicates that the user activity can be reliably determined with standard functionalities of the Android platform. In further research work, consideration should be given to how an appropriate activity trigger can be implemented while safeguarding privacy.

The testings also showed that the delay times when opening the messages vary greatly and that this can not be attributed to inappropriate user activities alone. It therefore seems unlikely that significant increases in opening rates can be achieved by only integrating activity-based context information as a trigger. Rather, this information is to be evaluated in combination with other context information.

It should be noted here that the number of study participants was too small for generalizable statements. Further studies are needed to extend the testing period and involve a larger number of subjects.

Furthermore, when interpreting the results, it should be noted that the participants of the study were explicitly asked to pay attention to push notifications or to provide feedback on incoming messages. It can be assumed that this fact also led to an impairment of the informative value of the test results. Further tests would therefore be necessary where such a bias is avoided and where the expected content of the push notification and its user value alone is the incentive to open these messages.

References

1. Accengage: The 2018 push notification & in-app message benchmark (2018). https://www.accengage.com/benchmark-opt-in-and-reaction-rates-of-push-notifi cations-and-in-app-messages-for-mobile-apps-2018-edition/
2. Adamczyk, P., Bailey, B.P.: If not now, when? In: Dykstra-Erickson, E., Tscheligi, M. (eds.) CHI 2004, CHI Letters, pp. 271–278. Association for Computing Machinery, New York (2004). https://doi.org/10.1145/985692.985727
3. Adamczyk, P., Iqbal, S.T., Bailey, B.P.: A method, system, and tools for intelligent interruption management. In: Dix, A., Dittmar, A. (eds.) TAMODIA 2005, pp. 123–126. Association for Computing Machinery, New York (2005). https://doi.org/10.1145/1122935.1122959
4. Adobe: Adobe PhoneGap Build (2019). https://build.phonegap.com/
5. Bailey, B.P., Konstan, J.A., Carlis, J.V.: Measuring the effects of interruptions on task performance in the user interface. In: SMC 2000 Conference Proceedings, pp. 757–762. IEEE, Piscataway (2002). https://doi.org/10.1109/ICSMC.2000.885940
6. Biel, J.I., Martin, N., Labbe, D., Gatica-Perez, D.: Bites 'n' bits. In: Proceedings of the ACM on Interactive, Mobile, Wearable and Ubiquitous Technologies, vol. 1, no. 4, pp. 1–33 (2018). https://doi.org/10.1145/3161161
7. Chang, Y.J., Tang, J.C.: Investigating mobile users' ringer mode usage and attentiveness and responsiveness to communication. In: Boring, S., Rukzio, E., Gellersen, H., Hinckley, K. (eds.) MobileHCI 2015, pp. 6–15. Association for Computing Machinery, New York (2015). https://doi.org/10.1145/2785830.2785852
8. Christoph, S., Dominik, H.: Using semantic web technology for ubiquitous location and situation modeling. Ann. GIS 10(2), 157–165 (2004). https://doi.org/10.1080/10824000409480667
9. CleverTap: Data-backed secrets to successful push notifications 2018 report - an in-depth analysis of 40 billion push notifications. https://clevertap.com/l/wp-push-notification-report-2018/
10. Cutrell, E., Czerwinski, M., Horvitz, E.: Notification, disruption, and memory: effects of messaging interruptions on memory and performance. In: INTERACT 2001, pp. 263–269. IOS Press, Amsterdam (2001)
11. Czerwinski, M., Cutrell, E., Horvitz, E.: Instant messaging and interruption: influence of task type on performance. In: Paris, C. (ed.) Proceedings of OZCHI 2000, pp. 361–367. CHISIG, Sydney (2000)
12. Czerwinski, M., Cutrell, E., Horvitz, E.: Instant messaging: effects of relevance and timing. In: McDonald, S., Waern, Y., Cockton, G. (eds.) People and Computers XIV – Usability or Else!, pp. 71–76. Springer, London (2000)
13. Dey, A.K.: Understanding and using context. Pers. Ubiquit. Comput. 5(1), 4–7 (2001). https://doi.org/10.1007/s007790170019
14. Dingler, T., Pielot, M.: I'll be there for you. In: Boring, S., Rukzio, E., Gellersen, H., Hinckley, K. (eds.) MobileHCI 2015, pp. 1–5. Association for Computing Machinery, New York (2015). https://doi.org/10.1145/2785830.2785840

15. Exler, A., Braith, M., Schankin, A., Beigl, M.: Preliminary investigations about interruptibility of smartphone users at specific place types. In: Lukowicz, P., Krüger, A., Bulling, A., Lim, Y.K., Patel, S.N. (eds.) Proceedings of the 2016 ACM International Joint Conference on Pervasive and Ubiquitous Computing Adjunct, pp. 1590–1595. ACM, New York (2016). https://doi.org/10.1145/2968219.2968554
16. Felt, A.P., Egelman, S., Wagner, D.: I've got 99 problems, but vibration ain't one. In: Yu, T., Enck, W., Jiang, X. (eds.) SPSM 2012, p. 33. Association for Computing Machinery, New York (2012). https://doi.org/10.1145/2381934.2381943
17. Fischer, J.E., Greenhalgh, C., Benford, S.: Investigating episodes of mobile phone activity as indicators of opportune moments to deliver notifications. In: Bylund, M. (ed.) Proceedings of the 13th International Conference on Human Computer Interaction with Mobile Devices and Services, p. 181. ACM, New York (2011). https://doi.org/10.1145/2037373.2037402
18. Fischer, J.E., Yee, N., Bellotti, V., Good, N., Benford, S., Greenhalgh, C.: Effects of content and time of delivery on receptivity to mobile interruptions. In: de Sá, M., Carriço, L.M., Correia, N. (eds.) Proceedings of the 12th International Conference on Human Computer Interaction with Mobile Devices and Services, p. 103. Association for Computing Machinery, New York (2010). https://doi.org/10.1145/1851600.1851620
19. Gillie, T., Broadbent, D.: What makes interruptions disruptive? A study of length, similarity, and complexity. Psychol. Res. **50**(4), 243–250 (1989). https://doi.org/10.1007/BF00309260
20. Github: Github: the world's leading software development platform (2019). https://github.com/
21. Google: Google APIs for android: detected activity (2018). https://developers.google.com/android/reference/com/google/android/gms/location/DetectedActivity#constants
22. Google: Firebase cloud messaging (2019). https://firebase.google.com/docs/cloud-messaging/
23. Heckmann, D.: Ubiquitous user modeling: Zugl.: Saarbrücken. Univ., Diss., 2006, Dissertationen zur Künstlichen Intelligenz (DISKI), vol. 297. Akad. Verl.-Ges. Aka, Berlin (2006). http://deposit.d-nb.de/cgi-bin/dokserv?id=2860787&prov=M&dok_var=1&dok_ext=htm
24. Ho, J., Intille, S.S.: Using context-aware computing to reduce the perceived burden of interruptions from mobile devices. In: Kellogg, W. (ed.) CHI 2005, Technology, Safety, Community, p. 909. ACM Press, New York (2005). https://doi.org/10.1145/1054972.1055100
25. Horvitz, E., Koch, P., Sarin, R., Apacible, J., Subramani, M.: Bayesphone: pre-computation of context-sensitive policies for inquiry and action in mobile devices. In: Ardissono, L., Brna, P., Mitrovic, A. (eds.) UM 2005. LNCS (LNAI), vol. 3538, pp. 251–260. Springer, Heidelberg (2005). https://doi.org/10.1007/11527886_33
26. Iqbal, S.T., Bailey, B.P.: Understanding and developing models for detecting and differentiating breakpoints during interactive tasks. In: Rosson, M.B. (ed.) Proceedings of the SIGCHI Conference on Human Factors in Computing Systems, p. 697. ACM Digital Library, ACM, New York (2007). https://doi.org/10.1145/1240624.1240732
27. Iqbal, S.T., Horvitz, E.: Notifications and awareness. In: Inkpen, K., Gutwin, C., Tang, J. (eds.) Proceedings of the 2010 ACM Conference on Computer Supported Cooperative Work, p. 27. ACM, New York (2010). https://doi.org/10.1145/1718918.1718926

28. Kreifeldt, J.G., Mccarthy, M.E.: Interruption as a test of the user-computer interface. In: Proceedings of the Seventeenth Annual Conference on Manual Control (JPL Publication 81–95). University of California, Los Angeles, 16–18 June 1981, pp. 655–667 (1981)

29. Kushlev, K., Proulx, J., Dunn, E.W.: Silence your phones. In: Kaye, J., Druin, A., Lampe, C., Morris, D., Hourcade, J.P. (eds.) CHI 2016, pp. 1011–1020. The Association for Computing Machinery, New York (2016). https://doi.org/10.1145/2858036.2858359

30. Lopez-Tovar, H., Charalambous, A., Dowell, J.: Managing smartphone interruptions through adaptive modes and modulation of notifications. In: Brdiczka, O., Chau, P., Carenini, G., Pan, S., Kristensson, P.O. (eds.) IUI 2015, pp. 296–299. The Association for Computing Machinery, New York (2015). https://doi.org/10.1145/2678025.2701390

31. Mark, G., Gudith, D., Klocke, U.: The cost of interrupted work. In: Czerwinski, M. (ed.) Proceedings of the SIGCHI Conference on Human Factors in Computing Systems, p. 107. ACM, New York (2008). https://doi.org/10.1145/1357054.1357072

32. Mehrotra, A., Hendley, R., Musolesi, M.: Prefminer: mining user's preferences for intelligent mobile notification management. In: Lukowicz, P. (ed.) Proceedings of the 2016 ACM International Joint Conference on Pervasive and Ubiquitous Computing Adjunct, pp. 1223–1234. ACM, New York (2016). https://doi.org/10.1145/2971648.2971747

33. Mehrotra, A., et al.: Understanding the role of places and activities on mobile phone interaction and usage patterns. In: Proceedings of the ACM on Interactive, Mobile, Wearable and Ubiquitous Technologies, vol. 1, no. 3, pp. 1–22 (2017). https://doi.org/10.1145/3131901

34. Mehrotra, A., Musolesi, M.: Intelligent notification systems: a survey of the state of the art and research challenges. http://arxiv.org/pdf/1711.10171v2

35. Mehrotra, A., Musolesi, M., Hendley, R., Pejovic, V.: Designing content-driven intelligent notification mechanisms for mobile applications. In: Mase, K., Langheinrich, M., Gatica-Perez, D., Gellersen, H., Choudhury, T., Yatani, K. (eds.) UbiComp 2015, pp. 813–824. Association for Computing Machinery, New York (2015). https://doi.org/10.1145/2750858.2807544

36. Mehrotra, A., Pejovic, V., Vermeulen, J., Hendley, R., Musolesi, M.: My phone and me. In: Kaye, J., Druin, A., Lampe, C., Morris, D., Hourcade, J.P. (eds.) CHI 2016, pp. 1021–1032. The Association for Computing Machinery, New York (2016). https://doi.org/10.1145/2858036.2858566

37. Mehrotra, A., Tsapeli, F., Hendley, R., Musolesi, M.: Mytraces: Investigating correlation and causation between users' emotional states and mobile phone interaction. In: Proceedings of the ACM on Interactive, Mobile, Wearable and Ubiquitous Technologies, vol. 1, no. 3, pp. 1–21 (2017). https://doi.org/10.1145/3130948

38. Obuchi, M., Sasaki, W., Okoshi, T., Nakazawa, J., Tokuda, H.: Investigating interruptibility at activity breakpoints using smartphone activity recognition API. In: Lukowicz, P., Krüger, A., Bulling, A., Lim, Y.K., Patel, S.N. (eds.) Proceedings of the 2016 ACM International Joint Conference on Pervasive and Ubiquitous Computing Adjunct, pp. 1602–1607. ACM, New York (2016). https://doi.org/10.1145/2968219.2968556

39. Okoshi, T., Nozaki, H., Nakazawa, J., Tokuda, H., Ramos, J., Dey, A.K.: Towards attention-aware adaptive notification on smart phones. Pervasive Mob. Comput. **26**, 17–34 (2016). https://doi.org/10.1016/j.pmcj.2015.10.004

40. Park, C., Lim, J., Kim, J., Lee, S.J., Lee, D.: Don't bother me. I'm socializing! In: Lee, C.P., Poltrock, S., Barkhuus, L., Borges, M., Kellogg, W. (eds.) CSCW 2017, pp. 541–554. The Association for Computing Machinery, New York (2017). https://doi.org/10.1145/2998181.2998189

41. Pejovic, V., Musolesi, M.: InterruptMe. In: Brush, A.J., Friday, A., Kientz, J., Scott, J., Song, J. (eds.) Proceedings of the 2014 ACM International Joint Conference on Pervasive and Ubiquitous Computing, pp. 897–908. ACM, New York (2014). https://doi.org/10.1145/2632048.2632062

42. Pielot, M.: Large-scale evaluation of call-availability prediction. In: Brush, A.J., Friday, A., Kientz, J., Scott, J., Song, J. (eds.) Proceedings of the 2014 ACM International Joint Conference on Pervasive and Ubiquitous Computing, pp. 933–937. ACM, New York (2014). https://doi.org/10.1145/2632048.2632060

43. Pielot, M., Dingler, T., Pedro, J.S., Oliver, N.: When attention is not scarce - detecting boredom from mobile phone usage. In: Mase, K., Langheinrich, M., Gatica-Perez, D., Gellersen, H., Choudhury, T., Yatani, K. (eds.) UbiComp 2015, pp. 825–836. Association for Computing Machinery, New York (2015). https://doi.org/10.1145/2750858.2804252

44. Pielot, M., de Oliveira, R., Kwak, H., Oliver, N.: Didn't you see my message? In: Jones, M., Palanque, P., Schmidt, A., Grossman, T. (eds.) Proceedings of the SIGCHI Conference on Human Factors in Computing Systems, pp. 3319–3328. ACM, New York (2014). https://doi.org/10.1145/2556288.2556973

45. Poppinga, B., Heuten, W., Boll, S.: Sensor-based identification of opportune moments for triggering notifications. IEEE Pervasive Comput. **13**(1), 22–29 (2014). https://doi.org/10.1109/MPRV.2014.15

46. PushBots: Push notifications, but so much better (2019). https://pushbots.com/

47. Rosenthal, S., Dey, A.K., Veloso, M.: Using decision-theoretic experience sampling to build personalized mobile phone interruption models. In: Lyons, K., Hightower, J., Huang, E.M. (eds.) Pervasive 2011. LNCS, vol. 6696, pp. 170–187. Springer, Heidelberg (2011). https://doi.org/10.1007/978-3-642-21726-5_11

48. Sahami Shirazi, A., Henze, N., Dingler, T., Pielot, M., Weber, D., Schmidt, A.: Large-scale assessment of mobile notifications. In: Jones, M., Palanque, P., Schmidt, A., Grossman, T. (eds.) Proceedings of the SIGCHI Conference on Human Factors in Computing Systems, pp. 3055–3064. ACM, New York (2014). https://doi.org/10.1145/2556288.2557189

49. Schilit, B., Adams, N., Want, R.: Context-aware computing applications. In: Workshop on Mobile Computing Systems and Applications, pp. 85–90. IEEE Computer Society, Los Alamitos (1995). https://doi.org/10.1109/WMCSA.1994.16

50. Tsubouchi, K., Okoshi, T.: People's interruptibility in-the-wild. In: Lee, S., Takayama, L., Truong, K. (eds.) UbiComp 2017, pp. 922–927. ACM = Association for Computing Machinery, New York (2017). https://doi.org/10.1145/3123024.3124556

51. Westermann, T., Möller, S., Wechsung, I.: Assessing the relationship between technical affinity, stress and notifications on smartphones. In: Boring, S., Rukzio, E., Gellersen, H., Hinckley, K. (eds.) MobileHCI 2015, pp. 652–659. Association for Computing Machinery, New York (2015). https://doi.org/10.1145/2786567.2793684

52. Zimmermann, A., Lorenz, A., Oppermann, R.: An operational definition of context. In: Kokinov, B., Richardson, D.C., Roth-Berghofer, T.R., Vieu, L. (eds.) CONTEXT 2007. LNCS (LNAI), vol. 4635, pp. 558–571. Springer, Heidelberg (2007). https://doi.org/10.1007/978-3-540-74255-5_42

Data Management Model for Internet of Everything

Lulwah AlSuwaidan[(⊠)]

College of Computer and Information Sciences,
Al-Imam Mohammad ibn Saud Islamic University,
Riyadh 11432, Saudi Arabia
lnsuwaidan@imamu.edu.sa

Abstract. Data has been everywhere because of the communication infrastructure available that consists of various dependent and independent entities including devices, people, and processes. The interconnected entities have changed the process of collecting and sharing information. This evolutionary paradigm of gathering, storing and analyzing data streams is called the Internet of Everything (IoE). The IoE is established on top of the IoT by adding the human element to the IoT network. In particular, the IoE can improve quality of lives via smart connection between people, processes, data, and things. This huge network and massive data exchanged among its particulars requires for intelligent, smart, and effective data management model. In this paper, we investigate the current state of data management for IoT/IoE and we found limited researches focused on enhancing the process of data management. Therefore, we introduce a data-driven data management model for IoT/IoE; the model ensures data governance, privacy, and includes advanced data processing. It also provides data services such as security and integrity.

Keywords: Data management · Internet of Everything ·
Internet of Things

1 Introduction

The recent development of sensing, communications, and analytics technologies, information is being generated, collected, managed and analyzed automatically rather than followed the traditional information processing process. This has been emerged with the rapid development of technologies such as Wireless Sensor Network (WSN), Radio Frequency Identification (RFID), and Complex Event Processing (CEP) [19]. Services such as accurate perception, monitoring and reaction open a new insights and new applications. This huge extension of network services and development of information systems have promoted a new type of network, called Internet of Things (IoT). Later, people have involved in the process of data exchange among network nodes which drives to the emergence of Internet of Everything (IoE). It can be shown as an area consisting of

© Springer Nature Switzerland AG 2019
I. Awan et al. (Eds.): MobiWIS 2019, LNCS 11673, pp. 331–341, 2019.
https://doi.org/10.1007/978-3-030-27192-3_26

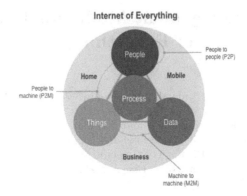

Fig. 1. IoE Cisco definition: the what, where, and how of the internet of everything.

trillions of intelligent sensor devices that are able to exchange data, and people are able to gain information while machines learn from other machine in the network. According to Cisco Systems, there will be around 37 billion new things will be connected within a global network by 2020 [2]. This huge network of devices, processes, data, and people has many challenges and issues specifically in managing the data that exchanged among devices and people.

Data management is a broad concept consisting of the architectures, practices, and procedures for correct management of the data lifecycle. In particular, data management in IoT/IoE is a middle layer between the objects and devices producing the data and the applications accessing the data for analysis purposes and services [3]. In this paper, we provide a novel data management model for the IoE. In addition, we present a data-driven management model for IoE that able to collect, manage, analyze, and preserve data. The model has an additional top-level services that enhance the performance and efficiency in managing organizational data.

The rest of this paper is organized as follows: Sect. 2 discusses the background and related works for IoT/IoE and data management. It also presents the challenges and issues of IoT/IoE. Section 3 introduces a data-driven management model for IoE based on the current challenges of IoT/IoE data management. It also gives an analysis of how can satisfy a set of services that added value for the process of data management. Finally, Sect. 4 concludes the paper.

2 Background

2.1 Internet of Everything

The recent revolution of the Internet of Thing (IoT) has forced to consider the process of data exchange between connected things. There has been a misunderstanding between IoT and IoE where the analysis clearly distinguishes between them. Cisco has compared the IoT to IoE as a network connecting physical

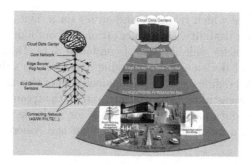

Fig. 2. The structure of the human neural system and its resemblance to the IoT/IoE architecture. [26]

objects (does not include the "people" and "process" components of IoE). IoT is a single technology transition, while IoE comprises many technology transitions (including IoT). Cisco has introduced this new concept which consists of four parts namely "things", "process", "people", and "data" as shown in Fig. 1 [2]. The independent devices of the past are now being connected to the Internet including machine-to-machine (M2M), person-to-machine (P2M), and person-to-person (P2P) systems. Ning and Wang [26] have illustrated the similarity of IoT/IoE architecture to the architecture of the human neural network (see Fig. 2). Cisco [5] has illustrated the future of IoE where it is basically based on the IoT growth since any added features would result in a greater network connectedness. The ITU Telecommunication Standardization Sector characterises the (IoE) as "a worldwide base for the data society, empowering propelled administrations by interconnecting (physical and virtual) things taking into account existing and advancing interoperable data and correspondence innovations" [21]. IoT/IoE has been an infrastructure in countries such as China, India, and Africa to invest in IoT/IoE for applications such as clean water, carbon discharge, and economy. IoE is also a crucial technology for public sector, Cisco's has pointed out to top 10 insights that have a value for the public sector. The analysis has focused on four primary drivers of IoE which include: employee productivity, cost reduction, citizen experience, and increased revenue [6].

2.2 Data Management

Data management has been of a great role in technologies such as IoT and IoE because of huge data the instantly exchanged among network entities. Generally, data management has stated by Weik [32] as "The controlling of data handling operations, such as the acquisition, analysis, translation, coding, storage, retrieval, and distribution of data, but not necessarily the generation and use of that data". In the current generation, data management has defined as an administrative process that includes acquiring, validating, storing, protecting, and processing required data to ensure the accessibility, reliability, and timeliness of the data for its users. SAS [1] has defined it as a composite of related concepts: Data access which retrieves and stores data, Data quality that refers to data accuracy and usability, Data integration for combining different types of data, Data federation for unique view of combined data, Data governance that defines the rules and decisions for managing organization's data, Master data management (MDM) defines, unifies and manages all of the data that is common and essential to all areas of an organization, and Data streaming which analyzes data and recognises data patterns and filters it for multiple uses as it flows into the organization. In a nutshell, data management is a coherent process of data collect.

2.3 IoE Challenges and Issues

IoE has encountered number of technologies affecting its process such as communication, remote monitoring, and security. Raj and Prakash [27] have reviewed and compared some of adopted technologies and reached a conclusion that most of the existence works focused on the disruptive architectures of the IoE in order to enhance its features, security and storage capacity. One of the challenges is node security especially in determining which device has attacked in the organization's network. In addition, securing the data that exchanged in the network is another issue. Sianaki et al. [30] claimed that the security of the nodes is particularly important as the system can be affected by malicious activities and the sensitive data can be manipulated or lost.

Data exchange and the process of continuous acquisition of data from multiple sources is another challenge. Sianaki et al. [30] discussed this in the health sector when collecting data from patients such as traditional data collection methods including heart and blood oxygen saturation detection or advanced methods such as accelerometers, gyroscopes, and surface electrodes. In term of IoE, people such as medical doctors or nurses also can be a source of data that might affect the overall accuracy. As a results, the data become more extensive and massive which leads to manage the big data and the compatibility of the different data architectures. This availability of massive data requires high effective, durable, and reliable storage which is still a very costly. In addition, IoT which is part of the IoE structure has encountered a challenge in how manage data effectively. This has discussed by Ning et al. [26] in their IoT layered architecture (see Fig. 3) where data have to be collected, processed, stored and analyzed. Data also have to be cleaned for accurate and reliable data structure. Thus, when the data have accurately collected and processed, a high-level information needs to be extracted, abstracted and inferred from raw data for decision supports.

In data management, there always been a focus on the process of data collection which is not enough. Galetto [13] has claimed that enterprises and organizations should understand from the start that data management and data analytics only will be successful when they first put some thought into how they will gain value from their raw data. They can then move beyond raw data collection with efficient systems for processing, storing, and validating data, as well as effective analysis strategies. In addition, another challenge of data management occurs at

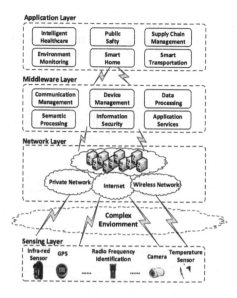

Fig. 3. Layered architecture of IoT [19].

the stage of categorizing data and determining the purpose from it. Each step of data collection and management must lead toward acquiring the right data and analyzing it in order to get the actionable intelligence necessary for making truly data-driven business decisions.

3 Data Management Model for Internet of Everything

As we have discussed previously, the IoT is the originate of the revolution of IoE. There are a massive efforts that enhanced the process of data management for IoT. Ma et. al. [19] have introduced a layered architecture of IoT (see Fig. 3) which is consisted of four layers: Sensing Layer which connects between physical and cyber worlds, Network Layer that translates the collected data to upper layers for further processing and higher-level abstraction, Middleware Layer which is the most important layer in IoT architecture which combines several major functions of data management and processing, it also provides service interfaces for applications in sensing and network layers, and lastly is the Application Layer that build on top of the three lower layers and provides domain-oriented IoT applications for end-users in various application domains. Furthermore, they have proposed a three-layered reference model for application design. The focus in this model is on the data itself specifically cleaning, analyzing and storage. Indeed, the data management requires more than these simple processes since the data in technologies such as IoT/IoE usually collected from different sources and requires high-end processes such as machine learning and artificial intelligent techniques. Nowadays, IoT applications such as smart cities that require data management have integrated these advanced techniques to enhance accuracy and efficiency.

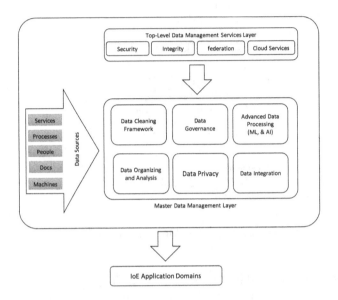

Fig. 4. IoE data-driven management model.

In this paper, we present a data-driven management model for IoE as it is shown in Fig. 4. The model has three main components: data sources layer, master data management layer, and top-level data management services layer. A detailed description of each layer and its function will be presented in the following:

– Data Sources Layer
Nowadays, data have been of various types and IoE deals with data that collected from different sources. In this model, we consider this variation by including five types of data sources: services, processes, people, documents, and machines. First, services can be one of important data sources; any organization provides case reports and statistics to each of its procedures which results in data of high benefits to all its departments. However, we found limited attention on considering services and their outcomes as a source of data. The concentrate is on direct data gathering of customer/employee satisfactions through web-based surveys and questioners [4,25]. Process as a source of data is critical specifically in IoT/IoE since it is the core of IoE between people, things and data as it is shown in Fig. 1 [33]. For example, smart homes have different processes that exchange data periodically to update the systems. The other type is the people which they could be of different levels: top-management, employee, customers, end-user. Human in IoE has a crucial

effect at the final stage of business decision, therefore they have involved in the process at early stage of data collection. Human input as a data can be behaviour, preferences, lifestyle, and any characteristics reflect people and result in better decision. Any organization has its rules and regulations documented in data archiving center; these documents and other ones collected from organization departments are source of data since they considered as indicators for further decisions. The last source of data is the core one which is machines or network sensors; each part in IoT/IoE follow M2M machine-to-machine [17,36]. The recent trend is not on the sensor technology or how data is changed, the trend is on how energy-efficient data gathering and preserve sensor lifetime [18,29,35].

– Master Data Management Layer
This layer includes the components required for preserving efficient data management for the organization. Data cleaning should be the first step in this layer because working, for example, with biased, duplicate, or errors in data would results in uncertain decisions. Moreover, there are different types of data such as text, spatial, temporal, or streaming data; each of which has its own cleansing techniques. Chu et al. [7] have presented the challenges while data cleaning process. In addition, Chu et al. [8] have integrated knowledge management and crowdsourcing as a technique for data cleansing. Once data has already cleansed, governing the data is the next step to govern the data with collection of practices and processes that guarantees the formal management of data assets within an organization. One of techniques for data governance is integrating ontology to better gain an awareness of the landscape of the data, processes, and organizational attributes. DeStefano [11] have proposed a tool based on linked data and ontology that enhanced data awareness within the organization and resulted in increasing the ability to govern corporate data assets, and in turn increased data quality. Machine learning and artificial intelligence have proven to be powerful for data processing. Mahdavinejad et al. [20] have reviewed various machine learning methods that applicable for IoT/IoE data by presenting a taxonomy of machine learning algorithms to illustrate how machine learning techniques are applied to the data in order to extract higher level information. They also reviewed the potential challenges of machine learning for IoT/IoE data analytics. Domingos [12] has claimed that the standard machine learning formulations is limited when processing the data. However, he stated the power of machine learning theory and practice with integration of assumptions, and promises to make machine learning for data management much easier and more effective. Markov logic, one of powerful techniques for machine learning, can effectively defines very deep probability distributions over non-i.i.d., multi-relational data. Learning structure in the case of Markov logic, a set of formulas in first-order logic-is intractable, as in more traditional representations, but can be done effectively using inductive logic programming techniques. One of the applications is leverages signal processing and machine-learning techniques into building management systems (BMS); Tushar et al. [31] have addressed the problem of IoT-based BMS by providing model that leverages signal processing

and machine-learning techniques. The model able to extract high-level building occupancy information through simple, low-cost IoT sensors and study how human activities impact a building's energy use-information that can be exploited to design energy conservation measures that reduce the building's energy consumption.

Moving to the lower box of Master Data Management Layer which consists of firstly data analysis component. We agreed on amounts of data that have been produced as IoT/IoE networks increases and can thus be the force of emergence of big data analytics approaches [16]. Marjani et al. [24] investigated the state-of-the-art research directed toward big IoT data analytics. In particular, they found the relationship between big data analytics and IoT; and therefore they proposed a new architecture for big IoT data analytics. As we have discussed IoT/IoE incorporates machine learning and parallel distributed systems such as clouds, clusters, and grids for big data storage, processing, and analytics which turns to Intelligent IoT (IIoT). In IIoT, end devices continuously produce and transmit data streams, and thus can increase network traffic between device-cloud communication and it increases in-network data transmissions. This requires additional efforts for big data processing, management, and analytics, [28] proposed a concentric computing model (CCM) paradigm consist of sensing systems, outer and inner gateway processors, and central processors (outer and inner) for the deployment of big data analytics applications in IIoT. When data has already analyzed, needing for data privacy is of high importance since ensuring consumer privacy and security has become a critical issue due to the interconnection of different smart devices in various communication networks and the information they carry. Desai et al. [10] have presented a recent and intensive review of privacy related research in the IoE enabled smart grid environment. Privacy policies and regulations have preserved the ICT environment specifically in IoT/IoE and their big data analytics. Majeed et al. [23] have discussed the effectiveness of the provision of privacy of individuals through privacy enhancing technologies (PETs). They stated how recently the individual's privacy has gained a considerable interest in both industry and academia since privacy enhancing technologies (PETs) constitute a technical means to protect information. Last component in this layer is data integration which simply refers to data unification. Daraio [9] have proposed Ontology-based Data Management (OBDM) approach to coordinate, integrate and maintain the data needed for Science, Technology and Innovation (STI) policy development. Golshan et al. [14] have found two challenges in data integration: develop good open source tools for different components of data integration pipelines, and provide practitioners with viable solutions for the long-standing problem of systematically combining structured and unstructured data. We have found a lack of maintaining data integrity in data management.

– Top-Level Data Management Service Layer
  This layer adds additional services to master data management layer which includes: security, integrity, federation, and cloud services. A Fog-to-Cloud (F2C) is a new concept released that combines the advantages of both the

centralized (Cloud) and distributed data management in a smart city. This can reduce communication latencies for real-time or critical services, decrease network data traffic, and apply different policies. In particular, the cloud and fog computing is a technology that provides on demand computational resources. Zahoor et al. [34] proposed a cloud-fog based model for resource management in smart grid. The model can identify the hierarchical structure of cloud-fog computing to provide different types of computing services for resource management in SG. The two components integrity and federation ensure the diversity of data sources and the techniques behind them especially data federation that preserves the data storage without requiring to immigrate data itself. Security is another crucial service in data management because IoT/IoE open fast data sharing without considering security issues. Majeed et al. [22] introduced a holistic approach to devising a secure IoE architecture for cross-culture communication organizations. It includes technological wearable devices, their security policies, communication protocols, data format and data encryption features. This approach considers secure IoE model which provides for a generic implementation after analyzing the critical security features to reduce the risk of data exploitations. Huang et al. [15] claimed the lack of focus in the previous work that concentrate on security of the management in IoT/IoE. Therefore, they proposed a decentralized security model called lightning network and smart contract (LNSC) based on the lightning network and smart contract in the blockchain ecosystem. It thus can be integrated with current scheduling mechanisms to enhance the security of trading IoT/IoE entities and devices.

4   Conclusion

In this paper, a Data-Driven Management Model for IoE has been proposed. This model provides a coherent data management process that results in data-driven business decisions. It has a top-level service layer which provides additional services to the management process. We have overcome some limitations and challenges in the current models such as security and integrating data from different sources. One of the issue is storage and migrating data from its original source, we have adopted cloud as a service to enhance the storage capabilities and preserving the space capacity. For future work, we intend to examine the model in real organization and measure its effectiveness and resolve any coming limitations.

References

1. Data Management: Manage your data as a valuable resource. https://www.sas.com/en_us/insights/data-management/data-management.html. Accessed 7 June 2019
2. The internet of everything global public sector economic analysis. https://www.cisco.com. Accessed 26 May 2019
3. Abu-Elkheir, M., Hayajneh, M., Ali, N.: Data management for the internet of things: design primitives and solution. Sensors 13(11), 15582–15612 (2013)

4. Benítez, J.A., et al.: A web-based tool for automatic data collection, curation, and visualization of complex healthcare survey studies including social network analysis. Comput. Math. Methods Med. **2017** (2017)

5. Bradley, J., Reberger, C., Dixit, A., Gupta, V., Macaulay, J.: Internet of everything (IoE): top 10 insights from Cisco's IoE value at stake analysis for the public sector. IEEE Commun. Lett. (2013)

6. Bradley, J., Reberger, C., Dixit, A., Gupta, V., Macaulay, J.: Internet of everything (IoE): top 10 insights from Cisco's IoE value at stake analysis for the public sector. Econ. Anal. (2013)

7. Chu, X., Ilyas, I.F., Krishnan, S., Wang, J.: Data cleaning: overview and emerging challenges. In: Proceedings of the 2016 International Conference on Management of Data, pp. 2201–2206. ACM (2016)

8. Chu, X., et al.: Katara: a data cleaning system powered by knowledge bases and crowdsourcing. In: Proceedings of the 2015 ACM SIGMOD International Conference on Management of Data, pp. 1247–1261. ACM (2015)

9. Daraio, C., et al.: Data integration for research and innovation policy: an ontology-based data management approach. Scientometrics **106**(2), 857–871 (2016)

10. Desai, S., Alhadad, R., Chilamkurti, N., Mahmood, A.: A survey of privacy preserving schemes in IoE enabled smart grid advanced metering infrastructure. Clust. Comput. **22**(1), 43–69 (2019)

11. DeStefano, R., Tao, L., Gai, K.: Improving data governance in large organizations through ontology and linked data. In: 2016 IEEE 3rd International Conference on Cyber Security and Cloud Computing (CSCloud), pp. 279–284. IEEE (2016)

12. Domingos, P.: Machine learning for data management: problems and solutions. In: Proceedings of the 2018 International Conference on Management of Data, SIGMOD 2018, pp. 629–629. ACM, New York (2018). https://doi.org/10.1145/3183713.3199515

13. Galetto, M.: What is data management? (2016). https://www.ngdata.com/what-is-data-management/. Accessed 7 June 2019

14. Golshan, B., Halevy, A., Mihaila, G., Tan, W.C.: Data integration: after the teenage years. In: Proceedings of the 36th ACM SIGMOD-SIGACT-SIGAI Symposium on Principles of Database Systems, pp. 101–106. ACM (2017)

15. Huang, X., Xu, C., Wang, P., Liu, H.: LNSC: a security model for electric vehicle and charging pile management based on blockchain ecosystem. IEEE Access **6**, 13565–13574 (2018)

16. Kaur, J., Wongthongtham, P., Abu-Salih, B., Fathy, S.: Analysis of scientific production of IoE big data research. In: 2018 32nd International Conference on Advanced Information Networking and Applications Workshops (WAINA), pp. 715–720. IEEE (2018)

17. Lindsey, S., Raghavendra, C., Sivalingam, K.M.: Data gathering algorithms in sensor networks using energy metrics. IEEE Trans. Parallel Distrib. Syst. **9**, 924–935 (2002)

18. Liu, Y., Lam, K.Y., Han, S., Chen, Q.: Mobile data gathering and energy harvesting in rechargeable wireless sensor networks. Inf. Sci. **482**, 189–209 (2019)

19. Ma, M., Wang, P., Chu, C.H.: Data management for internet of things: challenges, approaches and opportunities. In: 2013 IEEE International Conference on Green Computing and Communications and IEEE Internet of Things and IEEE Cyber, Physical and Social Computing, pp. 1144–1151. IEEE (2013)

20. Mahdavinejad, M.S., Rezvan, M., Barekatain, M., Adibi, P., Barnaghi, P., Sheth, A.P.: Machine learning for internet of things data analysis: a survey. Digit. Commun. Netw. **4**(3), 161–175 (2018)

21. Majeed, A.: Developing countries and internet-of-everything (IoE). In: 2017 IEEE 7th Annual Computing and Communication Workshop and Conference (CCWC), pp. 1–4. IEEE (2017)

22. Majeed, A., Bhana, R., Haq, A., Kyaruzi, I., Williams, M.: Devising a secure architecture of internet of everything (IoE) to avoid the data exploitation in cross culture communications. Int. J. Adv. Comput. Sci. Appl. (IJACSA) **7**(4) (2016)

23. Majeed, A., Bhana, R., Haq, A., Kyaruzi, I., Pervaz, S., Williams, M.L.: Internet of everything (IoE): analysing the individual concerns over privacy enhancing technologies (pets). Int. J. Adv. Comput. Sci. Appl. (IJACSA) **7**(3) (2016)

24. Marjani, M., et al.: Big iot data analytics: architecture, opportunities, and open research challenges. IEEE Access **5**, 5247–5261 (2017)

25. Murgan, M.G.: A critical analysis of the techniques for data gathering in legal research. J. Soc. Sci. Human. **1**(3), 266–274 (2015)

26. Ning, H., Wang, Z.: Future internet of things architecture: like mankind neural system or social organization framework? IEEE Commun. Lett. **15**(4), 461–463 (2011)

27. Raj, A., Prakash, S.: Internet of everything: a survey based on architecture, issues and challenges. In: 2018 5th IEEE Uttar Pradesh Section International Conference on Electrical, Electronics and Computer Engineering (UPCON), pp. 1–6. IEEE (2018)

28. ur Rehman, M.H., Ahmed, E., Yaqoob, I., Hashem, I.A.T., Imran, M., Ahmad, S.: Big data analytics in industrial IoT using a concentric computing model. IEEE Commun. Mag. **56**(2), 37–43 (2018)

29. Ren, J., Zhang, Y., Zhang, K., Liu, A., Chen, J., Shen, X.S.: Lifetime and energy hole evolution analysis in data-gathering wireless sensor networks. IEEE Trans. Industr. Inf. **12**(2), 788–800 (2015)

30. Sianaki, O.A., Yousefi, A., Tabesh, A.R., Mahdavi, M.: Internet of everything and machine learning applications: issues and challenges. In: 2018 32nd International Conference on Advanced Information Networking and Applications Workshops (WAINA), pp. 704–708. IEEE (2018)

31. Tushar, W., et al.: Internet of things for green building management: disruptive innovations through low-cost sensor technology and artificial intelligence. IEEE Sig. Process. Mag. **35**(5), 100–110 (2018)

32. Weik, M.H.: Data management. In: Weik, M.H. (ed.) Computer Science and Communications Dictionary, pp. 352–352. Springer, Boston (2001). https://doi.org/10.1007/1-4020-0613-6_4318

33. Wibisono, W., Kusuma, I.G.N.A., Ishida, Y., Winarno, I.: Towards an immunity-based approach for preserving energy of data-gathering processes in wireless sensor network environments. In: 2016 International Conference On Advanced Informatics: Concepts, Theory And Application (ICAICTA), pp. 1–6. IEEE (2016)

34. Zahoor, S., Javaid, N., Khan, A., Ruqia, B., Muhammad, F.J., Zahid, M.: A cloud-fog-based smart grid model for efficient resource utilization. In: 2018 14th International Wireless Communications & Mobile Computing Conference (IWCMC), pp. 1154–1160. IEEE (2018)

35. Zhang, J., Tang, J., Wang, T., Chen, F.: Energy-efficient data-gathering rendezvous algorithms with mobile sinks for wireless sensor networks. Int. J. Sens. Netw. **23**(4), 248–257 (2017)

36. Zhang, Y., He, S., Chen, J.: Data gathering optimization by dynamic sensing and routing in rechargeable sensor networks. IEEE/ACM Trans. Netw. **24**(3), 1632–1646 (2015)

Author Index

Printed in the United States
By Bookmasters